THE TIMES
Guide to the European Parliament 1984

Edited by
Alan Wood
Head of Parliamentary Staff, *The Times*

Times Books

Published by Times Books Limited
16 Golden Square
London W1R 4BN

Acknowledgement
In compiling this guide, the editor, *The Times* and Times Books
wish to acknowledge their indebtedness for the assistance and
cooperation given by the Directorate General of Information
and Public Relations of the European Parliament based in
Luxembourg, the staffs of the offices of the Parliament in the
member states (and particularly that in the United Kingdom),
the Secretariats and press officers of the Political Groups at the
European Parliament, and Conservative Central Office and
Labour Party Headquarters in the United Kingdom.
                                                            AHW

Typesetting by
Rowland Phototypesetting
Bury St Edmunds
Suffolk

Printed in the UK by
St Edmundsbury Press
Bury St Edmunds
Suffolk

British Library Cataloguing in Publication Data

The Times Guide to the European Parliament
   – 1984
   1. European Parliament – Periodicals
   I. Wood, Alan,   1919–
   341.24'22'05   JN36

   ISBN 0-7230-0258-4

Contents

Foreword

by M. Pierre Pflimlin, homme de l'Europe
President of the European Parliament, July 1984

M. Pflimlin, a prominent French politician ever since the last war and a leading figure in various European political institutions, was elected President of the European Parliament on July 24, 1984, the first day of the first session of the second directly-elected Parliament. Only two ballots were required. From 1979–84 he was one of the Vice-Presidents of the first directly-elected Parliament and also vice-chairman of the European People's Party – the Christian Democratic group. He served in the nominated Parliament from 1959–67 and for the same period was a member of the Council of Europe's Consultative Assembly, holding office as its President from 1963–66. Amid holding various senior Ministerial offices in France, he was Prime Minister for a short time in 1958. He was Mayor of Strasbourg 1959–83 where the Parliament holds its plenary sessions, and is now its Honorary Mayor.

The newly-elected European Parliament must, in my view, bring home to the citizens of Europe the recognition of the evolutionary process on which the European Community is engaged. We are attempting to alter the fundamental relationships between the peoples of Europe, for the relationships that we have traditionally pursued too often led us into wars with one another.

Despite past and current difficulties, the balance of advantages of the Community is positive. But that is not enough. What the youth of Europe is demanding is not only that we pull Europe out of the rut, but that we step out anew on a path to a united Europe.

The last Parliament made an important contribution with its draft treaty on European Union. It is essential that the new Parliament plays its part in the developments which will follow from the Fontainebleau summit.

The peoples of the Community of Ten – soon, I hope, to be Twelve – know too little of the United Europe which is emerging, and too little of their own Parliament. This new Times Guide to the European Parliament will play a valuable role in informing them.

The 12 vice-presidents of the Parliament elected in two ballots are:

Signora Maria Cassanmagnago Cerretti, Italy, EPP
Herr Siegbert Alber, Germany, EPP
Lady Elles, United Kingdom, ED
Mr Hans Nord, Netherlands, LD
Mr Patrick Lalor, Ireland, RDE
Herr Horst Seefeld, Germany, Soc

Signor Mario Dido', Italy, Soc
Mr Winston Griffiths, United Kingdom, Soc
Signor Guido Fanti, Italy, Comm
Mr Spyridon Plaskovitis, Greece, Soc
Mme Nicole Pery, France, Soc
Mr Pøul Møller, Denmark, ED

Second direct elections in the European Community

The second direct elections in the ten states of the European Community to send 434 members to the European Parliament were held on June 14 and June 17, 1984. Some 114.4m out of a European electorate of 200.5m went to the polls to return a Parliament which while sustaining a centre-right majority was considerably different in composition and character from the outgoing elected Parliament.

In many respects the turnout was disappointing, particularly in the United Kingdom, once again the lowest in the European Community, at 32.56 per cent, compared with 32.3 per cent in 1979, and where, for the first time, the electorate had been subjected to non-political newspaper and television advertisements simply designed to encourage people to vote. By and large the campaigns in each of the member states evolved around national politics rather than on the major issues facing the European Community, even its budgetary quarrels.

The fall in support in France for the Socialists and the Communists had the most dramatic impact leading quite swiftly to a change of Prime Minister. M. Pierre Mauroy made way for the 37-year-old M. Laurent Fabius whom it was hoped would restore some of that nation's faith in President Mitterand.

Thanks to the gains by the Labour Party in the United Kingdom, where Mrs Thatcher's Conservative Government seemed to be buffeted by big and little local difficulties, notably a prolonged coal mining dispute, the Socialist emerged once again as the largest group in the European Parliament. Both the European People's Party (Christian Democratic) and European Democratic (Conservative) Groups were smaller but with the Liberals and the European Democratic Alliance (renamed from European Progressive Democrats) together being of the same strength, the centre-right just held to its majority after Euro elections in which the Communist Group lost seven seats.

But it is on the fringes and the way the MEPs there adapt to the proceedings and procedures at Strasbourg that will determine how this new Parliament establishes itself under M. Pierre Pflimlin, the veteran French politician and respected European, who reached its Chair after two ballots.

The election in Germany of seven 'Greens' who proceeded to combine with other ecologists, produced a new 'Rainbow' Group – Arc-en-Ciel – and it decided to operate with four co-chairmen. The election in France of 10 National Front MEP's led by M. Jean-Marie Le Pen, a French presidential candidate in 1974, aroused some sincere, symbolic but somewhat muted protests and token demonstrations against racism – like the wearing of white roses – in the chamber on the first day. However, M. Le Pen, being joined by five members from Italy and one from Greece was able under the rules to form a new right-wing group – Droites Européennes – to get the benefits of a secretariat and other facilities. And not surprisingly he leads it.

M. le Pen even stood for the Presidency of the Parliament and after being decisively ignored by the other groups promptly announced his group of 16 would back M. Pflimlin. This brought a challenge from Mrs Barbara Castle, the UK Labour leader, as to whether M. Pflimlin wished to become President with that backing, but in such a situation the whole Parliament was quickly brought around to realizing that both the Front and the Greens had been democratically elected. M. Pflimlin was duly elected and was as warmly received by Parliament as any of his predecessors.

Although the July plenary session left one or two loose ends to be sorted out, the composition of the political groups, compared with those in the outgoing Parliament, emerged as follows:

Socialists 130 (124); European People's Party (Christian Democratic) 110 (117); European Democratic (Conservative) 50 (63); Communist and Allies 41 (48); Liberal and Democratic 31 (38); European Democratic Alliance 29 (22); Arc-en-Ciel 20 (–); Droites Européennes 16 (1); Non-attached 7 (10). In the outgoing Parliament, there were 12 MEPs in the CDI Group for the Technical Coordination and Defence of Independent Groups and Members. A table setting out the membership of the groups from the various EEC states is on page 8.

New group leaders were appointed, mostly the week before the Parliament met. The failure of the Free Democrats (FDP) to obtain five per cent of the poll in Germany meant they lost their four European seats in the Liberal Group including that held by Herr Martin Bangemann, the group leader. Mme Simone Veil, former President of the Parliament, succeeded him but Herr Bangemann soon found himself back in office – as Germany's Economics Minister.

Both the Socialist and EPP Groups are led by Germans. Herr Rudi Arndt defeated Mr Ernest Glinne of Belgium, leader in the last Parliament, by 67 votes to 54, to head the former, and Herr Egon Klepsch obtained 98 votes to nine in returning to lead the EPP as he did in the first half of the last Parliament. Sir Henry Plumb had already been firmly installed as the Conservative Group leader well before the European elections. The Communists unanimously elected Signor Gianni Cervetti of Italy as chairman to replace Signor Guido Fanti. Here it should not be forgotten that in Italy, for the first time, the Communists polled more than the Christian Democrats in an election.

Finally, the European Democratic Alliance re-elected its leader, M. Christian de la Malène of France.

As in 1979, the highest turnouts were in Belgium, Luxembourg and Italy. There were smaller turnouts in Greece, Germany, France, Netherlands, Ireland (where Labour lost its four seats) and the UK. The first-past-the-post electoral system used in England, Scotland and Wales, but not in Northern Ireland, brought renewed demands from the Liberal and Social Democratic Alliance and from the Liberal Group as a whole for a uniform voting system throughout the Community.

In polling nearly 2.6m votes or 18.5 per cent of the British turnout, the Alliance obtained not a single seat, a situation wholly unrepeated elsewhere in the Community. In Luxembourg there were 174,000 votes cast for that country's six seats and in Ireland, 1,120,416 votes were cast for its 15 seats. The Liberal Group is to campaign to ensure change in time for the next elections in June 1989.

The list system employed on continental Europe threw up its usual changes of personalities what with the election in Italy and Luxembourg of Ministers who quickly gave way to others lower down their lists, and also the election in Italy of some MEPs in two constituencies. That brought in other members.

In the United Kingdom, Labour won 15 seats at the expense of the Conservatives, the boundaries of the 78 seats in England, Scotland and Wales only having been finalized shortly before the election. The three seats in Northern Ireland were retained by the sitting MEPs while in the other three countries the Conservatives have 45 compared to the 60 won in 1979 and Labour 32 compared with 17 won five years ago. Mrs Winifred Ewing retained the Highlands and Islands for the Scottish National Party, returning to the Parliament and becoming a committee chairman.

There are 232 members of the previous Parliament in the new Parliament. The membership includes 75 women, compared with 67 elected in 1979 plus two in the Greek elections of 1981. The number of dual mandates has fallen considerably from 125 in 1979 to 49 in the 1984 Parliament.

Group membership just before 1984 elections

	B	DK	D	GR	F	IRL	I	L	NL	UK	Total
Socialist	7	4	35	10	23	4	14	1	9	17	124
EPP (Christian Democrat)	10	1	42	8	9	4	30	3	10		117
European Democrat (Conservative)	—	2	—	—	—	—	—	—	—	61	63
Communist and Allies	—	1	—	4	19	—	24	—	—	—	48
Liberal and Democratic	4	3	4	—	15	1	5	2	4	—	38
European Progressive Democrat	—	1	—	—	15	5	—	—	—	1	22
Group for Technical Coordination	2	4	—	—	—	1	4	—	—	1	12
Non-attached	1	—	—	2	—	—	4	—	2	1	10
Totals	24	16	81	24	81	15	81	6	25	81	434

Group membership after June 1984 elections

The composition of the political groups at the first plenary session of the new European Parliament held in Strasbourg from July 24–27 1984 was as follows:

	B	DK	D	GR	F	IRL	I	L	NL	UK	Total
Socialist (Soc)	7	4	33	10	20	—	12	2	9	33	130
EPP (Christian Democratic)	6	1	41	9	9	6	27	3	8	—	110
European Democratic (Conservative) ED	—	4	—	—	—	—	—	—	—	46	50
Communist and Allies (Comm)	—	1	—	4	10	—	26	—	—	—	41
Liberal and Democratic (LD)	5	2	—	—	12	1	5	1	5	—	31
European Democratic Alliance (RDE – formerly DEP)	—	—	—	—	20	8	—	—	—	1	29
Arc-en-Ciel (ARC)	4	4	7	—	—	—	3	—	2	—	20
Droites-Européennes (DR)	—	—	—	1	10	—	5	—	—	—	16
Non-attached (NI)	2	—	—	—	—	—	3	—	1	1	7
Totals	24	16	81	24	81	15	81	6	25	81	434

B – Belgium; DK – Denmark; D – Germany; GR – Greece; F – France; IRL – Ireland; I – Italy; L – Luxembourg; NL – Netherlands; UK – United Kingdom.

Political group membership in 1979

Distribution of seats among the political groups of the European Parliament after direct elections in June, 1979, and on the first session of that Parliament in July 1979:

	B	DK	D	GR	F	IRL	I	L	NL	UK	Total
Socialist (Soc)	7	4	35	—	21	4	13	1	9	18	112
EPP (Christian Democratic)	10	—	42	—	9	4	30	3	10	—	108
European Democratic (ED) (Conservative)	—	3	—	—	—	—	—	—	—	61	64
Communist and Allies (Comm)	—	1	—	—	19	—	24	—	—	—	44
Liberal and Democratic (LD)	4	3	4	—	17	1	5	2	4	—	40
European Progressive Democrats (DEP)	—	1	—	—	15	5	—	—	—	1	22
Group for Technical Coordination (CDI)	1	4	—	—	—	1	5	—	—	—	11
Non-attached (NI)	2	—	—	—	—	—	4	—	2	1	9
Totals	24	16	81	—	81	15	81	6	25	81	410

B – Belgium; DK – Denmark; D – Germany; GR – Greece; F – France; IRL – Ireland; I – Italy; L – Luxembourg; NL – Netherlands; UK – United Kingdom.

Leaders of the political groups

Herr Rudi Arndt
Germany
Socialist

Herr Egon Klepsch
Germany
European People's Party

Sir Henry Plumb
United Kingdom
European Democratic

Signor Giovanni Cervetti
Italy
Communist and Allies

Mme Simone Veil
France
Liberal and Democratic

M Jean-Marie Le Pen
France
Droites-Européennes

M Christian de la Malène
France
European Democratic Alliance

The new Arc-en-Ciel group decided to have
four co-chairmen:
Fru Else Hammerich, Denmark
Mr Bram van der Lek, Netherlands
Mr Paul Staes, Belgium
Mr Jaak Vandemeulebroucke, Belgium

Members elected to the European Parliament

In this list of members elected to the European Parliament in the second direct elections of the European Community held on June 14–17, 1984, a * denotes those who were members of the outgoing elected Parliament.

The abbreviations used to designate the political groups of the European Parliament are: ARC – Arc-en-Ciel (Rainbow Group); Comm – Communist and Allies; DR – Droites Européennes; ED – European Democratic (Conservative); EPP – European People's Party (Christian Democratic); LD – Liberal and Democratic; NI – Non-attached (independents); RDE – European Democratic Alliance (formerly DEP – European Progressive Democrats); Soc – Socialist. Membership is that at the September 1984 session.

Abbreviations of the political parties of MEPs in the member states of the European Community are set out at the end of this list.

Name	Member state	Political group	Party
A			
ABELIN, Jean-Pierre	France	EPP	UDF–RPR
*ABENS, Victor	Luxembourg	Soc	POSL
*ADAM, Gordon	United Kingdom	Soc	Lab
*ADAMOU, Dimitrios	Greece	Comm	KKE
*AERSSEN, Jochen van	Germany	EPP	CDU
*AIGNER, Heinrich	Germany	EPP	CSU
*ALAVANOS, Alexandros	Greece	Comm	KKE
*ALBER, Siegbert	Germany	EPP	CDU
*ALMIRANTE, Giorgio	Italy	DR	MSI–DN
AMADEI, Giuseppe	Italy	Soc	PSDI
ANASTASSOPOULOS, Georgios	Greece	EPP	ND
D'ANCONA, Mevr Hedy	Netherlands	Soc	PvdA
ANDREWS, Niall	Ireland	RDE	F–Fáil
ANGLADE, Mme Marie-Madeleine	France	RDE	UDF/RPR (CNIP)
*ANTONIOZZI, Dario	Italy	EPP	DC
ANTONY, Bernard	France	DR	FN
*ARNDT, Rudi	Germany	Soc	SPD
AVEROF-TOSITSAS, Evangelos	Greece	EPP	ND
AVGERINOS, Paraskevas	Greece	Soc	PASOK
B			
BACHY, Jean-Paul	France	Soc	PS
BACKER, Mevr Rika de	Belgium	EPP	CVP–EVP
BAGET BOZZO, Gianni	Italy	Soc	PSI
*BALFE, Richard	United Kingdom	Soc	Lab
BANOTTI, Ms Mary	Ireland	EPP	F–Gael
*BARBARELLA, Signora Carla	Italy	Comm	PCI
BARDONG, Otto	Germany	EPP	CDU
BARINGDORF, Friedrich-Wilhelm Graefe zu	Germany	ARC	Grüne
BARRETT, Sylvester	Ireland	RDE	F–Fáil
*BARTOLOMEI, Mario di	Italy	LD	PLI/PRI
BARZANTI, Roberto	Italy	Comm	PCI
*BATTERSBY, Robert	United Kingdom	ED	C
BAUDIS, Dominique	France	EPP	UDF/RPR
BAUDOUIN, Denis	France	RDE	UDF/RPR
BEAZLEY, Christopher	United Kingdom	ED	C

Name	Member state	Political group	Party
*BEAZLEY, Peter	United Kingdom	ED	C
BERNARD-REYMOND, Pierre	France	EPP	UDF/RPR (CDS)
*BERSANI, Giovanni	Italy	EPP	DC
BESSE, Jean	France	Soc	PS
*BETHELL, Lord	United Kingdom	ED	C
*BETTIZA, Vincenzo	Italy	LD	PLI
*BEUMER, Bouke	Netherlands	EPP	CDA
*BEYER DE RYKE, Luc	Belgium	LD	PRL
*BISMARCK, Philipp von	Germany	EPP	CDU
BLOTTNITZ, Frau Undine-Uta Bloch von	Germany	ARC	Grüne
*BLUMENFELD, Erik	Germany	EPP	CDU
*BOCKLET, Reinhold	Germany	EPP	CSU
*BØGH, Jørgen	Denmark	ARC	Folkebe-vaegelsen
BOMBARD, Alain	France	Soc	PS
*BONACCINI, Aldo	Italy	Comm	PCI
*BONDE, Jens-Peter	Denmark	ARC	Folkebe-vaegelsen
*BONINO, Signora Emma†	Italy	NI	PR
*BOOT, Mevr Elise	Netherlands	EPP	CDA
BORGO, Franco	Italy	EPP	DC
*BOSERUP, Fru Bodil	Denmark	Comm	SF
BOUTOS, Ioannis	Greece	EPP	ND
BRAUN-MOSER, Frau Ursula	Germany	EPP	CDU
BRINKMEIER, Jürgen Georg	Germany	Soc	SDP
*BROK, Elmar	Germany	EPP	CDU
*BROOKES, Miss Beta	United Kingdom	ED	C
*BUCHAN, Mrs Janey	United Kingdom	Soc	Lab
*BUTTAFUOCO, Antonio	Italy	DR	MSI–DN

C

CAMARET, Michel de	France	DR	FN
CARIGNON, Alain	France	RDE	UDF/RPR
*CAROSSINO, Angelo	Italy	Comm	PCI
CASINI, Carlo	Italy	EPP	DC
CASSANMAGNAGO CERRETTI, Signora Maria Luisa	Italy	EPP	DC
CASSIDY, Bryan	United Kingdom	ED	C
*CASTELLINA, Signora Luciana	Italy	ARC	PCI
*CASTLE, Mrs Barbara	United Kingdom	Soc	Lab
*CATHERWOOD, Sir Frederick	United Kingdom	ED	C
CERVETTI, Giovanni	Italy	Comm	PCI
CHABOCHE, Dominique	France	DR	FN
*CHAMBEIRON, Robert	France	Comm	PCF
*CHANTERIE, Raphaël	Belgium	EPP	CVP–EVP
*CHARZAT, Mme Gisèle	France	Soc	PS
CHIABRANDO, Mauro	Italy	EPP	DC
CHINAUD, Roger	France	LD	UDF/RPR (PR)
CHIUSANO, Vittorino	Italy	EPP	DC
CHOURAQUI, Mme Nicole	France	RDE	UDF/RPR (RPR)
CHRISTENSEN, Ib	Denmark	ARC	Folkebe-vaegelsen
CHRISTIANSEN, Ejner Hovgaard	Denmark	Soc	S
CHRISTODOULOU, Efthymios	Greece	EPP	ND
CIANCAGLINI, Michelangelo	Italy	EPP	DC

† resigned September 11, 1984

Name	Member state	Political group	Party
*Cinciari Rodano, Signora Maria Lisa	Italy	Comm	PCI
*Clinton, Mark	Ireland	EPP	F–Gael
*Cohen, Robert	Netherlands	Soc	PvdA
Collinot, Michel	France	DR	FN
*Collins, Kenneth	United Kingdom	Soc	Lab
Columbu, Michele	Italy	ARC	UV–PSDA
Cornelissen, Peter	Netherlands	EPP	CDA
*Costanzo, Roberto	Italy	EPP	DC
Coste-Floret, Alfred	France	EPP	UDF/RPR (RPR)
Cot, Jean-Pierre	France	Soc	PS
*Cottrell, Richard	United Kingdom	ED	C
*Courcy Ling, John de	United Kingdom	ED	C
Crawley, Mrs Christine	United Kingdom	Soc	Lab
*Croux, Lambert	Belgium	EPP	CVP–EVP
Cryer, Robert	United Kingdom	Soc	Lab
*Curry, David	United Kingdom	ED	C

D

*Dalsass, Joachim	Italy	EPP	SVP
Daly, Mrs Margaret	United Kingdom	ED	C
*Dankert, Pieter	Netherlands	Soc	PvdA
Debatisse, Michel	France	EPP	UDF/RPR
Deniau, Jean-François	France	LD	UDF/RPR
Deprez, Gérard	Belgium	EPP	PSC–PPE
*Dido', Mario	Italy	Soc	PSI
Dimitriadis, Chrysanthos	Greece	DR	EPEN
*Donnez, Georges	France	LD	UDF/RPR
*Douro, Marquess of	United Kingdom	ED	C
Ducarme, Daniel	Belgium	LD	PRL
Dupuy, Mme Anne-Marie	France	RDE	UDF/RPR
*Dury, Mme Raymonde	Belgium	Soc	PS

E

Ebel, Manfred	Germany	EPP	CDU
Elles, James	United Kingdom	ED	C
*Elles, Lady	United Kingdom	ED	C
Elliott, Michael	United Kingdom	Soc	Lab
*Ephremidis, Vassilios	Greece	Comm	KKE
*Ercini, Sergio	Italy	EPP	DC
*Estgen, Nicolas	Luxembourg	EPP	PCS
Evrigenis, Dimitrios	Greece	EPP	ND
*Ewing, Mrs Winifred	United Kingdom	RDE	SNP
*Eyraud, Louis	France	Soc	PS

F

Faith, Mrs Sheila	United Kingdom	ED	C
*Fajardie, Roger	France	Soc	PS
Falconer, Alexander	United Kingdom	Soc	Lab
*Fanti, Guido	Italy	Comm	PCI
Fanton, André	France	RDE	UDF/RPR
Fatous, Léon	France	Soc	PS
*Fellermaier, Ludwig	Germany	Soc	SDP
*Ferranti, Basil de	United Kingdom	ED	C
*Fich, Ove	Denmark	Soc	S
Fitzgerald, Gene	Ireland	RDE	F–Fáil
Fitzsimons, Jim	Ireland	RDE	F–Fáil

11

Name	Member state	Political group	Party
*FLANAGAN, Sean	Ireland	RDE	F–Fáil
FLESCH, Mme Colette	Luxembourg	LD	PD
FLOSSE, Gaston	France	RDE	UDF/RPR
*FOCKE, Frau Katharina	Germany	Soc	SPD
FONTAINE, Mme Nicole	France	RDE	UDF/RPR
FORD, Glyn	United Kingdom	Soc	Lab
FORMIGONI, Roberto	Italy	EPP	DC
*FRANZ, Otmar	Germany	EPP	CDU
*FRIEDRICH, Bruno	Germany	Soc	SPD
*FRIEDRICH, Ingo	Germany	EPP	CSU
*FRÜH, Isidor	Germany	EPP	CDU
*FUILLET, Mme Yvette	France	Soc	PS

G

Name	Member state	Political group	Party
GADIOUX, Mme Colette	France	Soc	PS
GAIBISSO, Gerardo	Italy	EPP	DC
*GALLAND, Yves	France	LD	UDF/RPR (PR)
GALLO, Max	France	Soc	PS
*GALLUZZI, Carlo	Italy	Comm	PCI
GATTI, Natalino	Italy	Comm	PCI
*GAUTIER, Fritz	Germany	Soc	SPD
*GAWRONSKI, Jas	Italy	LD	PRI
GAZIS, Nikolaos	Greece	Soc	PASOK
GERONTOPOULOS, Kyriakos	Greece	EPP	ND
*GIAVAZZI, Giovanni	Italy	EPP	DC
*GIUMMARRA, Vincenzo	Italy	EPP	DC
GLEZOS, Emmanouil	Greece	Soc	PASOK
*GLINNE, Ernest	Belgium	Soc	PS
*GREDAL, Fru Eva	Denmark	Soc	S
*GREMETZ, Maxime François	France	Comm	PCF
*GRIFFITHS, Winston	United Kingdom	Soc	Lab
GROENENDAAL, Mevr Jessica	Netherlands	LD	VVD
GUARRACI, Anselmo	Italy	Soc	PSI
*GUCHT, Karel de	Belgium	LD	PVV–ELD
GUERMEUR, Guy	France	RDE	UDF/RPR

H

Name	Member state	Political group	Party
*HABSBURG, Otto	Germany	EPP	CSU
*HAHN, Wilhelm	Germany	EPP	CDU
*HAMMERICH, Fru Else	Denmark	ARC	Folkebe-vaegelsen
*HÄNSCH, Klaus	Germany	Soc	SPD
HAPPART, José	Belgium	NI	PS
HÄRLIN, Benni	Germany	ARC	Grüne
HEINRICH, Frau Brigitte	Germany	ARC	Grüne
HEMELDONCK, Mevr Marijke van	Belgium	Soc	SP
*HERMAN, Fernand	Belgium	EPP	PSC–PPE
HERSANT, Robert	France	EPP	UDF/RPR
*HEUVEL-BLANK, Mevr Ien van den	Netherlands	Soc	PvdA
HINDLEY, Michael	United Kingdom	Soc	Lab
*HOFF, Frau Magdalene	Germany	Soc	SPD
*HOFFMANN, Mme Jacqueline	France	Comm	PCF
*HOFFMANN, Karl-Heinz	Germany	EPP	CDU
HOON, Geoffrey	United Kingdom	Soc	Lab
*HOWELL, Paul	United Kingdom	ED	C
HUCKFIELD, Leslie	United Kingdom	Soc	Lab
HUGHES, Stephen	United Kingdom	Soc	Lab
*HUME, John	United Kingdom	Soc	SDLP

Name	Member state	Political group	Party
*HUTTON, Alasdair	United Kingdom	ED	C

I

IODICE, Antonio	Italy	EPP	DC
IPPOLITO, Felice	Italy	Comm	PCI
†IVERSEN, John	Denmark	Comm	SF

J

JACKSON, Mrs Caroline	United Kingdom	ED	C
*JACKSON, Christopher	United Kingdom	ED	C
*JAKOBSEN, Erhard	Denmark	EPP	CD
JEPSEN, Fru Marie	Denmark	ED	KF
JOSPIN, Lionel	France	Soc	PS
JUPPÉ, Alain	France	RDE	UDF/RPR

K

KILBY, Michael	United Kingdom	ED	C
*KLEPSCH, Egon Alfred	Germany	EPP	CDU
*KLINKENBORG, Jan	Germany	Soc	SPD
KLÖCKNER, Michael	Germany	ARC	Grüne
KUIJPERS, Willy	Belgium	ARC	VU–EVA
*KYRKOS, Leonidas	Greece	Comm	KKE-es

L

*LALOR, Patrick	Ireland	RDE	F–Fáil
LAMBRIAS, Panayiotis	Greece	EPP	ND
*LANGES, Horst	Germany	EPP	CDU
*LECANUET, Jean	France	EPP	UDF/RPR (UDF)
LE CHEVALLIER, Jean-Marie	France	DR	FN
LEHIDEUX, Mme Martine	France	DR	FN
LEK, Bram van der	Netherlands	ARC	PSP
LEMASS, Mrs Eileen	Ireland	RDE	F–Fáil
*LEMMER, Gerd Ludwig	Germany	EPP	CDU
*LENTZ-CORNETTE, Mrs Marcelle	Luxembourg	EPP	PCS
*LENZ, Frau Marlene	Germany	EPP	CDU
LE PEN, Jean-Marie	France	DR	FN
LIENEMANN, Mme Marie-Noëlle	France	Soc	PS
*LIGIOS, Giosuè	Italy	EPP	DC
*LIMA, Salvatore	Italy	EPP	DC
*LINKOHR, Rolf	Germany	Soc	SPD
*LIZIN, Mrs Anne-Marie	Belgium	Soc	PS
*LOMAS, Alfred	United Kingdom	Soc	Lab
LONGUET, Gérard	France	LD	UDF/RPR (PR)
*LOO, Charles-Emile	France	Soc	PS
*LOUWES, Hendrik	Netherlands	LD	VVD
*LUSTER, Rudolf	Germany	EPP	CDU
*‡LYNGE, Finn	Denmark	Soc	Siumut

M

*McCARTIN, John Joseph	Ireland	EPP	F–Gael
McGOWAN, Michael	United Kingdom	Soc	Lab
McMAHON, Hugh	United Kingdom	Soc	Lab
McMILLAN-SCOTT, Edward	United Kingdom	ED	C

† Takes seat on Jan 1, 1985, when Greenland leaves European Community
‡ sits until Dec 31, 1984 as representative of Greenland which then leaves EEC

Name	Member state	Political group	Party
McSharry, Ray	Ireland	RDE	F–Fáil
*Maffre-Baugé, Emmanuel	France	Comm	PCF
*Maher, Thomas	Ireland	LD	Ind
*Maij-Weggen, Mevr Johanna	Netherlands	EPP	CDA
*Malangré, Kurt	Germany	EPP	CDU
Malaud, Philippe	France	RDE	UDF/RPR (CNIP)
*Malène, Christian de la	France	RDE	UDF/RPR (RPR)
Mallet, Jacques	France	EPP	UDF/RPR (UDF)
Mancel, Jean-François	France	RDE	UDF/RPR (RPR)
*March, Mme Danielle de	France	Comm	PCF
*Marchais, Georges	France	Comm	PCF
*Marck, Pol	Belgium	EPP	CVP–EVP
Marinaro, Signora Francesca	Italy	Comm	PCI
*Marshall, John	United Kingdom	ED	C
Martelli, Claudio	Italy	Soc	PSI
Martin, David	United Kingdom	Soc	Lab
*Martin, Mme Simone	France	LD	UDF/RPR (PR)
Massari, Renato	Italy	Soc	PSDI
Mattina, Vincenzo	Italy	Soc	PSI
Mavros, Georgios	Greece	Soc	PASOK
*Megahy, Thomas	United Kingdom	Soc	Lab
*Mertens, Meinolf	Germany	EPP	CDU
Metten, Alman	Netherlands	Soc	PvdA
Michelini, Alberto	Italy	EPP	DC
*Mihr, Karl-Heinrich	Germany	Soc	SPD
*Miert, Karel van	Belgium	Soc	SP
Mita, Ciriaco de	Italy	EPP	DC
Mizzau, Alfeo	Italy	EPP	DC
Molinari, Emilio	Italy	NI	DP
*Møller, Pøul	Denmark	ED	KF
*Moorhouse, James	United Kingdom	ED	C
Moravia, Alberto	Italy	Comm	PCI
Moroni, Gianni	Italy	Soc	PSDI
Morris, David	United Kingdom	Soc	Lab
*Motchane, Didier	France	Soc	PS
Mouchel, Jean	France	RDE	UDF/RPR (RPR)
Muhlen, Ernest	Luxembourg	EPP	PCS
Münch, Werner	Germany	EPP	CDU
*Muntingh, Hemmo J.	Netherlands	Soc	PvdA
Musso, François	France	RDE	UDF/RPR (RPR)

N

Name	Member state	Political group	Party
Natta, Alessandro	Italy	Comm	PCI
Newens, Stanley	United Kingdom	Soc	Lab
Newman, Edward	United Kingdom	Soc	Lab
*Newton Dunn, William	United Kingdom	ED	C
*Nielsen, Jørgen Brøndlund	Denmark	LD	V
*Nielsen, Fru Tove	Denmark	LD	V
*Nord, Hans R	Netherlands	LD	VVD
*Nordmann, Jean-Thomas	France	LD	UDF/RPR (PR)
*Normanton, Tom	United Kingdom	ED	C

Name	Member state	Political group	Party
Novelli, Diego	Italy	Comm	PCI

O

*O'Donnell, Thomas	Ireland	EPP	F–Gael
*O'Hagan, Lord	United Kingdom	ED	C
Oppenheim, Fru Jeanette	Denmark	ED	KF
*d'Ormesson, Olivier	France	DR	FN

P

*Paisley, Ian	United Kingdom	NI	Dem U
*Pajetta, Giancarlo	Italy	Comm	PCI
*Pannella, Marco	Italy	NI	PR
*Pantazi-Tzifa, Ka Konstantina	Greece	Soc	PASOK
*Papapietro, Giovanni	Italy	Comm	PCI
Papoutsis, Christos	Greece	Soc	PASOK
Parodi, Eolo	Italy	EPP	DC
Pasty, Jean-Claude	France	RDE	UDF/RPR (RPR)
*Pasquale, Pancrazio de	Italy	Comm	PCI
*Patterson, Ben	United Kingdom	ED	C
*Pearce, Andrew	United Kingdom	ED	C
*Pelikan, Jiri	Italy	Soc	PSI
*Penders, Jean J. M.	Netherlands	EPP	CDA
*Pery, Mme Nicole	France	Soc	PS
*Peters, Johannes Wilhelm	Germany	Soc	SPD
*Petronio, Francesco	Italy	DR	MSI–DN
Peus, Frau Gabriele	Germany	EPP	CDU
*Pfennig, Gero	Germany	EPP	CDU
*Pflimlin, Pierre	France	EPP	UDF/RPR (CDS)
Piermont, Frau Dorothee	Germany	ARC	Grüne
*Pininfarina, Sergio	Italy	LD	PLI
*Piquet, René	France	Comm	PCF
Pirkl, Fritz	Germany	EPP	CSU
Pisoni, Ferruccio	Italy	EPP	DC
Pisoni, Nino	Italy	EPP	DC
Pitt, Terence	United Kingdom	Soc	Lab
*Plaskovitis, Spyridon	Greece	Soc	PASOK
*Plumb, Sir Henry	United Kingdom	ED	C
Pomilio, Mario	Italy	EPP	DC
*Poniatowski, Michel	France	LD	UDF/RPR (UFE)
Pons, Bernard	France	RDE	UDF/RPR (RPR)
Pordea, Gustave	France	DR	FN
Pötschki, Hans	Germany	EPP	CDU
*Pöttering, Hans-Gert	Germany	EPP	CDU
*Prag, Derek	United Kingdom	ED	C
*Pranchère, Pierre	France	Comm	PCF
*Price, Peter	United Kingdom	ED	C
*Prout, Christopher	United Kingdom	ED	C
*Provan, James	United Kingdom	ED	C

Q

*Quin, Ms Joyce	United Kingdom	Soc	Lab

R

*Rabbethge, Frau Renate-Charlotte	Germany	EPP	CDU

Name	Member state	Political group	Party
RAFTERY, Thomas	Ireland	EPP	F–Gael
RAGGIO, Andrea	Italy	Comm	PCI
REICHLIN, Alfredo	Italy	Comm	PCI
REMACLE, Marcel	Belgium	Soc	PS
RIGO, Mario	Italy	Soc	PSI
*RINSCHE, Günter	Germany	EPP	CDU
*ROBERTS, Dame Shelagh	United Kingdom	ED	C
ROELANTS DU VIVIER, François	Belgium	ARC	Ecolo–V
*ROGALLA, Dieter	Germany	Soc	SPD
ROMEO, Rosario	Italy	LD	PLI/PRI
ROMEOS, Georgios	Greece	Soc	PASOK
*ROMUALDI, Pino	Italy	NI	MSI–DN
ROOIJ, Mevr Yvonne van	Netherlands	EPP	CDA
ROSSETTI, Giorgio	Italy	Comm	PCI
*ROSSI, André	France	LD	UDF/RPR (PR)
ROTHE, Frau Mechthild	Germany	Soc	SPD
ROTHLEY, Willi	Germany	Soc	SPD
ROUX, Jean-Pierre	France	RDE	UDF/RPR (RPR)
*RYAN, Richie	Ireland	EPP	F–Gael

S

Name	Member state	Political group	Party
*SABY, Henri	France	Soc	PS
SAKELLARIOU, Joannis	Germany	Soc	SPD
*SALISCH, Frau Heinke	Germany	Soc	SPD
*SÄLZER, Bernhard	Germany	EPP	CDU
*SCHINZEL, Dieter	Germany	Soc	SPD
*SCHLEICHER, Frau Ursula	Germany	EPP	CSU
*SCHMID, Gerhard	Germany	Soc	SPD
SCHMIT, Mme Lydie	Luxembourg	Soc	POSL
SCHÖN, Konrad	Germany	EPP	CDU
SCHREIBER, Heinz	Germany	Soc	SPD
SCHWALBA-HOTH, Frank	Germany	ARC	Grüne
*SCOTT-HOPKINS, Sir James	United Kingdom	ED	C
*SCRIVENER, Mme Christiane	France	LD	UDF/RPR (PR)
*SEAL, Barry	United Kingdom	Soc	Lab
*SEEFELD, Horst	Germany	Soc	SPD
*SEELER, Hans-Joachim	Germany	Soc	SPD
*SEGRE, Sergio	Italy	Comm	PCI
*SEIBEL-EMMERLING, Frau Lieselotte	Germany	Soc	SPD
*SELIGMAN, Madron	United Kingdom	ED	C
SELVA, Gustavo	Italy	EPP	DC
*SHERLOCK, Alexander	United Kingdom	ED	C
*SIMMONDS, Richard	United Kingdom	ED	C
SIMONS, Frau Barbara	Germany	Soc	SPD
*SIMPSON, Anthony	United Kingdom	ED	C
SMITH, Llewellyn	United Kingdom	Soc	Lab
SPÄTH, Leopold	Germany	EPP	CDU
*SPINELLI, Altiero	Italy	Comm	PCI
*SQUARCIALUPI, Signora Vera	Italy	Comm	Ind. Sin.
STAES, Paul	Belgium	ARC	Agalev
STARITA, Giovanni	Italy	EPP	DC
STAUFFENBERG, Franz Ludwig Graf von	Germany	EPP	CSU
STEVENSON, George	United Kingdom	Soc	Lab
STEWART, Kenneth	United Kingdom	Soc	Lab
*STEWART-CLARK, Sir John	United Kingdom	ED	C
STIRBOIS, Jean-Pierre	France	DR	FN

Name	Member state	Political group	Party
*Sutra de Germa, Georges	France	Soc	PS

T

Name	Member state	Political group	Party
*Taylor, John David	United Kingdom	ED	OUP
*Thareau, Bernard	France	Soc	PS
Thome-Patenôtre, Mme Jacqueline	France	RDE	UDF/RPR (RPR)
Tognoli, Carlo	Italy	Soc	PSI
Toksvig, Claus	Denmark	ED	KF
*Tolman, Teun	Netherlands	EPP	CDA
Tomlinson, John	United Kingdom	Soc	Lab
Tongue, Miss Carole	United Kingdom	Soc	Lab
Topmann, Günter	Germany	Soc	SPD
Tortora, Enzo	Italy	NI	PR
Toussaint, Michel	Belgium	LD	PRL
Tripodi, Antonino	Italy	DR	MSI–DN
Trivelli, Renzo	Italy	Comm	PCI
Trupia, Signora Lalla	Italy	Comm	PCI
*Tuckman, Frederick	United Kingdom	ED	C
*Turner, Amédée	United Kingdom	ED	C
Tzounis, Ioannis	Greece	EPP	ND

U

Name	Member state	Political group	Party
Ulburghs, Jef	Belgium	NI	SP

V

Name	Member state	Political group	Party
Valenzi, Maurizio	Italy	Comm	PCI
*Vandemeulebroucke, Jaak	Belgium	ARC	VU–EVA
*Vanneck, Sir Peter	United Kingdom	ED	C
Varfis, Grigorios	Greece	Soc	PASOK
*Vayssade, Mme Marie-Claude	France	Soc	PS
*Veil, Mme Simone	France	LD	UDF/RPR (RPR)
Verbeek, Herman	Netherlands	ARC	PPR
*Vergeer, Willem	Netherlands	EPP	CDA
*Verges, Paul	France	Comm	PCF
Vernier, Jacques	France	RDE	UDF/RPR (RPR)
*Vernimmen, Willy	Belgium	Soc	SP
*Vetter, Heinz Oskar	Germany	Soc	SPD
*Vgenopoulos, Nikolaos	Greece	Soc	PASOK
*Viehoff-Maag, Mevr Phili	Netherlands	Soc	PvdA
Visser, Ben	Netherlands	Soc	PvdA
Vittinghoff, Kurt	Germany	Soc	SPD
Vries, Gijs de	Netherlands	LD	VVD
*Vring, Thomas von der	Germany	Soc	SPD

W

Name	Member state	Political group	Party
Waal, Leendert van der	Netherlands	NI	SGP
*Wagner, Manfred	Germany	Soc	SPD
*Walter, Gerd	Germany	Soc	SPD
*Wawrzik, Kurt	Germany	EPP	CDU
*Weber, Frau Beate	Germany	Soc	SPD
*Wedekind, Rudolf	Germany	EPP	CDU
*Welsh, Michael	United Kingdom	ED	C
West, Norman	United Kingdom	Soc	Lab
*Wettig, Klaus	Germany	Soc	SPD

Name	Member state	Political group	Party
*WIECZOREK-ZEUL, Frau Heidemarie	Germany	Soc	SPD
WIJSENBEEK, Florus	Netherlands	LD	VVD
WINTER, August de	Belgium	LD	PVV–ELD
*WOGAU, Karl von	Germany	EPP	CDU
WOLFF, Claude	France	LD	UDF/RPR (UDF)
*WOLTJER, Eisso P.	Netherlands	Soc	PvdA
*WURTZ, Francis	France	Comm	PCF

Y

YANNAKOU, Ka Marietta	Greece	EPP	ND

Z

*ZAGARI, Mario	Italy	Soc	PSI
ZAHORKA, Hans-Jürgen	Germany	EPP	CDU
*ZARGES, Axel	Germany	EPP	CDU

Member state political parties

Belgium
Agalev ......Anders gaan arbeiden,
leven en vrijen
CVP–EVP..Christelijke Volkspartij
(Europese Volkspartij)
PSC–PPE...Parti social-chrétien
(Parti Populaire Européen)
Ecolo-V ....Ecologistes Confédérés
pour l'organisation de
lutte originales – Verts
FDF–RW...Front démocratique des
Francophones
(Rassemblement Wallon)
PRL ....Parti des réformes et
de la liberté
PVV–ELD Partij voor vrijheid en
vooruitgang (Europese
Liberalen en Demokraten)
SP ....Socialistische Partij
PS ....Parti socialiste
VU–EVA ..Volksunie – Europese
Vrije Alliantie

Denmark
CD ....Centrum-Demokrater
FRP ....Fremskridtspartiet
KF ....Det konservative folkeparti
S ....Socialdemokratiet
SF ....Socialistisk folkeparti
V ....Venstre, Danmarks
liberale parti
Siumut ......Greenland party
Also Folkebevaegelsen
mod EF, the anti-EEC movement

France
CDS ....Centre des Démocrates
Sociaux
CNIP ....Centre National des
Indépendants Paysans
FN ....Front National
PCF..........Parti communiste français
PR ....Parti Républicain
PS ....Parti socialiste
RPR ....Rassemblement pour la
République
UDF.........Union démocratique
française
UDF/RPR Union de l'Opposition

Germany
CDU ....Christlich-Demokratische
Union
CSU ....Christlich-Soziale Union
Grüne ....Die Grünen
SPD ....Sozialdemokratische Partei
Deutschlands

Greece
EPEN ....Ethniki Politiki Enossis
ND...........Nea Dimokratia
PASOK.....Panelliniko Socialistiko Kinima
KKE.........Kommounistiko Komma
Hellados
KKE-es.....Kommounistiko Komma
Hellados – essoterikou

Ireland (Eire)
F-Fáil........Fianna Fáil Party
F-Gael ......Fine Gael Party
Ind ....Independent

Italy
DC...........Democrazia cristiana
DP ....Democrazia proletaria
Ind. Sin. ....Independenti di Sinistra
MSI–DN ...Movimento sociale italiano
– Destra Nazionale
PCI ....Partito comunista italiano
PLI ....Partito liberale italiano
PR ....Partito radicale
PRI ....Partito republicano italiano
PSDI ....Partito socialista
democratico italiano
PSI...........Partito socialista italiano
SVP..........Sudtiroler Volkspartei
(Partito popolare sudtirolese)
UV–PSDA Union Valdotaine – Partito
sardo d'azione

Luxembourg
PCS..........Parti chrétien social
DP ....Parti démocratique
POSL ....Parti ouvrier socialiste

Netherlands
CDA ....Christen Democratisch Appèl
PPR ....Politieke Partij Radikalen
PSP ....Pacifistisch Socialistische Partij
PvdA ....Partij van de Arbeid
SGP ....Staatkundig Gereformeerde
Partij
VVD ....Volkspartij voor Vrijheid
en Democratie

United Kingdom
C ....Conservative Party
Dem U ......Democratic Unionist Party (NI)
Lab ....Labour Party
OUP ....Official Ulster Unionist
Party (NI)
SDLP ....Social Democratic and
Labour Party (NI)
SNP..........Scottish National Party

EP committee membership

In spite of representations that separate committees should be established on fisheries and on human rights, the European Parliament decided to maintain its existing 17 committees plus the Committee on the Verification of Credentials which is provided for in its standing orders. Membership of the 18 committees is as follows, with the vice-chairmanships given in order of precedence:

Committee on Agriculture, Fisheries and Food (45 members)
Chairman: Mr Teun Tolman (Netherlands, EPP).
Vice-Chairmen: M. Louis Eyraud (France, Soc), Herr Freidrich-Wilhelm Graefe zu Baringdorf (Germany, ARC), M. Jean Mouchel (France, RDE).
SOC (12) Castle, Crawley, Eyraud, Guarraci, Morris, Romeos, Rothe, Sutra de Germa, Thareau, Vernimmen, Wettig, Woltjer.
EPP (12) Bocklet, Borgo, Clinton, Dalsass, Debatisse, Früh, Marck, Mertens, F. Pisoni, N. Pisoni, Stavrou, Tolman.
ED (5) Battersby, Jepsen, Plumb, Provan, Simmonds.
COMM (5) Adamou, Gatti, Marinaro, Maffre-Baugé, Pranchère.
LD (3) S. Martin, Maher, B. Nielsen.
RDE (4) Fanton, McSharry, Mouchel, Musso.
ARC (2) Graefe zu Baringdorf, Christensen.
DR (1) Stirbois.
NI (1) Happart.

Political Affairs Committee (45 members)
Chairman: Sgr Roberto Formigoni (Italy, EPP).
Vice-Chairmen: Herr Klaus Hänsch (Germany, Soc), Sir James Scott-Hopkins (United Kingdom, ED), M. Jean-François Deniau (France, LD).
SOC (14) Amadei, Charzat, B. Friedrich, Glinne, Hänsch, van den Heuvel-Blank, Jospin, Lomas, Martelli, Newens, Plaskovitis, Seefeld, Van Miert, Walter.
EPP (12) Antoniozzi, Bernard-Reymond, Blumenfeld, Boutos, Croux, de Mita, Formigoni, Habsburg, Klepsch, Lenz, Penders, Pöttering.
ED (5) Bethell, Lady Elles, Prag, Scott-Hopkins, Vanneck.
COMM (4) Cervetti, Ephremidis, Piquet, Segre.
LD (3) Bettiza, Deniau, Gawronski.
RDE (3) Anglade, Coste-Floret, Flanagan.
ARC (2) Hammerich, Piermont.
DR (1) Le Pen.
NI (1) Paisley.

Budgets Commitee (42 members)
Chairman: M. Jean-Pierre Cot (France, Soc).
Vice-Chairmen: Mr Richie Ryan (Ireland, EPP), Mr David Curry (United Kingdom, ED), Signora Carla Barbarella (Italy, Comm).
SOC (12) Abens, Arndt, Cot, Dankert, Fich, Fuillet, Hoff, Pitt, Rigo, Tomlinson, Varfis, von der Vring.
EPP (10) Bardong, Chiusano, Christodoulou, Cornelissen, Deprez, Langes, Mizzau, Pfennig, Ryan, Schön.
ED (5) Catherwood, Curry, Douro, J. Elles, Normanton.
COMM (4) Barbarella, Boserup, Chambeiron, Spinelli.
LD (4) di Bartolomei, Louwes, Rossi, Scrivener.
RDE (3) Lalor, Malaud, Pasty.
ARC (1) Bonde.
DR (2) Antony, Chaboche.

Committee on Economic and Monetary Affairs and Industrial Policy (42 members)
Chairman: Dr Barry Seal (United Kingdom, Soc).
Vice-Chairmen: M. Jean-François Mancel (France, RDE), Dr Philipp von Bismarck (Germany, EPP), Mr Peter Beazley (United Kingdom, ED).
SOC (13) Besse, Falconer, Gautier, Gredal, van Hemeldonck, Mattina, Mavros, Metten, Mihr, Quin, Rogalla, Seal, Wagner.
EPP (11) Abelin, Beumer, von Bismarck, Ercini, Franz, I. Friedrich, Herman, Raftery, Starita, Wedekind, von Wogau.
ED (5) P. Beazley, Cassidy, de Ferranti, Oppenheim, Patterson.
COMM (5) Bonaccini, Kyrkos, de March, Novelli, Trupia.
LIB (4) de Vries, de Gucht, T. Nielsen, Wolff.
RDE (2) Juppé, Mancel.
DR (2) Chaboche, Romualdi.

Committee on Energy, Research and Technology (30 members)
Chairman: M. Michel Poniatowski (France, LD).
Vice-Chairmen: Herr Bernhard Sälzer (Germany, EPP), Mr Gordon Adam (United Kingdom, Soc), Mr Madron Seligman (United Kingdom, ED).
SOC (9) Adam, Glezos, Lienemann, Linkohr, Lizin, Schinzel, Smith, Viehoff, West.
EPP (7) Ciancaglini, Estgen, Mallet, Münch, Rinsche, Sälzer, Späth.
ED (4) Møller, Seligman, Toksvig, Turner.
COMM (3) Ippolito and two others.
LD (2) Pininfarina, Poniatowski.
RDE (2) Carignon, Fitzsimons.
ARC (2) Molinari, Staes.
DR (1) Petronio.

Committee on External Economic Relations (25 members)
Chairman: Dame Shelagh Roberts (United Kingdom, ED).
Vice-Chairmen: Mr Michael Hindley (United Kingdom, Soc), Herr Jochen van Aerssen (Germany, EPP), Mme Jacqueline Thome-Patenôtre (France, RDE).
SOC (7) Brinkmeier, Ford, Hindley, Motchane, Massari, Seeler, Wieczorek-Zeul.
EPP (7) van Aerssen, Costanzo, Mühlen, Tzounis, Van Rooij, Zahorka, Zarges.
ED (3) Kilby, Moorhouse, Roberts.
COMM (2) Galluzzi, Reichlin.
LD (3) Chinaud, de Winter, Toussaint.
RDE (1) Thome-Patenôtre.
ARC (1) Heinrich.
DR (1) de Camaret.

Committee on Legal Affairs and Citizens' Rights (25 members)

Chairman: Mme Marie-Claude Vayssade (France, Soc).
Vice-Chairmen: Mr Dimitrios Evrigenis (Greece, EPP),
M. Georges Donnez (France, LD), Mr Nikolaos Gazis
(Greece, Soc).
SOC (7) Gazis, Hoon, Rothley, Vayssade, Vetter,
Zagari, Lynge.
EPP (5) Casini, Evrigenis, Fontaine, Malangré,
Stauffenberg.

ED (3) O'Hagan, Price, Prout.
COMM (2) Barzanti, Gremetz
LD (1) Donnez.
RDE (2) de la Malène, Pons.
ARC (1) Schwalba-Hoth.
DR (2) Petronio, Pordea.
NI (2) Tortora, Ulburghs.

Committee on Social Affairs and Employment (30 members)

Chairman: Mr Michael Welsh (United Kingdom, ED).
Vice-Chairmen: Frau Heinke Salisch (Germany, Soc), Mr
John McCartin (Ireland, EPP), Mr Alexandros Alavanos
(Greece, Comm).
SOC (10) d'Ancona, Bachy, Dido', Dury. E. H.
Christiansen, Megahy, Peters, Salisch, Stewart,
Vgenopoulos.
EPP (8) Brok, Chanterie, Ciancaglini, Gaibisso,
Yannakou, Iodice, Maij-Weggen, McCartin.

ED (3) Stewart-Clark, Tuckman, Welsh.
COMM (3) Alavanos, J. Hoffmann, Raggio.
LIB (2) Groenendaal, Lonquet.
RDE (2) Fitzgerald, Chouraqui.
ARC (1) Harlin.
DR (1) Le Chevallier.

Committee on Regional Policy and Regional Planning (28 members)

Chairman: Signor Pancrazio de Pasquale (Italy, Comm).
Vice-Chairmen: M. Daniel Ducarme (Belgium, LD), Mr
Edward Newman (United Kingdom, Soc), Signor Mauro
Chiabrando (Italy, EPP).
SOC (9) Avgerinos, Gadioux, Griffiths, Hume, D.
Martin, Moroni, Newman, Sakellariou, Schreiber.
EPP (7) Anastassopoulos, Boot, Chiabrando,
Giummarra, Ligios, O'Donnell, Pötschki.

ED (3) C. Beazley, Hutton, Taylor.
COMM (2) de Pasquale, Verges.
LIB (2) Romeo, Ducarme.
RDE (2) Barrett, Lemass.
ARC (2) Columbu, Vandemeulebroucke.
DR (1) Almirante.

Transport Committee (24 members)

Chairman: Mr Georgios Anastassopoulos (Greece, EPP).
Vice-Chairmen: Herr Jan Klinkenborg (Germany, Soc),
Herr Karl-Heinz Hoffmann (Germany, EPP), Mr Leslie
Huckfield (United Kingdom, Soc).
SOC (9) Cryer, Fatous, Huckfield, Klinkenborg,
Papoutsis, Remacle, Stevenson, Topmann, Visser.
EPP (6) Baudis, Braun-Moser, Ebel, K-H. Hoffmann,
Lambrias, Starita.

ED (3) Faith, Marshall, Newton Dunn.
COMM (2) Carossino, Rossetti.
LDE (1) Wijsenbeek.
RDE (1) Roux (F).
DRS (1) Buttafuoco.
NI (1) van der Waal.

Committee on the Environment, Public Health and Consumer Protection (31 members)

Chairman: Frau Beate Weber (Germany, Soc).
Vice-Chairmen: Frau Ursula Schleicher (Germany,
EPP), Frau Undine-Uta Bloch von Blottnitz (Germany,
ARC), Mr Kenneth Collins (United Kingdom, Soc).
SOC (9) Bombard, Collins, Hughes, Muntingh, Schmid,
Tognoli, Tongue, Vittinghoff, Weber.
EPP (7) Alber, Banotti, Dalsass, Lentz-Cornette,
Michelini, Parodi, Schleicher.

ED (4) Cottrell, Caroline Jackson, Pearce, Sherlock.
COMM (3) Moravia, Mme Squarcialupi and another.
LIB (2) Nordmann, Veil.
RDE (2) Dupuy, Vernier.
ARC (3) Bloch von Blottnitz, van der Lek, Roelants du
Vivier.
DR (1) Collinot.

Committee on Youth Affairs, Culture, Education, Information and Sport (24 members).

Chairman: Mrs Winifred Ewing (United Kingdom,
RDE).
Vice-Chairmen: M. Roger Fajardie (France, Soc), Sgr
Gustavo Selva (Italy, EPP), Sgr Giovanni Papapietro
(Italy, Comm).
SOC (6) Elliott, Fajardi, Gallo, McMahon, Pelikan,
Seibel-Emmerling.
EPP (7) Gerontopoulos, Hahn, Hersant, Münch, Peus,
Pomilio, Selva.

Ed (3) Brookes, Howell, McMillan-Scott.
COM (2) Fanti, Papapietro.
LIB (1) Groenendaal.
RDE (2) Baudouin, Ewing.
ARC (2) Bøgh, Klöckner.
DR (1) Tripodi.

Development and Cooperation Committee (42 members)

Chairman: Frau Katharina Focke (Germany, Soc).
Vice-Chairmen: Sgr Giovanni Bersani (Italy, EPP), M.
Francis Wurtz (France, Comm), Mr John de Courcy Ling
(United Kingdom, ED).
SOC (13) Baget Bozzo, Balfe, Buchan, Cohen,
Fellermaier, Focke, Loo, McGowan, Pantazi, Pery,
Saby, Simons, Schmid.
EPP (10) Bersani, Cassanmagnago Cerretti, de Backer,
Lemmer, Luster, Michelini, Pirkl, Rabbethge, Vergeer,
Wawrzik.

ED (4) De Courcy Ling, Christopher Jackson, Simpson,
Daly.
COMM (4) Pajetta, Cinciari Rodano, Trivelli, Wurtz.
LD (3) Beyer de Ryke, Flesch, Galland.
RDE (3) Andrews, Flosse, Guermeur.
ARC (3) Castellina, Kuijpers, Verbeek.
DR (1) d'Ormesson.
NI (1) Pannella.

21

EP COMMITTEE MEMBERSHIP

Budgetary Control Committee (30 members)
Chairman: Herr Heinrich Aigner (Germany, EPP).
Vice-Chairmen: Mr David Martin (United Kingdom, Soc), Fru Bodil Boserup (Denmark, Comm), Mr Robert Battersby (United Kingdom, ED).
SOC (10) Dankert, Fellermaier, Fuillet, Martin, Pitt, Schreiber, Sutra de Germa, Varfis, Wettig, Hoff.
EPP (8) Aigner, Bardong, Giummarra, Marck, Ryan, Schön, Cornelissen, Lentz-Cornette.

ED (3) Battersby, Price, Simmonds.
COMM (3) Barbarella, Boserup, Gatti.
LD (2) Scrivener, Flesch.
RDE (2) Mouchel, Guermeur.
ARC (1) Harlin.
DR (1) Dimitriadis.

Committee on the Rules of Procedure and Petitions (25 members)
Chairman: Sgr Giuseppe Amadei (Italy, Soc).
Vice-Chairmen: M. Raphaël Chanterie (Belgium, EPP), Mme Raymonde Dury (Belgium, Soc), Herr Frank Schwalba-Hoth (Germany, ARC).
SOC (8) Adam, Bombard, Dury, Gazis, Griffiths, Pelikan, Rogalla, Rothley.
EPP (6) Anastassopoulos, Boot, Chanterie, Lima, Malangré, Wedekind.

ED (3) Cottrell, Patterson, Prout.
COMM (2) Cinciari Rodano, de Pasquale.
LD (2) Donnez, Toussaint.
RDE (1) McSharry.
ARC (1) Schwalba-Hoth.
DR (1) Romualdi.
NI (1) Bonino.

Institutional Affairs Committee (30 members)
Chairman: Sgr Altiero Spinelli (Italy, Comm).
Vice-Chairmen: M. Lambert Croux (Belgium, EPP), Herr Hans-Joachim Seeler (Germany, Soc), Sgr Jas Gawronski (Italy, LD).
SOC (9) Amadei, Dido', Hansch, Mavros, Mehagy, Seeler, Sutra de Germa, Van Miert, Zagari.
EPP (8) van Aerssen, Cassanmagnago Cerretti, Croux, Evrigenis, Giavazzi, Lecanuet, Stauffenberg, Zarges.

EDE (3) Prag, Stewart-Clark, Toksvig.
COMM (3) Ephremidis, Fanti, Spinelli.
LD (3) Gawronski, de Gucht, Nord.
RDE (2) Fitzgerald, Musso.
ARC (1) Columbu.
DR (1) de Camaret.

Committee on Women's Rights (25 members)
Chairman: Frau Marlene Lenz (Germany, EPP).
Vice-Chairmen: Ms Christine Crawley (United Kingdom, Soc), Signora Maria Lisa Cinciari Rodano (Italy, Comm), Ka Marietta Yannakou (Greece, EPP).
SOC (9) Crawley, Lizin, Newman, Pantazi, Quin, Salisch, Schmid, Vayssade, Wieczorek-Zeul.
EPP (7) Braun-Moser, Cassanmagnago Cerretti, de Backer-Van Ocken, Fontaine, Yannakou, Lenz, Maij-Weggen.

ED (3) Faith, Caroline Jackson, Jepsen.
COMM (2) Cinciari Rodano, Trupia.
LD (1) Groenendaal.
RDE (1) Lemass.
ARC (1) Heinrich.
DR (1) Lehideux.

Verification of Credentials Committee (9 members)
Chairman: Herr Dieter Rogalla (Germany, Soc).
Vice-Chairmen: Signora Maria Luisa Cassanmagnago Cerretti (Italy, EPP), Mr Geoffrey Hoon (United Kingdom, Soc), Herr Kurt Malangré (Germany, EPP).
SOC (2) Hoon, Rogalla.

EPP (2) Cassanmagnago Cerretti, Malangré.
ED (1) Price.
COMM (1) Barzanti.
LD (1) Wijsenbeek.
RDE (1) Flanagan.
ARC (1) Bloch von Blottnitz.

Victory even with an austerity programme

By Ian Murray
The Times correspondent in Brussels

The centre right Belgian coalition government went into the European elections knowing it must have made itself unpopular by its tough austerity programme, but hopeful it could still command a majority of the vote. Thanks solely to the Flemish vote, it managed to do so.

For all that it likes to call itself the centre of the European Community, Belgium, like every other country, almost succeeded in ignoring totally the European dimension of its campaign. The austerity programme was the background against which the battle was fought. The weapons used depended largely on which side of the linguistic frontier the voters lived.

In Flanders, which is now the wealthier part of the country, old resentments against French-speaking Wallonia won further support for the regional parties. In Wallonia, where the stricken steel and coal industries had left desperately high unemployment, voters showed their resentment against the Flemish-dominated government by voting Socialist instead of for the regional parties.

There was also a real swing to the Socialists in Flanders and the leader of their list, Karel van Miert, proved to be the most popular of all the 432 candidates in the country. For all that, the ruling coalition could take heart that despite having introduced the most stringent austerity programme most Belgians can remember, it is still capable of easily winning any general election. Even in Wallonia, the left could only hope for the slimmest of majorities.

The real losers in the coalition were the Flemish Christian Democrats, a party with classless traditions which has been an essential member of any Belgian Government since the war. It continued to try to occupy the centre ground of Belgian politics, which meant that its support was eroded from both sides. Those on the left voted Socialist or Ecologist: those on the right voted Liberal or for the regional Volksund Party.

In Wallonia, the Christian Democrats held their own alongside the Liberals. The old protest votes, which succeeded in sending both a Brussels and a Walloon regionalist to Strasbourg, were transferred to the Socialists and to the Ecologists.

The annihilation of the Walloon regionalists was enormously helped by the fact that one of their most popular leaders, José Happart, rebel mayor of what is meant to be a Flemish commune, decided to stand as a Socialist. He was rewarded by scoring the highest number of personal votes cast by French speakers.

There was also a strong personal vote for one independent candidate who had succeeded in winning the 'hopeless' last place on the French speaking list. He was Roger Nols, mayor of the Brussels commune of Schaerbeek, who was standing on an anti-immigration ticket. He won so many personal votes that he was awarded a seat even though the proportional system meant only three out of the 11 on the list got through. This extreme right tendency echoed that in neighbouring France and underlined the widespread belief that immigration was a prime cause of unemployment.

The other worrying splinter vote for the government was the support given on both sides of the linguistic frontier to the ecologist movement, opposed as it was to deployment of nuclear missiles. This had won national seats in the last general election but its support had obviously continued to grow, particularly in Flanders. In consequence, both communities returned a Green candidate to the European Parliament.

Among the voters were presumably the 377 British and Irish nationals who had taken advantage of the Belgian offer to vote in European elections (since both countries usually deny this right to non-residents). The fact that this tiny number from among the 20 000 strong British/Irish community indicated the low level of interest among them.

The independent Liberal candidate who won a seat, thanks to a high turnout for him personally because of his right-wing immigration policies, decided after the election to give up his seat to an official member of the party. Having made his point through the election, he decided he wanted to go back to just being the mayor of his town.

23

THE CAMPAIGN IN DENMARK

Significant victory for Conservatives

by George Clark
former European political correspondent of
The Times

As a result of the more sophisticated propaganda campaigns mounted by all parties, the Euro-election turnout in Denmark increased from 47.8 per cent in 1979 to 52.3 per cent this time. Though one commentator called it 'a boring argument', with the pro- and anti-EEC groupings fairly evenly balanced, there was a lot of venom in the speeches of the tub-thumpers campaigning for the Popular Movement against the EEC. They were often accused of engaging in 'smear tactics' and producing misleading statistics to persuade the hesitating voters to rally behind their banners.

This anti-EEC coalition of minor parties was, at the end of the day, able to rejoice in the prospect of its representation being increased from five to six. But the really significant victory went to the Conservative People's Party which increased its share of the vote by 6.8 per cent, doubling its representation. Its MEPs – Fru Marie Jepsen, Mr Pøul Møller, Mr Claus Toksvig and Fru Jeanette Oppenheim – were a welcome addition to the strength of the European Democratic Group (Conservatives) in the European Parliament. Mr Møller, a member of the bureau of the ED Group, is also a Vice-President of the Parliament.

Mr Toksvig, who came second to Mr Møller in the popular voting list (130 728 votes to Mr Møller's 134 069 – the highest personal vote in Denmark), is a newcomer to the political stage. A former television commentator and correspondent in New York and later in London for the Danish broadcasting service, he was one of the best known candidates on the hustings.

'It is relatively easy to become a well-known face when one works in television,' he said, 'but it is extremely important to win the respect of the voters.'

The Social Democrats who, like the Labour Party in Britain, have reservations about membership of the EEC, lost some votes to the anti-EEC movement but still held their three seats. But for the relatively new anti-tax Progress Party (Fremskridt), the election was a disaster. Not only was its leader, Mr Mogens Glistrup, a tax lawyer, serving three-and-a-half years' prison sentence for tax offences, but the party's vote dropped from 100 702 to 68 747.

As a result, with only 3.5 per cent of the poll, compared with 5.8 per cent in 1979, the party lost its one seat in Strasbourg. Mr Glistrup saved up some of his 'liberty days' in order to leave prison and take part in television and radio discussion programmes and to address meetings.

Although some in his party thought it was a mistake to make him top candidate in their list, he polled nearly 60 000 votes, way ahead of any of his colleagues. And the party itself, though defeated, did better than opinion pollsters had predicted.

The party was formed in 1972 in protest against high income taxation, appealing chiefly to the middle class vote. Its object was to abolish income tax and limit central and local government services. Defence spending was to be drastically reduced (in fact, it was a political joke, spread around the world, that defence policy was to be a gramophone record which would be broadcast continuously on the outbreak of war, announcing 'We surrender' – in Russian!) In recent years, the party has lost public support and the European result confirmed the trend.

In Greenland, Mr Finn Lynge, who sat in the Parliament in the Socialist group, was candidate for the Siumut Party and won again with 55 per cent of the 9 772 votes cast. When Greenland leaves the Community in January 1985, he will be replaced in Parliament by Mr John Iversen of the Socialist People's Party.

The Venstre Liberals retained their two seats, and it was an encouragement to the Coalition Government led by Mr Pøul Schluter, Conservative, that all four parties in the coalition improved their share of the votes (Conservatives, Centre Democrats, Kristeligt Folkeparti and Venstre) – a welcome endorsement in a country where governments have not lasted very long in the years since the war.

Only a grain of comfort for Left

by Diana Geddes
The Times correspondent in Paris

In France, the European elections may mark a watershed in French political life. The ruling coalition of Communists and Socialists suffered a severe blow from which neither may never fully recover, while the two main opposition parties have been left reeling by the spectacular breakthrough of the extreme right National Front.

The great winner of the elections was undoubtedly the National Front. It obtained 11 per cent of the vote, the same as the Communists, having never previously won more than 2 per cent in a national election, though it had scored some notable successes in local elections over the preceding year. It was the best extreme right test score since the Poujadists won 12.5 per cent in the parliamentary elections in 1956. Could the Front's success be sustained, however, or was it just a flash in the pan – a vote of exasperation and protest cast by a rag-bag of disillusioned voters in the safe knowledge that it would have no direct bearing on their lives?

An analysis of those who voted for the National Front indicated that M. Jean-Marie Le Pen, the colourful, ex-paratrooper head of the movement, might well have succeeded in building up a solid core of supporters, equally spread across all age groups and drawn from all socio-economic groups, though with preponderance among the small self-employed. M. Le Pen did particularly well in the big towns where the National Front's cherished themes of law and order and immigration were uppermost in people's minds. In Marseilles, Perpignan, Nice, Toulon and Aix-en-Provence, the National Front won more than 20 per cent of the vote.

Two factors made it difficult to assess the importance of the National Front's score, or that of the other major parties. However, first, 43 per cent of the electorate chose not to vote at all – a record for any French election, national or local – and second, the vote was by proportional representation and that certainly helped to boost the National Front's share of the vote above that which it might expect in a national election.

The Communists were left severely shaken by the collapse of their support in the elections – four points down from the 15 per cent obtained in the presidential elections three years ago, and half the level in the 1979 European elections. Some Communists sought solace in the high abstention rate, claiming that a large section of their traditional supporters felt so disillusion by the Government's failure to keep its promises, that they decided to stay away from the polls altogether.

The underlying reasoning was clear: that those lost sheep would return to the fold once the Government changed its policies so as to conform with the undertakings jointly made by the Communists and Socialists in 1981; or, alternatively, once the Communists left the Government and thereby freed themselves of all responsibility for rising unemployment, falling standards of living, cuts in social services, etc.

However, another section of the Communist Party considered that too facile. It felt that what appeared to be a steadily continuing decline of the party, which had reached its lowest level in more than 50 years, could only be stopped if the underlying structural causes for that decline were identified and tackled – and that meant changing certain fundamental aspects of the party itself.

The party was immediately plunged into an impassioned and sometimes bitter debate, with widely divergent views being expressed, on what steps the party should take to ensure what many believed to be its very survival. One hotly debated issue was whether the party should continue to participate in government, as the vast majority of its supporters seemed to wish, or whether it should cut its losses and leave what was increasingly looking like a sinking ship. If the party was to leave the Government, however, it must look as if it were pushed out: it must avoid the opprobrium of breaking the union of the left a second time.

THE CAMPAIGN IN FRANCE

In the 1981 presidential and legislative elections, the Socialists benefited directly from the decline in the Communist vote. In the European elections that did not happen, however, and the Socialists saw their own proportion of the vote fall sharply to a mere 21 per cent. The combined vote of all the left-wing parties totalled only 36 per cent in the European elections, compared with 47 per cent in the first round of the 1981 presidential elections and 56 per cent in the parliamentary elections in the same year. The electorate's message was clear: they did not like the Government's policies.

But did that mean that the policies themselves were not good? The Government, which had expected to do badly in the elections, argued that it was simply a case of a sick man not liking the medicine he was being given, and insisted that it had no intention of changing its policies which were only just beginning to bear fruit. But it knew that it was engaged in a desperate race against time if it were to produce sufficiently good results to win back its lost supporters in time for the 1986 parliamentary elections.

Not all Socialists agreed with the Government's analysis of the election results. Some, like the left-wing Cérès faction within the party, felt that the policies themselves were wrong, and were encouraged by the Government's defeat at the polls to say so even more loudly than before. Others also disagreed, but kept quiet, fearing that the still very young party, formed only twelve years earlier, would simply disintegrate if it suffered a further severe defeat in 1986, unless an immediate determined effort were made to keep it united.

The only grain of comfort that the left could derive from the elections was that their sharp decline had not seemed to benefit the two main opposition parties, the Gaullist RPR and the centre-right UDF, which had joined forces to form a single list headed by Mme Simone Veil, former President of the European Parliament and one of the most popular French political figures.

Mme Veil's list obtained only 43 per cent of the vote, one point less than the two parties had obtained separately in the European elections in 1979, and well short of the 50 per cent plus goal at which some opposition leaders were originally aiming. Disillusionment with the left had clearly not turned voters back to the traditional opposition parties which they had rejected in 1981.

The opposition was not in a position to reap the fruits of the left's decline. Its own ranks were in disarray, with neither no clear leader nor any clear policies, save that of an indefatigable onslaught against the Government, and it now found itself challenged from its own extreme right. How should it react? Should it join ranks with the National Front, or should it rather seek to isolate it?

All the main parties were forced to engage in a fundamental reappraisal of their positions and policies in the aftermath of the political upheaval caused by the European elections.

West Germany turns somewhat Green

by Michael Binyon
The Times correspondent in Bonn

The elimination of the Free Democrats from the European Parliament and a surge of support for the Greens – these were the main results of the European Election in West Germany. The electorate also delivered a firm rebuff to both the Christian Democratic coalition Government and the Social Democratic opposition, after a campaign that dwelt more on the Government's domestic record after a year in office than on the future of Europe.

The final results gave the FDP 4.8 per cent of the vote – less than the minimum 5 per cent needed under West German election law to win seats at Strasbourg. It was the first time since the founding of the Federal Republic that the party had been eliminated in a national election, and it led to questioning both within the FDP and outside the party of the future role of Germany's smallest party.

The Greens, on the other hand, were jubilant at winning 8.2 per cent – their highest total in a national poll, and a measure of their increased support since their entry into the Bundestag at the general election March 1983. They were the only party to campaign against the European Community as it now is, but insisted they would try to change it from inside rather than lead Germany out of the EEC.

The established parties dismissed the support for the Greens – a loose alliance of pacifists, ecologists, left-wing radicals and feminists – as a normal protest vote. But the Greens won a significant share of the young people's vote, especially in university towns, and captured up to 14 per cent of the vote in some cities. Campaigning hard on environmental issues, they clearly found an echo in today's Germany.

With seven seats at Strasbourg, the party announced plans to form a new faction with Dutch and Belgian ecologists to hasten the 'Greening' of Europe. The Greens are led by Friedrich-Wilhelm Graefe zu Baringdorf, a farmer of no party allegiance, and include the woman editor of the radical Berlin newspaper *Tageszeitung* and a Berlin journalist who was sentenced to two-and-a-half years imprisonment for publishing material deemed to further the cause of terrorism, but released pending appeal.

Chancellor Helmut Kohl described the results of the election as 'unsatisfactory' and a rebuff to his party, which did worse than when it was in opposition at the last European election. The percentage achieved by the CDU fell from 39.1 to 37.5, while the Christian Social Union, the CDU's sister party in Bavaria, suffered a fall from 10.1 to 8.5 per cent.

For the Social Democrats the result was an even greater disappointment. They failed, as an opposition party, to exploit the Government's domestic difficulties, and presented a tired and divided image to the electorate. Herr Willy Brandt, the party chairman, blamed the relatively low turnout – 56.8 per cent compared with 67.5 in 1979 – for the SPD's poor showing, and said the European Community was still not convincing enough to voters.

The Free Democrats found their worst fears confirmed, and after the loss of all four seats at Strasbourg, the party was wracked by internal argument and criticism of Herr Hans-Dietrich Genscher, the party leader. He announced, as a consequence, that he would step down in 1985 instead of the following year. Herr Martin Bangemann, who had been leader of the Liberals in the Parliament at Strasbourg, was expected to succeed Herr Genscher. He was the party's choice a few weeks later to succeed Otto Graf Lambsdorff, the FDP Economics Minister who was forced to resign after being sent for trial on charges of corruption.

The election campaign in Germany was more lively than in several countries but still failed to make much impact on the electorate. Cynics said the reason why all political parties were so eager to get a large turnout was their need for money. Under the federal financing of elections, each vote cast for a party brought a corresponding subsidy to fill the party coffers.

As in many countries, 'Europe' was hardly an issue. Virtually all Germans are in favour of the European Community, which for West Germany has become almost an ersatz father-land, giving the Federal Republic influence and political weight it would be hesitant to use in isolation.

Campaign arguments, therefore, did not turn on the benefits of the Community to Germany, the country's very high contributions or the wrangling over the budget. The Social Democrats largely supported the line taken by Chancellor Kohl on this score, and were as interested as he was in getting Europe moving again.

The main importance of the election was as a national test of the Government's popularity fifteen months after the general election. The SPD openly called on voters to use the poll as such, and to give a clear rebuff to the conservative policies pursued by the Kohl Government.

For the opposition, the timing of the election could not have been more opportune. Chancellor Kohl's coalition was grappling with the worst outbreak of industrial unrest for many years, had barely recovered from the fiasco of the abortive proposals for an amnesty for those evading taxes on political donations, and was nervous at the impending charges against Count Lambsdorff and their political repercussions.

The themes that dominated the campaign were unemployment, cutbacks in social security, the economy, the environment and European integration and security – roughly in that order of importance. The Social Democrats deliberately played down the defence issue, probably realizing that the party was still too divided on this, and that voters had become satiated with arguments for or against the Nato missiles.

Instead, the SPD hit hard at the Government's unpopular cutbacks in state benefits and the lavish social security network, and made the most of the political divisons and public anxieties over the engineering strike.

The Christian Democrats defended their year in office by pointing to clear evidence of economic recovery while accusing the opposition of endangering this through encourage-ment of trade union intransigence on the demands for a 35-hour week.

The CDU also went to lengths to project itself as the real party for Europe in Germany, the inheritor of the Adenauer legacy in building the European Community. Both Herr Kohl and his ministers spoke out forcefully for a stronger, more united, more imaginative Europe. The Chancellor made much of the Franco–German alliance as the kernel of Europe, and promised new joint initiatives with France to get the Community going again – if necessary without Britain and those less enthusiastic members. However, he did not spell out any concrete initiatives.

All parties spent heavily on the campaign. The CDU and SPD each spend around DM 30m, the CSU DM 13m, the FDP DM 7m, and the Greens about DM 1m. Herr Kohl campaigned hard, travelling round the country to election rallies. The SPD chartered a train for whistle-stop campaigning by Herr Brandt, Herr Hans-Jochen Vogel, the party's par-liamentary leader, and other speakers.

Perhaps the most imaginative attempt to give some zest to a campaign that even European-minded Germans found boring was 'Katharina's Circus', named after Frau Katharina Focke, leader of the SPD candidates. Inside the travelling big top, jugglers, acrobats and animal tamers tried to get the party's European message across with a little more bravura than the normal town hall rally.

THE CAMPAIGN IN GREECE

Big parties have a popularity duel

by Mario Modiano
The Times correspondent in Athens

The ruling Socialists and opposition Conservatives in Greece are adjusting their sights and reviewing their tactics in the light of the European election results. The ostensible rejoicing over their respective 'victory' has long died down, and both parties admit privately that the outcome was, if anything, disappointing.

The Panhellenic Socialist Movement (PASOK), the party of Mr Andreas Papandreou, the Prime Minister, was ahead again with over two-fifths of the total vote, but lost no less than 13.5 per cent of its following since 1981. The New Democracy Party (NDP), led by Mr Evangelos Averof-Tositsas, scored modest gains over its 1981 performance, but it failed to beat PASOK and thereby force it into an early general election.

Among the lesser parties the pro-Soviet Communist Party of Greece (KKE) saw its eagerness for a show of strength, that would have increased its bargaining power towards the Socialists, overruled by Moscow's desire that Mr Papandreou's Socialist Government should be left undisturbed to continue destablizing the West from within. Its campaign was low key, so its position remained almost unchanged.

Greek voters, of course, were supposed to be electing their 24 representatives for the European Parliament. However, the two big parties turned the election into a popularity duel, and fostered polarization to squeeze out of the race the third parties which would otherwise have been favoured by the system of simple proportional representation.

However, two small parties managed to survive: the Communist Party of the Interior (KKEes), better known as the Eurocommunists, who managed to reelect the charismatic Leonidas Kyrkos as MEP, and the National Political Union (EPEN), a new extreme right-wing party representing supporters of the jailed ex-dictator, George Papadopoulos.

Lost in the maelstrom of polarization was the Party of Social Democracy (KODISO) of Mr John Pesmazoglou, described as 'the most European of Greeks', who lost his Strasbourg seat and promptly resigned as leader of his party, and the right-wing party of Progressives of Mr Spyras Markezinis, which also lost its seat in the European Parliament.

The election campaign was fought passionately by the two big parties on national rather than European issues. Its results, therefore, bear comparison only with those of the national elections of October 18, 1981, rather than the previous European elections held in Greece on the same date.

It was the NDP that first challenged PASOK to this duel. A Government defeat would have enabled it to invoke the constitutional provision compelling the President to proclaim immediate elections in case of a 'manifest disparity' between the composition of Parliament and the will of the electorate.

PASOK picked up the gauntlet almost with relief. By transposing the battle to the full spectrum of issues, it was spared the need to explain its contradictory European policies. Above all, it enabled the Socialists to stop the drift on their left by brandishing the spectre of a right-wing comeback in case of a PASOK defeat.

Socialist losses were equally divided between the parties on their right and left. The drift on the right did not turn into a massive flight by centre voters, the same voters who caused PASOK's strength to double twice between 1974 and 1981. Disappointed as these moderate voters may be of the Government's poor performance and concerned by its Marxist rhetoric, this was still not enough for them to overcome their almost atavistic aversion for the right-wing.

Perhaps the most intriguing twist in the election was that PASOK lost heavily to the NDP in the big cities – mainly Athens, Piraeus and Salonika – which are traditionally left-leaning. It maintained a strong position in the countryside where the farmer's lot has substantially improved thanks to European Community financing, the origin of which the PASOK Government is careful to conceal from the beneficiaries.

THE CAMPAIGN IN GREECE

In the cities, the more sophisticated voter felt the need to express his resentment for PASOK's over-exposure on state television, the arrogance with which it wields power and, above all, the absence of dialogue before it takes decisions that affect the lives of millions. Attitudes such as these made PASOK's promise of 'power to the people' sound hollow.

Mainly in the cities, the housewife feels the pinch of soaring prices, the school-leaver stumbles on the heightening wall of unemployment, the small businessman is harrassed by bureaucracy, the patient finds no hospital bed, and the man-in-the-street chokes with pollution and indignation over the declining quality of city life. The NDP assumed it would win because of all these signs of swelling opposition – the gigantic campaign rallies, the results of professional union elections, the changes in the student vote. But it misread the city-dweller's reactions, hoping that it reflected a nationwide state of mind. It did not.

The NDP cashed in on disappointment, but it was a vote against PASOK, not a vote in favour of the NDP. The NDP campaign addressed itself more to its established clientele than the centrist voters it wished to attract from PASOK. Evidence of this is that part of its gains the NDP in turn lost to the extreme right EPEN. The results proved that the Conservatives, after 32 months of Socialist rule, had failed to regain enough credibility as an alternative to the PASOK rule.

This failure is bound to revive the leadership crisis that has tormented this party since its leader, Mr Averof-Tositsas, who is 74, underwent heart surgery in London in 1982. The operation was a success, but a swarm of contenders jockeyed for position in the succession struggle. The rivalry was hastily swept under the rug to convey an image of unity in view of the European elections.

Now NDP cadres who feel that the party should become more appealing to the centre voter in order to win the next general election (not due until October 1985), insist that this cannot be done under the leadership of Mr Averof-Tositsas who, rightly or wrongly, had acquired a reputation as a hardliner.

PASOK itself is in for some soul-searching. If this had been a general election, it would have barely maintained its majority in Parliament. A loss of its centrist voters on the right could easily topple the delicate balance, or force it to coalesce with KKE. Analysts believe PASOK will continue to rely on its radical rhetoric to keep its left happy, while its actions will be such as not to alienate its right.

And, ah yes, of course there was a European dimension in this election. Its greatest benefit from Europe was that both sides lined up high-powered lists of candidates for the European Parliament. In the case of the NDP, Mr Averof-Tositsas himself led the list to underline the importance of the contest, but he is eventually expected to resign his Strasbourg seat and cede it to the runner-up.

The average Greek does not really understand what the European Parliament is all about. With a Government ideologically hostile to what party propaganda refers to as 'the Europe of monopolies', the public here is mostly kept in the dark about European issues. Perhaps the best known facts among Greeks about Greek MEP's is that they get a lot of travelling done, and very handsome salaries to boot!

Loss of four seats a major blow for Labour

by Richard Ford
The Times correspondent in Ireland

The Republic of Ireland honeymoon with the EEC has ended and the turnout in the Euro poll reflected that and disenchantment with the country's three major political parties. Only 48 per cent of the electorate bothered to vote compared with 63 per cent five years earlier despite the benefits – about Irish £4000m – that membership has brought to the country.

Like elsewhere, politicians had to fight against voter apathy, and domestic rather than European issues dominated the campaign. When the results were declared, Dr Garret FitzGerald's Fine Gael party must have given a collective sigh of relief that the electorate had not turned decisively against it after seventeen months as a senior partner in coalition government.

The results confirmed the trend that Fine Gael's party machine now rivals Mr Charles Haughey's Fianna Fáil in professionalism, leaving the junior coalition government partner, Labour, with little but envy for their rival's organizational skill. Labour's loss of all its four seats in Europe was a major blow, leaving the Republic as the only country in the EEC without representation in a left-wing group at Strasbourg.

With unemployment at more than 210000, high taxation and inflation of 10.1 per cent, Fianna Fáil saw the election as a golden opportunity to attack the coalition government and get the electorate to deliver a damning verdict on Dr FitzGerald's leadership. From the outset, Mr Haughey made it clear he saw the poll as hastening the Government's downfall, and adverts in newspapers urged the electorate to vote against bad government and for Fianna Fáil. The opposition also brought the issue of Ireland's neutrality into the campaign and took an increasingly hard line on the report of the New Ireland Forum, insisting that Britain call a conference which would lead to a united Ireland governed from Dublin.

Fine Gael and Labour expected revenge from an electorate after months of economic austerity and at times ineffective leadership. It was widely believed that the administration postponed local government elections due on the same day as the Euro poll because it was afraid of the ground it would lose. However, Fianna Fáil failed to get the huge anti-government endorsement it desired, though the party did achieve a majority of seats, allowing Mr Haughey to say he had got the overall majority he had sought since becoming leader of the party in 1979. But it was only a modest success, giving the party no guarantee that in a general election they would win an overall majority of seats in the Dail.

Its overall percentage of first preference votes was, at 39.2 per cent, still 1 per cent behind the combined totals of Fine Gael and Labour and the party was unable to capitalize on anger among the electorate, particularly concern over high taxation and high unemployment. In areas crucial for victory in a general election they had little success. In Dublin, where there are 48 Dail seats, they found themselves unable to regain ground, particularly south of the city. Fianna Fáil still needs to widen its support among the urban middle-class voters but the problem facing Mr Haughey is that while his hard line Republicanism increases support in the west of the country, it does not appeal to the urban voter, who has been giving his support to Dr FitzGerald.

While Fine Gael's increasing professionalism enabled it to manage its vote well enough to increase its seats from four to six, it still lost support in Dublin and its Labour partner suffered a major setback by losing the four seats it had surprisingly won in 1979. Though Labour lost those seats, it is ironic that its percentage share of the vote dropped less than the two main parties. Nevertheless, the loss was a psychological blow, hitting moral and party finances and confirming the view that its senior partner in government is making gains at its expense.

The party, suffering from poor organization, was hit hardest by anti-Government feeling with the result that opposition to continuing in the coalition is likely to grow within the organization. Inevitably, Labour's poor showing led to speculation about the long-term future of the Government though it is likely to run its full term of office and into a general election in 1987. But Labour will increase pressure for more concessions from Fine Gael and action on inexpensive policies, particularly in the area of social reform.

Labour wants movement on reforming the Republic's contraceptive laws, changes in legislation affecting women and particularly the abolition of the status of illegitimacy and action on unemployment and taxation levels. Dr FitzGerald has promised that there is much legislation currently being drafted and that future sessions of the Dail will be busy with emphasis on reform.

Because Labour is in government it has been unable to attract the protest vote which in the EEC election went to the Workers Party, Sinn Fein and independents. The Workers Party did not make the gains it expected but Sinn Fein got 4.9 per cent of first preference votes although its eight candidates lost their deposits. Its involvement in community work, particularly in Dublin, where it has been active in groups fighting the drugs problem, paid dividends and they have gained support among disaffected voters and the young.

It is this tide of disaffection and alienation, seemingly wanting change, that Labour should be able to attract and which, along with the apathy revealed during the campaign, serves as a warning to the Republic's two major parties.

One vote which showed an overwhelming majority was on a referendum giving the Dail power to legislate for non-nationals living in the Republic to vote in presidential and general elections. The referendum will be followed by legislation giving 12000 British citizens living in Ireland voting rights. Dr FitzGerald was delighted that the referendum was passed by an overwhelming majority: more than 75 per cent of the electorate voted 'Yes', with 24 per cent opposing.

Reminder provided by funeral in Rome

by Peter Nicholls
The Times correspondent in Rome

The European elections will have their place in Italian political history if only for the fact that the Communists, for the first time, overtook the Christian Democrats to become the country's biggest single party. That was a fact, even if the extent of the lead was a genuine photo-finish: the margin was a mere 0.3 per cent.

The question which remains is whether the Communist success means that a new page has been turned or that the results amount to little more than footnote to history. There have been elections at regional and local government level since the European competition but they were not wide enough or decisive enough to give much indication as to the resilience of the Communist advance.

It was natural to suppose that the Communists gained from the fact that Enrico Berlinguer, the party secretary, died of a stroke in the midst of the campaign. He was given a huge funeral in Rome and the cortège passed close to the Roman forum where the body of the murdered Caesar was burned. Naturally that setting provided a reminder of the most famous case in ancient history of the use of a dead man for political purposes, namely Mark Antony's harangue to the people of Rome over Caesar's body. But it would be an over-simplification to suppose that the Communists gained simply because of the sentimental force provided by the death of their leader.

That was an element, but its true weight is extremely difficult to judge. In the polling booths there was undoubtedly a tendency on the part of some voters to react to this possibility by giving their vote to the Christian Democrats in order to counter-balance the effect of the possible emotional attraction of voting Communist.

This indirect effect of Berlinguer's death explains what was the most surprising result after the Communist gains, namely, that the smaller parties performed disappointingly. For several years now there have been signs of an increasingly important role for the smaller parties which have indeed been, in general, effectively led. The Republican, Senator Giovanni Spadolini, became the first Prime Minister not to have been drawn from the Christian Democrat ranks since the end of the war. He was followed in the Prime Minister's post by Signor Bettino Craxi, who was the first Socialist to hold the post.

Signor Craxi arrived at the head of a five-party coalition without any ministerial experience. He had, however, behind him his work in changing the fissionomy of Italian socialism. His aim as secretary was to prepare his party for governmental responsibilities and to build it up as an alternative to Communism. The traditionally divided Socialist Party, with a tendency in a part of its membership to feel the attraction of the Communists, appeared under his leadership to be far more disciplined and along the lines of Craxi's own thinking.

And so he arrived at the Prime Ministership in August 1983 with a reputation for strong-mindedness combined with managerial skills. Some people feared him and he was frequently portrayed by the cartoonists as a latter-day Mussolini. He has been at pains to correct this image of himself even if neither he nor his associates would deny a somewhat brusque manner. His 10 per cent of the total vote when he took over the party was small compared with the 30 per cent controlled by the Communists. He nevertheless looked set to extend his base and, to justify the new character he had imposed on his party, his gains would have had to come from the Communists rather than from his allies in government.

The prestige and the practical powers of the Prime Ministership in electoral terms were thought to assure him an advance in the European elections. In the event, he made no progress. Instead of gaining support for his party, he must have paid the price for having accepted the stationing of cruise missiles in Sicily and the general unpopularity of his coalition.

Senator Spadolini, meanwhile, who had substantially increased the support for his

Republican Party as Prime Minister, allied himself with the Liberals for the European election. This coupling, too, provided a disappointment – and this despite the fact that the Republicans and Liberals kept their campaign strictly on European rather than on national issues.

Perhaps that was a part of their problem. Italians are probably the most convinced Europeans of the whole Community but this did not prevent them from turning the European elections into as much a national as a Community affair. The Communists themselves expressed this idea clearly with their slogan: 'What Italy do you want in Europe?' and this was followed by a list of the scandals at present in the public eye, beginning with the illegal masonic lodge 'Propaganda 2' which at one point threatened to topple the Government.

The total political effect of all these elements which emerged from the European elections was a shift backward towards a concentration of strength behind the two biggest parties – the Communists and the Christian Democrats. (Until these elections one would have written Christian Democrats and Communists.) The slight advantage in terms of absolute support won by the Communists had a psychological importance rather than political weight.

As frequently happens in Italian affairs, a setback for the coalition offered hopes of a better performance by the Government as a consequence of the shock administered by the voters. In a sense, Signor Craxi is strengthened for having emerged with a disappointing result. But this is only true in immediate tactical terms. He will need to do better than this in the early future if he wishes to remain the arbiter of the situation.

Luxembourg has its magnificent six

by Ian Murray
The Times correspondent in Brussels

For the second time running, Luxembourg took advantage of the fact that European elections were being held in order to stage its own general election. This meant that the voting there was probably the most accurate indication of local political feeling. There could have been no tactical voting to send warning signals to the government.

Thus the sharp swing to the left against the centre right coalition was a very real one, doubtless born of the anger caused by problems in the steel industry and disenchantment among the largely conservative farming community at the way EEC-imposed dairy quotas were hitting incomes. That the recession was making itself felt in opulent Luxembourg was proof of how deep it had gone, and the general mood was that the best alternative was to vote Socialist.

This meant that on a European level the Liberal Party, which had formed a coalition with the Socialists since the last election, lost one of its two seats to the Socialists. At a national level it forced the dominant Christian Democrats to consider forming the next government as either a grand alliance of all parties or as a straight partnership with the Socialists.

The Christian Democrats had little to worry about on their own account. They retained their three seats in Europe and lost out only marginally in the national parliament. They remained an essential senior partner in any government and the most representative party in their country.

The tiny size of the electorate (smaller than any average British constituency) means that the Luxemburger, with six members to represent him, has the loudest individual voice in the European Parliament. It also means that good support for smaller parties is not enough to win a seat since there are not enough available for all. Thus although the Luxembourg Ecologists won nearly as high a percentage of the vote as their colleagues in Belgium and West Germany, they did not succeed in sending a member to the Parliament. Nevertheless, their success shows how wide the Green movement has become.

Luxembourg retains a very special interest in the European Parliament and is still fighting a case through the European Court (which is based in Luxembourg) to try to force members to return there for at least some of the full sessions. The Parliament building has even been enlarged so that it can accommodate members from Spain and Portugal as and when those two countries join. For the Luxemburger, the Grand Duchy remains the logical seat of the Parliament.

Decision on missiles overshadowed campaign

by Robert Schull
The Times correspondent in The Hague

The 1984 European elections had the dubious distinction in this traditionally European-minded country of provoking the lowest turnout on record for an election in the Netherlands. Only just over half of the 10 million strong electorate bothered to vote, nearly 8 per cent less than in the 1979 election.

Instead of being seen as in contradiction with Dutch European-mindedness, this electoral apathy was explained by some observers as a deliberate decision not to vote for a Parliament that has no real powers. As one observer put it: 'Perhaps those who stayed away were the true Europeans.'

A more plausible explanation seems to be a total lack of interest – also on the part of the media – in the activities of the European Parliament as was demonstrated by an opinion poll conducted only a few months before the election. This disclosed that only 30 per cent of the population was aware that elections were being held in 1984 and only 10 per cent could identify these as European elections.

Interest in the election was hardly stimulated by the election campaign which passed largely unnoticed in spite of the considerable financial means the parties had at their disposal. Most Dutch voters would be hard put to name even a few of Holland's 25 MEPs, with the possible exception of Mr Pieter Dankert, then its President.

Politically speaking, the campaign was largely overshadowed by the Dutch Cabinet decision on cruise missiles, which was taken a fortnight before the election, culminating in a debate, carried by the Government in the Lower House on the eve of polling day, which in the Netherlands was on Thursday, June 14.

Not surprisingly the cruise missile issue also dominated the various explanations proffered concerning the election result.

It was particularly noted that if these had been national elections the ruling centre right coalition of Christian Democrats and conservative Liberals would have lost their parliamentary majority. Nonetheless, although Prime Minister Ruud Lubbers' Christian Democrats suffered a loss of two seats in the European Parliament in comparison with the 1979 election, they did marginally better than in the 1982 national election, contrary to expectations. In this respect, the result of the Christian Democrats is thought to have been enhanced by Mr Lubbers' skilful handling of the cruise missile debate.

For the junior coalition partners, the Liberals, the opposite is true. They gained one seat in the European Parliament but lost nearly 5 per cent of the vote compared to the 1982 national election. Labour, the main opposition party, emerged as the overall winner, displacing the Christian Democrats as the largest Dutch political party in the European Parliament and confirming its position as the largest political party in the Netherlands since the 1982 national elections.

Labour gains were not, however, either as spectacular as opinion polls had led people to believe or as could have been expected for an opposition party, particularly in the wake of the highly controversial Cabinet cruise missile decision. In this respect, it was felt that Labour attempts to turn a European Parliament vote for Labour into a vote against cruise missiles misfired.

In all, nine parties took part in the European elections of which four were represented in the previous Parliament and five in the new Parliament. One of the parties in the previous

Parliament, the left liberal Democrats '66, confirmed the electoral disaster that befell it in the 1982 national election and lost both its seats in the European Parliament.

A seat was won, however, for the first time by a combined list of three small right-wing Calvinist parties. In the 1979 election they had presented themselves separately. The Greens appeared on the Dutch political scene for the first time. A combined list of the Greens, who are not represented in the national parliament, with three small left-wing parties is represented for the first time in the European Parliament with two seats.

A party that did not win a seat was the Centrum Party, the Dutch equivalent of the National Front. There was concern, however, at the fact that with 2.8 per cent of the vote, this party, which has one seat in the Lower House in The Hague, has trebled its electoral support since the 1982 national elections.

Voting in the Netherlands was, as in national elections, on the basis of proportional representation. Dutch citizens living in other EEC countries were allowed to vote by mail while Dutch civil servants (such as diplomats) stationed in third countries also had the right to vote. Nationals from EEC countries living in the Netherlands also had the right to vote in the Dutch election provided they did not exercise that right in their own country.

The best news came after the result

by Philip Webster
of *The Times* political staff

The second direct election to the European Parliament was held in the United Kingdom on June 14, 1984, and proved no more successful than the first in capturing the interest of the electorate. Quite irrespective of the showing of the individual parties, it was by any yardstick of democratic involvement a failure. If ever confirmation were needed that the spirit of the European Community flickers low in Britain, here was it.

No one expected a rush to the polls. But it was generally anticipated that the pitiful turnout of 1979 (31.6 per cent), for an election held only one month after the general election of that year when the country's political energies were sapped, would be easily surpassed. However, that did not happen. By the time the last votes were counted on Monday, June 18, it was evident that there had been another nationwide display of stupendous indifference. The official turnout figure for the 81 seats in England, Scotland, Wales and, Northern Ireland was 32.56 per cent, by far the lowest in the ten countries of the Community. In England, Scotland and Wales, it came to 31.8 per cent. There were no close rivals for the wooden spoon.

But if their apathy threshold had barely altered, the voters of Britain made significant changes in the political balance of the contingent they sent to Strasbourg. In numerical terms the story was simple. The Conservatives won the election with 5 426 866 votes (40.8 per cent) and 45 seats. It lost 15 of the seats it had held since 1979 to the Labour Party, which received in total 4 865 224 votes (36.5 per cent) and won 32 seats, compared with just 17 in 1979. The Liberal–Social Democratic Party Alliance, which had emerged as the third force in British politics in the previous Parliament's term, fared no better in terms of seats than had the Liberals on their own in 1979. With a combined total across the three countries of 2 591 659 votes (19.5 per cent), it won not a single seat and was again unrepresented in Strasbourg.

Its best hope of winning a seat had been in the Highlands and Islands constituency but it was thwarted, ironically, not by one of the main parties, but by that remarkable warrior from the Scottish National Party, Mrs Winnie Ewing, who held on to the seat with a substantially increased majority. In Northern Ireland (see page 44) the three members who had represented the province in the previous five years – the Rev. Ian Paisley, of the Democratic Unionist Party, Mr John Taylor, of the Official Unionists, and Mr John Hume, of the Social Democratic and Labour Party – were all reelected.

The election produced some personal triumphs, notably that by Mrs Barbara Castle, undoubtedly still the best known of the British contingent. The former Labour Cabinet minister, at the age of 72, changed seats from Greater Manchester North to the theoretically marginal Greater Manchester West, won it with a thumping 37 698 majority, and was promptly reelected leader of the Labour group at Strasbourg.

It brought defeat to nine of the sitting Tory MEPs and two former Labour MEPs. Among those who had to say goodbye was Mr Adam Fergusson, the Conservative foreign affairs spokesman. It means a Conservative contingent whose independence from the party at Westminster seems certain to grow. Only one Tory, Mr Tom Normanton, will retain the 'dual mandate' as a member of both Parliaments, compared with eight in the last Parliament. Only four Conservatives with experience of the Commons remain – Mr Normanton, Sir James Scott-Hopkins, former leader of the Tory delegation, Mr Basil de Ferranti, who left Westminster in 1964 and now chairs his family company, and a newcomer, Mrs Sheila Faith, MP for Belper, 1979–83.

Twenty-two of Labour's team are new to the Parliament. They include three left-wing former MPs defeated at the 1983 general election, Mr Robert Cryer, Mr Leslie Huckfield and Mr Stanley Newens, and a former Foreign Office minister, Mr John Tomlinson.

From the bald figures, the Conservative Party was able to claim, with justice, actual victory, and that a swing against it since the 1983 general election (5.5 per cent) was no higher than might be expected one year into a new term. But it was Labour, the least European of the three parties, which only a year earlier had gone to the country on a pledge to take Britain out of the Community and from whom the pro-EEC wing had largely defected in the previous few years, that was able to derive the most satisfaction. It had set itself the relatively modest aims of achieving between 25 to 30 seats and confirming itself as the main opposition to Mrs Thatcher's government. In both it succeeded.

For the Alliance there was disappointment but not despair. As a new force it suffered from the volatility of its support, the fact that unlike its rivals it had no hard core of voters who would turn out regardless of the occasion, and from an electoral system that gives little chance to any party whose support is so widely spread throughout the vast Euro-constituencies. The only certain loser in Britain was the European Parliament.

To understand why Labour was justly entitled to claim that it was on the march again after an election result which, if repeated at a general election, would still have left Mrs Margaret Thatcher in Downing Street with a comfortable overall majority, one needs to delve back briefly into that party's turbulent history and to recall the events which led to the rise of the Alliance.

Ever since its 1979 general election defeat, Labour had been in turmoil. Its left wing, led by Mr Tony Benn, made huge ground against the right on both policy and organizational fronts. It moved towards policies of outright unilateral nuclear disarmament and withdrawal from the European Community, and at the same time decided that all its MPs should submit themselves during each Parliament to a vote by the activists in their constituencies to decide whether they should be allowed to stand again at the next election. It was seen by many on the right as a fetter on their independence and it was feared that many whom the left considered 'unsound' would be unseated.

It was also decided that the sole right of electing the party leader should be taken away from the MPs and given to an electoral college composed of the trade unions, the constituency activists and the MPs. On November 11, 1980, shortly before the electoral college was activated, Mr James Callaghan resigned the leadership and Mr Michael Foot, then aged 67, beat Mr Denis Healey to take over.

Ten days later Dr Owen, the former Labour foreign secretary, announced that he was not standing for reelection to the shadow cabinet, and Mrs Shirley Williams, another highly popular former Cabinet minister, announced that she would not be a candidate at the next election.

The break was not far away. A special one-day conference at Wembley, London, in early 1981 settled the composition of the electoral college and gave only 30 per cent of the votes to the MPs, the rest going to the unions and the constituencies. The following day Mr Roy Jenkins, the former Labour cabinet minister who had become President of the European Commission in January 1977, and who had first spoken in 1979 of the need for a new radical centre in British politics, formed with Dr Owen, Mrs Williams and Mr William Rodgers, a new Council for Social Democracy. (They were the 'Gang of Four'.) It soon became the SDP and, in alliance with the Liberals, was chalking up a series of incredible by-election successes by the end of the year.

Labour had lost some of its most senior and respected figures but the troubles continued with a bitter contest between Mr Benn and Mr Healey for the deputy leadership of the party. By the time of the general election in June, 1983, the die was cast. Although the Alliance had dropped back sharply since the heady days of its formation, its achievement in securing one-quarter of the votes cast contributed to Labour (which was reconciled to defeat even before the campaign began), losing scores of seats to the Conservatives on minority votes.

In the end Labour managed only 209 seats, its worst showing since 1935, and Mrs Thatcher was returned with a landslide 144-seat majority. As pertinent for Labour was the fact that it finished just two percentage points ahead of the Alliance in the total of votes cast. It lost a quarter of its 1979 vote, falling back from 36.9 per cent to 27.6 per cent, the lowest share ever won by the principal opposition party; it lost deposits in one out of five of all the seats it contested. The bell for Labour was tolling.

In the aftermath of the election Mr Jenkins, the first elected leader of the SDP, stood down and was succeeded by Dr David Owen. At the autumn conference of the Labour Party, Mr Neil Kinnock was elected to replace Mr Foot. The party was given internal warnings that it had a year in which to reestablish itself in the public mind as the undisputed alternative to the Tories. It was against that background that Labour's performance in the European elections had to be judged. Its aim of confirming itself as the alternative government was decisively achieved. It increased the gap between itself and the Alliance, just 2 per cent in June, 1983, to 17 per cent. And the Alliance, which on its 1983 votes stood second in 32 of the 78 British constituencies, managed to hold on to that position in only 13 of them.

Labour regarded its showing viz-a-viz the Alliance just as important as making inroads into the Conservative majority. Mr Robin Cook, Labour's spokesman on Europe, in a statement after the results were declared, exulted: 'The Alliance may be able to raise a flash-in-the-pan at a by-election when the electorate is reduced to a negative protest vote, but it is Labour that comes out on top in a national election when the electorate has a chance to cast a positive vote for change.'

In that remark Mr Cook was referring to an event which occurred on the same day as the European elections and which gave the Alliance considerable consolation for its disappointment in that poll. Against all the predictions, the Social Democrats scored a sensational victory in a by-election at Portsmouth South, overturning a Conservative majority of 12335 and maintaining the Alliance's fine performance, superior to that of Labour, in the by-elections held at that stage of the parliament.

Its complaint against the injustices of the electoral system has become a familiar, even boring, refrain after major elections. But it is undeniable that the European poll once again raised questions about a system which left a fifth of the people who troubled to vote without anyone to represent them at Strasbourg and which inevitably has the effect of distorting the balance of political forces inside the European Parliament.

The Alliance saw no point in raising a fuss about it before or during the campaign, rightly perceiving the public's lack of enthusiasm for debates about electoral systems. But in the immediate flush of outrage that followed the declaration of the results, it was quickly calling in aid psephological studies showing that it would have won 14 seats under an PR system. No wonder its leaders were left crying foul. It was a crazy, bankrupt, horrendous system, said Dr Owen.

And doubtless those studies understated the Alliance case. One of the key factors in its poor showing was the knowledge, shared by its leaders and constituency activists, that it was up against a brick wall and that there would be little tangible reward for their efforts. A PR system, any PR system, would galvanize the Alliance – and that is probably the reason it will never get one unless it achieves power, or a share of it, in Britain.

The Alliance suffered from the tranquillity of the campaign. It did its best, befitting the most pro-European of the contenders, to enthuse the voters. It got off the mark first by calling in its candidates to London on the May Day bank holiday, and inviting along the media to hear its leaders address them. Aiming to make a virtue of its Europeanism, it published its manifesto a full week before its rivals and pledged to 'lift the sights' of the electorate to the advantage and potential of the Community.

But the nation did not really want to know. The Alliance, with far less money to spend than its rivals and a much less efficient countrywide organization, was always at a disadvantage. It had always relied on a significant proportion of protest votes, people who did not like the other parties but felt they should do their democratic duty and vote. In the European election, they were under no such obligation. In by-elections its shortage of resources could be overcome by concentrating its forces on single constituencies. In general elections the acknowledged importance of the occasion will bring the voters out in any case.

For the Conservative Party there was disappointment at the loss of seats, but not surprise. The scale of the reverses was along the lines forecast by the party's own private polls, and the falls of only 1.6 per cent in its share of the vote since the general election hardly amounted to an earthquake.

It, too, was able to take consolation from the failure of the Alliance to take off. An SDP-Liberal surge in its heartlands would have caused far more nervousness than the Labour recovery that did in fact take place. Mr John Gummer, the party chairman, was able to claim that the Conservatives had done better in the elections than any other sitting government in Europe, and indeed many Conservative MPs were privately voicing the opinion that a year in which the Government had slipped on a number of so-called 'banana skins' had not ended too badly.

Almost from the start of Mrs Thatcher's second term, there were uncharacteristic stumbles. An unseemly behind-the-scenes row over the choice of the new Commons Speaker, in which the Prime Minister did not get her way, was followed by an unsuccessful attempt by the Government to make an example of MPs in its campaign to restrict public sector pay. The Prime Minister's decision to elevate William Whitelaw, her trusted deputy, to the House of Lords soon after the election disenchanted the voters of Penrith and the Border and almost gave the Alliance a shock victory in a by-election.

The resignation of Mr Cecil Parkinson from the Cabinet brought further unwelcome publicity; the invasion of Grenada, a Commonwealth country, by the United States against British wishes brought humiliation; and the decision to ban trade union membership at the government communications centre at Cheltenham brought hostility.

On top of all that, the revolts of leading Conservatives like Mr Edward Heath, the former Prime Minister, against the legislation to 'cap' the rates and to abolish the 1985 elections to the Greater London Council and the metropolitan county councils in advance of their abolition brought further embarrassment.

But when the short-term political repercussions for the individual parties had been digested, it seemed certain that the most abiding message of the campaign in Britain, the way the parties chose to fight it, the result and, above all, the turnout, was the one it sent to the European Community. Britain's electors, or those of them who bothered to turn up and vote, gave a thumbs-down by their choice to the idea of closer European integration espoused only by the Alliance parties. Some 76 per cent of the votes cast went either to a Labour Party which retained withdrawal from the Community as an option in its manifesto, or a Conservative Party whose attitude towards the EEC in the years beforehand had been less than warm-hearted.

One did not have to look too far for explanations for the turnout. In the previous five years the British had read and heard little which reflected credit on the European Parliament. The only stories to have made any impact through the mass circulation newspapers were those which concerned the alleged extravagances of the MEPs, or their 'perks', or the apparently endless dispute over where the Parliament should sit. In a country which expects much of its legislature, the European Parliament was seen, albeit somewhat inaccurately, as a virtually powerless talking-shop.

Both main parties, too, made much of their opposition to any enlargement of its powers, a key element in any move towards a more closely united Europe. Indeed, the Prime Minister declared at the outset of the Conservative campaign that she was against any increase in the Parliament's powers or of any weakening of the right of individual governments to block changes with which they disagreed through the use of the national veto. Most important of all, of course, was the apparently low esteem in which the Community and its institutions were held in Britain at the time the election took place, a condition to which the debilitating battle over the net deficit between Britain's payments to and receipts from the EEC had undoubtedly contributed in the previous five years.

A short review of that saga is necessary. Every since Mrs Thatcher had gone to Dublin in November, 1979, when the forecast deficit for the following year had risen to an unacceptable £120m, and declared in the most non-communitaire terms that Britain wanted her money back, the issue of the UK contribution had consumed the Community.

Mrs Thatcher's performance in Dublin was one that cast her as the villian of the piece in European eyes, and as the dispute rumbled on through the early 1980s to the Fontainebleau summit which immediately followed the June 1984 elections, that was how she continued to be regarded. For Mrs Thatcher it was a straight conflict between right and wrong; it was grotesque that the third poorest country in the EEC should make the biggest contribution. She set out in 1979 to achieve a 'broad balance' between Britain's receipts and contributions and declared that she could not accept 'half a loaf'.

When Dublin broke down, she warned her Community partners that she was not afraid of 'precipitating a crisis', that she had little room for manoeuvre, that she was prepared to consider suspending Britain's budget payments. She gave them 'one last chance'. Whatever the justice of Britain's case – and there could be little doubt but that she was suffering an inequity – the manner of the Prime Minister's approach was not conducive to good relations and could only have stoked the embers of latent anti-Europeanism in Britain.

For the anti-Market forces in the Labour Party, the Dublin summit was a gift. The policy changes which were to lead to it taking up its withdrawal stance in the 1983 general election began within days of the summit when left-wingers on the policy-forming national executive committee, buoyed by the anti-EEC climate that Mrs Thatcher had helped to engender, set in motion a study of the alternatives to membership.

For the next five years, at summit after summit, Britain's demand for a long-term settlement to the budgetary imbalance and the problem of runaway farm spending dominated the agenda to the exclusion of much else. Although Mrs Thatcher continued to search for a permanent solution, Britain's rebate continued to be the subject of an annual, damaging haggle, with Britain usually getting back around two-thirds of its contributions. The twelve months preceding the 1984 election saw that process reach an unhappy, painful climax, but with an outcome that may at least offer some hope for the future.

By the summer of 1983, when the heads of government met in Stuttgart, the prospect of the Community running out of money was real indeed. It needed an increase in its 'own resources', the proceeds from a 1 per cent cross-Community levy of VAT calculated on a common basket of goods and services, to survive financially. Such a rise required the agreement of all member states. The British Government, seizing its chance, made plain that its assent to an increase would be dependent on the Community taking measures to control agricultural spending and a fairer deal for Britain on the budget. It had the lever it needed, but it was to be another year of acrimonious wrangling before an acceptable settlement could be reached.

The Athens summit in December, 1983, came and went without agreement, and then came the explosion at Brussels the following March. Mrs Thatcher refused to go along with anything other than the permanent arrangement she had so long sought. President Mitterand, in the chair, castigated her for her intransigence. The summit collapsed. Britain's 1983 rebate of £457m, agreed at Stuttgart, was frozen. Mrs Thatcher threatened retaliation. Draft legislation to enable Britain to withhold its contributions from the Community had already been prepared.

The Community had been to the brink but it wished to go no further. The desire for a solution to its internal differences quickly reasserted itself. Talks were called by the French Government to get negotiations going again. Mrs Thatcher's unspoken threat to withhold Britain's twice-monthly payment to Brussels, which many ministers and MPs regarded as unconstitutional, was quietly dropped.

Early in April, 1984, the Community at last appeared to begin to get to grips with agricultural overproduction. A deal to cut milk output was not welcomed by many British farmers but it pleased Mrs Thatcher and most of her ministers. The change in the atmosphere came too late, however, to have an appreciable effect on an electorate conditioned to almost permanent bickering between Britain and the remainder of the Community. Were they to be blamed if they took a less than charitable view of the Community and all its work, or questioned the point in voting?

Then there was the attitude of the parties. Lack of commitment to the Community did not diminish the importance of the elections to Labour. Coming just a year after its shattering election defeat and nine months after the installation of a new leader in Mr Kinnock, the poll was crucial as an indicator of the party's recovery – the one nationwide test of opinion in Britain between the 1983 general election and the next.

Labour's deep dilemma – how a profoundly anti-EEC party could go out and ask for votes to send its representatives to the European Parliament – was far more easily and successfully handled than ever seemed possible. The party and Mr Kinnock had taken steps to modify the commitment, contained in its 1983 manifesto, to withdraw from the Community within the lifetime of a Parliament. At the annual conference in the autumn of 1983, Labour changed its stance. It accepted that for the term of the next Parliament, Britain would be an EEC member and that at the end of it membership would have spanned fifteen years.

It downgraded its withdrawal commitment to a position that Britain must retain the 'option' to withdraw, a posture it readopted in its European manifesto. Mr Kinnock himself made a notable contribution in February, 1984, when he called for a transformation of the Community on new principles and a new 'Messina conference' similar to that which led to the formation of the Community, 'to reject, rewrite or revise the Treaty of Rome'.

Labour's position, however, was less than lukewarm and it was no shock that party strategists chose to treat the elections as a national referendum on the first year of Mrs Thatcher's second term. Unemployment, the future of the health service, the Government's alleged assault on the independence of local government, even defence – the issue which had proved so damaging for Labour at the general election – were to be given preference to European issues.

There was little alternative. The vast majority of the troops Labour was sending into battle were strongly anti-Market. Two of its unfortunate pro-EEC stalwarts in the previous parliament, Mr Brian Key (Yorkshire South) and Mr Derek Enright (Leeds) had been denied the right of standing again by their anti-EEC constituency parties. Another of their number, Mr Michael Gallagher, had defected to the SDP.

Even so, Labour's campaign, given the importance it attached to doing well, was energetically fought – at least nationally. In line with the youthful campaigning image it was projecting under the new leadership, it organized Eurofests in several big cities at which television celebrities joined party leaders for afternoons of politics and entertainment. A campaign bus toured the country and there was even a £2500 contest run by the party to find 'a better song for Europe' in which hundreds took part. The showbiz style may have drawn scorn from Labour's opponents but the party clearly enjoyed it and it appeared to serve them well. Being the acknowledged anti-EEC party clearly did Labour little harm.

The Conservatives were far less keen than Labour or the Alliance to raise the political temperature. Mrs Thatcher kept a lower profile than Mr Kinnock, Mr David Steel, the Liberal leader, and Dr Owen, and seemed happy to leave her party chairman, Mr John

Gummer, in charge. Knowing that they must suffer some losses on the almost freakish 1979 result, there was no advantage to the Tories in elevating the importance of the poll. Perceiving the country's lack of interest, unwilling to risk creating a situation in which the Alliance bandwagon might conceivably roll, the Tories were happy to rely on their bedrock support.

The strategy succeeded, allowing the party to claim justly that if a general election had been held on the same day Mrs Thatcher would have been home for a comfortable third term. But for the Alliance and the Tory Euro-enthusiasts, the tactics were galling. Mr Edward Heath, the former Prime Minister, who led Britain into the Community and is its staunchest defender, accused his party of failing to mount an effective campaign. Appearing on television on results night, he said that on his 8000-mile campaign tour he went to places where his party had done absolutely nothing about the election. He lamented: 'The Conservative Party just did not fight this election all-out on a European basis. I am sad about it: they didn't.'

If the campaign in the United Kingdom, which Labour and the Conservatives launched on May 21 and the Alliance a week earlier, had a European strand it was the relative claims of each party to be able to change the Community for its own good and that of Britain. From the start, Mrs Thatcher made much of the rebates she had managed to secure and scoffed at Labour for failing to get a 'penny piece' when it was in office. Labour, in its manifesto, described itself as the only party with the determination to fight for reform and attacked Mrs Thatcher for throwing away Britain's negotiating position. Mr Gummer seized throughout on the anti-market antecedents of Labour candidates. Early on he alleged that only six had been identified from election literature as committed supporters of the Community. Mrs Thatcher attacked the 'Eurofanatics' of the Alliance, whom she said wanted to see the British character submerged in Europe, and the 'Europhobes' of Labour who wanted Britain out.

Good knockabout electioneering material. Unfortunately the campaign rarely rose above that level to a deeper examination of the Community. For the Alliance, Dr Owen and Mr Steel made the most of their Europeanist credentials. Too many British leaders, they said in the foreword to their manifesto, had concealed an inability to provide imaginative direction to the Community behind a surly anti-Europeanism. 'We have no patience with these attempts to play to the gallery of outdated nationalism,' they said.

A bonus for Mrs Thatcher during the campaign was the world economic summit held in London early in June which gave her the opportunity of being seen in her role as a world statesman. The opposition parties made the best of it by calling on the summit to launch a strategy of world reflation in the certain knowledge that it would not, and to give themselves something to complain about afterwards.

It was national issues, however, that moved the parties and the voters. A Harris Research Centre poll for ITN carried out as voters left the polls on June 14 indicated that more than half those who voted did so to express views on domestic political issues, 19 per cent because they always voted and only 29 per cent because they regarded European issues as important.

Ironically, but consistently, it appears that the fractional increase in overall turnout was due to a small rise in those voting in Greater London and the six metropolitan counties threatened with extinction by legislation due to have been brought in in late 1984. Labour did notably well in those areas, which suggested that the interest of Labour activists had been aroused by the threat of abolition. In London the swing to Labour was 8.5 per cent, well above the national level, and there were some unexpected gains in the capital.

A miners' strike had been proceeding in Britain for twelve weeks when the European campaign got under way, and could not fail to be an issue. Labour's tactics were to criticize the Tories for not intervening to bring the National Union of Mineworkers and the National Coal Board together, but it also feared the damage that the nightly television scenes of violence on the picket lines could do to the party's prospects. Mr Kinnock strongly condemned the violence after one particularly bad incident.

Come June 14, it was apparent that the dispute had brought out the Labour activists. The swing to the party was well above average in most of the mining areas (10.3 per cent in South Yorkshire, 9.2 per cent in South Wales and 9.1 per cent in Durham), but not in Nottingham-shire where the miners had continued to work during the dispute.

As the campaign drew to its close, the tenor of the messages from the parties had not varied. At his last press conference, Mr Kinnock called on his supporters 'to inflict a major defeat on the Tory government.' Mr David Steel accused his opponents of fighting an escapist campaign. Peace, security, jobs and economic recovery all depended on a united Europe working together, but Labour had escaped into triviality and frivolity and the Conservatives into nostalgia and patriotic posturing, he said. Mr Steel warned: 'The real danger is not

Britain leaving Europe but Europe leaving Britain.' In the Conservatives' last election broadcast, Mrs Thatcher spoke with pride of the way she had 'fought Britain's corner' in the budget negotiations. *Plus ça change . . ..*

The battle was over. More than 270 candidates had fought it. It had attracted some coverage in the quality press, but little in the popular newspapers or, in truth, on television until the results started rolling in on the Sunday night. One other party with something to cheer was Britain's own 'Greens'. The Ecology Party attracted 71 000 votes in Britain, nearly three times its share of the vote in the general election.

It was a classic irony that the war between Britain and her partners over the budget which had so dogged the Community for five years came to a sudden end less than two weeks after the elections. The Community's leaders at Fontainebleau at last put together a deal which guaranteed Britain an annual rebate on its contributions in return for an increase in 'own resources' from 1 per cent to 1.4 per cent.

Far more important than the figures was the prospect, admittedly uncertain, that the agreement opened up, of a Community free from the curse of almost constant rows about money. The 1983 rebate was unblocked, a further cash payment of £600m for 1984 agreed upon and an annual 66 per cent rebate of Britain's total contribution guaranteed. Reporting to the House of Commons on the outcome, the Prime Minister said: 'This is a successful culmination of our long and persistent efforts to correct the budget inequity and to put the United Kingdom's refunds on a lasting basis.' The outcome was good for Britain and good for the Community, she averred.

The Prime Minister added: 'It will make possible a relaunching of the Community in which Britain will play a full role; will give an impetus to enlargement, thus strengthening democracy in Spain and Portugal; and remove what has been a constant source of friction in our relations with the Community ever since we joined.' Mrs Thatcher was promising better days ahead.

True, difficulties will never be far away. The new formula for calculating Britain's rebates applies only so long as the 'own resources' rate remains at 1.4 per cent and no one was predicting that that would be able to endure for more than a few years. but as the Prime Minister warned: 'You would not expect us to agree to a change from 1.4 per cent unless this new system continues or an even more satisfactory one takes its place.'

The European Community after years of crisis will be hoping that Mrs Thatcher's optimistic words about the future will come true. It badly needs to turn its mind to matters other than money such as transforming itself into a real common market, not only of goods but of services, too; removal of the obstacles to travel and work inside the Community; and joint action to strengthen Europe's defences.

If the Community moves forward, so too will the European Parliament. It is to be earnestly hoped that the elections of 1989 will be something more than the glorified opinion poll that the 1984 event turned out to be and that the abysmal turnouts of the previous two elections will not be repeated. There is a way, but is there a will? A proportional representation (PR) system of voting, bringing Britain into line with her partners, would surely give the elections a new legitimacy and meaning for millions whose votes are otherwise wasted. The strongest argument against PR – that it has tended to produce a succession of weak and unstable governments – does not apply to the European Parliament whose members do not govern.

PR systems may be more complicated than Britain's much-cherished first-past-the-post; yet all other west European countries have managed to live with them. So has Northern Ireland in all but its Westminster elections. It would be insulting to suggest that the British electors could not do so equally well – and it is an electoral scandal to deny them the opportunity to try.

Astonishing vote for Ulster's 'Big Man'

by Richard Ford
The Times correspondent in Belfast

Few countries can have gone to the polls as often in the last three years as the people of Northern Ireland. When they cast their votes in the European election on June 14 it was the fourth time since 1981 and the turnout at 65.4 per cent was the highest in the United Kingdom.

The poll was essentially a replay of the Northern Ireland Assembly and general elections, with contests within the nationalist and loyalist communities rather than between them. And even as the results were declared, politicians from both sides of the community were turning their thoughts to the next round of this long-running struggle. In 1985, the local government elections will see the proponents of constitutional nationalism and militant-force Republicanism, along with the brash Democratic Unionists and staider Official Unionists, fight again for the hearts and minds of their respective communities.

Interest in the European poll centred mainly on the struggle between the Social Democratic and Labour Party and Provisional Sinn Fein, political wing of the Provisional IRA, for leadership of the Nationalist and Roman Catholic communities. But equally fascinating was the contest in the Loyalist community to show whether the Official Unionists could consolidate their lead over the Democratic Unionists.

Issues were aplenty: the report of the New Ireland Forum together with speculation that the Government might be preparing a move to break the political stalemate; the growing electoral strength of Provisional Sinn Fein; the future of the Northern Ireland Assembly and maintaining or breaking the union with Britain. Amid these essentially local issues, European matters were raised, particularly by Mr John Hume, who, to the confusion of his SDLP supporters, successfully stuck to EEC affairs throughout the campaign. While the Rev. Ian Paisley of the DUP and Mr Danny Morrison of PSF urged withdrawal from the Community, Mr John Taylor of the Official Unionists was less vehement in his opposition to the EEC and Mr Hume positively enthusiastic for the benefits.

But the concern of most voters seems to have been stopping the advance of Provisional Sinn Fein and its candidate, Mr Morrison, the advocate of using the 'ballot box and Armalite', in their bid to take power. Fear of the Provisionals and and uncertainty over their position in the wake of the New Ireland Forum brought Loyalists flocking to Mr Paisley's banner. He gathered a huge 230 251 votes by campaigning on a smash Sinn Fein and anti-Forum platform. Neither was his huge personal vote harmed by the furore over remarks made by a DUP Assembly member who suggested that Roman Catholics and their priests should be incinerated at public expense.

Even the Official Unionists, whose candidate had neither the personality nor the vote-getting appeal of Ulster's 'Big Man' were astonished at the size of Mr Paisley's vote. Although Mr Taylor was elected, his party had hoped to run Mr Paisley close on first preference votes by a strategy of presenting him as the voice of moderate responsible Unionism in contrast to the larger-than-life, flamboyant Mr Paisley, with his fondness for bellowing 'No surrender' and his dramatic stunts.

Concern over PSF also showed in the Nationalist community where SDLP party workers were anxious to halt the momentum of the Provisional IRA political wing. The party kept to European issues, stressing Mr John Hume's record in Europe, his personal qualifications, and in a low key campaign reaped a reward of 151 399 first preference votes, increasing the party's percentage share of the vote from 17.9 per cent in June 1983 to 22.1 per cent twelve months later. Mr Hume benefited from Alliance voters who deserted their party to stop PSF, whose vote at 91 476 was below the psychologically important 100 000 figure. Although PSF percentage share of the vote dropped by 0.1 per cent compared with the 1983 general election, their claim that they could match Mr Hume on first preference votes was a bad misreading of the situation.

Many questions, however, remain unanswered. Despite Mr Paisley's success in reversing the decline in his party's fortunes, it is yet to be proved that his personal vote can be translated into a sustained revival of the DUP. The size of his vote was also interpreted as a warning to the Government not to move too far or fast in its response to the Forum. As Mr Paisley loudly proclaimed after singing the hymn 'Praise God From Whom All Blessings Flow': 'There will be no united Ireland – Ulster is British.'

The scale of his victory may herald the end of the Revival of Official Unionist fortunes, open the barely concealed divisions within the party and end the recent signals of moderation that have been coming from the party leader. The OUP will be under extreme pressure to retreat to a more uncompromising position, particularly with the local government elections approaching.

Mr Hume's success increases his party's image as a one-man band, but he believes it will rejuvenate the organization and give it greater confidence in future electoral contests with PSF. The public perception is that the SDLP soundly saw off the treat from PSF and this will undoubtedly help, although the scale of Mr Hume's victory may decrease the pressure on Britain to act.

Though disappointed by their result, PSF believe the real battle is in May 1985. But before then they may encounter moral problems among supporters and perhaps a reopening of the debate on the Armalite and ballot box approach. Mr Gerry Adams, party president, admitted that some action by the Provisional IRA may have caused voters to desert the party but the organization must hope that Mr John Hume's prediction – that the only way they can go is down – is unfounded. The result also showed that the four other candidates standing for smaller parties were squeezed by the big battalions in the intracommunal fight that remains the dominant feature of Northern Ireland politics.

Results of voting in the second direct elections to the European Parliament

BELGIUM

Polling day: June 17

Electorate: 6975677   (1979 electorate: 6800584)

Valid votes: 5725837   Turnout: 92.2%   (1979 valid votes: 5442867   turnout: 91.4%)

Seats: 24

Party	1984			1979		
	Votes	% of poll	Seats	Votes	% of poll	Seats
Socialist (SP)	980668	17.1	4	698889	12.8	3
Socialist (PS)	762377	13.3	5	575823	10.6	4
Christian People's (CVP)	1134012	19.8	4	1607941	29.5	7
Social Christian (PSC)	436126	7.6	2	445909	8.2	3
Reform and Freedom (PRL)	540597	9.4	3	372904	6.9	2
Freedom and Progress (PVV)	494585	8.6	2	512363	9.4	2
People's Union, Flanders (VU–EVA)	484925	8.5	2	324540	6.0	1
Ecologists (Agalev)	246879	4.3	1	77986	1.4	—
Ecologists (Ecolo–V)	220704	3.9	1	107837	2.0	—
Walloon Rally (PWE)	142871	2.5	—	414613	7.6	2
Others	282093	5.0	—	304062	5.6	—
Totals	5725837		24	5442867		24

Voting system: Regional list, PR. One Flemish constituency of 13 seats and one Walloon constituency of 11 seats. Voting in those constituencies was as follows:

College Electoral Francophone (Wallonia) (11 seats)

Party	1984			1979	
	Votes	% of poll	Seats	% of poll	Seats
Democrates–Chrétiens (PSC)	436126	19.5	2	21.2	3
Socialistes (PS)	762377	34	5	27.4	4
Liberaux (PRL)	540597	24.1	3	17.8	2
Regionalistes Bruxellois (FDF)	142871	6.4	—	19.7	2
Regionalistes Wallons (PWE)	51899	2.3	—	—	—
Communistes (PCB)	61604	2.8	—	5	—
Ecologistes (Ecolo–V)	220704	9.9	1	5.1	—
Extreme Gauche (PTB)	13079	0.6	—	0.4	—
Trotskystes Pos (LRT)	10498	0.5	—	0.3	—
Totals	2239755	—	11	—	11

College Electoral Neerlandophone (Flanders) (13 seats)

Party	1984			1979	
	Votes	% of poll	Seats	% of poll	Seats
Democrates–Chrétiens (CVP)	1134012	32.5	4	48.1	7
Socialistes Flamands (SP)	980668	28.1	4	20.9	3
Liberaux (PVV)	494585	14.2	2	15.3	2
Regionalistes Flamands (VU)	484925	13.9	2	9.7	1
Communistes Flamands (KPB)	25765	0.7	—	1.2	—
Ecologistes (Agalev)	246879	7.1	1	2.3	—
Front Flamand (Vlaamsblok)	73222	2.1	—		
Extreme–Gauche (PvdA)	30578	0.9	—	1.1	—
Trotskystes Sap (Ral)	15448	0.4	—	0.3	—
Totals	3486082	—	13		

RESULTS OF VOTING

Those elected were:

WALLONIA

Socialists (5 seats)
*Raymonde Dury
*Ernest Glinne
José Happart
*Anne-Marie Lizin
Marcel Remacle

Liberals (3 seats)
*Luc Beyer de Ryke
Roger Nols
Michel Toussaint

Christian Democrats (2 seats)
Gérard Deprez
*Fernand Herman

Ecologist (1 seat)
François Roelants du Vivier

FLANDERS
Socialists (4 seats)
Jef Ulburghs
*Marijke van Hemeldonck
*Karel van Miert
*Willy Vernimmen

Christian Democrats (4 seats)
Rika de Backer
*Raf Chanterie
*Lambert Croux
*Pol Marck

Freedom and Progress (2 seats)
*Karel de Gucht
August de Winter

People's Union (2 seats)
Willy Kuijpers
*Jaak Vandemeulebroucke

Ecologist (1 seat)
Paul Staes

DENMARK

Polling day: June 14

Electorate: 3 804 660   (34 649 in Greenland)   1979 electorate: 3 725 235   (29 188 in Greenland)

Valid votes: 2 002 726   Turnout: 52.2%   (1979: 1 754 850   turnout: 47.8%)

Seats: 16

Party	Votes	1984 % of poll	Seats	Votes	1979 % of poll	Seats
Conservative People's	414 177	20.8	4	245 309	14.1	2
Popular Movement against EC	413 808	20.8	4	365 760	20.1	4
Social Democracy	387 098	19.4	3	382 487	21.9	3
Liberal	248 397	12.5	2	252 767	14.5	3
Socialist People's	183 580	9.2	1†	81 991	4.7	1
Centre Democracy	131 984	6.6	1	107 790	6.2	1
Progress	68 747	3.5	—	100 702	5.8	1
Others	142 489	7.2	—	208 272	12.7	—
GREENLAND						
Siumut	7 359	—	1	5 053	—	1
Others	4 983	—	—	4 719	—	—
Totals	2 002 622	100	16	1 754 850	100	16

Voting system: National list, with all Denmark a 15-seat constituency – 16 from January 1, 1985. PR. In Greenland, simple majority (first-past-the-post) system.
†The Socialist People's Party gets a second seat when Greenland (represented by Siumut) leaves the European Community on January 1, 1985.

Those elected were:

Conservative People's Party (4 seats)
Marie Jepsen
*Pøul Møller
Jeanette Oppenheim
Claus Toksvig

Social Democracy (3 seats)
*Ove Fich
*Eva Gredal
Ejner Hovgaard Christiansen

Socialist People's Party (1 seat)
*Bodil Boserup
John Iversen (from 1.1.1985)

GREENLAND
Siumut
*Finn Lynge (until 1.1.1985)

Popular Movement against EEC (4 seats)
*Jørgen Bøgh
*Jens-Peter Bonde
Ib Christensen
*Else Hammerich

Liberal Party (2 seats)
*Jørgen Brøndlund Nielsen
*Tove Nielsen

Centre Democracy (1 seat)
*Erhard Jakobsen

FRANCE

Polling day: June 17

Electorate: 36 880 688   (1979 electorate: 35 180 531)

Valid votes: 20 180 934   Turnout: 56.7%   (1979 valid votes: 20 253 307   turnout: 60.7%)

Seats: 81

Party	Votes	1984 % of poll	Seats	Votes	1979 % of poll	Seats
Union of Opposition (UDF/RPR)	8 683 596	43.0	41	—	—	—
Union for France in Europe	—	—	—	5 666 979	27.9	26
Defence of France's interests in Europe	—	—	—	3 301 980	16.2	15
Socialist (PS)	4 188 875	20.8	20	4 763 026	23.4	21
Communist (PCF)	2 261 312	11.2	10	4 153 710	20.4	19
National Front	2 210 344	11.0	10	—	—	—
Europe–Ecology (Verts)	680 080	3.4	—	—	—	—
Others	2 156 737	10.6	—	2 367 612	12.1	—
Totals	20 180 944		81	20 253 307		81

Voting system: PR national list. Minimum of 5 per cent needed to obtain seat.

Those elected were:

Union of the Opposition (UDF/RPR) (41 seats)
*Simone Veil
Bernard Pons
*Jean Lecanuet
*Christian de la Malène
*Michel Poniatowski
Alain Juppé
*Pierre Pflimlin
Philippe Malaud
*André Rossi
Nicole Chouraqui
*Georges Donnez
Alain Carignon
Jean-François Deniau
André Fanton
Dominique Baudis
Jean-Pierre Roux
Roger Chinaud
Alfred Coste-Floret
Nicole Fontaine
Gaston Flosse
*Yves Galland
Jean-François Mancel
Robert Hersant
Anne-Marie Dupuy
Claude Wolff
Jean Mouchel
Pierre Bernard-Reymond
Jacques Vernier
*Christiane Scrivener
Denis Baudouin
*Jean-Thomas Nordmann
Jean-Claude Pasty
Gérard Longuet
Madeleine Anglade
Jacques Mallet
Guy Guermeur
Michel Debatisse
Jacqueline Thome-Patenôtre
*Simone Martin
François Musso
Jean-Pierre Abelin

Socialist (20 seats)
Lionel Jospin
*Nicole Pery
Jean-Pierre Cot
*Gisèle Charzat
Max Gallo
*Roger Fajardie
*Bernard Thareau
*Didier Motchane
*Alain Bombard
*Yvette Fuillet
Léon Fatous
Jean-Paul Bachy
*Henri Saby
*Georges Sutra de Germa
*Marie-Claude Vayssade
Jean Besse
*Charles-Emile Loo
Colette Gadioux
*Louis Eyraud
Marie-Noëlle Lienemann

French Communist Party (10 seats)
*Georges Marchais
*Danielle de March
*René Piquet
*Paul Verges
*Emmanuel Maffre-Baugé
*Jacqueline Hoffmann
*Pierre Pranchère
*Francis Wurtz
*Robert Chambeiron
*Maxime Gremetz

National Front (10 seats)
Jean-Marie Le Pen
Michel de Camaret
Jean-Pierre Stirbois
G. A. Pordea
*Olivier d'Ormesson
Bernard Antony
Dominique Chaboche
J.-M. Le Chevallier
Martine Lehideux
Michel Collinot

49

GERMANY

Polling day: June 17

Electorate: 44 451 981   (1979 electorate: 42 751 940)

Valid votes: 24 841 302   Turnout: 56.8%   (1979 valid votes: 27 847 109   turnout: 65.7%)

Seats: 81

Party	Votes	1984 % of poll	Seats	Votes	1979 % of poll	Seats
Christian Democratic Union (CDU)	9 308 411	37.5	34	10 883 085	39.1	34
Christian Social Union (CSU)	2 109 130	8.5	7	2 817 120	10.1	8
Social Democrats (SPD)	9 296 417	37.4	33	11 370 045	40.8	35
Liberals (FDP)	1 192 624	4.8	—	1 662 621	6.0	4
Die Grünen (Ecologists)	2 025 972	8.2	7	893 683	3.2	—
Pacifists	313 108	1.3	—			
Extreme Right (NDP)	198 633	0.8	—			
Women's Party	94 463	0.4	—			
Traditionalists (DZ)	93 921	0.4	—			
Democratic Ecologists (Ö–DP)	77 026	0.3	—			
Citizens (WMB)	52 753	0.2	—			
European Federalists (EPP)	34 500	0.1	—			
EAP	30 874	0.1	—			
Bayernpartei	23 539	0.1	—			
Others	—	—	—	220 555	0.8	—
Totals	24 851 371	—	81	27 847 109	—	81

Voting system: PR on the national or Länd list system. SPD and Die Grünen used national lists and CDU and CSU used Länd lists. There are three MEPs for Berlin.

Those elected were:

CDU/CSU (41 seats)

CDU (34 seats)
*Jochen van Aerssen
*Siegbert Alber
Otto Bardong
*Philipp von Bismarck
*Erik Blumenfeld
Ursula Braun-Moser
*Elmar Brok
Manfred Ebel
*Otmar Franz
*Isidor Früh
*Wilhelm Hahn
*Karl-Heinz Hoffmann
*Egon Klepsch
*Horst Langes
*Gerd Lemmer
*Marlene Lenz
*Rudolf Luster
*Kurt Malangré
*Meinolf Mertens
Werner Münch
Gabriele Peus
*Gero Pfennig
Hans Pötschki
*Hans-Gert Pöttering
*Renate-Charlotte Rabbethge
*Günter Rinsche
*Bernhard Sälzer
*Konrad Schön
Leopold Späth
*Kurt Wawrzik
*Rudolf Wedekind
*Karl von Wogau
Hans-Jürgen Zahorka
*Axel Zarges

Social Democrat Party (33 seats)
*Rudi Arndt
Jürgen Brinkmeier
*Ludwig Fellermaier
*Katharina Focke
*Bruno Friedrich
*Fritz Gautier
*Klaus Hänsch
*Magdalene Hoff
*Jan Klinkenborg
*Rolf Linkohr
*Karl-Heinrich Mihr
*Johannes Peters
*Dieter Rogalla
Mechthild Rothe
Willi Rothley
Joannis Sakellariou
*Heinke Salisch
*Dieter Schinzel
*Gerhard Schmid
Heinz Schreiber
*Horst Seefeld
*Hans-Joachim Seeler
*Lieselotte Seibel-Emmerling
Barbara Simons
Günter Topmann
*Heinz Oskar Vetter
Kurt Vittinghoff
*Thomas von der Vring
*Manfred Wagner
*Gerd Walter
*Beate Weber
*Klaus Wettig
*Heidemarie Wieczorek-Zeul

CSU (7 seats)
*Heinrich Aigner
*Reinhold Bocklet
*Ingo Friedrich
*Otto Habsburg
Fritz Pirkl
*Ursula Schleicher
Franz von Stauffenberg

Ecologists (7 seats)
Undine Bloch von Blottnitz
Friedrich-Wilhelm Graefe zu Baringdorf
Benedikt Härlin
Brigitte Heinrich
Michael Klöckner
Dorothee Piermont
Frank Schwalba-Hoth

In the Federal Länder, the union parties, the SPD, FDP and Greens, achieved the following percentage of the vote during the direct elections for the European parliament (1979 results are in brackets):

Bundesland	Total vote	CDU/CSU	SPD	FDP	Grüne
Schleswig-Holstein	57.6	44.4	39.9	4.5	8.2
	(65.6)	(47.9)	(43.7)	(5.2)	(2.7)
Hamburg	58.3	36.6	42.0	4.9	12.7
	(66.4)	(36.9)	(52.2)	(6.3)	(3.5)
Niedersachsen	61.1	43.0	40.5	4.9	8.2
	(70.0)	(45.8)	(44.7)	(5.3)	(3.6)
Bremen	55.1	31.0	48.0	4.5	11.8
	(66.3)	(32.7)	(53.0)	(8.3)	(4.7)
Nordrhein-Westfalen	59.3	42.8	41.7	4.2	8.0
	(67.4)	(45.8)	(44.6)	(5.8)	(3.0)
Hessen	59.0	41.4	41.8	5.0	7.8
	(66.5)	(44.8)	(45.4)	(6.2)	(2.8)
Rheinland-Pfalz	76.4	46.6	38.6	5.0	6.6
	(78.1)	(49.2)	(41.1)	(6.4)	(2.4)
Baden-Württemberg	48.3	50.9	27.3	7.1	10.1
	(59.2)	(52.3)	(34.3)	(8.1)	(4.5)
Bayern	46.1	57.2	27.6	4.0	6.8
	(58.9)	(62.5)	(29.2)	(4.7)	(2.9)
Saarland	78.5	42.6	43.6	3.9	6.6
	(81.1)	(46.4)	(44.0)	(5.8)	(2.4)
Berlin	56.8	46.0	37.4	4.8	8.2
	(65.7)	(49.2)	(40.8)	(6.0)	(3.2)

GREECE

Polling day: June 17

Electorate: 7790309 (1981 electorate: 6806851 – first European elections in Greece were on October 18, 1981)

Valid votes: 5956060 Turnout: 77.2% (1981 valid votes: 5753478 turnout: 78.6%)

Seats: 24

Party	Votes	1984 % of poll	Seats	Votes	1981 % of poll	Seats
Socialist (PASOK)	2476491	41.58	10	2278030	40.12	10
New Democracy (ND)	2266568	38.05	9	1779462	31.34	8
Communist (KKE)	693304	11.64	3	729052	12.84	3
Communist, Interior (KKE-es)	203813	3.42	1	300841	5.29	1
Extreme Right Wing (EPEN)	136642	2.29	1	—	—	—
Others	179242	3.02	—	666993	10.41	%
Totals	5956060	100	24	5753478	100	24

Voting system: National list. PR.

Those elected were:

Socialist (10 seats)
Paraskevas Avgerinos
Nikolaos Gazis
Emmanouil Glezos
Georgios Mavros
*Konstantina Pantazi-Tzifa
Christos Papoutsis
*Spyridon Plaskovitis
Georgios Romeos
Grigorios Varfis
*Nikolaos Vgenopoulos

Communist (3 seats)
*Dimitrios Adamou
*Vassilios Ephremidis
Alexandros Alavanos

Extreme Right Wing (1 seat)
Chrysanthos Dimitriadis

New Democracy (9 seats)
Georgios Anastassopoulos
Evangelos Averof-Tositsas
Ioannis Boutos
Efthymios Christodoulou
Dimitrios Evrigenis
Kyriakos Gerontopoulos
Marietta Yannakou
Panayiotis Lambrias
Ioannis Tzounis

Communist, Interior (1 seat)
*Leonidas Kyrkos

IRELAND

Polling day: June 17

Electorate: 2 413 404   (1979 electorate: 2 188 798)

Valid votes: 1 120 416   Spoiled votes: 27 329   Turnout: 47.6%   (1979 valid votes: 1 339 072   Spoiled votes: 53 213   turnout: 63.6%)

Seats: 15

Party	1984 Votes	1984 % of poll	1984 Seats	1979 Votes	1979 % of poll	1979 Seats
Fianna Fáil	438 946	39.2	8	464 451	34.7	5
Fine Gael	361 034	32.2	6	443 652	33.1	4
Independents	113 067	10.1	1	189 499	14.1	2
Labour	93 656	8.4	—	193 898	14.5	4
Sinn Féin	54 672	4.9	—	—	—	—
Workers'	48 449	4.3	—	43 942	3.3	—
Democratic Socialist	5 350	0.5	—	—	—	—
Green Alliance	5 242	0.5	—	—	—	—
Community Democrats of Ireland	—	—	—	3 630	0.27	—
Totals	1 120 416	—	15	1 339 072	—	15

Voting system: Regional list. Country divided into four constituencies and seats allotted on PR.

Those elected were:

Fianna Fáil (8 seats)
Niall Andrews
Sylvester Barrett
Gene Fitzgerald
*Jim Fitzsimons
*Sean Flanagan
*Patrick Lalor
Eileen Lemass
Ray McSharry

Independent (1 seat)
*Thomas Maher

Fine Gael (6 seats)
Mary Banotti
*Mark Clinton
*Joe McCartin
*Tom O'Donnell
Thomas Raftery
*Richie Ryan

Voting details in Ireland's four constituencies

DUBLIN
4 seats

	1984			1979		
Electorate	704873			618454		
Total poll	288831	41.0%		304068	49.16%	
Spoiled votes	6153	0.9%		8653	2.84%	
Total valid poll	282678	40.1%		295415	47.77%	
Quota	56536			59084		
Candidates	12			13		

First preferences	Number	% of poll	Seats	Number	% of poll	Seats
Fianna Fáil	94350	33.4	2	84008	28.4	1
Fine Gael	89674	31.7	2	89658	30.4	1
Labour	28384	10.0	—	87150	29.5	2
Workers' Party	19590	6.9	—	—	—	—
Sinn Fein	14604	5.2	—	11915	4.0	—
Democratic Socialist Party	5350	1.9	—	—	—	—
Green Alliance	5242	1.9	—	—	—	—
Independent	—	—	—	21760	7.4	—
Other	25484	9.0	—	915	0.3	—

Elected: Andrews (FF), Banotti (FG), Lemass (FF), Ryan (FG). All elected after 8th count. No candidate reached quota.

LEINSTER
3 seats

	1984			1979		
Electorate	545878			486248		
Total poll	268491	49.2%		322312	66.3%	
Spoiled votes	9197	1.7%		15416	4.8%	
Total valid poll	259292	47.5%		306896	63.1%	
Quota	64824			—		
Candidates	9			—		

First preferences	Number	% of poll	Seats	Number	% of poll	Seats
Fianna Fáil	113512	43.8		127327	41.9	1
Fine Gael	94877	36.6		125021	40.7	1
Labour	30773	11.9		40072	13.1	1
Workers' Party	8943	3.4		—	—	—
Sinn Fein	11189	4.3		14476	4.7	—

Elected: Clinton (FG), Fitzsimons (FF), Lalor (FF).

MUNSTER
5 seats

First preference	1984 Number	% of poll	Seats	1979 Number	% of poll	Seats
Electorate	691076			641625		
Total poll	349179	50.5%		445192	69.4%	
Spoiled votes	6216	0.9%		14597	3.3%	
Total valid poll	342963	49.6%		430595	67.1%	
Quota	57161			71766		
Candidates	9			13		
Fianna Fáil	133521	38.9	2	161370	37.5	2
Fine Gael	98068	28.6	2	115609	26.8	1
Labour	26162	7.6	—	53614	12.5	1
Workers' Party	17304	5.6	—			
Sinn Fein	12829	3.7	—	11526	2.7	—
Independent	55079	16.0	1	86208	20.0	1
Other	—	—	—	2268	0.5	—

Elected: Barrett (FF), Fitzgerald (FF), Maher (Ind), O'Donnell (FG), Raftery (FG).

CONNACHT–ULSTER
3 seats

First preference	1984 Number	% of poll	Seats	1979 Number	% of poll	Seats
Electorate	471577			442471		
Total poll	241244	51.2%		320713	72.5%	
Spoiled votes	5763	1.2%		14547	4.5%	
Total valid poll	235481			306166	69.2%	
Quota	58871			76542		
Candidates	11			11		
Fianna Fáil	97563	41.4	2	91746	30.0	1
Fine Gael	78415	33.3	1	113364	37.0	1
Labour	8337	3.5	—	13062	4.3	—
Workers' Party	2612	1.1	—	—	—	—
Sinn Fein	16050	6.8	—	6025	2.0	—
Independent	—	—	—	81522	26.6	1
Other	32504	13.79	—	447	0.1	—

Elected: Flanagan (FF), McCartin (FG), McSharry (FF).

Details of the eight counts in Dublin

Quota: 56 536

Name/party	1st count Votes	2nd count Transfer of Fettes's Votes	Result	3rd count Transfer of de Courcy Ireland's Votes	Result	4th count Transfer of Ross's Votes	Result	5th count Transfer of Noonan's Votes	Result	6th count Transfer of Loftus's Votes	Result	7th count Transfer of Geraghty's Votes	Result	8th count Transfer of Tunney's Votes	Result
Andrews, Niall (FF)	32 512	+180	32 692	+144	32 836	+428	33 264	+1 375	34 639	+2 034	36 673	+2 189	38 862	+13 083	51 945
Banotti, Mary (FG)	42 660	+611	43 271	+793	44 064	+2 590	46 654	+267	46 921	+3 648	50 569	+1 990	52 559	+755	53 314
Cluskey, Frank (Lab)	28 384	+462	28 846	+988	29 834	+1 068	30 902	+1 082	31 984	+3 701	35 685	+11 366	47 051	+1 403	48 454
de Courcy Ireland, John (DSP)	5 350	+772	6 112	−6 112	—	—		—		—		—		—	
Dublin Bay Loftus, Sean (Ind)	17 385	+1 113	18 498	+1 298	19 796	+1 780	21 576	+1 719	23 295	−23 295	—	—		—	
Fettes, Christopher (Green)	5 242	−5 242	—	—		—		—		—		—		—	
Geraghty, Des (WP)	19 590	+490	20 080	+1 016	21 096	+636	21 732	+4 403	26 135	+3 165	29 300	−29 300	—	—	
Lemass, Eileen (FF)	31 350	+113	31 483	+107	31 590	+300	31 890	+1 121	33 011	+1 891	34 902	+1 932	36 834	+17 069	53 903
Noonan, Jim (SF)	14 604	+126	14 730	+114	14 844	+115	14 959	−14 959	—	—		—		—	
Ross, Shane (Ind)	8 099	+603	8 703	+903	9 605	−9 605	—	—		—		—		—	
Ryan, Richie (FG)	47 014	+372	47 386	+399	47 785	+1 787	49 572	+242	49 814	+3 229	53 043	+1 389	54 432	+1 327	55 759
Tunney, Jim (FF)	30 488	+100	30 588	+53	30 641	+204	30 845	+1 124	31 969	+1 523	33 492	+1 813	35 305	−35 305	—
Non-transferable:		280		30		697		3 626		4 104		8 621		1 669	

Details of the four counts in Leinster

Quota: 64 824

Name/party	1st count Votes	2nd count Transfer of Carroll, Dwyer, McManus & Sharkey's Votes Result	3rd count Transfer of Bolger's Votes Result	4th count Transfer of Clinton's Surplus Result
Bolger, Deirdre (FG)	33 208	+1 362=34 570	−34 570	
Carroll, John (SF)	4 396	−4 396= —	—	
Clinton, Mark (FG)	61 669	+1 490=63 159	+28 932=92 091	−27 267=64 824
Dwyer, Jim (SF)	2 245	−2 245= —	—	
Fitzsimons, Jim (FF)	57 321	+2 707=60 028	+996=60 994	+2 941=63 935
Keating, Justin (Lab)	30 773	+4 535=35 308	+2 148=37 756	+15 796=53 552
Lalor, Patrick (FF)	56 191	+2 989=59 189	+748=59 928	+1 349=61 277
McManus, Liz (WP)	8 943	−8 943= —	—	
Sharkey, Martin (SF)	4 548	−4 548= —	—	
Non-transferable:		7 049	1 476	7 181

57

Details of seven counts in Munster

Quota: 57161	1st count	2nd count		3rd count		4th count		5th count		6th count		7th count	
		Transfer of Behal's		Transfer of Sherlock's		Transfer of Maher's		Transfer of Desmond's		Transfer of O'Donnell's		Transfer of Raftery's	
Name/party	Votes	Votes	Result	Votes	Result	Surplus	Result	Votes	Result	Surplus	Result	Surplus	Result
Barrett, Sylvester (FF)	47622	+1325	=48947	+1048	=49995	+188	=50183	+1836	=52019	+344	=52363	+645	=53008
Behal, Richard (SF)	12829	−12829	—		—		—		—		—		—
Davern, Noel (FF)	42863	+1237	=44100	+1297	=45397	+306	=45703	+1941	=47644	+355	=47999	+695	=48694
Desmond, Eileen (Lab)	26162	+981	=27080	+4294	=31374	+786	=32160	−32160		—		—	
Fitzgerald, Gene (FF)	43036	+951	=43987	+2192	=46179	+319	=46498	+2958	=49456	+273	=49729	+849	=50578
Maher, T. J. (Ind)	55079	+1761	=56840	+3298	=60138	−2977	=57161	—	57161		57161		57161
O'Donnell, Tom (FG)	53832	+481	=54313	+1376	=55689	+234	=55923	+10614	=66537		66537		66537
Raftery, Tom (FG)	44236	+165	=44401	+1405	=45806	+263	=46069	+6584	=52653	+7315	=59968	−2807	=57161
Sherlock, Joe (WP)	17304	+2641	=19945	−19945		—		—		—		—	
Non-transferable:		3350		5035		881		8227		8287		958	

Details of nine counts in Connacht–Ulster

Quota: 58871

Name/party	1st count (Recount) Votes	2nd count — Transfer of Brick's Votes / Result	3rd count — Transfer of McGing's Votes / Result	4th count — Transfer of Fullerton's Votes / Result	5th count — Transfer of O'Foighil's Votes / Result	6th count (Recount) — Transfer of Higgins Votes / Result	7th count — Transfer of O'Caolain's Votes / Result	8th count — Transfer of Murrin's Votes / Result	9th count — Transfer of McCartin's Surplus / Result
Blaney, Neil (Ind. FF)	32504	+371=32875	+747=33622	+1757=35379	+231=35610	+1730=37340	+3075=40415	+1909=42324	+2106=44430
Brick, Jimmy (WP)	2612	-2612	—	—	—	—	—	—	—
Flanagan, Sean (FF)	40760	+257=41017	+407=41424	+191=41615	+173=41788	+869=42657	+364=43021	+894=43915	+2095=46010
Fullerton, Eddie (SF)	5771	+125= 5896	+810= 6706	-6706	—	—	—	—	—
Higgins, Michael D. (Lab)	8337	+868= 9205	+196= 9401	+186= 9587	+401= 9988	-9988	—	—	—
McCartin, Joe (FG)	51164	+129=51293	+252=51545	+207=51752	+3239=54991	+2256=57247	+514=57761	+18913=76674	-17803=58871
McGing, Mary (SF)	4176	+118= 4294	-4294	—	—	—	—	—	—
McSharry, Ray (FF)	56803	+152=56955	+297=57252	+466=57718	+178=57896	+844=58740	+708=59448	59448	59448
Murrin, Joe (FG)	20107	+97=20204	+211=20415	+153=20568	+2633=23190	+1964=25154	+305=25459	-25459	—
O'Caolain, Caoimhghin (SF)	6103	+55= 6158	+1009= 7167	+2876=10043	+116=10159	+258=10417	-10417	—	—
O'Foighil, Pol (FG)	7144	+70= 7214	+68= 7282	+41= 7323	-7323	—	—	—	—
Non-transferable:		370	297	829	363	2067	5451	3743	13602

ITALY

Polling day: June 17

Electorate: 44 438 303   1979 electorate: 42 193 369

Valid votes: 35 098 046   Turnout: 83.4%   (1979 valid votes: 35 042 601   turnout: 84.9%)

Invalid votes: 1 945 649   Unmarked votes: 709 951

Seats: 81

Party	Votes	1984 % of poll	Seats	Votes	1979 % of poll	Seats
Communist (PCI)	11 693 415	33.3	27	10 345 284	29.6	24
Christian Democracy (DC)	11 574 318	33.0	26	12 753 708	36.4	29
Socialist (PSI)	3 935 966	11.2	9	3 858 295	11.0	9
Social Movement (MSI)	2 274 489	6.5	5	1 907 800	5.4	4
Liberal (PLI)	—	—	—	1 270 152	3.5	3
Republican (PRI)	2 137 768	6.1	5	895 558	2.6	2
Social Democrat (PSDI)	1 224 003	3.5	3	1 512 425	4.3	4
Radical (PR)	1 197 858	3.4	3	1 283 512	3.7	3
Proletarian Democracy (DP)	505 037	1.4	1	252 342	0.7	1
South Tyrol People's (SVP)	198 850	0.6	1	196 373	0.6	1
Sardinian Action (UV–PSDA)	193 055	0.5	1	167 642	0.4	—
Liga Veneta	163 287	0.5	—	—	—	—
PDUP	—	—	—	406 656	1.2	1
Others	—	—	—	192 724	0.5	—
Totals	35 098 046	100	81	35 042 601	100	81

Voting system: Regional list with five constituencies

Those elected were:

Communist party (27 seats)
*Carla Barbarella
*Angelo Carossino
*Luciana Castellina†
Giovanni Cervetti
*Maria Cinciari Rodano
*Pancrazio de Pasquale
*Guido Fanti
*Carlo Galluzzi
Natalino Gatti
*Felice Ippolito
Francesca Marinaro
Alberto Moravia†
Alessandro Natta
Diego Novelli
*Giancarlo Pajetta
*Giovanni Papapietro
Andrea Raggio
Alfredo Reichlin
Giorgio Rossetti
*Sergio Segre
*Altiero Spinelli†
Renzo Trivelli
Lalla Trupia
Maurizio Valenzi

† Elected to two constituencies. Replacements are:
*Aldo Bonaccini
Roberto Barzanti
*Vera Squarcialupi

Liberal and Republican Parties (5 seats)
*Vincenzo Bettiza (PLI)
*Mario di Bartolomei (PRI)
*Jas Gawronski (PRI)
*Sergio Pininfarina (PLI)
Rosario Romeo (PRI)

Socialist Party (9 seats)
Gianni Baget Bozzo
*Mario Dido'
Anselmo Guarraci
Claudio Martelli
Vincenzo Mattina
*Jiri Pelikan
Mario Rigo
Carlo Tognoli
*Mario Zagari

Christian Democrats (26 seats)
Giulio Andreotti
*Dario Antoniozzi
*Giovanni Bersani
Franco Borgo
Carlo Casini
*Maria Luisa Cassanmagnago Cerretti
Mauro Chiabrando
Vittorino Chiusano
Michelangelo Ciancaglini
*Roberto Costanzo
Ciriaco de Mita
Arnaldo Forlani**
Roberto Formigoni
Gerardo Gaibisso
*Vincenzo Giummarra
Antonio Iodice
*Giosuè Ligios
*Salvatore Lima
Alberto Michelini
Eolo Parodi
Ferruccio Pisoni
Nino Pisoni
Mario Pomilio
Oscar Scalfaro**
Gustavo Selva
Giovanni Starita

Social Movement (5 seats)
*Giorgio Almirante
*Antonio Buttafuoco
*Franco Petronio
*Pino Romualdi
Antonio Tripodi

Social Democratic Party (3 seats)
Giovanni Moroni
Franco Nicolazzi**
Pierluigi Romita**

Proletarian Democracy (1 seat)
Emilio Molinari

Sardinian Action Party (1 seat)
Michele Columbu

Radical Party (3 seats)
Enzo Trotora†
*Marco Pannella

† Elected to two constituencies. Replacement:
*Emma Bonino

South Tyrol People's Party (1 seat)
*Joachim Dalsass

** Italian Ministers Andreotti, Forlani and Scalfaro (DC) and Nicolazzi and Romita (PSDI) did not take their seats in the EP. The Christian Democrats Sergio Ercini, Alfeo Mizzau and Giovanni Giavazzi, and the Social Democrats Giuseppe Amadei and Renato Massari replaced them.

Voting details in Italy's five regional constituencies

Italy, North-West (Italia Nord Occidentale)
Piedmonte, Valle d'Aosta, Liguria and Lombardia

Party	Votes	1984 % of poll	Seats	Votes	1979 % of poll	Seats
PCI	3 138 246	31.7	7	2 853 836	28.7	7
DC	3 213 010	32.5	7	3 421 015	34.3	8
PSI	1 217 232	12.3	3	1 239 077	12.4	3
MSI	450 255	4.5	1	333 209	3.4	1
PLI ⎫	897 300	9.1	2	624 488	6.3	2
PRI ⎭				297 419	3.0	1
PSDI	324 481	3.3	1	467 343	4.7	1
PR	397 498	4.0	1	410 140	4.1	1
DP	189 482	1.9	1	91 235	0.9	1
UV–PSDA	35 324	0.4	—	79 385	0.8	—
PDUP	—	—	—	110 771	1.1	—
Other	30 226	0.3	—	29 781	0.3	—
Totals	9 893 054	—	23	9 957 699	—	25

The following were elected, with preference in brackets:

PCI (7 seats): Pajetta (524 886), Novelli (336 145), Cervetti (110 034), Carossino (89 690), Marinaro (88 279), Bonaccini (66 868), Squarcialupi (47 681). Spinelli and Moravia opted to take seats won in Central Italy.
DC (7 seats): Formigoni (452 103), Scalfaro (396 377), Cassanmagnago (194 097), Chiusano (157 478), Pisoni (157 106), Parodi (155 715), Chiabrando (138 083).

PSI (3 seats): Tognoli (336 401), Pelikan (80 583), Dido' (71 490).
PLI/PRI (2 seats); Pininfarina (171 321), Gawronski (149 852).
PSDI (1 seat): Romita (36 501).
MSI (1 seat): Petronio (94 631).
PR (1 seat): Tortora (131 602).
DP (1 seat): Molinari (22 220).

RESULTS OF VOTING

Italy North-East (Italia, Nord Orientale)
Veneto, Trentino-Alto Adige, Friuli Venezia-Giulia, Emilia-Romagna

Party	Votes	1984 % of poll	Seats	Votes	1979 % of poll	Seats
PCI	2 352 153	32.9	6	2 145 156	30.3	5
DC	2 426 067	34.0	5	2 599 360	36.7	6
PSI	729 821	10.2	1	757 238	10.7	2
MSI	288 015	4.0	—	190 517	2.7	—
PLI/PRI	469 022	6.6	1	455 519	3.7	1
					2.8	—
PSDI	252 922	3.5	1	323 028	4.6	1
PR	202 544	2.8	—	251 624	3.5	1
DP	104 388	1.4	—	37 977	0.5	—
SVP	198 850	2.8	1	196 199	2.8	1
UV–PSDA	15 026	0.2	—	46 991	0.7	—
Liga Ven.	113 807	1.6	—	—	—	—
PDUP	—	—	—	59 769	0.8	—
Totals	7 152 615	—	15	7 063 378	—	17

The following were elected, with preferences in brackets:

PCI (6 seats): Natta (212 980), Fanti (99 407), Castellina (89 635), Trupia (89 635), Rossetti (55 075), Gatti (48 585).
DC (5 seats): Forlani (322 152), Borgo (186 661), Selva (167 612), F. Pisoni (120 275), Bersani (115 825).

PSI (1 seat): Rigo (75 436).
PLI/PRI (1 seat): Bettiza (57 816).
PSDI (1 seat): Nicolazzi (19 922).
SVP (1 seat): Dalsass (132 899).

Italy, Central (Italia Centrale)
Toscana, Umbria, Marche and Lazio

Party	Votes	1984 % of poll	Seats	Votes	1979 % of poll	Seats
PCI	2 973 778	41.5	7	2 587 609	36.4	6
DC	2 088 194	29.1	5	2 256 976	31.7	5
PSI	763 745	10.6	2	741 502	10.4	1
MSI	471 001	6.6	1	392 804	5.5	1
PLI ⎫	363 946	5.1	1	186 830	2.6	—
PRI ⎭				205 376	2.9	1
PSDI	192 099	2.7	—	281 469	4.0	1
PR	214 016	3.0	1	262 482	3.7	1
DP	85 077	1.2	—	48 324	0.6	—
UV–PSDA	9 963	0.1	—	12 156	0.2	—
Liga Ven.	7 272	0.1	—	20 879	—	—
PDUP	—	—	—	116 795	1.7	1
Totals	7 169 091		17	7 113 202	—	17

The following were elected, with preferences in brackets:

PCI (7 seats): The late Enrico Berlinguer (715 320) (Galuzzi elected with 53 524 preferences), Spinelli (172 455), Moravia (130 621), Segre (86 519), Barbarella (73 971), Rodana (55 617), Barzanti (42 337). Castellini took seat won in NW Italy.
DC (5 seats): Andreotti (490 727), Casini (162 394), Michelini (138 385), Gaibisso (116 734), Starita (95 801).

PSI (2 seats): Martelli (246 895), Zagari (70 182).
MSI (1 seat): Romualdi (119 940).
PLI/PRI (1 seat): Bartolomei (51 818).
PR (1 seat): Bonino (14 948).

Italy, South (Italie Meridionale)
Abruzzi, Molise, Campania, Puglia, Basilicata and Calabria

Party	Votes	1984 % of poll	Seats	Votes	1979 % of poll	Seats
PCI	2215663	30.3	5	1871129	25.7	4
DC	2677596	36.6	6	3046006	41.8	7
PSI	833139	11.4	2	757812	10.4	2
MSI	756906	10.3	2	690348	9.4	1
PLI }	222098	3.0	1	106822	1.5	—
PRI }					1.5	—
PSDI	309368	4.2	1	312095	4.3	1
PR	211176	2.9	1	203167	2.8	—
DP	81664	1.1	—	46489	0.7	—
UV–PSDA	10480	0.1	—	14597	0.2	—
Liga Ven.	7003	0.1	—	—	—	—
PDUP	—	—	—	78253	1.1	—
Others	—	—	—	40901	0.6	
Totals	7325093		18	7167619	—	15

The following were elected, with preferences in brackets:

PCI (5 seats): Reichlin (541268), Valenzi (326148), Papapietro (227976), Ippolito (190820), Trivelli (153422).
DC (6 seats): Mita (1052847), Costanzo (307989), Iodice (235220), Ciancaglini (182421), Pomilio (168681), Antoniozzi (151911).

PSI (2 seats): Mattina (279234), Bozzo (176121).
MSI (2 seats): Almirante (500722), Tripodi (106187).
PSDI (1 seat): Moroni (101543).
PR (1 seat): Pannella (91547).
PLI/PRI (1 seat): Romeo (70727).

Italy, Islands (Italie Insulae)
Sicilia and Sardegna

Party	Votes	1984 % of poll	Seats	Votes	1979 % of poll	Seats
PCI	1013575	28.5	2	864809	24.9	2
DC	1169451	32.9	3	1418457	40.5	3
PSI	392029	11.0	1	358471	10.3	1
MSI	308312	8.7	1	298313	8.5	1
PLI }	185407	5.2	—	89814	2.6	—
PRI }					2.6	—
PSDI	145133	4.1	—	119454	3.5	—
PR	172624	4.9	—	149641	4.3	—
DP	44426	1.2	—	23676	0.7	—
UV–PSDA	122262	3.4	1	11513	0.3	—
Liga Ven.	4979	0.1	—	—	—	—
PDUP	—	—	—	34413	1.0	—
Others				26915	0.8	
Totals	3558193		8	3395476	—	7

The following were elected, with preferences in brackets:

PCI (2 seats); Pasquale (236052), Raggio (139119).
DC (3 seats): Lima (256289), Ligios (186914), Liummarra (167764).

PSI (1 seat): Guarracci (139504).
MSI (1 seat): Buttafuoco (98703).
UV–PSDA (1 seat): Columbu (36787).

RESULTS OF VOTING

Italian valid votes cast in the nine other member states of the European Community

Party	1984 (41.7% turnout)		1979 (35.7% turnout)	
	Votes	% of poll	Votes	% of poll
PCI	69232	36.3	36805	30.6
DC	41976	22.0	32506	27.7
PSI	26939	14.1	12846	10.1
MSI	8870	4.6	3865	3.0
PLI	6311	3.3	3446	2.7
PRI			2269	1.8
PSDI	15932	8.4	10880	8.6
PR	4717	2.5	4211	3.3
DP	9916	5.2	4641	3.7
SVP	1642	0.9	977	0.8
UV–PSDA	2944	1.5	—	—
Liga Ventea	2332	1.2	—	—
Others	—	—	12184	10.0
TOTALS	190811		124630	

LUXEMBOURG

Polling day: June 17 (Voting compulsory and coinciding with a general election)

Electorate: 214434   (1979: 212740)

Each elector has six votes. Valid votes are, therefore, estimated at:
1984: 162898 (turnout 87%) and 1979: 169787 (turnout 88.9%)

Seats: 6

Party	1984			1979		
	Votes	% of poll	Seats	Votes	% of poll	Seats
Christian Socialist People's (PCS)	345586	34.9	3	352296	36.2	3
Socialist Workers (POSL)	296382	29.9	2	211106	21.6	1
Democratic	218481	22.1	1	274307	28.1	2
Greens (Grüne)	60152	6.1	—	—	—	—
Communist	40395	4.1	—	48813	5.0	—
Independent Socialist	25355	2.6	—	—	—	—
Revolutionary Communist	3791	0.4	—	—	—	—
Others	—	—	—	78857	9.1	—
Totals	990142	—	6	965379	—	6

Voting system: National list, PR.

Those elected were:

Christian Socialist People's Party (3 seats)

	Preference vote
†Jacques Santer	22432
†Fernand Boden	18415
†Jean Spautz	15771

Democratic Party (1 seat)

Colette Flesch	22239

Socialist Workers' Party (2 seats)

*Victor Abens	18045
†Jacques Poos	13440

† Did not take seats and were replaced respectively by: Nicolas Estgen, Marcella Lentz-Cornette, Ernest Muhlen and Lydie Schmit.

THE NETHERLANDS

Polling day: June 14

Electorate: 10 476 161   (1979 electorate: 9 799 761)

Valid votes: 5 297 621   Turnout: 50.6%   (1979 valid votes: 5 667 303   turnout: 58.1%)

Seats: 25

Party	Votes	1984 % of poll	Seats	Votes	1979 % of poll	Seats
Labour Party (PvdA)	1 785 399	33.7	9	1 722 240	30.4	9
Christian Democrats (CDA)	1 590 601	30.0	8	2 017 743	35.6	10
Liberal Freedom and Democracy Party (VVD)	1 002 825	18.9	5	914 787	16.2	4
Green Progressive Alliance	296 516	5.6	2	—	—	—
Coalition of Protestants	275 824	5.2	1	—	—	—
Democrats '66 (Ind)	120 848	2.3	—	511 967	9.5	2
Ecologists	67 423	1.3	—	—	—	—
Extreme-Droite (Centrum Partij)	134 888	2.6	—	—	—	—
Conservateurs	23 297	0.4	—	—	—	—
Others	—	—	—	500 566	8.3	—
Totals	5 297 621		25	5 667 303		25

Voting system: National lists, PR.

Those elected were:

PvdA (Labour Party)
*P. Dankert
*Mme I. van den Heuvel-Blank
*E. P. Woltjer
Mme H. d'Ancona
*H. J. Muntingh
*Mme P. J. Viehoff-Maag
*R. Cohen
B. Visser
A. Metten

CDA (Christian Democrats)
*B. Beumer
*W. J. Vergeer
*T. Tolman
*J. J. M. Penders
*Mme J. R. H. Maij-Weggen
Mme Y. M. C. Th. van Rooij
*Mme E. C. A. M. Boot
P. A. M. Cornelissen

VVD (Liberals)
*H. R. Nord
*H. J. Louwes
Mme J. E. S. Groenendaal
G. M. de Vries
F. A. Wijsenbeek

Green Progressive Alliance
B. van der Lek
H. A. Verbeek

Droite confessionnelle (Coalition of Protestants)
L. van der Waal

UNITED KINGDOM
England, Scotland and Wales   78 seats

Polling day: June 14

Electorate: 41 917 313   (1979 electorate: 40 529 970)

Votes cast: 13 312 898   Turnout: 31.8%   (1979 votes cast: 12 873 852   turnout: 31.8%)

Party	Votes	1984 % of poll	Seats	Votes	1979 % of poll	Seats
Conservative	5 426 866	40.8	45	6 508 493	50.6	60
Labour	4 865 224	36.5	32	4 253 207	33.0	17
Alliance*	2 591 659	19.5	—	1 690 599	13.1	—
Scot Nat	230 594	1.7	1	247 836	1.9	1
Pl. Cymru	103 031	0.8	—	83 399	0.6	—
Others	95 524	0.7	—	90 318	0.7	—
Totals	13 312 898	—	78	12 873 852	—	78

*Only Liberal candidates stood in 1979

Voting System: Simple majority, or first-past-the-post.

Those elected were:

Conservative (45 seats)
*Robert Battersby
Christopher Beazley
*Peter Beazley
*Lord Bethell
*Miss Beta Brookes
Bryan Cassidy
*Sir Fred Catherwood
*Richard Cottrell
*John de Courcy Ling
*David Curry
*The Marquess of Douro
*Mrs Margaret Daly
*Lady Elles
James Elles
Mrs Sheila Faith
*Basil de Ferranti
*Paul Howell
*Alasdair Hutton
Mrs Caroline Jackson
*Christopher Jackson
Michael Kilby
Edward McMillan-Scott
*John Marshall
*James Moorhouse
*William Newton Dunn
*Tom Normanton
*Lord O'Hagan
*Ben Patterson
*Andrew Pearce
*Sir Henry Plumb
*Derek Prag
*Peter Price
*Christopher Prout
*James Provan
*Dame Shelagh Roberts
*Sir James Scott-Hopkins
*Madron Seligman
*Dr Alexander Sherlock
*Richard Simmonds
*Anthony Simpson
*Sir John Stewart-Clark
*Fred Tuckman
*Amédée Turner QC
*Sir Peter Vanneck
*Michael Welsh

Labour (32 seats)
*Gordon Adam
*Richard Balfe
*Mrs Janey Buchan
*Mrs Barbara Castle
*Kenneth Collins
Mrs Christine Crawley
Robert Cryer
Michael Elliott
Alec Falconer
Glyn Ford
*Winston Griffith
Michael Hindley
Geoffrey Hoon
Leslie Huckfield
Stephen Hughes
*Alfred Lomas
Michael McGowan
Hugh McMahon
David Martin
David Morris
*Thomas Megahy
Stanley Newens
Eddie Newman
Terry Pitt
*Ms Joyce Quin
*Barry Seal
Llewellyn Smith
George Stevenson
Kenneth Stewart
John Tomlinson
Ms Carol Tongue
Norman West

Scottish National Party (1 seat)
*Mrs Winifred Ewing

UK constituency results

Results in the 78 European constituencies of England, Scotland and Wales contested under the first-past-the-post electoral system were as follows. A more detailed table of voting is at the end of the constituency results. In the result tables * denotes an MEP in the outgoing Parliament, although not necessarily in the same seat as before because of boundary changes and selection reasons.

In the six seats with no boundary changes and the seven seats with minor changes, the 1979 European electorates and voting figures are given. The 1983 figures are the general election voting totals in the Westminster seats making up the Euro constituency.

Abbreviations used are:

C – Conservative; Lab – Labour; L/All – Liberal Alliance; SDP/All – Social Democrat/Alliance; SNP – Scottish National Party; PlC – Plaid Cymru; Ecol – Ecology Party; CAEF – Cornish and European Federalist; CBJ – Campaign for British Justice; Ecol/Chr – Ecology/Christian; FJC – For Jesus and His Cross; FRP – Federal Republican Party; Wes Reg – Wessex Regionalist.

BEDFORDSHIRE SOUTH

Electorate: 524 963

Luton South; Milton Keynes; North Hertfordshire; North Luton; South West Hertfordshire; Stevenage; West Hertfordshire.

*Beazley, P. (C)	72 088	43.5%
Cochrane, W. (Lab)	57 106	34.5%
Dixon, P. (L/All)	36 444	22.0%
C majority	14 982	9.1%

Total vote: 165 638 (31.6%).

1983 Total vote: 397 597 (77.0%). C 187 119 (47.1%); All 117 110 (29.4%); Lab 92 348 (23.2%); Others 1 020 (0.3%). C maj 70 009 (17.6%).

BIRMINGHAM EAST

Electorate: 548 899

The Birmingham seats of Edgbaston, Erdington, Hall Green, Hodge Hill, Northfield, Selly Oak, Small Heath, Sparkbrook and Yardley.

Crawley, Mrs C. (Lab)	76 377	49.4%
*Forster, Miss N. (C)	54 994	35.5%
Bennett, D. (SDP/All)	21 927	14.2%
Howlett, Miss D. (FJC)	1 440	0.9%
Lab majority	21 383	13.9%

Total vote: 154 738 (28.2%).

1873 Total vote: 373 089 (67.8%); C 150 087 (40.2%); Lab 149 258 (40.0%); All 70 719 (19.0%); Others 3 025 (0.8%). C maj 829 (0.2%).

BIRMINGHAM WEST

Electorate: 518 707

Aldridge Brownhills; Birmingham Ladywood; Birmingham Perry Barr; Sutton Coldfield; Walsall North; Walsall South; West Bromwich East; West Bromwich West.

Tomlinson, J. (Lab & Co-op)	61 946	45.2%
Hart, C. (C)	55 702	40.6%
Binns, J. (SDP/All)	19 422	14.2%
Lab majority	6 244	4.6%

Total vote: 137 070 (26.4%).

1983 Total vote: 363 311 (70.3%). C 152 652 (42.0%); Lab 139 574 (38.4%); All 69 920 (19.2%); Others 1 165 (0.3%). C maj 13 078 (3.5%).

BRISTOL

Electorate: 569 765

Bath: the Bristol seats of East, North West, South, and West; Kingswood; Northavon; Wansdyke.

*Cottrell, R. (C)	94 652	46.1%
Berry, R. L. (Lab)	77 008	37.5%
Farley, P. (SDP/All)	33 698	16.4%
C majority	17 644	8.6%

Total vote: 208 358 (36%).

1983 Total vote: 423 746 (75.0%). C 191 607 (45.2%); Lab 116 709 (27.6%); All 111 534 (26.3%). C maj 74 898 (17.7%).

CAMBRIDGE AND BEDFORDSHIRE NORTH

Electorate: 523 899

Cambridge; Huntingdon, Mid Bedfordshire; North Bedfordshire; North East Cambridgeshire; Peterborough; South West Cambridgeshire.

*Catherwood, Sir F. (C)	86 117	53.4%
Bottomley, H. (Lab)	38 901	24.1%
Duff, A. (L/All)	36 341	22.5%
C majority	47 216	29.3%

Total vote: 161 359 (30.8%).

1983 Total vote: 386 313 (74.9%). C 197 728 (51.2%); All 117 382 (30.4%); Lab 69 463 (18.0%); Others 1 740 (0.4%). C maj 80 346 (20.8%).

CHESHIRE EAST

Electorate: 498 568

*Normanton, T. (C)	71 182	45.8%
Stephenson, A. (Lab)	52 806	34.0%
Corbett, J. P. (SDP/All)	31 374	20.2%
C majority	18 376	11.8%

Total vote: 155 362 (31.2%).

1983 Total vote: 369 497 (75.0%). C 174 446 (47.2%); Lab 101 693 (27.5%); All 92 180 (25.0%); Others 1 158 (0.3%).

67

RESULTS OF VOTING

CHESHIRE WEST

Electorate: 539 761

Birkenhead; City of Chester; Eddisbury; Ellesmere Port and Neston; Halton; Wallasey; Wirral South; Wirral West.

*Pearce, A. (C)	74 597	43.9%
Hansom, D. G. (Lab)	64 887	38.2%
Owen, E. (SDP/All)	30 470	17.9%
C majority	9 710	5.7%

Total vote: 169 954 (31.5%).

1983 Total vote: 395 575 (73.7%). C 179 777 (45.4%); Lab 126 412 (32.0%); All 89 049 (22.5%); Others 337 (0.1%). C maj 53 365 (13.5%).

CLEVELAND AND YORKSHIRE NORTH

Electorate: 566 083

Hartlepool; Langbaurgh; Middlesborough; Redcar; Richmond (Yorks); Skipton and Ripon; Stockton North; Stockton South.

*Vanneck, Sir P. (C)	73 217	40.7%
Tinnion, P. F. (Lab & Co-op)	70 592	39.3%
Beever, C. (SDP/All)	35 916	20.0%
C majority	2 625	1.4%

Total vote: 179 725 (31.8%).

1983 Total vote: 399 886 (71.2%). C 169 792 (43.0%); Lab 121 209 (30.3%); All 108 473 (27.1%); Others 412 (0.1%). C maj 48 583 (12.1%).

CORNWALL AND PLYMOUTH (same)

Electorate: 506 004 (489 803)

Falmouth and Camborne; North Cornwall; Plymouth Devonport; Plymouth Drake; Plymouth Sutton; St Ives; South East Cornwall; Truro.

Beazley, C. (C)	81 627	42.5%
Marks, J. (SDP/All)	63 876	33.3%
Cosgrove, J. (Lab)	35 952	18.7%
Parkyn, A. (Ind)	5 645	5.5%
Trevallim, R. (Ind)	2 981	
Whetter, J (CAEF)	1 892	
C majority	17 751	9.2%

No change.
Total vote: 191 973 (37.9%)

1979 Total vote: 171 600 (35.0%). C 94 650 (55.2%); Lab 36 681 (21.4%); L 23 105 (13.5%); Others 17 164 (10.0%). C maj 57 969 (33.8%).

1983 Total vote: 387 661 (76.8%). C 187 010 (48.2%); All 149 857 (38.7%); Lab 47 142 (12.2%); Others 3 652 (0.9%). C maj 37 153 (9.6%).

COTSWOLDS, THE

Electorate: 527 081

Banbury; Cheltenham; Cirencester and Tewkesbury; Gloucester; Stratford-on-Avon; Stroud; Witney.

*Plumb, Sir H. (C)	94 740	53.5%
Burton, Miss M. (L/All)	45 798	25.8%
Royall, Mrs J. A. (Lab)	36 738	20.7%
C majority	48 942	27.7%

Total vote: 177 276 (33.6%).

1983 Total vote: 390 965 (75.3%). C 210 561 (53.9%); All 122 112 (31.2%); Lab 56 691 (14.5%); Others 1 601 (0.4%). C maj 88 449 (22.6%).

CUMBRIA AND LANCASHIRE NORTH
(minor)

Electorate: 547 433 (531 948)

Barrow and Furness; Carlisle; Copeland; Lancaster; Morecambe and Lunesdale; Penrith and the Border; Westmorland and Lonsdale; Workington; Wyre.

Faith, Mrs I. S. (C)	86 127	45.8%
Atkinson, J. R. (Lab)	62 332	33.1%
Brooks, Mrs K. C. (L/All)	39 622	21.1%
C majority	23 795	12.7%

No change.
Total vote: 188 081 (34.4%).

1979 Total vote: 185 183 (34.8%). C 104 471 (56.4%); Lab 62 485 (33.7%); L 16 631 (9.0%); Others 1 596 (0.9%). C maj 41 986 (22.7%).

1983 Total vote: 410 030 (75.2%). C 197 767 (48.2%); Lab 113 876 (27.8%); All 97 274 (23.7%). C maj 83 891 (20.5%).

DERBYSHIRE

Electorate: 553 020

Amber Valley; Ashfield; Bolsover; Derby North; Derby South; Erewash; High Peak; West Derbyshire.

Hoon, G. W. (Lab)	79 466	43.5%
*Spencer, T. (C)	72 613	39.7%
Elles, Miss J. (SDP/All)	30 824	16.8%
Lab majority	6 853	3.8%

Total vote: 182 903 (33.1%).

1983 Total vote: 409 605 (74.5%). C 169 387 (41.4%); Lab 141 025 (34.4%); All 93 882 (22.9%); Others 5 311 (1.3%). C maj 28 362 (6.9%).

DEVON (same)

Electorate: 560 807 (533 237)

Exeter; Honiton; North Devon; South Hams; Teignbridge; Tiverton; Torbay; Torridge and West Devon.

*O'Hagan, Lord (C)	110 121	54.7%
Driver, P. (L/All)	53 519	26.6%
Gorbutt, D. A. (Lab)	30 017	14.9%
Christie, P. (Ecol)	6912	3.8%
Rous, Lady (Wes Reg)	659	
C majority	56 602	28.1%

No change.
Total vote: 210 228 (35.9%).

1979 Total vote: 205 422 (38.5%). C 127 032 (61.8%); L 41 010 (20.0%); Lab 37 380 (18.2%). C maj 86 022 (41.9%).

1983 Total vote 422 135 (76.3%). C 231 426 (54.8%); All 150 639 (35.7%); Lab 37 134 (8.8%); Others 2936 (0.7%). C maj 80 787 (19.1%).

DORSET EAST AND HAMPSHIRE WEST

Electorate: 565 709

Bournemouth East; Bournemouth West; Christchurch; New Forest; North Dorset; Poole; Romsey and Waterside; South Dorset.

Cassidy, B. (C)	109 072	57.6%
Goss, J. (L/All)	49 181	26.0%
James, D. T. (Lab)	31 223	16.4%
C majority	59 891	31.6%

Total vote: 189 476 (33.5%).

1983 Total vote: 403 500 (72.5%). C 238 929 (59.2%); All 118 952 (29.5%); Lab 40 675 (10.1%); Others 4944 (1.2%). C maj 119 977 (29.7%).

DURHAM

Electorate: 530 104

Bishop Auckland; Blaydon; City of Durham; Darlington; Easington, North Durham; North West Durham; Sedgefield.

Hughes, S. S. (Lab)	106 073	57.9%
Fletcher-Vane, R. (C)	44 846	24.5%
Foote Wood, C. (L/All)	32 307	17.6%
Lab majority	61 227	33.4%

Total vote: 183 226 (34.6%).

1983 Total vote: 383 472 (72.6%). Lab 174 146 (45.4%); C 116 038 (30.3%); All 92 882 (24.2%); Others 406 (0.1%). Lab maj 58 108 (15.2%).

ESSEX NORTH EAST

Electorate: 574 022

Braintree; Harwich; North Colchester; Rochford; Saffron Walden; South Colchester and Malden; Southend East; Southend West.

*Curry, D. M. (C)	97 138	55.6%
Stapleton, B. L. (Lab)	42 836	24.5%
Ross, A. E. (SDP/All)	34 769	19.9%
C majority	54 302	31.1%

Total vote: 174 743 (30.4%).

1983 Total vote: 411 930 (72.7%). C 226 568 (55.0%); All 126 337 (30.6%); Lab 58 228 (14.1%); Others 797 (0.3%). C maj 100 231 (24.3%).

ESSEX SOUTH WEST

Electorate: 557 704

Basildon; Billericay. Brentwood and Ongar; Castle Point; Chelmsford; Epping Forest; Harlow; Thurrock.

*Sherlock, Dr A. (C)	72 190	45.8%
O'Brien, C. (Lab)	56 169	35.6%
Morris, A. (L/All)	29 385	18.6%
C majority	16 021	10.2%

Total vote: 157 744 (28.3%).

1983 Total vote: 405 924 (73.0%). C 198 364 (48.9%); All 117 342 (28.9%); Lab 87 372 (21.5%); Others 2846 (0.7%). C maj 81 022 (19.9%).

GREATER MANCHESTER CENTRAL

Electorate: 507 941

Altrincham and Sale; Davyhulme; the Manchester seats of Blackley, Central, Gorton, Withington, and Wythenshawe; Stretford.

Newman, E. (Lab)	76 830	50.8%
Sewell, T. (C)	48 753	32.2%
Wedell, G. (L/All)	24 192	16.0%
Martin, K (Ind)	1430	1.0%
Lab majority	28 077	18.6%

Total vote: 151 205 (29.8%).

1983 Total vote: 353 158 (69.6%). Lab 147 672 (41.8%); C 126 918 (35.9%); All 75 974 (21.5%); Others 2594 (0.8%). Lab maj 20 754 (5.9%).

RESULTS OF VOTING

GREATER MANCHESTER EAST

Electorate: 510 586

Ashton under Lyne; Cheadle; Denton and Reddish; Hazel Grove; Oldham Central and Royton; Oldham West; Stalybridge and Hyde; Stockport.

Ford, J. G. (Lab)	65 101	42.7%
Thornber, K. (C)	56 450	37.0%
Gaskin, Mrs B. (SDP/All)	27 801	18.2%
Shipley, M. J. (Ecol)	3 158	2.1%
Lab majority	8 651	5.7%

Total vote: 152 475 (29.9%).

1983 Total vote: 369 263 (72.5%). C 147 129 (39.8%); Lab 123 388 (33.4%); All 97 302 (26.4%); Others 1 444 (0.4%). C maj 23 741 (6.4%).

GREATER MANCHESTER WEST

Electorate: 528 896

Bolton North East; Bolton South East; Bolton West; Bury North; Bury South; Eccles; Salford East; Worsley.

*Castle, Mrs B. (Lab)	93 740	55.9%
*Hopper, W. (C)	56 042	33.4%
Boddy, J. (SDP/All)	17 894	10.7%
Lab majority	37 698	22.5%

Total vote: 167 676 (31.7%).

1983 Total vote: 390 397 (74.2%). Lab 161 573 (41.4%); C 149 242 (38.2%); All 78 094 (20.0%); Others 1 488 (0.4%). Lab maj 12 331 (3.2%).

HAMPSHIRE CENTRAL

Electorate: 524 649

Aldershot; Basingstoke; Eastleigh; North West Hampshire; Southampton; Itchen; Southampton Test; Winchester.

*de Ferranti, B. (C)	84 086	51.8%
Jacobs, F. (SDP/All)	39 265	24.2%
Castle, M. V. (Lab)	39 228	24.0%
C majority	44 821	27.6%

Total vote: 162 577 (31%).

1983 Total vote: 387 073 (74.8%). C 198 608 (51.3%); All 120 408 (31.1%); Lab 67 558 (17.5%); Others 499 (0.1%). C maj 78 200 (20.2%).

HEREFORD AND WORCESTER (same)

Electorate: 560 654 (522 406)

Bromsgrove; Hereford; Leominster; Mid Worcestershire; South Worcestershire; West Gloucestershire; Worcester; Wyre Forest.

*Scott-Hopkins, Sir J. (C)	84 077	48.3%
Nielson, P. E. S. (Lab)	44 143	25.3%
Phillips, I. D. (L/All)	37 854	21.7%
Norman, Mrs F. (Ecol)	8 179	4.7%
C majority	39 934	23.0%

No change.
Total vote: 174 253 (31.1%).

1979 Total vote: 181 580 (34.8%). C 106 271 (58.5%); Lab 49 888 (27.5%); L 25 421 (14.0%). C maj 56 383 (31.0%).

1983 Total vote: 414 342 (75.2%). C 216 807 (52.4%); All 125 553 (30.3%); Lab 68 562 (16.5%); Others 3 420 (0.8%). C maj 91 254 (22.1%).

HERTFORDSHIRE

Electorate: 505 206

Broxbourne; Hertford and Stortford; Hertsmere; St Albans; South West Hertfordshire; Watford; Welwyn Hatfield.

*Prag, D. (C)	87 603	51.5%
McWalter, A. (Lab)	41 671	24.5%
Beckett, Mrs F. (SDP/All)	40 877	24.0%
C majority	45 932	27.0%

Total vote: 170 151 (33.7%).

1983 Total vote: 381 359 (76.1%). C 200 659 (52.6%); All 110 387 (28.9%); Lab 67 853 (17.8%); Others 2 460 (0.7%). C maj 90 272 (23.7%).

HUMBERSIDE

Electorate: 503 080

Beverley; Bridlington; Brigg and Cleethorpes; Great Grimsby; Hull East; Hull North; Hull West.

*Battersby, R. (C)	61 952	43.3%
Crampton, P. D. (Lab)	53 937	37.7%
Unwin, S. W. (SDP/All)	27 318	19.0%
C majority	8 015	5.6%

Total vote: 143 207 (28.5%).

1983 Total vote: 381 408 (70.2%). C 149 594 (42.6%); Lab 104 366 (29.7%); All 96 423 (27.4%); Others 1 025 (0.3%). C maj 45 228 (12.9%).

KENT EAST (minor)

Electorate: 554808 (559857)

Ashford; Canterbury; Dover; Faversham; Folkestone and Hythe; Maidstone; North Thanet; South Thanet.

*Jackson, C. (C)	92340	52.5%
*Enright, D. (Lab)	43473	24.7%
Kinch, A. (SDP/All)	34601	19.7%
Dawe, S. (Ecol)	5405	3.1%
C majority	48867	27.8%

No change.
Total vote: 175819 (31.7%).

1979 Total vote: 181305 (32.4%). C 117267 (64.8%); Lab 40060 (22.1%); L 20190 (11.1%); Others 3788 (2.1%). C maj 77207 (42.6%).

1983 Total vote: 450849 (72.3%). C 247755 (55.0%); All 126034 (28.0%); Lab 73370 (16.3%); Others 3690 (0.7%). C maj 121721 (27.0%).

KENT WEST

Electorate: 565693

Dartford; Gillingham; Gravesham; Medway; Mid Kent; Sevenoaks; Tonbridge and Malling; Tunbridge Wells.

*Patterson, G. B. (C)	85414	49.0%
Woodhams, A. (Lab)	50784	29.1%
Billenness, P. (L/All)	33306	19.1%
Bunyan, Mrs C. (Ecol)	4991	2.9%
C majority	34630	19.9%

Total vote: 174495 (30.9%).

1983 Total vote: 414398 (74.1%). C 220793 (53.3%); All 108069 (26.1%); Lab 83381 (20.1%); Other 2155 (0.5%). C maj 112724 (27.2%).

LANCASHIRE CENTRAL

Electorate: 524132

Blackpool North; Blackpool South; Chorley; Fylde; Preston; Ribble Valley; South Ribble; West Lancashire.

*Welsh, M. (C)	82370	50.4%
Jones, Ms H. (Lab)	56175	34.4%
*Gallagher, M. (SDP/All)	24936	15.2%
C majority	26195	16.0%

Total vote: 163481 (31.2%).

1983 Total vote: 385634 (74.1%). C 193319 (50.1%); Lab 102441 (26.6%); All 87669 (22.7%); Others 2205 (0.6%). C maj 90878 (23.6%).

LANCASHIRE EAST

Electorate: 534542

Blackburn; Burnley; Heywood and Middleton; Hyndburn; Littleborough and Saddleworth; Pendle; Rochdale; Rossendale and Darwin.

Hindley, M. J. (Lab)	75711	44.6%
*Kellet-Bowman, E. (C)	67806	39.9%
Lishman, G. (L/All)	26320	15.5%
Lab majority	7905	4.7%

Total vote: 169837 (31.8%).

1983 Total vote: 371220 (69.8%). C 156357 (42.1%); Lab 144447 (38.9%); All 67736 (18.3%); Others 2680 (0.7%). C maj 11910 (3.2%).

LEEDS

Electorate: 526133

Elmet; the Leeds seats of Central, East, North East, North West, and West, Morley and Leeds South; Pudsey.

McGowan, M. (Lab)	70535	42.3%
Holt, J. G. (C)	60178	36.1%
Cooksey, S. J. (L/All)	36097	21.6%
Lab majority	10357	6.2%

Total vote: 166810 (31.7%).

1983 Total vote: 367811 (69.9%). C 140086 (38.1%); Lab 119314 (32.4%); All 105209 (28.6%); Other 3202 (0.9%). C maj 20772 (5.6%).

LEICESTER

Electorate: 564350

Bosworth; Leicester East; Leicester South, Leicester West; Loughborough; North Warwickshire; Nuneaton; Rutland and Melton.

*Tuckman, F. (C)	72508	41.3%
Soulsby, P. (Lab)	69616	39.8%
Simmonds, D. (SDP/All)	29656	17.0%
Barratt, A. (Ind C)	3249	1.9%
C majority	2892	1.7%

Total vote: 175029 (31%).

1983 Total vote: 420595 (74.8%). C 196765 (46.8%); Lab 126320 (30.0%); All 92645 (22.0%); Others 4865 (1.2%). C maj 70445 (16.8%).

LINCOLNSHIRE

Electorate: 551 904

Bassetlaw; East Lindsey; Gainsborough and Horncastle; Grantham; Holland with Boston; Lincoln; Newark; Stamford and Spalding.

*Newton Dunn, W. (C)	92 606	52.3%
Sewell, C. (Lab)	47 161	26.6%
Purves, G. (L/All)	37 244	21.1%
C majority	45 445	25.7%

Total vote: 177 011 (32.1%).

1983 Total vote 402 758 (74.0%). C 207 136 (51.4%); All 114 002 (28.3%); Lab 80 356 (20.0%); Others 1 264 (0.3%). C maj 93 134 (23.1%).

LONDON CENTRAL

Electorate: 543 825

Chelsea; City of London and Westminster South; Fulham; Hampstead and Highgate; Holborn and St Pancras; Islington North; Islington South and Finsbury; Kensington; Westminster North.

Newens, A. S. (Lab & Co-op)	77 842	43.2%
*Fergusson, A. (C)	64 545	35.8%
Wistrich, E. (SDP/All)	30 269	16.8%
Porrit, J. (Ecol)	5 945	4.2%
Maynard, R. (CBJ)	1 569	
Lab majority	13 297	7.4%

Total vote: 180 170 (33.1%).

1983 Total vote: 341 798 (62.1%). C 142 319 (41.6%); Lab 113 794 (33.3%); All 77 136 (22.6%); Others 8 549 (2.5%). C maj 28 525 (20.5%).

LONDON EAST (same)

Electorate: 537 831 (541 938).

Barking; Dagenham, Hornchurch; Ilford North; Ilford South; Newham North East; Romford, Upminster, Wanstead and Woodford.

Tongue, Miss C. (Lab)	73 870	45.6%
*Tyrrell, A. (C)	61 711	38.1%
Horne, Mrs J. (SDP/All)	26 379	16.3%
Lab majority	12 159	7.5%

Labour gain from C.
Total vote: 161 960 (30.1%).

1979 Total vote: 159 647 (29.5%). C 77 940 (48.8%); Lab 64 925 (40.7%); L 16 782 (10.5%). C maj 13 015 (8.2%).

1983 Total vote: 368 631 (77.6%). C 165 626 (44.9%); Lab 109 179 (29.6%); All 88 731 (24.1%); Others 5 095 (1.4%). C maj 56 447 (15.3%).

LONDON NORTH

Electorate: 564 359

Chipping Barnet; Edmonton; Enfield North; Enfield Southgate; Finchley; Hendon North; Hendon South; Hornsey and Wood Green; Tottenham.

*Marshall, J. (C)	74 846	41.4%
Large, E. (Lab)	69 993	38.7%
Skinner, J. (L/All)	31 344	17.3%
Lang, P. (Ecol)	4 682	2.6%
C majority	4 853	2.7%

Total vote: 180 865 (32.1%).

1983 Total vote 387 044 (68.8%). C 184 569 (47.7%); Lab 113 596 (29.3%); All 84 302 (21.8%); Others 4 577 (1.2%). C majority 70 973 (18.4%).

LONDON NORTH EAST (same)

Electorate: 513 781 (518 912)

Bethnal Green and Stepney; Bow and Poplar; Chingford; Hackney North and Stoke Newington; Hackney South and Shoreditch; Leyton; Newham North West; Newham South; Walthamstow.

*Lomas, A. (Lab)	79 907	61.8%
Batchelor, M. (C)	27 242	21.1%
Heppell, J. (L/All)	17 344	13.4%
Lambert, Mrs J. (Ecol)	4 797	3.7%
Lab majority	52 665	40.7%

No change.
Total vote: 129 290 (25.2%).

1979 Total vote: 106 083 (20.4%). Lab 61 044 (57.5%); C 36 200 (34.1%); L 8 839 (8.3%). Lab maj 24 804 (23.4%).

1983 Total vote: 304 758 (59.3%). Lab 130 915 (43.0%); C 87 627 (28.7%); All 70 391 (23.1%); Others 15 825 (5.2%). Lab maj 43 288 (14.3%).

LONDON NORTH WEST

Electorate: 518 365

Brent East; Brent North; Brent South; Harrow East; Harrow West; Hayes and Harlington; Ruislip-Northwood; Uxbridge.

*Bethell, Lord (C)	69 803	43.1%
Healy, Ms P. (Lab)	62 381	38.6%
Ketteringham, A. (L/All)	29 609	18.3%
C majority	7 422	4.6%

Total vote: 161 793 (31.2%).

1983 Total vote: 360 429 (69.9%). C 170 826 (47.4%); Lab 97 490 (27.1%); All 90 834 (25.2%); Others 1 279 (0.3%). C maj 73 336 (22.5%).

LONDON SOUTH AND SURREY EAST

Electorate: 505393

Carshalton and Wallington; Croydon Central; Croydon North East; Croydon North West; Croydon South; East Surrey; Reigate; Sutton and Cheam.

*Moorhouse, J. (C)	82122	53.3%
Mackinlay, A. (Lab)	37465	24.3%
Parry, J. (L/All)	34546	22.4%
C majority	44657	29.0%

Total vote: 154133 (30.5%).

1983 Total vote: 356887 (71.0%). C 199056 (55.8%); All 101133 (28.3%); Lab 54263 (15.2%); Others 2435 (0.7%). C maj 97923 (27.5%).

LONDON SOUTH EAST

Electorate: 561984

Beckenham; Bexleyheath; Chislehurst; Eltham; Erith and Crayford; Greenwich; Old Bexley and Sidcup; Orpington; Ravensbourne; Woolwich.

*Price, P. (C)	81508	44.6%
Cowan, S. J. (Lab)	61493	33.7%
Fryer, J. (L/All)	38614	21.2%
Turner, W. (Marx)	989	0.5%
C majority	20015	10.9%

Total vote: 182604 (32.5%).

1983 Total vote 405034 (72.4%). C 200844 (49.6%); All 118563 (29.3%); Lab 83184 (20.5%); Others 2443 (0.6%). C maj 82281 (20.3%).

LONDON SOUTH INNER

Electorate: 530672

Dulwich; Lewisham Deptford; Lewisham East; Lewisham West; Norwood; Peckham; Southwark and Bermondsey; Streatham; Vauxhall.

*Balfe, R. (Lab & Co-op)	77661	50.9%
Miller, Mrs D. (C)	46180	30.3%
Daly, J. (SDP/All)	25391	16.7%
Owens, Mrs J. (Ecol)	3281	2.2%
Lab & Co-op majority	31481	20.6%

Total vote: 152513 (28.7%).

1983 Total vote: 342514 (64.0%). Lab 138712 (40.4%); C 117829 (34.4%); All 80329 (23.4%); Others 5644 (1.6%). Lab maj 20883 (6.0%).

LONDON SOUTH WEST

Electorate: 499273

Battersea; Epsom and Ewell; Kingston upon Thames; Mitcham and Morden; Putney; Surbiton; Tooting; Wimbledon.

*Roberts, Dame S. (C)	70490	41.6%
Pollack, Miss A. J. (Lab)	63623	37.6%
Twigg, D. (L/All)	32268	19.0%
Willington, Mrs S. (Ecol)	3066	1.8%
C majority	6867	4.0%

Total vote: 169447 (33.9%).

1983 Total vote: 354914 (77.1%). C 169888 (47.9%); Lab 94651 (26.7%); All 85263 (24.0%); Others 5112 (1.4%). C maj 75237 (21.2%).

LONDON WEST

Electorate: 516661

Brentford and Isleworth: Ealing Acton; Ealing North; Ealing Southall; Feltham and Heston; Hammersmith; Richmond and Barnes; Twickenham.

Elliott, M. N. (Lab)	79554	40.8%
*Hord, B. (C)	74325	38.1%
Layton, C. (SDP/All)	36687	18.8%
Sutherland, Mrs D. (Ecol)	4361	2.2%
Lab majority	5229	2.7%

Total vote: 194927 (37.7%).

1983 Total vote: 380699 (73.8%). C 166462 (43.7%); Lab 112697 (29.6%); All 95696 (25.1%); Others 5844 (1.6%). C maj 53765 (14.1%).

MERSEYSIDE EAST

Electorate: 537285

Knowsley North; Knowsley South; Leigh; Liverpool Garston; Makerfield; St Helens North; St Helens South; Wigan.

Huckfield, L. (Lab)	87086	61.2%
Galbraith, T. (C)	38047	26.7%
Bishop, T. (SDP/All)	17259	12.1%
Lab majority	49039	34.5%

Total vote: 142392 (26.5%).

1983 Total vote: 389198 (72.4%). Lab 200808 (51.6%); C 108204 (27.8%); All 78160 (20.1%); Others 2026 (0.5%). Lab maj 92604 (23.8%).

RESULTS OF VOTING

MERSEYSIDE WEST

Electorate: 551532

Bootle; Crosby; the Liverpool seats of Broadgreen, Mossley Hill, Riverside, Walton, and West Derby; Southport.

Stewart, K. (Lab)	65915	42.3%
*Hooper, Miss S. (C)	52718	33.8%
Clark, P. (L/All)	37303	29.9%
Lab majority	13197	8.5%

Total vote: 155936 (28.3%).
1983 Total vote: 392621 (70.9%). Lab 145143 (37.0%); C 130538 (33.2%); All 108080 (27.5%); Others 8860 (2.3%). Lab maj 14605 (3.7%).

MIDLANDS CENTRAL

Electorate: 533798

The Coventry seats of North East, North West, South East, and South West; Meriden; Rugby and Kenilworth; Solihull; Warwick and Leamington.

*de Courcy Ling, J. (C)	67884	44.5%
Blackman, D. J. (Lab & Co-op)	55155	36.2%
Langmead, P. (SDP/All)	27912	18.3%
Enstone, A. (FRP)	1494	1.0%
C majority	12720	8.3%

Total vote: 152445 (28.6%).
1983 Total vote 387914 (73.2%). C 179019 (46.1%); Lab 114686 (29.6%); All 92315 (23.8%); Others 1894 (0.5%). C maj 64333 (16.6%).

MIDLANDS WEST

Electorate: 533796

Dudley East; Dudley West: Halesowen and Stourbridge; Warley East; Warley West; Wolverhampton North East; Wolverhampton South East; Wolverhampton South West.

Pitt, T. J. (Lab)	74091	50.7%
Burnside, A. (C)	54406	37.2%
Carter, C. (L/All)	17709	12.1%
Lab majority	19685	13.5%

Total vote: 146206 (27.4%).
1983 Total vote: 382689 (71.8%). C 157143 (41.1%); Lab 142962 (37.4%); All 80999 (21.1%); Others 1585 (0.4%). C maj 14181 (3.7%).

NORFOLK (minor)

Electorate: 543214 (504605)

Great Yarmouth, the Norfolk seats of Mid, North, North West, South, and South West; Norwich North, Norwich South.

*Howell, P. (C)	95459	49.8%
Heading, A. E. B. (Lab)	58602	30.6%
Williams, L. (SDP/All)	37703	14.7%
C majority	36857	19.2%

No change.
Total vote: 191764 (35.3%).
1979 Total vote: 172192 (34.1%). C 102981 (59.8%); Lab 52406 (30.4%); L 16805 (9.8%). C maj 50575 (29.4%).
1983 Total vote 403675 (75.2%). C 200865 (49.8%); All 112636 (27.9%); Lab 88871 (22.0%); Others 1303 (0.3%). C maj 88229 (21.9%).

NORTHAMPTONSHIRE

Electorate: 547188

Blaby; Corby; Daventry; Harborough; Kettering; Northampton North; Northampton South; Wellingborough.

*Simpson, A. (C)	88668	49.8%
Dickie, J. (Lab)	48809	27.4%
Goodhart, Mrs C. (SDP/All)	37421	21.0%
Bryant, Mrs A. (Chr/Ecol)	3330	1.8%
C majority	39859	22.4%

Total vote: 178228 (32.6%).
1983 Total vote: 408635 (75.8%). C 211721 (51.8%); All 105329 (25.8%); Lab 89202 (21.8%); Others 2383 (0.6%). C maj 106392 (26.0%).

NORTHUMBRIA

Electorate: 512979

Berwick-upon-Tweed; Blyth Valley; Hexham; Newcastle upon Tyne Central; Newcastle upon Tyne North; Tynemouth; Wallsend; Wansbeck.

*Adam, G. (Lab)	78417	42.6%
Crichton, C. (C)	62717	34.1%
Scott, G. (L/All)	42946	23.3%
Lab majority	15700	8.5%

Total vote: 184080 (35.9%).
1983 Total vote: 376239 (73.5%). C 133057 (35.4%); Lab 130299 (34.6%); All 111999 (29.8%); Others 884 (0.2%). C maj 2758 (0.7%).

NOTTINGHAM

Electorate: 554 473

Broxtowe; Gedling; Mansfield; Nottingham East; Nottingham North; Nottingham South; Rushcliffe; Sherwood.

Kilby, M. (C)	82 500	45.3%
Coates, K. (Lab)	66 374	36.5%
Melton, K. (L/All)	33 169	18.2%
C majority	16 126	8.8%

Total vote: 182 043 (32.8%).

1983 Total vote: 387 100 (70.3%). C 185 618 (48.0%); Lab 119 663 (30.9%); All 78 510 (20.3%); Others 3 309 (0.8%). C maj 55 955 (17.1%).

SHROPSHIRE AND STAFFORD

Electorate: 562 823

Cannock and Burntwood; Ludlow; Newcastle-under-Lyme; Shropshire; Shrewsbury and Atcham; South Staffordshire; Stafford; The Wrekin.

*Prout, C. (C)	82 291	46.5%
Hallam, D. J. A. (Lab)	57 359	32.4%
Burman, R. (L/All)	37 209	21.1%
C majority	24 932	14.1%

Total vote: 176 859 (31.4%).

1983 Total vote: 419 182 (75.5%). C 201 666 (48.1%); All 110 403 (26.3%); Lab 106 766 (25.5%); Others 347 (0.1%). C maj 91 263 (21.7%).

OXFORD AND BUCKINGHAMSHIRE

Electorate: 542 343

Aylesbury; Beaconsfield; Buckingham; Chesham and Amersham; Henley; Oxford East; Oxford West and Abingdon; Wycombe.

Elles, J. (C)	94 136	52.8%
Liddle, R. (SDP/All)	45 055	25.3%
Power, J. G. (Lab)	39 164	22.0%
C majority	49 081	27.5%

Total vote: 178 355 (32.9%).

1983 Total vote: 393 927 (73.6%). C 217 605 (55.2%); All 112 299 (28.5%); Lab 61 782 (15.7%); Others 2 241 (0.6%). C maj 105 306 (26.7%).

SOMERSET AND DORSET WEST

Electorate: 540 393

Bridgwater: Somerton and Frome; Taunton; Wells; Weston-super-Mare; West Dorset; Woodspring; Yeovil.

Daly, Mrs M. (C)	98 928	50.9%
Moore, R. (L/All)	58 677	30.2%
Linden, Mrs J. (Lab)	36 836	18.9%
C majority	40 251	20.7%

Total vote: 194 441 (36%).

1983 Total vote: 404 672 (76.2%). C 215 704 (53.3%); All 141 469 (35.0%); Lab 47 049 (11.6%); Others 450 (0.1%). C maj 74 235 (18.3%).

SHEFFIELD

Electorate: 558 984

Chesterfield; North East Derbyshire; the Sheffield seats of Attercliffe, Brightside, Central, Hallam, Heeley, and Hillsborough.

Cryer, R. (Lab)	93 530	56.8%
Grayson, D. (C)	47 247	28.7%
Holmstedt, Miss M. (L/All)	23 935	14.5%
Lab majority	46 283	28.1%

Total vote: 164 712 (29.5%).

1983 Total vote: 393 179 (70.6%). Lab 173 807 (44.2%); C 120 932 (30.8%); All 96 976 (24.7%); Others 1 464 (0.3%). Lab 52 875 (13.4%).

STAFFORDSHIRE EAST

Electorate: 563 376

Burton; Mid Staffordshire; North West Leicestershire; South Derbyshire; South East Staffordshire; Stoke-on-Trent Central; Stoke-on-Trent North; Stoke-on-Trent South.

Stevenson, G. W. (Lab)	76 753	44.7%
*Moreland, R. (C)	68 886	40.1%
Fox, R. (SDP/All)	26 093	15.2%
Lab majority	7 867	4.6%

Total vote: 171 732 (30.5%).

1983 Total vote: 416 609 (74.5%). C 176 277 (42.3%); Lab 146 525 (35.2%); All 92 666 (22.2%); Others 1 141 (0.3%). C maj 29 752 (7.1%).

75

RESULTS OF VOTING

SUFFOLK

Electorate: 516050

Bury St Edmunds; Central Suffolk; Ipswich; South East Cambridgeshire; South Suffolk; Suffolk Coastal; Waveney.

*Turner, A. (C)	88243	54.0%
Moszczynski, W. (Lab)	41145	25.2%
Leakey, C. (L/All)	34084	20.9%
C majority	47098	28.8%

Total vote: 163472 (31.7%).

1983 Total vote: 379863 (74.7%). C 201926 (53.1%); All 98387 (25.9%); Lab 79315 (20.9%); Others 235 (0.1%). C maj 103539 (27.3%).

SURREY WEST

Electorate: 504923

Chertsey & Walton; Esher; Guildford; Molesey Valley; North West Surrey; South West Surrey; Woking.

*Douro, Marquess of (C)	96675	59.2%
Mortimer, E. (SDP/All)	44087	27.0%
Vaz, K. (Lab)	22531	13.8%
C majority	52588	32.2%

Total vote: 163293 (32.3%).

1983 Total vote: 362575 (72.7%). C 217075 (60.0%); All 107316 (29.6%); Lab 36409 (10.0%); Others 1775 (0.4%). C maj 109759 (30.4%).

SUSSEX EAST (minor)

Electorate: 537397 (535564)

Bexhill and Battle: Brighton Kemptown; Brighton Pavilion; Eastbourne; Hastings and Rye; Hove; Lewes; Wealden.

*Stewart-Clark, Sir J. (C)	102287	57.9%
Busby, J. (SDP/All)	36666	20.8%
Spillman, H. (Lab)	32213	18.2%
Evelyn, Mrs E. (Ecol)	5401	3.1%
C majority	65621	37.1%

No change.
Total vote: 176567 (32.9%).

1983 Total vote: 378465 (70.9%). C 220859 (58.4%); All 103040 (27.2%); Lab 51301 (13.5%); Others 3265 (0.9%). C maj 117819 (31.2%).

SUSSEX WEST

Electorate: 531934

Arundel; Chichester; Crawley; Horsham; Mid Sussex; Shoreham; Worthing.

*Seligman, M. (C)	104257	58.7%
Walsh, Dr J. (L/All)	46755	26.3%
Rees, G. C. (Lab)	22857	12.9%
Ahern, D. (Ecol)	3842	2.2%
C majority	57502	32.4%

Total vote: 177711 (33.4%).

1983 Total vote: 384655 (73.1%). C 230234 (59.9%); All 112801 (29.3%); Lab 37867 (9.8%); Others 3753 (1.0%). C maj 117433 (30.6%).

THAMES VALLEY

Electorate: 519564

East Berkshire; Reading East; Reading West; Slough; Spelthorne; Windsor and Maidenhead; Wokingham.

*Elles, Lady (C)	74928	52.1%
Bastin, R. B. (Lab)	36123	25.1%
Bradnock, R. (L/All)	32704	22.8%
C majority	38805	27.0%

Total vote: 143755 (27.7%).

1983 Total vote: 367665 (72.1%). C 197474 (53.7%); All 98516 (26.8%); Lab 64020 (17.4%); Others 7655 (2.1%). C maj 98958.

TYNE AND WEAR

Electorate: 543955

Gateshead East; Houghton and Washington; Jarrow; Newcastle upon Tyne East; South Shields; Sunderland North; Sunderland South; Tyne Bridge.

*Quin, Miss J. (Lab)	89024	60.3%
Cook, R. (C)	39610	26.8%
Carroll, B. (SDP/All)	19081	12.9%
Lab majority	49414	33.5%

Total vote: 147715 (27.2%).

1983 Total vote: 366709 (67.4%). Lab 180777 (49.3%); C 104183 (28.4%); All 81749 (22.3%); Lab maj 76594 (20.9%).

WIGHT AND HAMPSHIRE EAST

Electorate: 544 189

East Hampshire; Fareham; Gosport; Havant; Isle of Wight; Portsmouth North; Portsmouth South.

*Simmonds, R. (C)	96 666	51.7%
Ludford, Mrs S. (L/All)	53 738	28.8%
Phillips, J. A. (Lab)	36 445	19.5%
C majority	42 928	22.9%

Total vote: 186 849 (34.3%).

1983 Total vote: 393 397 (73.4%). C 218 475 (55.5%); All 130 594 (33.2%); Lab 42 874 (10.9%); Others 1 454 (0.4%). C maj 87 881 (22.3%).

WILTSHIRE

Electorate: 531 501

Devizes; Newbury; North Wiltshire; Salisbury; Swindon; Wantage; Westbury.

Jackson, Mrs C. (C)	86 873	47.5%
Ainslie, J. (L/All)	60 404	33.1%
Whiteside, P. (Lab)	35 457	19.4%
C majority	26 469	14.4%

Total vote: 182 734 (34.4%).

1983 Total vote: 394 990 (75.1%). C 204 715 (51.8%); All 134 449 (34.0%); Lab 53 610 (13.6%); Others 2 216 (0.6%). C maj 70 266 (17.8%).

YORK

Electorate: 517 592

Boothferry; Glanford and Scunthorpe; Harrogate; Ryedale; Scarborough; Selby; York.

McMillan-Scott, E. (C)	80 636	51.0%
Haines, Mrs S. (Lab)	44 234	28.0%
Howard, M. (SDP/All)	33 356	21.0%
C majority	36 402	23.0%

Total vote: 158 226 (30.6%).

1983 Total vote: 369 936 (72.3%). C 193 471 (52.3%); All 95 806 (25.9%); Lab 79 828 (21.6%); Others 831 (0.2%). C maj 113 643 (30.7%).

YORKSHIRE SOUTH

Electorate: 516 431

Barnsley Central Barnsley East; Doncaster Central; Doncaster North; Don Valley; Rotherham; Rother Valley; Wentworth.

West, N. (Lab)	98 020	66.4%
Pickley, Mrs R. (C)	30 271	20.5%
Eden, D. (SDP/All)	19 306	13.1%
Lab majority	67 749	45.9%

Total vote: 147 597 (28.6%).

1983 Total vote: 355 082 (69.2%). Lab 185 723 (52.3%); C 95 836 (27.0%); All 73 523 (20.7%). Lab maj 89 887 (25.3%).

YORKSHIRE SOUTH WEST

Electorate: 518 423

Barnsley West and Penistone; Colne Valley; Dewsbury; Hemsworth; Huddersfield; Normanton; Pontefract and Castleford; Wakefield.

*Megahy, T. (Lab)	88 464	55.4%
Lodge, A. (C)	44 291	27.7%
Crossley, J. (L/All)	26 964	16.9%
Lab majority	44 173	27.7%

Total vote: 159 719 (30.8%).

1983 Total vote: 350 040 (67.7%). Lab 159 510 (45.6%); C 118 599 (33.9%); All 71 105 (20.3%); Others 826 (0.2%). Lab maj 40 911.

YORKSHIRE WEST

Electorate: 560 190

Batley and Spen; Bradford North; Bradford South; Bradford West; Calder Valley; Halifax; Keighley; Shipley.

*Seal, B. (Lab)	86 259	47.8%
Bruce, I. (C)	65 405	36.2%
Lyons, E. (SDP/All)	28 709	15.9%
Lab majority	20 854	11.6%

Total vote: 180 373 (32.2%).

1983 Total vote: 412 519 (74.2%). C 166 117 (40.3%); Lab 138 470 (33.6%); All 101 764 (24.7%); Others 6 168 (1.4%). C maj 27 647 (6.7%).

SCOTLAND

GLASGOW (minor)

Electorate: 518 178 (534 414)

The Glasgow seats of Cathcart, Central, Garscadden, Govan, Hillhead, Maryhill, Pollok, Provan, Shettleston, and Springburn.

*Buchan, Mrs J. (Lab)	91 015	59.3%
Chadd, Miss S. (C)	25 282	16.5%
Mason, C. (L/All)	20 867	13.6%
MacLeod, N. (SNP)	16 456	10.7%
Lab majority	65 733	42.8%

No change.
Total vote: 153 620 (29.6%).

1979 Total vote: 150 839 (28.2%). Lab 73 846 (49.0%); C 41 144 (27.3%); SNP 24 776 (16.4%); L 11 073 (7.3%). Lab maj 32 702 (21.7%).

1983 Total vote: 355 504 (68.4%). Lab 186 221 (52.4%); All 72 340 (20.4%); C 67 318 (19.0%); SNP 27 762 (7.8%); Other 1 863 (0.4%). Lab maj 113 881 (32.0%).

HIGHLANDS AND ISLANDS (minor)

Electorate: 307 265 (298 802)

Argyll and Bute; Caithness and Sutherland; Inverness, Nairn and Lochaber; Moray; Ross, Cromarty and Skye; Orkney and Shetland; Western Isles.

*Ewing, Mrs W. (SNP)	49 410	41.9%
Johnston, R. (L/All)	33 133	28.1%
Webster, D. (C)	18 847	16.0%
McArthur, Rev J. (Lab)	16 644	14.1%
SNP majority	16 277	13.8%

No change.
Total vote: 118 034 (38.4%).

1979 Total vote: 117 722 (39.4%). SNP 39 991 (34.0%); L 36 109 (30.7%); C 30 776 (26.1%); Lab 10 846 (9.2%). SNP maj 3 882 (3.3%).

1983 Total vote: 216 718 (71.3%). All 74 005 (34.2%); C 67 481 (31.1%); SNP 46 990 (21.7%); Lab 28 242 (13%). All maj 6 524 (3.0%).

LOTHIANS

Electorate: 526 068

The Edinburgh seats of Central, East, Leith, Pentlands, South and West; Linlithgow; Livingston; Midlothian.

Martin, D. W. (Lab)	74 989	40.4%
Henderson, I. (C)	49 065	26.4%
Mabon, Dr J. D. (SPD/All)	36 636	19.7%
Stevenson, Dr D. (SNP)	22 331	12.0%
Hendry, Miss L. (Ecol)	2 560	1.4%
Lab majority	25 924	14.0%

Total vote: 185 581 (35.3%).

1983 Total vote: 375 648 (71.8%). Lab 129 752 (34.5%); C 113 670 (30.3%); All 101 373 (27.0%); SNP 29 398 (7.8%); Others 1 455 (0.4%). Lab maj 16 082 (4.3%).

SCOTLAND MID AND FIFE

Electorate: 528 529

Clackmannan; Falkirk East; Falkirk West; Stirling; Central Fife; Dunfermline East; Dunfermline West; Kirkcaldy; North East Fife; Perth and Kinross.

Falconer, A. (Lab)	80 038	42.7%
*Purvis, J. (C)	52 872	28.2%
Jones, Mrs J. (SNP)	30 511	16.3%
Wedderburn, A. (SDP/All)	24 220	12.9%
Lab majority	27 166	14.5%

Total vote: 187 641 (35.5%).

1983 Total vote: 384 066 (80.9%). Lab 133 752 (34.8%); C 110 331 (28.7%); All 91 900 (23.9%); SNP 46 015 (12.0%); Others 2 068 (0.6%). Lab maj 23 421 (6.1%).

SCOTLAND NORTH EAST

Electorate: 548 711

Aberdeen North; Aberdeen South; Banff and Buchan; Gordon; Kincardine and Deeside; Angus East; Dundee East; Dundee West; North Tayside.

*Provan, J. (C)	53 809	34.2%
Doran, F. (Lab)	44 638	28.4%
Hood, D. (SNP)	33 448	21.3%
Philip, I. (SDP/All)	25 490	16.2%
C majority	9 171	5.8%

Total vote: 157 385 (28.7%).

1983 Total vote: 383 972 (70.7%). C 134 265 (35.0%); Lab 85 697 (22.3%); All 83 160 (21.7%); SNP 79 942 (20.8%); Others 908 (0.2%). C maj 48 568 (12.7%).

SCOTLAND SOUTH

Electorate: 484 760

Ayr: Carrick, Cumnock and Doon Valley; Clydesdale; Cunninghame South; Dumfries; Galloway and Upper Nithsdale; East Lothian; Roxburgh and Berwickshire; Tweeddale, Ettrick and Lauderdale.

*Hutton, A. (C)	60 843	37.0%
Stewart, R. (Lab & Co-op)	57 706	35.1%
Buchanan, Mrs E. (L/All)	23 598	14.4%
Goldie, I. (SNP)	22 242	13.5%
C majority	3 137	1.9%

Total vote: 164 389 (33.9%).

1983 Total vote: 362 648 (75.5%). C 123 787 (34.1%); Lab 110 637 (30.5%); All 94 342 (26.0%); SNP 33 882 (9.4%). C maj 13 150 (3.6%).

STRATHCLYDE EAST

Electorate: 498 458

Cumbernauld and Kilsyth; East Kilbride; Glasgow; Rutherglen; Kilmarnock and Loudoun; Monklands East; Monklands West; Motherwell North; Motherwell South.

*Collins, K. (Lab)	90 792	58.6%
Leslie, G. (SNP)	27 330	17.7%
Leckie, R. (C)	24 857	16.1%
de Seume, Ms P. (L/All)	11 883	7.7%
Lab majority	63 462	40.9%

Total vote: 154 862 (31.1%).

1983 Total vote: 372 807 (75.2%). Lab 183 740 (49.3%); All 77 244 (20.7%); C 75 596 (20.3%); SNP 35 823 (9.6%); Other 404 (0.2%). Lab maj 106 496 (28.6%).

STRATHCLYDE WEST

Electorate: 499 162

Clydebank and Milngavie; Cunninghame North; Dumbarton; Eastwood; Greenock and Port Glasgow; Paisley North; Paisley South; Renfrew West and Inverclyde; Strathkelvin and Bearsden.

McMahon, H. (Lab)	70 234	40.8%
Lait, Miss J. (C)	47 196	27.4%
Herriot, Mrs J. (SNP)	28 866	16.8%
Herbison, D. (SDP/All)	25 955	15.0%
Lab majority	23 038	13.4%

Total vote: 172 251 (34.5%).

1983 Total vote: 373 417 (75.2%). Lab 132 613 (35.5%); C 108 906 (29.1%); All 98 603 (26.4%); SNP 32 163 (8.6%); Other 1 132 (0.4%). Lab maj 23 707 (6.4%).

WALES

WALES MID AND WEST

Electorate: 533 644

Carmarthen; Ceredigion and Pembroke North; Llanelli; Pembroke; Brecon and Radnor; Gower; Neath; Swansea East; Swansea West.

Morris, D. (Lab)	89 362	41.6%
Lewis, D. (C)	52 910	24.7%
Lloyd, D. (L/All)	35 168	16.4%
Williams, Dr P. (PlC)	32 880	15.3%
Smith, Miss M. (Ecol)	4 266	2.0%
Lab majority	36 452	16.9%

Total vote: 214 586 (40.2%).

1983 Total vote: 408 900 (77.1%). Lab 151 462 (37.0%); C 128 948 (31.5%); All 90 979 (22.3%); PIC 34 580 (8.5%); Other 2 931 (0.7%). Lab maj 22 514 (5.5%).

WALES NORTH (same)

Electorate: 516 153 (493 181)

Alyn and Deeside; Clwyd North West; Clwyd South West; Delyn; Wrexham; Caernarfon; Conwy; Meirionnydd Nant Conwy; Ynys Mon; Montgomery.

*Brookes, Miss B. (C)	69 139	31.6%
Ellis, T. (SDP/All)	56 861	26.0%
Campbell, I. (Lab)	54 768	25.0%
Iwan, D. (PlC)	38 117	17.4%
C majority	12 278	5.6%

No change.
Total vote: 218 885 (42.4%).

1979 Total vote: 176 960 (35.9%). C 74 173 (41.9%); Lab 46 627 (26.3%); PlC 34 171 (19.3%); L 21 989 (12.4%). C maj 27 546 (15.6%).

1983 Total vote: 397 300 (77.6%). C 148 244 (37.3%); All 98 937 (24.9%); Lab 94 029 (23.7%); PIC 55 603 (14.0%); Other 487 (0.1%). C maj 49 307 (12.4%).

WALES SOUTH

Electorate: 509 434

The Cardiff seats of Central, North, South and Penarth, and West; Vale of Glamorgan; Bridgend; Ogmore; Pontypridd; Aberavon.

*Griffiths, W. J. (Lab)	99 936	57.1%
Pattman, Miss J. (C)	55 678	28.5%
Davis, Mrs J. (L/All)	26 588	13.6%
Huws, Dr D. (PlC)	13 201	6.8%
Lab majority	44 258	22.7%

Total vote: 195 403 (38.4%).

1983 Total vote 375 492 (73.9%). Lab 142 763 (38.2%); C 127 088 (33.8%); All 90 887 (24.2%); PIC 12 627 (3.4%); Other 2 127 (0.6%). Lab maj 15 675 (4.0%).

WALES SOUTH EAST (minor)

Electorate: 565 739 (545 152)

Blaenau Gwent; Islwyn; Monmouth; Newport East; Newport West; Torfaen; Caerphilly; Cynon Valley; Merthyr Tydfil and Rhymney; Rhondda.

Smith, L. (Lab)	131 916	61.2%
Whyatt, R. (C)	36 359	16.9%
Lindley, C. (SDP/All)	28 330	13.1%
Morgan, S. (PlC)	18 833	8.7%
Lab majority	95 557	44.3%

No change.
Total vote: 215 438 (38.1%).

1979 Total vote: 167 756 (31.1%). Lab 93 093 (54.8%); C 51 478 (30.3%); PlC 12 469 (7.3%); L 10 534 (6.2%); Other 2 182 (1.3%). Lab maj 41 615 (24.5%).

1983 Total vote: 427 294 (75.8%). Lab 215 604 (50.5%); C 95 030 (22.2%); All 92 555 (21.7%); PIC 22 499 (5.2%); Other 1 606 (0.4%). Lab maj 120 574 (28.2%).

United Kingdom (excluding Northern Ireland)

	C	Lab	*All	SNP PIC	Others	Totals
ENGLAND	4 880 009	3 963 186	2 242 930	—	88 698	11 174 823
	(5 817 992)	(3 536 261)	(1 444 204)		(86 310)	(10 884 767)
% of poll	43.7 (53.5)	35.5 (32.5)	20.1 (13.3)	—	0.8(0.5)	—
Number of MEPs	42 (54)	24 (12)	—	—	—	66
SCOTLAND	332 771	526 056	201 782	230 594	2 560	1 293 763
	(430 772)	(421 968)	(178 433)	(247 836)	—	(1 279 049)
% of poll	25.7 (33.7)	40.7 (33.0)	15.6 (14.0)	17.8 (19.4)	0.2 (—)	—
Number of MEPs	2 (5)	5 (2)	—	1 (1)	—	8
WALES	214 086	375 982	146 947	103 031	4 266	844 312
	(259 729)	(294 978)	(67 962)	(83 399)	(4 008)	(710 076)
% of poll	25.4 (36.6)	44.5 (41.5)	17.4 (9.6)	12.2 (11.7)	0.5 (0.6)	—
Number of MEPs	1 (1)	3 (3)	—	—	—	4
Totals	5 426 866	4 865 224	2 591 659	333 625	95 524	13 312 989
	(6 508 493)	(4 253 207)	(1 690 599)	(331 235)	(90 318)	(12 873 852)
% of poll	40.8 (50.6)	36.5 (33.0)	19.5 (13.1)	2.5 (2.6)	0.7 (0.7)	—
Number of MEPs	45 (60)	32 (17)	— (—)	1 (1)	—	78

1979 figures given in parentheses. *In 1979 only Liberals stood.   In 1984 31.8% of electorate of 41 917 313 voted.

NORTHERN IRELAND

Electorate: 1 064 035   (1979 electorate: 1 029 490)

Total poll: 696 971   (1979 total poll: 586 060 turnout: 56.9%)

Spoiled votes: 11 654   (1979 spoiled votes: 13 821 turnout: 2.4% of poll)

Valid poll: 685 317   (1979 valid poll: 572 239 turnout: 55.6%)

Quota: 171 330   (1979 quota: 143 060)   Seats: 3

Name and party	1984 1st pref	% of poll	Seats	1979 1st pref	% of poll	Seats
*Paisley, Rev I. (Dem U)	230 251	33.6	1	170 688	29.8	1
*Hume, J. (SDLP)	151 399	22.1	1	140 622	24.6	1
*Taylor, J. D. (OUP)	147 169	21.5	1	125 169	21.9	1
Morrison, D. (PSF)	91 476	13.3	—	—	—	—
Cook, D. (All)	34 046	5.0	—	39 026	6.8	—
Kilfedder, J. (UDUP)	20 092	3.0	—	—	—	—
Lynch, S. (WP)	8 712	1.3	—	—	—	—
McGuigan, C. (Ecol)	2 172	0.3	—	—	—	—

Voting system: PR. All 17 Ulster parliamentary constituencies make up the single multi-member European constituency with single transferable voting system.

The quota is calculated by dividing the total number of valid votes by the number of seats plus one (4) and then adding one to the result.

The following were elected:

The Rev Ian Paisley (Dem U)
John Hume, SDLP
John Taylor, OUP

Vote analysis (elected members):

	Votes	Multiples of quota
Paisley	230 251	1.34
Hume	151 399	0.88
Taylor	147 169	0.85

1983 Total vote: 764 928 (72.8%). OUP 259 952 (34.0%); DUP 152 749 (20.0%); SDLP 137 012 (17.9%); PSF 102 701 (13.4%); Alliance NI 61 275 (8.0%); Other 51 236 (6.7%). First-past-the-post voting system.

Details of four counts in Northern Ireland

Name/party	1st count Votes	2nd count Transfer of Paisley's Surplus	Result	3rd count Transfer of Lynch and McGuigan's Votes	Result	4th count Transfer of Kilfedder and Cook's Votes	Result
Paisley, Ian (DUP)	230 251	−58 921	171 330	—	171 330	—	171 330
Hume, John (SDLP)	151 399	+265	151 664	+4646	156 310	+26 946	183 256
Taylor, John (OUP)	147 169	+38 545	185 714	—	185 714	—	185 714
Morrison, Danny (PSF)	91 476	+49	91 525	+1119	92 644	+435	93 079
Cook, D. (All)	34 046	+846	34 892	+2509	37 401	−37 401	—
Kilfedder, James (UDUP)	20 092	+18 201	38 293	+560	38 854	−38 854	—
Lynch, Seamus (WP)	8712	+101	8813	−8813	—	—	—
McGuigan, Colin (Ecol)	2172	+64	2236	−2236	—	—	—
Non-transferable:		847	847	+2215	3062	+48 874	51 936

THE FIRST SESSION IN STRASBOURG
Rebates and the budget again dominate events

By Alan Wood,
Head of Parliamentary Staff, *The Times*

M. Pierre Pflimlin, in acknowledging his election as President on the first day of the first session of the newly elected European Parliament, felt that the people of Europe knew too little about its activities. By the end of the week, the Parliament's decision to block the United Kingdom's rebate of £457m on its 1983 contributions to the Community budget, plus some rebate for Germany, certainly put it in the headlines, particularly in Britain. The move provoked criticism from Mrs Thatcher, the British Prime Minister, and President Mitterand of France, who had striven so hard to get the rebate issue settled.

There was an immediate strong reaction from the British contingent in Strasbourg – with Tory and Labour voting en bloc against further withholding of the rebate – along with some invective from the Foreign Office and from the House of Commons a few days later. While the Parliament's decision, even when considered calmly, which far too many people seemed unprepared to do, was undoubtedly viewed then as mistaken, the MEPs were serving notice in a resolution carried by 214 votes to 70 with three abstentions, that they would not allow any decision to be taken regarding the Community's budget without their consent.

The resolution blocking the refund and that for Germany as well set out the Parliament's reservations about the methods agreed by the EEC Heads of Government at the Fontainebleau summit very shortly after the Euro elections, for injecting permanency into the system of refunds to the UK in such a way that the Parliament would not be able to set them aside as it had done before and was now doing again.

The devising of this mechanism was hailed as an important achievement by both Mrs Thatcher, the Prime Minister, and Mr Malcolm Rifkind, Minister of State for Foreign Affairs, when they were tackled in the Commons about the European Parliament's action. Mr Rifkind thought the Parliament had been inept while the Opposition considered the decision should be matched by one from Britain to withhold contributions of a like sum. However, the Government frowned on such a course of action.

Immediate reaction at Strasbourg from the European Democratic (Conservative) Group led by Sir Henry Plumb was particularly hostile. In wheeling and dealing earlier in the week over the election of the new President, the Conservatives agreed to back M. Pflimlin, after Lady Elles had stood down following the first ballot, if the Christian Democrats of the EPP group promised to back a Tory candidate for the next presidency. This was duly honoured but the centre right concord seemed somewhat tattered after the EPP votes that came to be cast in favour of withholding the UK rebate until there had been a satisfactory agreement on the supplementary budget for 1984 which the British Government had been opposing.

Parliament was only able to take the decision it did, because after the Budget Committee of the previous Parliament had, on July 12, approved the release of the United Kingdom's rebate, the outgoing Socialist President, Mr Pieter Dankert, had not officially signed it away. There was much conjecture as to why he had not signed – it probably cost him the chairmanship of the Budgets Committee which he had sought after relinquishing the Presidency. But he had, within the Socialist Group, an enlarged British Labour group to contend with, and they certainly caused a stir. The reactions of some of them, particularly the ex-MPs, was revealing, ranging from looking upon the EP as a kindergarten to the other end of the lifespan – a graveyard! One said it reminded him of his days on a local council – everything fixed before entering the chamber.

The ill-feeling created by the Parliament's decision both in the United Kingdom itself and among its MEPs is unfortunate. The Government's insistence on stricter budgetary and financial control and a reshaping of the Community budget so that the common agricultural policy swallows a lower proportion of the funds reflects in objective, if not in actual method, the expressed wish of the first directly elected Parliament. By its votes it had sought to demonstrate that it wanted less spent on agriculture and more on the regional and social funds and on overseas aid, to which the European Parliament consistently attaches considerable importance.

The Marquess of Douro, Conservative spokesman on the budget, pointed out that the United Kingdom's action so far in blocking a supplementary budget for 1984 had reduced the EEC Commission's demands from £2600m to about £1300m. That, he maintained, showed the United Kingdom was right to apply pressure on the Commission. Mr John Marshall, another Conservative, described the Parliament's action as manna to the anti-Marketeers of the United Kingdom.

Mrs Barbara Castle, leader of the British group of Labour MPs and senior vice-chairman of the Socialist Group, revealed the lack of solidarity in the group's proceedings by voicing British disagreement with a paragraph in a Socialist motion welcoming the general results of Fontainebleau. It was an opportunity tragically missed, declared Mrs Castle. Mrs Thatcher had meekly accepted an increase in the Community's own resources for a few weak words about the need for controlling expenditure. 'Oh, what a fall there was, my countrymen!' exclaimed Mrs Castle.

The UK contingent did not have its feelings assuaged by contentions from the leaders of other political groups that repayment was only put off until the supplementary budget for 1984 had been agreed – until the gap had been filled. This important vote and the Fontainebleau decisions undoubtedly ensure that the EEC budget restructuring certainly dominates the first half of the new Parliament. And it is not only the English, the Scots and the Welsh who have noted that besides a new French President of the Parliament, there is a new French President of the Commission, M. Jacques Delors, the former French Finance Minister. At least the election of the former ensures one thing – the continuance of plenary sessions at Strasbourg.

Much other important business was accomplished. Besides the Presidency, other votes determined the choice of vice-presidents and quaestors, who look after the interests of MEPs in the running of the Parliament. Important committee chairmanships had to be settled along with vice-chairmanships and composition of committees. Unlike five years ago, this operation was carried out more swiftly and at the end of the week practically everything had been determined. In the constitution of the committees it was noticeable that Sir Henry Plumb, ex-President of the National Farmers Union, joined Mrs Castle among the membership of the all-important Agriculture Committee.

Group meetings, mostly prior to the session, had put in place the leaders of the main political groups. The election of the Greens in some member states, particularly Germany, and the National Front and other right-wingers in France, Italy and Greece, led to the formation of two new groups – the Arc-en-Ciel (Rainbow) Group, and the Droites Européennes. The former, to demonstrate the broad sweep of its multi-party consensus, chose to have a syndicate of four co-chairpersons; the latter with 16 members from three countries preferred to be led by M. Jean-Marie Le Pen, ex-member of the French National Assembly and one-time presidential candidate. The formation of the groups means each enjoys the benefit of full secretariat facilities and representation on the Parliament's committees.

The title of 'Arc-en-Ciel' (Rainbow) was taken to reflect the fact that the 20 MEPs in it represent a federation of four distinct political groups comprising members from five states and ten political parties or movements. They are committed, they say, to finding alternatives to the existing European Community, whether by changing it or leaving it. Their aim in working together is to secure equal rights and privileges for MEPs from democratic parties and movements who opt not to join one of the established political groups.

The Droites Européennes faced demonstrations and protests and M. Le Pen was subjected to interruptions when he pressed the need for an overall Community emigration policy. But the fact remains that, thanks to the list system, these groups are there for at least five years at the strength they enjoyed in July, provided of course they do not fall apart either through dissension or by over-using the list system to bring in new members to give a changing outlook.

The European Progressive Democrats (DEP) of the last Parliament also decided upon a change of name, to European Democratic Alliance. This immediately brought protests from the European Democratic (Conservative) Group over possible unhelpful confusion between the two, especially in label initials. This reference book sticks to ED for the Conservatives as used over the last five years following their decision that 'Conservative' was a trifle non-U for Europe, and employs RDE for the new alliance.

In proceedings gracefully presided over by 78 year-old Mme Jacqueline Thome-Patenôtre of France, in place of the oldest member, Mr Nikolaos Gazis of Greece who was ill, two ballots were required before M. Pflimlin emerged as the new President. Mme Thome-Patenôtre is International Vice-President of the European Movement and in her speech opening the session, she considered the turnout at the June elections was rather poor reflecting a certain disappointment among the general public of Europe.

'We have five years before us in which to restore its faith,' she said. The Parliament, with its draft treaty for European Union, had given Europe new hope. The more international tensions deteriorated, the more important it was for Europeans to unite.

There were seven candidates in the first ballot for the Presidency in which 207 votes were needed for an absolute majority of the 413 valid votes cast. The outcome was: M. Pflimlin (France, EPP) 165; Mr Pieter Dankert (Netherlands, Soc) 123; Lady Elles (United Kingdom, ED) 44; Signor Giancarlo Pajetta (Italy, Comm) 37; Frau Undine-Uta Bloch von Blottnitz (Germany, ARC) 17; M. Le Pen (France, DR) 16, and Signor Altiero Spinelli (Italy, Comm) 11.

In the second ballot, in which four of the above-named candidates stood down, an absolute majority of 202 was needed. Of the 403 valid votes cast, M. Pflimlin obtained 221, Mr Dankert 133 and Signor Spinelli, 49. The victor was warmly welcomed by all the political groups and in accepting office, M. Pflimlin believed that Europe, despite severe problems, still had a good chance. 'First there is our economic potential' he said. 'We are the greatest commercial power in the world. Then there are Europe's resources in intelligence and imaginative and innovative capacity. These are our trump cards.'

He declared: 'If we are not a dynamic Assembly, if through our Assembly there does not blow strongly the wind which arises from the depth of our people who want the Community to get out of a rut and prepare for our youth a future of prosperity, peace and security, we will not be worthy of the mandate with which we have been entrusted. It is inevitable, and often very necessary, that we should argue, but at least let us unite at critical moments so that there emerges from this Assembly the new impetus that Europe needs.'

The two ballots for the 12 vice-presidencies proved eventful because after the first, Herr Rudi Arndt, the new German chairman of the Socialist Group, protested that his group, although the largest and entitled to five of the vice-presidencies, had obtained none. Adjournments of the session and consultations produced the required Socialist quota in the second ballot.

In the first ballot there were 413 valid votes with Signora Maria Cassanmagnago Cerretti (Italy, EPP) obtaining 270 (making her the senior Vice-President), Herr Siegbert Alber (Germany, EPP) 251, Lady Elles (United Kingdom, ED) 246, Mr Hans Nord (Netherlands, LD) former Secretary-General of the EP, 234, and Mr Patrick Lalor (Ireland, F–Fáil) 212, over 10 other candidates. These stood again in the second ballot and out of 404 valid votes (thus requiring an absolute majority of 202) the following were elected: Herr Horst Seefeld (Germany, Soc) 295; Signor Mario Dido' (Italy, Soc) 282, Mr Winston Griffiths (United Kingdom, Soc), Signor Guido Fanti (Italy, Comm) 264, Mr Spyridon Plaskovitis (Greece, Soc) 255, Mme Nicole Pery (France, Soc) 250, and Mr Pøul Møller (Denmark, ED) 214.

The five quaestors elected were Mr Ernest Glinne (Belgium, Soc), Herr Kurt Wawrzik (Germany, EPP), Mr Thomas Maher (Ireland, LD), Mr Anthony Simpson (United Kingdom, ED) and Signor Angelo Carossino (Italy, Comm).

The composition of the groups was almost entirely settled, although by the end of the session the Socialists were still undetermined over a dispute about the membership of Mr José Happart of Belgium. Three of his colleagues, in view of the unresolved situation, indicated they would not be taking part formally in the activities of the group, but for the purposes of setting out the relative strengths of the political groups in the Parliament, the three have been included in the Socialist Group total, but not Mr Happart.

The rebate decision on the final day might hardly provide that impetus but it did at that time stimulate more interest in its proceedings. Somehow or other Europe's budgetary problems have to be solved and the sheer desperation was highlighted in speeches by Dr Garret Fitzgerald, the Irish Prime Minister and President of the European Council until the end of 1984, and by Mr Christopher Tugendhat, the EEC Commissioner for the budget and financial control. Five years ago at the first session of the first elected European Parliament, Mr Tugendhat, one of the UK's two Commissioners, was uttering warnings of the early exhaustion of the EEC's 'own resources' of customs duties, levies on trade in foodstuffs and up to 1 per cent on VAT. Here he was, in nearing the end of an eight-year stint on the Commission, pointing out that that exhaustion was upon them.

The Irish Prime Minister said the failure of the Budget Council to provide for the interim financial needs of the Community this year caused deep concern. The situation was grave. Nine member states had adopted a common position on the need for additional financing. Although he did not say so, everyone knew the odd one out was the United Kingdom.

Significantly, he declared: 'It is of course, right that the member states in the Budget Council should seek to satisfy themselves that all possible savings will be made in the Community budget on the basis of policies that have been laid down for 1984 by the Council, with the concurrence of Parliament. But this having been done, whatever remaining shortfall emerges must be provided for.'

During his speech, he conceded that the primary responsibility for most of the failures of the Community fell on member Governments in the manner in which they had conducted themselves in the Council of Ministers in its various forms. There was a certain injustice in the fact that as governments they had escaped some of their share of the blame for the deficiencies of the Community and that a disproportionate share of the blame had been visited by the people upon the European Parliament.

Some MEPs nodded their agreement with this comment. Important developments were lying ahead. Dr Fitzgerald mentioned some, like the functions of a new ad hoc committee on institutional affairs which the heads of government had decided to set up. Comprised of political figures from member states, that committee was being chaired by Senator Dooge, Leader of the Irish Senate and a former Foreign Minister. Part of its functions, according to Dr Fitzgerald, will be to make suggestions for the improvement of European cooperation and the decision-making arrangements of the Community's institutions and the inter-relationships between them. Another committee is to promote the identity of Europe and its image both for its citizens and for the rest of the world.

These are all grand things, but in the immediate future MEPs will have to contend with more practical day-to-day problems like easing border bureaucracy, cheaper air fares and various environmental issues. Negotiations for the accession of Spain and Portugal have to be completed and when that happens the European Parliament will be joined by MEPs from those two countries. Although added strain is bound to be imposed on the Parliament's effectiveness, the evidence of the first five years is just sufficient to impart a note of optimism. The next five years will tell.

Women in the European Parliament

The European Parliament has 18 committees and women are in the chairs of six of them. There are three women vice-presidents, and Mme Simone Veil, former President of the Parliament, is the new leader of the Liberal and Democratic Group.

There are 76 women MPs out of the 434, compared with 67 elected in 1979, plus two more who came after the Greek elections in 1981. The EP Committee on Women's Rights, chaired by Frau Marlene Lenze of Germany (EPP) has 25 members of whom 23 are women.

Member states send the following number of women members: Belgium 4, Denmark 6, France 17, Germany 16, Greece 2, Ireland 2, Italy 8, Luxembourg 2, the Netherlands 7 and the United Kingdom 12. The three women vice-presidents are Signora Cassanmagnago Cerretti (Italy, EPP), the senior vice-president, Lady Elles (United Kingdom, ED) and Mme Nicole Pery (France, Soc).

The other five committee chairmanships are: External Economic Relations – Dame Shelagh Roberts (United Kingdom, ED); Legal Affairs and Citizens Right – Mme Marie-Claude Vayssade (France, Soc); Environment, Public Health and Consumer Protection – Frau Beate Weber (Germany, Soc); Youth Affairs, Culture, Education, Information and Sport – Mrs Winifred Ewing (United Kingdom, RDE); Development and Cooperation – Frau Katharina Focke (Germany, Soc).

The leader of the British group of Labour MPs, Mrs Barbara Castle, has become the senior vice-chairman of the Socialist group.

The European Parliament

The biographical information on the members of the European Parliament has been compiled from information supplied to *The Times* by the Directorate-General of Information and Public Relations of the European Parliament and its offices in the EEC member states, the Secretariats and Press Officers of the Political Groups of the Parliament, and Conservative Central Office and Labour Party Headquarters in the United Kingdom. Occupations and political group membership are those at the time of election to the Parliament. Addresses and telephone numbers were those available for publication at the July 1984 plenary session at Strasbourg, and for some MEPs, especially among the new ones, are subject to change.

All MEPs can also be contacted at the EP political group offices in Brussels, at the Palais de l'Europe in Strasbourg during plenary sessions, the various offices of the European Parliament in the member states, and through their political party headquarters.

ABELIN, JEAN-PIERRE
France, EPP (UDF/RPR)

M. Jean-Pierre Abelin was elected to the EP in 1984. Employee of the Banque de France. Vice-chairman, Vienne County Council, Chatellerault county councillor since 1977, and town councillor since 1983. Vienne deputy (UDF), 1978–81. Born Sep 3 1950.

Address: La Chapelle d' Autoigué, 86100 Chatellerault.

ABENS, VICTOR
Luxembourg, Soc (POSL)

Mr Victor Abens was elected to the EP in 1979 and became a vice-chairman of the Socialist Group in 1984, having served on its bureau in the last Parliament. Member, Luxembourg Chamber of Deputies, 1946–81; Mayor of Vianden, 1946–81. Member, Parliamentary Assembly of Council of Europe. Born Oct 16 1912. Industrialist.

Address: 48, Grand-rue, Vianden. Tel: 84006.

ADAM, GORDON
UK, Northumbria, Soc (Lab)

Mr Gordon Adam, a mining engineer, elected to the EP in 1979, became a vice-chairman of the EP Energy, Research and Technology Committee in July 1984. Born Mar 28 1934; educated Leeds University. BSc, PhD, E Eng. Member, Whitley Bay Borough Council, 1971–74; former member North Tyneside Metropolitan District Council. In general elections fought Tynemouth, 1966, and Berwick-upon-Tweed, February 1974 and November 1973 by-election.

Addresses: 2 Queen's Road, Whitley Bay, Tyne and Wear, NE26 3BJ. Tel: (0632) 528616. Newgate Chambers, Newgate Street, Newcastle-upon-Tyne NE1 5RE. Tel: (0632) 329944

ADAMOU, DIMITRIOS
Greece, Comm (KKE)

Mr Dimitrios Adamou, a journalist, was elected to the EP in 1981, re-elected in 1984. Born Oct 20 1914. Editor of *Risospastis* since 1981.

Address: Samarinas 2, Sepolia, Athens. Tel: (1) 5143072.

AERSSEN, JOCHEN VAN
Germany, EPP (CDU)

Herr Jochen van Aerssen was a member of the Bundestag, 1976–81, and has been a member of the EP since 1977; elected to it in 1979. A vice-chairman of the EP Committee on External Economic Relations in the last Parliament and reappointed in July, 1984. Born Apr 15 1941; studied at universities of Bonn, Cologne and Freiburg. Appointed Doctor of Law, 1970. Member of CDU since 1964; member, Rhineland CDU 'Land' executive, Kleve CDU district executive and North Rhine-Westphalia 'Land' Assembly, 1970–76. President, North Rhine-Westphalia 'Europa Union' from 1978.

Address: Elfgenweg 33, 4000 Düsseldorf 11. Tel: (0211) 594188.

AIGNER, HEINRICH
Germany, EPP (CSU)

Herr Heinrich Aigner has been a member of the EP since 1961; elected in 1979. Chairman of EP Committee on Budgetary Control since 1979, reappointed 1984. Member of the Bundestag 1957–80. Former senior executive officer, Bavarian Ministry of Agriculture; vice-chairman, Deutsche Stiftung in Berlin. Born May 25 1924.

Address: Erzherzog-Karl-Strasse 6, 8450 Amberg (Oberptfalz). Tel: (09621) 25575.

ALAVANOS, ALEXANDROS
Greece, Comm (KKE)

Mr Alexandros Alavanos was elected to the EP in 1984 and became a vice-chairman of the EP Committee on Social Affairs and Employment in July 1984. Born May 22 1950.

Address: Eleftheriou Venizelou 49a, 15236 Palaia Pendeli.

ALBER, SIEGBERT
Germany, EPP (CDU)

Herr Siegbert Alber was elected a Vice-President of the EP in July 1984. MEP since 1977; elected in 1979 becoming a vice-chairman of EPP group and leader of the German Christian Democrats. Chaired EP committee of inquiry into treatment of toxic and dangerous substances by EEC and its member states. Member, Bundestag, 1969–80; assemblies of Council of Europe and WEU, 1970–77. Chairman, Stuttgart CDU, 1971–79. Born Jul 27 1936. Read law and became junior legal official and public prosecutor.

Address: Gammertinger Strasse 35, 7000 Stuttgart 80. Tel: (0711) 725445.

ALMIRANTE, GIORGIO
Italy, DR (MSI-DN)

Sgr Giorgio Almirante was elected to the EP in 1979. Italian MP since 1948. Journalist. One of the founders of the Italian Social Movement and is its National Secretary. Has been member of several parliamentary committees including the Committees on Home Affairs, Constitutional Affairs (four times) and Education. During the fourth legislature, he was the most fervent opposer to the regional electoral Bill. Chairman of the party's parliamentary group. Born Jun 27 1914; arts degree.

Addresses: Camera dei Deputati, 00100 Roma. Via Quattro Fontane 109, 00100 Roma. Tel: 4740382.

AMADEI, GIUSEPPE
Italy, Soc (PSDI)

Sgr Giuseppe Amadei, member of the Italian Chamber of Deputies from 1960, holding office as State Under Secretary for Industry, Commerce and Craft, and also for Finance, joined the nominated EP in 1976; elected in 1979, left in 1980 being re-elected in 1984. Has chaired Chamber of Deputies commission on education and the arts; at present Presidential Secretary, Chamber of Deputies, and member of the finance and treasury commission. Vice-President, Interparliamentary Group for Italy. Member, national executive, PSDI. Since 1980 in assemblies of WEU and Council of Europe.

Address: Direzione PSDI, Via Santa Maria in Via 12, 00187 Roma.

ANASTASSOPOULOS, GEORGIOS
Greece, EPP (ND)

Mr Georgios Anastassopoulos was elected to the EP in 1984 and became chairman, EP Transport Committee, in July 1984. Journalist. In 1978, he was first Greek appointed to Council of International Federation of Journalists, to which he was re-elected in 1980 and 1982. Born 1935; educated Athens College and Faculty of Law, Athens University. Worked for many newspapers and following the dictatorship became General Manager of the Athens News Agency. Acting Secretary of State attached to President's Office in the 1977 and 1981 caretaker governments. President, Association of Editors of Athens Daily Newspapers.

Address: Pindou 27, 15451 N. Psychiko.

89

ANCONA, MEVR HEDY d'
Netherlands, Soc (PvdA)

Mevr Hedy d'Ancona was elected to the EP in 1984. Former Secretary of State for emancipation measures; member of the First Chamber for seven years. Born Mar 1 1937.

Address: Amstel 274, 1017 AM Amsterdam.

ANDREWS, NIALL
Ireland, RDE (F-Fáil)

Mr Niall Andrews, elected to the EP in 1984, has been a member of the Dail since 1977. Former television programmes officer with RTE. Minister of State, Department of the Environment, Oct to Dec 1982. Member, Parliamentary assembly of Council of Europe since 1981. Married. Born Aug 1938.

Address: 48 Westbrook Road, Dublin 14.

ANGLADE, MME MARIE-MADELEINE
France RDE (UDF/RPR)

Mme Marie-Madeleine Anglade, who became an MEP in 1984, is Deputy Mayor of Paris with responsibility for employment; Regional councillor of Paris. General secretary, Compagnie Française de Journaux, since 1972; vice-chairman, National Committee of French Muslims, 1965–75. Born Jul 5 1921. Secretary General of Republican Unity Group in National Assembly; Member, National Committee of CNIP political party in France. Lawyer.

Address: 12, rue d'Uzès, 75002 Paris.

ANTONIOZZI, DARIO
Italy, EPP (DC)

Sgr Dario Antoniozzi, a lawyer, was elected to the EP in 1979, being a member of the nominated Parliament from 1972 and a vice-chairman, EPP Group, 1976–79. Member of Italian Parliament, 1953–79. Many times Under-Secretary of State for Transport, for Posts and Telecommunications, for Tourism and Entertainment, for the Merchant Marine and for Agriculture and Forestry. Minister for Tourism and Entertainment, then Minister for Cultural Assets and the Environment. Former National Councillor for the DC; assistant political secretary in 1976, and director of the Office for International Relations. Born Dec 11 1923.
Addresses: Via Nomentana 373, 00162 Roma. Tel: (06) 837078-8393661. Via Caroprese 33, 87100 Cosenza. Tel: (0984) 36196.

ANTONY, BERNARD
France, DR (FN)

M. Bernard Antony, known as Romain Marie, was elected to the EP in 1984. Professor of literature. Born Nov 28 1944. Chairman, Christianity-Solidarity committees.

Address: 61, avenue Lucien Coudert, 81100, Castres.

ARNDT, RUDI
Germany, Soc (SPD)

Herr Rudi Arndt, elected to the EP in 1979, was elected leader of the Socialist Group in July 1984, having previously been its senior vice-chairman. Mayor of Frankfurt, 1972–77. Lawyer. Member of Frankfurt municipal council for six years; in Landtag of Hesse for 16 years, and for eight years represented Hesse in the Bundesrat. Between 1964 and 1972 he was Minister of State for the economy and Minister of State for finance in Hesse. Member, Hesse SPD executive. Born Mar 1 1927.

Addresses: Europe-Buro, Fischerfeldstrasse 7-11, 6000 Frankfurt/Main. Tel: (0611) 291096. Mörfelder Landstrasse 278, 6000 Frankfurt/Main 70. Tel: (0611) 6311473.

91

AVEROF-TOSITSAS, EVANGELOS
Greece, EPP (ND)

Mr Evangelos Averof-Tositsas, who became an MEP in 1984, has been chairman of the New Democracy Party since 1981. Liberal MP for Ioannina, 1946–60, National Radical Union (ERE) MP, 1956–64, and New Democracy MP, 1974–77. Minister for Supplies, 1949–50; Minister for Economic Affairs, 1950–51; Secretary of State for Finance, 1951–52; Minister of Agriculture, 1956 and 1967; Foreign Affairs, 1956–63; Defence, 1974. Deputy Leader of Government, Jun to Oct 1981. Born 1910; educated Lausanne University. Doctor of law and political and economic science. Resigned in July 1984 and succeeded by **Mr Konstantinos Stavrou**.

Address: Dimokritou 10, 10673 Athens.

AVGERINOS, PARASKEVAS
Greece, Soc (PASOK)

Mr Paraskevas Avgerinos was elected to the EP in 1984. Founder member of PASOK (Pan-Hellenic Socialist Movement) and a minister since 1981. A doctor. Born 1927.

Address: Knossou 10, 17564 P. Faliro.

BACHY, JEAN-PAUL
France, Soc (PS)

M. Jean-Paul Bachy, teacher, elected to the EP in 1984. Born Mar 30 1947. Member, PS national secretariat for businesses. Maître Assistant, National Conservatoire of Arts and Crafts.

Address: 10, avenue Pierre Brossolette, 94300 Vincennes.

BACKER, MEVR RIKA DE
Belgium, EPP (CVP-EVP)

Mevr Rika de Backer was elected to the EP in 1984. Lawyer. Member of the Belgian Senate 1974–81. Born Feb 1 1923.

Address: Amerikalei 110, 2000 Antwerpen. Tel: (03) 238 32 20 and (03) 889 14 08.

BAGET BOZZO, GIANNI
Italy, Soc (PSI)

Sgr Gianni Baget Bozzo, a priest and theologian, was elected to the EP in 1984. Born Mar 8 1925 in Savona. Founder and director of the theological magazine *Renovatio*.

Address: Via Corsica 9, 16100 Genova. Tel: (010) 56 44 83.

BALFE, RICHARD
UK, London South Inner, Soc (Lab)

Mr Richard Balfe, elected to the EP in 1979, became deputy leader of group of Labour MPs in 1984. Born May 14 1944; educated Brook Secondary Modern, Sheffield, and London School of Economics. BSc Hons, Fellow of the Royal Statistical Society and of the Royal Institute of Public Administration. Member, Greater London Council, 1973–77. Parliamentary candidate, Paddington South, 1970. Member, London Regional Executive of Labour Party. Member, EP Committee on Development and Cooperation, from July 1984; former member, Political Affairs Committee.

Address: 259 Barry Road, Dulwich, London SE22 0JT. Tel: (01) 299-0868. c.o. RACS Ltd, 147 Powis Street, London SE18 6JN. Tel: (01) 855-2128.

93

BANOTTI, MS MARY
Ireland, EPP (F-Gael)

Ms Mary Banotti, a nurse, was elected to the EP in 1984. Has worked in Europe and Africa. Presenter of television programme on social welfare and writer on social policy matters. Active campaigner for family law reform. Chairs a treatment centre for alcoholism and founder member of hostel for battered wives.

Address: 8 Cambridge Avenue, Ringsend, Dublin 4.

BARBARELLA, SIGNORA CARLA
Italy, Comm (PCI)

Signora Carla Barbarella was elected to the EP in 1981 and became a vice-chairman of its Budgets Committee, being reappointed in July 1984. Worked from 1965–72 at Euratom and then at the Council of Ministers of the EEC, as principal administrator; official of the National Alliance of Smallholders; member of the staff of the Emilia-Romagna Regional Administration. Born Feb 4 1940; degree in political science.

Addresses: Via dei Giubbonari 74, 00188 Roma. Tel: 6567101. Via delle Botteghe Oscure 4, 00186 Roma. Tel: (06) 6711.

BARDONG, OTTO
Germany, EPP (CDU)

Herr Otto Bardong, a professor, was elected to the EP in 1984. Member of Rheinland-Pfalz legislative assembly since 1975 where he has been acting chairman of the political-cultural committee and a member of the budget and finance committees. Born Oct 2 1935.

Address: Höhenstrasse 9, 6520 Worms.

BARINGDORF, FRIEDRICH-WILHELM GRAEFE ZU
Germany, ARC (Grüne)

Herr Friedrich-Wilhelm Graefe zu Baringdorf was elected to the EP in 1984 and became a vice-chairman of its Agriculture Committee. Teacher and farmer. Was member of Evangelical Young Farmers of the Westphalian/Lippisch Young Farmers. Took leading role in formulating 'alternative' agricultural policy. In recent years, concentrated activities on workers' cooperative, Bauernblatt. A fifth of his farm at Ravensberger Huegelland, in the Herford district, has been turned over to organic farming, producing vegetables, grain and potatoes. Born Nov 29 1942.

Address: Am Berninghoff 2, 4905 Spenge.

BARRETT, SYLVESTER
Ireland, RDE (F-Fáil)

Mr Sylvester Barrett, elected to the EP in 1984, has been a member of the Dail since 1968. Minister for the Environment 1977–79; Minister for Defence 1980–81; Minister of State, Department of Finance, 1982. Born May 1926. Married.

Address: Kilmorane, Ennis, Co. Clare.

BARTOLOMEI, MARIO DI
Italy, LD (PLI/PRI)

Sgr Mario di Bartolomei, a journalist, was a member of the last Parliament and was re-elected in 1984. Member, Chamber of Deputies and of national executive of PRI. Born May 17 1931.

Addresses: Camera dei Deputati, 00100 Roma. Tel: (06) 67179705. Via Cassia 1041, 00189 Roma. Tel: (06) 3667458.

BARZANTI, ROBERTO
Italy, Comm (PCI)

Sgr Roberto Barzanti, elected to the EP in 1984, was mayor of Siena (1969–74) and is now deputy mayor. From 1974 to 1979 he was regional assessor for Tuscany. Student of literature and history. Born Jan 24 1939.

Address: c/o Commune di Siena, 53100 Siena.

BATTERSBY, ROBERT
UK, Humberside, ED (C)

Mr Robert Battersby became a vice-chairman of the EP Committee on Budgetary Control in July 1984, and a member of the EP Agriculture Committee. Elected to the EP in 1979. A principal administrator with the European Commission 1973–79, working on EEC fisheries policy and before that on European Coal and Steel Community loans. Previously sales director, GKN Contractors Ltd. Born Dec 14 1924; educated First Park Grammar School, Sheffield; Edinburgh University and Cambridge University; also studied at Sorbonne and Toulouse University. Fellow of Institute of Linguists.

Addresses: West Cross, Rockshaw Road, Merstham, Surrey RH1 3BZ. Tel: (07374) 3783. 28 First Avenue, Bridlington, N Humberside. Tel: 72489.

BAUDIS, DOMINIQUE
France, EPP (UDF/RPR)

M. Dominique Baudis, television journalist, was elected in 1984. Presenter, Journal Télévisé Soir 3, 1981, and TF1's journal télévisé, 1978–80. Formerly French TV's Middle East correspondent, he covered the war in Lebanon and was wounded by a Palestinian patrol. Interviewed Anwar Sadat, Menachem Begin and Yasser Arafat. Born Apr 14 1947. Mayor of Toulouse; Midi-Pyrénées regional councillor.

Address: Maire de Toulouse, Hôtel de Ville, 31000 Toulouse.

BAUDOUIN, DENIS
France, RDE (UDF/RPR)

M. Denis Baudouin, a journalist, became an MEP in 1984. Director general of information at Paris City Hall since 1977. Born Feb 14 1923. President Pompidou's public relations consultant 1970–73. Managing director, SOFIRAD, 1973–77. Member, economic and social council, 1969–74.

Address: Hotel de Ville de Paris, 75004 Paris RP.

BEAZLEY, CHRISTOPHER
UK, Cornwall and Plymouth, ED (C)

Mr Christopher Beazley, elected to the EP in 1984, became a member of the Parliament's Regional Policy Committee in July 1984. Has been Nuffield Research Fellow at the School of European Studies, Sussex University. Born Sep 5 1952; educated Shrewsbury School and Bristol University. Working on comparative study of history throughout EEC to produce teaching materials on European history. Was research assistant to MEP. Vice-chairman, since 1980, Lewes and Eastbourne branch of European Movement. Wealden district councillor, 1979–83.

Address: Martletts, 8 South Lynn Drive, Eastbourne, Sussex BN21 2JF. Tel: 0323-639626.

BEAZLEY, PETER
UK, Bedfordshire South ED (C)

Mr Peter Beazley, MEP for Bedfordshire 1979–84, won this seat in 1984; became a vice-chairman, EP Economic and Monetary Affairs Committee in July 1984. Member, bureau, ED group, since 1982. Had 31 years' service with Imperial Chemical Industries, 17 of them spent abroad in Frankfurt, Brussels, Portugal, South America and South Africa. Research Fellow, Royal Institute of International Affairs. Born Jun 9 1922; educated Highgate School and St John's College, Oxford.

Address: 'Rest Harrow', 14 The Combe, Ratton, Eastbourne, Sussex BN20 9DB. Tel: (0323) 54460.

BERNARD-REYMOND, PIERRE
France, EPP (UDF/RPR)

M. Pierre Bernard-Reymond, elected to the EP in 1984, was Foreign Secretary with responsibility for European affairs, 1978–81. Hautes Alps deputy (UDF), 1971–81; county councillor, 1973–79. Born Jan 16 1944. Deputy Mayor of Gap (Hautes Alpes) from 1971.

Address: Mairie de Gap, 05000 Gap.

BERSANI, GIOVANNI
Italy, EPP (DC)

Sgr Giovanni Bersani, a lawyer, was reappointed a vice-chairman of the EP Committee on Development and Cooperation in July 1984, having held that position in the previous Parliament. Elected to the EP 1979; member since 1960, a former Vice-President. Member, DC national council, since 1947. Born Jul 22 1914. Member, Chamber of Deputies, 1948–76; of Senate, since 1976. Under Secretary of State for Labour and Social Security, 1952–53. National leader of Christian Workers' Association since 1947; member, Bologna municipal council.

Addresses: Via delle Lame 118, 40122 Bologna. Tel: 266963/237419. Via di Frino 4, 40136 Bologna. Tel: 344484.

BESSE, JEAN
France, Soc (PS)

M. Jean Besse was elected to the EP in 1984. Member, PS steering committee. Born Oct 23 1943. Deputy regional director of youth and sports of Lower Normandy. Troarn (Calvados) county councillor.

Address: 19, rue Ecuyère, 14000 Caen.

BETHELL, LORD
UK, London North-West, ED (C)

Lord Bethell is a prominent campaigner for lower air fares in Europe, being chairman of 'Freedom of the Skies'. Elected to the EP in 1979; in nominated Parliament, 1975–79. Member, EP Political Affairs Committee; chairman, EP human rights working group. Co-author of booklet 'Consumers in Europe – a Conservative view'. Born Jul 19 1938; educated Harrow and Pembroke College, Cambridge. On editorial staff of *The Times Literary Supplement*, 1962–64; a script editor in BBC Drama Department, 1964–67. A Lord-in-Waiting (Government whip and a junior Government spokesman), House of Lords, 1970–71. Freelance writer and a translator from Russian and Polish.

Address: 73 Sussex Square, London W2 2SS

BETTIZA, VINCENZO
Italy, LD (PLI)

Sgr Vincenzo Bettiza was elected to the EP in 1979 and was a vice-chairman of the Liberal and Democratic Group until 1984. Member of the nominated Parliament. Journalist; on editorial board of *Il Nuovo Giornale*. Senator, 1976–79. Was correspondent of *La Stampa* and *Corriere della Sera* in various capitals of the World, including Moscow. Born Jun 7 1927.

Addresses: Via Anelli 5, 20122 Milano. Tel: (2) 54 53 33 22. Via Moscova 40/1, 20121 Milano.

BEUMER, BOUKE
Netherlands, EPP (CDA)

Mr Bouke Beumer was elected to the EP in 1979. Member of the Dutch Second Chamber 1975–79. Director of NW Overijssel Regional Council, 1962–66; Burgomaster of Midwolda, 1966–75. Born Nov 21 1934; studied economics at Rotterdam, 1952–58. Chairman, EP Committee on Youth Culture, Education, Information and Sport, 1982–84.

Addresses: Wilhelminastraat 24a, 8019 An Zwolle. Tel: (038) 21 31 71. Oude Middelhorst 9, 9751 Tk Hareen (Gr). Tel: (050) 343181.

BEYER DE RYKE, LUC
Belgium, LD (PRL)

Mr Luc Beyer de Ryke became an MEP in July 1980; re-elected 1984. Member, political bureau, PRL; East Flanders Provincial Council, 1961–65; Ghent Municipal Council, 1965–79. Journalist. Born Sep 9 1933.

Address: 19A, avenue de Gui, 1180 Bruxelles. Tel: (02) 374 30 70.

BISMARCK, PHILIPP VON
Germany, EPP (CDU)

Herr Philipp von Bismarck, an industrialist, was elected to the EP in 1979, joined the nominated EP in 1978. A vice-chairman, EP Committee on Economic and Monetary Affairs and Industrial Policy from July 1984; served on committee in previous Parliament. Member of Bundestag, 1969–79. Member, CDU national executive. Held office in Lower Saxony CDU and chaired CDU Economic Council. President of Hanover Chamber of Industry and Commerce 1967–71. Born Aug 19 1913.

Address: Bundeshaus, Zimmer 912 NH, 5300 Bonn 1. Tel: (0228) 163352–163378.

BLOTTNITZ, FRAU UNDINE-UTA BLOCH VON
Germany, ARC (Grüne)

Frau Undine-Uta Bloch von Blottnitz, elected to the EP in 1984, became a vice-chairman of the EP Committee on the Environment, Public Health and Consumer Protection. Housewife. Has campaigned against the building of atomic energy establishments at Dragahn and Gorleben. Born Aug 20 1936.

Address: 3131 Untergut Lüchow-Grabow. Tel: (05864) 349 and (05864) 303.

BLUMENFELD, ERIK
Germany, EPP (CDU)

Herr Erik Blumenfeld was a member of the Bundestag 1961–80, and of the EP since 1973 (elected in 1979), and the North Atlantic Assembly, since 1971. Deputy chairman, Hamburg 'Land' CDU (chairman 1958–68). Born Mar 27 1915. Owner of Messrs Blumenfeld and Co. Member, supervisory board of Albingia Rechtsschutz-Versicherungs AG, Hamburg; vice-president, Hamburg Chamber of Commerce, 1946–54. Member, Hamburg city Parliament, 1946–55 and 1966–70.

Addresses: Bundeshaus 5300 Bonn 1. Tel: (0228) 163860. Blumenstrasse 5, 2000 Hamburg 60.

BOCKLET, REINHOLD
Germany, EPP (CSU)

Herr Reinhold Bocklet was elected to the EP in 1979. Lectured in political science at the Geschwister-Scholl Institute (Munich University). Committee member, CDU-CSU Youth Organization (JU) for Bavaria 1969–79 and of same organization at Federal Republic level from 1973; deputy Federal chairman of this organization and JU representative in the EC working-party of the European Young Christian-Democrats from 1977. Member, CSU Regional Association for Upper Bavaria, since 1975. Born Apr 5 1943. Married.

Address: Grasslfingerstrasse 22a, 8038 Gröbenzell. Tel: (08142) 5523.

BØGH, THE REV JØRGEN
Denmark, ARC (Folkebevaegelsen)

The Rev Jørgen Bøgh, was elected to the EP in 1979 and held office as chairman of the Group for the Technical Coordination and Defence of Independent Groups and Members. In New Parliament joined ARC Group. Former dean of Aarhus. For many years, member of the SDP but disagreed with that party on Common Market issue. He has been a teacher at the Askov High School; headmaster of the 'free' teachers' training school at Ollerup; and leader of civil defence training, 1952–62. During the German Occupation, he was involved in the formation of the Danish Youth Council. Born Jun 6 1917.

Address: Langhaergårdsvej 52, 3460 Birkerød.

BOMBARD, ALAIN
France, Soc (PS)

M. Alain Bombard became an MEP in 1981.
Biologist. Director, laboratory ships 'Coryphène',
1958–60, and 'Captain Cap', 1960–62; chairman,
aquaculture committee, Provence-Alpes-Côte
d'Azur regional council. Author of works about the
sea. Born Oct 27 1924. Var county councillor since
1979.

Address: Le Mas, Ile des Embiez, 83140 Six Fours.

BONACCINI, ALDO
Italy, Comm (PCI)

Sgr Aldo Bonaccini was elected to the EP in 1979.
Served on Economic and Social Committee of
EEC; was secretary of Trade Union of
Metallurgical and Mechanical Workers and
thereafter of Trade Union of Chemical Workers
(Province of Milan). Secretary, Workers
Association of Milan and later of Lombardy.
Member, CGIL (Federation of Italian Trade
Unions) being in charge of economics (1969–73)
and international policy (1973–79). On executive of
European Confederation of Trade Unions,
1974–79. Born Jun 27 1920.

Address: Via Raffaele Balestra 44, 00152 Roma.

BONDE, JENS-PETER
Denmark, ARC (Folkebevaegelsen)

Mr Jens-Peter Bonde was elected to the EP in 1979;
member of its Budgets Committee. Contested the
European elections on the list of the anti-EEC
popular movement in Denmark. He was largely
responsible for starting up the movement's journal,
Det ny Notat (The New Report) which he produced
with other enthusiasts in a disused hairdresser's
salon in Noerrebro, Copenhagen. Born Mar 27
1948.

*Address: Nørrebrogade 140 III, 2200 København
N. Tel: (01) 81 83 15.*

BONINO, SIGNORA EMMA
Italy, NI (PR)

Signora Emma Bonino elected to the EP in 1979 became an Italian MP in 1976. Member and coordinator of the Centre for Information on Sterilization and Abortion since 1975. Member of Committee on Labour–Social Security. Secretary, Parliamentary Group of Partito Radicale. Born Mar 9 1948. Member, secretariat, 'Friends of the Earth'.

Address: Camera dei Deputati, 00100 Roma. Tel: 6793286.

BOOT, MEVR ELISE
Netherlands, EPP (CDA)

Mevr Elise Boot, who became an MEP in 1979, was on the academic staff of the Europe Institute, University of Utrecht, 1967–79. Served on National Council and executive of European Movement in Netherlands and central executive of International European Movement. Former member, Utrecht Provincial States Assembly. Born Aug 2 1932.

Addresses: Parkstraat 29, 3581 PC Utrecht. Tel: (030) 32 23 76. Kerkdwarsstraat 5, 3581 RG Utrecht. Tel: (030) 31 77 80.

BORGO, FRANCO
Italy, EPP (DC)

Sgr Franco Borgo, elected to the EP in 1984, has been chairman of the Vicenza Farmers' Association; Chamber of Commerce assessor on agriculture, and a member of the party's regional committee in Veneto. Member, Veneto regional council, since 1970 and was chairman of its committee on culture and vocational training. At present he is provincial adviser of the Cooperative Union. Since 1981, chairman, Veneto Farmers' Regional Federation. Born Oct 10 1932.

Address: Via Campogallo 10, 36060 Schiavon (Vicenza).

BOSERUP, FRU BODIL
Denmark, Comm (SF)

Fru Bodil Boserup, elected to the EP in 1979, has been treasurer of the Communist and Allies Group since then; is also a vice-chairman of the EP Committee on Budgetary Control. Former member, Copenhagen City Council. First became prominent in the Socialist People's Party in 1972 in debates on the EEC. Strongly against the Common Market, she is pressing for greater attention to be given to women's causes. Born Jun 24 1921.

Address: Damstien 32, 2720 Vanløse. Tel: (01) 740402.

BOUTOS, IOANNIS
Greece, EPP (ND)

Mr Ioannis Boutos, a lawyer, was elected to the EP in 1984. Liberal MP for Messinia, 1950–56; National Radical Union MP, 1961–64; New Democracy MP, 1974–77. Secretary of State for Coordination, 1961–68; Secretary of State attached to the Prime Minister's Office in the Government of National Unity, 1974; Minister of Commerce, 1974; acting Minister for Coordination, 1975; Minister of Agriculture, 1976–77; Finance, 1977–78; Agriculture, 1978–80; and Coordination, May–Oct, 1980, when he retired on health grounds. Born 1925; educated Athens University and London School of Economics.

Address: Santaroza 1, 10564 Athens.

BRAUN-MOSER, FRAU URSULA
Germany, EPP (CDU)

Frau Ursula Braun-Moser was elected to the EP in 1984. Wetterau district councillor and former Bad Vilbel town councillor. Born May 25 1937. Economist.

Address: Erzweg 55, 6368 Bad Vilbel.

BRINKMEIER, JÜRGEN
Germany, Soc (SPD)

Herr Jürgen Brinkmeier, a retired senate official, was elected to the EP in 1984. Until 1981 state director (state secretary) in Berlin. SPD chairman, Newkölln district; state treasurer of Berlin SPD. Born Apr 16 1935.

Address: Hannemanstrasse 34, 1000 Berlin 47.

BROK, ELMAR
Germany, EPP (CDU)

Herr Elmar Brok became an MEP in June 1980; re-elected 1984. Journalist. Deputy Federal chairman of the Junge Union; member of the federal committee for foreign policy and of the management committee of East Westphalia-Lippe CDU. Born May 14 1946.

Address: Thomas-Mann-Strasse 15, 4800 Bielefeld 17. Tel: (0521) 33 14 56.

BROOKES, MISS BETA
UK, North Wales, ED (C)

Miss Beta Brookes was elected an MEP in 1979; became a member, EP Committee on Youth, Culture, Education, Information and Sport in July, 1984. Secretary to a tourism company; formerly social worker with Denbighshire County Council. Born Jan 21 1932; educated Lowther College, Abergele, University of Wales and Alliance Française, Paris. Awarded American State Department Scholarship to study politics in United States. Parliamentary candidate for Widnes, 1955; Warrington, 1963 by-election; and Manchester Exchange 1964.

Addresses: The Cottage, Wayside Acres, Bodelwyd-dan, nr Rhyl, Clwyd, North Wales. Tel: St Asaph 583189. Conservative Office, 3 Llewelyn Road, Colwyn Bay, Clwyd LL29 7AP. Tel: (0492) 33878.

BUCHAN, MRS JANEY
UK, Glasgow, Soc (Lab)

Mrs Janey Buchan was elected to the EP in 1979; secretary, Labour group of MEPs, from 1984. Former chairman of Labour Party in Scotland and of the Scottish Gas Consumers' Council. For many years she was chairman of a local consumer group. Served on Strathclyde Regional Council, being former vice-chairman of its education committee. Married to Norman Buchan, Westminster Labour MP for Paisley South. Born Apr 30 1926.

Address: 72 Peel Street, Glasgow G11 5LR, Scotland. Tel: (041) 339 2583.

BUTTAFUOCO, ANTONIO
Italy, DR (MSI-DN)

Sgr Antonio Buttafuoco was elected to the EP in 1979; member of Italian Parliament 1972–76. Party member since its foundation; member of Central Committee. Member of the Sicilian Regional Assembly, 1951–71, being chairman of the parliamentary group, 1958–63. Deputy Secretary, Sicilian Regional Assembly, 1963–67. Town councillor for eight years. Mayor of Nissoria since 1968. Chairman, board of directors of Nissoria's bank Cassa Rurale ed Artigiana S. Giuseppe. Born Apr 20 1923; degree in political and social sciences.

Addresses: Via Zara 4, 94013 Leonforte (Enna). Tel: 0935/61737-61621. Via San Giorgio 3, 94010 Nissoria (Enna). Tel: 0935/69210-69203.

CAMARET, MICHEL DE
France, DR (FN)

M. Michel de Camaret, a diplomat, was elected to the EP 1984. Was French ambassador to the Council of Europe at Strasbourg, 1968–72; consul general in Sao-Paolo, 1972–77, and ambassador extraordinary to Burma, 1977–81. Member, permanent French mission to United Nations in New York, 1955–63. Born Oct 18 1915.

Address: 15 boulevard Beauséjour, 75016 Paris.

CARIGNON, ALAIN
France, RDE (UDF/RPR)

M. Alain Carignon, Mayor of Grenoble since 1983, was elected to the EP in 1984. Grenoble county councillor, 1976; re-elected 1982. Rhône-Alpes regional councillor. Former member, industry section, Economic and Social Council. Adviser to Ombudsman, Aimé Paquet, 1974–75, and to Jérome Monod, secretary general of the RPR, 1978–80. Chairman of an intercommunal group for research, planning and improvement in the Grenoble region. Born Feb 23 1949.

Address: Mairie de Grenoble, 38021 Grenoble.

CAROSSINO, ANGELO
Italy, Comm (PCI)

Sgr Angelo Carossino, elected to the EP in 1979, was elected one of the EP's five quaestors in July 1984; a vice-chairman of the EP Committee on Transport until 1984, when he remained a member of the committee. Factory worker. Mayor of Savona, 1957–68; party regional secretary, 1967–75; Regional Councillor for Liguria, 1970; and chairman of the Regional Council for Liguria 1975–79. Elected member of the Central Committee at the XI Party Congress, he entered the party leadership at the XIV Party Congress. Born Feb 21 1929.

Address: Via Privata Lanfranco 34 B, Casa A/1, 17011 Albisola Capo (Savona). Tel: (019) 44364.

CASINI, CARLO
Italy, EPP (DC)

Sgr Carlo Casini, elected to the EP in 1984, is a graduate in jurisprudence and became a magistrate in Empoli, then assistant public prosecutor in Florence, and in 1973 was elected a member of the Law Council of Tuscany. A judge in the Court of Appeal from 1977. Now a member of Chamber of Deputies. Born Mar 4 1935.

Address: Via della Canonica 1, 50122 Firenze. Tel: (055) 57 17 54.

CASSANMAGNAGO CERRETTI, SIGNORA MARIA LUISA
Italy, EPP (DC)

Signora Maria Luisa Cassanmagnago Cerretti became Senior Vice-President of the EP in July 1984, having held office as a Vice-President, 1982–84. Member of EP since 1976; elected in 1979, and a vice-chairman of the EPP Group, 1979–82. A vice-chairman of the EP Committee on Verification of Credentials from July 1984. Member, Italian Chamber of Deputies, 1972–79. Member, DC national council, since 1980, and on executive of DC women's movement since 1963. Adviser on social services to Milan provincial administration, 1963–72. Born Apr 7 1929; graduate in economics and commerce.
Addresses: Via Emanuele Filiberto 190, 00185 Roma. Tel: 7577607. Via Della Mendola 57, 00135 Roma. Tel: 32 82 154.

CASSIDY, BRYAN
UK, Dorset East and Hampshire West, ED (C)

Mr Bryan Cassidy, director-general of a trade association and a member of the council of the CBI, was elected to the EP in 1984. Became a member of its Economic and Monetary Affairs Committee in July 1984. Member, Greater London Council since 1981, being Conservative spokesman on industry and employment. Born Feb 17 1934; educated Sidney Sussex College, Cambridge, Married with three children.

Address: 97 Portland Road, London W11 4LN. Tel: (01) 584-2256.

CASTELLINA, SIGNORA LUCIANA
Italy, ARC (PCI)

Signora Luciana Castellina was elected to the EP in 1979 on PDUP list and became a vice-chairman of CDI group for defence of independent groups. Elected in 1984 on Communist list. Member, Chamber of Deputies, since 1976. Journalist, editor of daily newspaper *Il Manifesto*. Member of the Committee on Justice and the Interparliamentary Committee on the general guidance and supervision of the broadcasting services. Born Aug 9 1929; degree in jurisprudence. President, Union of Italian Women.

Address: Camera dei Deputati, Palazzo Raggi, Via del Corso 173, 00100 Roma. Tel: 67179591-9492. Via San Valentino 32, 00197 Roma.

CASTLE, MRS BARBARA
UK, Greater Manchester West, Soc (Lab)

Mrs Barbara Castle has been leader, UK Labour Party Group at EP since 1979. Vice-chairman (1979–84) and senior vice-chairman, Socialist Group, since July 1984. Elected for this seat in 1984; MEP for Greater Manchester, North 1979–84. Labour MP for Blackburn (1945–79). Member, NEC Labour Party (1950–79), chairman (1958–59). Minister of Overseas Development, 1964–65; of Transport, 1965–68; First Secretary of State and Secretary of State for Employment and Productivity, 1968–70. Secretary of State for Social Services, 1974–76. Born Oct 6 1911. Journalist.

Addresses: British Labour Group, 2 Queen Anne's Gate, London SW1. Tel: (01) 222-1728. Hell Corner Farm, Grays Lane, Ibstone, nr. High Wycombe, Bucks, HP14 3XX. Tel: (049-163) 464.

CATHERWOOD, SIR FREDERICK
UK, Cambridge and Bedfordshire North, ED (C)

Sir Frederick Catherwood, elected in 1979, is vice-chairman of ED group. Member, EP Budgets Committee since July 1984; former chairman, EP External Economic Relations Committee. Director-General, National Economic Development Council, 1966–71; previously Chief Economic Adviser, Department of Economic Affairs. Ex-managing director of John Laing and Son Ltd; director, Goodyear Tyre and Rubber Company (UK) Ltd. Chartered accountant. Former chairman, British Overseas Trade Board, British Institute of Management, Mallinson-Denny Ltd and Wittenborg Automat Ltd. B. Jan 30 1925; educ. Shrewsbury School, Clare Coll. Cambridge.

Address: Shire Hall, Castle Hill, Cambridge CB3 0AW. Tel: (0223) 317672.

CERVETTI, GIOVANNI
Italy, Comm (PCI)

Sgr Giovanni Cervetti, elected to the EP in 1984, was elected chairman of the Communist and Allies Group in July 1984. Secretary, Lombardy region of Communist Party and member of its national executive. Born Sep 12 1933.

Address: c/o Comitato Regionale Lombardo, Via Volturno 33, 20124 Milano.

CHABOCHE, DOMINIQUE
France, DR (FN)

M. Dominique Chaboche is vice-president of the National Front. Elected to the EP 1984. Born May 12 1937.

Address: 2, square Saint Florentin, 78150 Le Chesnay.

CHAMBEIRON, ROBERT
France, Comm (PCF)

M. Robert Chambeiron was elected to the EP in 1979 and has been a vice-chairman of EP Legal Affairs Committee. Retired civil servant; director of a cultural organization. Secretary-General of l'Union progressiste. Born May 22 1915. Deputy for Vosges in National Assembly 1945–58. Officer, Legion of Honour.

Address: 16, rue Gustave Zédé, 75016 Paris. Tel: 647 7189.

CHANTERIE, RAPHAËL
Belgium, EPP (CVP–EVP)

Mr Raphaël Chanterie, a member of the outgoing elected Parliament, was on the bureau of the EPP. A teacher, 1963–70. Born Nov 22 1942.

Addresses: Eikenlaan 26, 8790 Waregem. Tel: (056) 60 35 87. EUCDW, Albertinaplein 2, 1000 Brussel. Tel: (02) 512 33 98.

CHARZAT, MME GISÈLE
France, Soc (PS)

Mme Gisèle Charzat was first elected to the EP in 1979; member, bureau of Socialist Group; vice-chairman of EP Political Affairs Committee until 1984. Born Feb 17 1941. Journalist on economic affairs and teacher in higher education. Member, PS Central Committee, 1977–79.

Addresses: 63 rue Lauriston, 75116 Paris. Résidence de la Verte Vallée, Appartement 209, 14510 Houlgate.

CHIABRANDO, MAURO
Italy, EPP (DC)

Sgr Mauro Chiabrando was elected to the EP in 1984. Became member of Piedmont regional council in 1970, being re-elected in 1975 and 1980. Has also worked in Turin's municipal administration. Has been provincial secretary of DC in Turin. Holds diplomas in land surveying and agronomy. Born Mar 29 1984.

Address: Strada Baudenasca 8, 10064 Pinerolo (Torino).

CHINAUD, ROGER
France, LD (UDF/RPR)

M. Roger Chinaud was elected to the EP in 1984. Assistant to the Mayor of Paris and Mayor, 18th arrondissement; Ile-de-France regional councillor. Born Sep 6 1934. Paris deputy (independent republican group), 1973–81. International vice-president, Pan-European Union, since 1976.

Address: 1, rue Villersexel, 75007 Paris.

CHIUSANO, VITTORINO
Italy, EPP (DC)

Sgr **Vittorino Chiusano**, elected to the EP in 1984, is chairman of Fiat-France and Fiat's railway division in Savigliano. Now in charge of relations with the European institutions for the Fiat group. He had experience of working in France and Britain before joining Fiat. From 1968–77, he was secretary to the board of directors and to the Fiat Group's steering committee. During this period he was also director of foreign relations. Member, board of Teksid, of the Rome-France Bank, of the G. Agnelli Foundation, the Censis Foundation of Rome and of the 'La Stampa' publishing firm. Born Feb 27 1925.

Address: Corso Re Umberto, 5/bis, 10121 Torino.

CHOURAQUI, MME NICOLE
France, RDE (UDF/RPR)

Mme **Nicole Chouraqui**, a Deputy Mayor of Paris, and an economist, was an MEP 1979–80; re-elected 1984 when she became a vice-chairman of the European Democratic Alliance (formerly DEP) group. Born Mar 18 1938. Assistant general secretary of the RPR; member, political bureau, Radical Socialist Party, 1970–77. Financial analyst, Banque de l'Union parisienne, 1960–66. Councillor, City of Paris; Regional Councillor of Ile de France.

Address: Hôtel de Ville de Paris, 75004 Paris RP.

CHRISTENSEN, IB
Denmark, ARC (Folkebevaegelsen)

Mr **Ib Christensen** was elected to the EP in 1984. Chairman, Single-Tax Party (Retsforbundet) which he represented in the Danish Parliament 1973–75 and from 1978–79 when his party lost all seats. Member, European Parliament, 1978–79. He has been a member of the Council of Europe and a leading figure in the One World organization, the UN Association and various Nordic organizations. Born Mar 15 1930.

Address: Folkebevaegelsen mod EF, Gørtlervej 26, 8900 Randers. Tel: (06) 42 68 53.

CHRISTIANSEN, E. HOVGAARD
Denmark, Soc (S)

Mr E. Hovgaard Christiansen, elected to the EP in 1984, has been secretary-general of the Social Democratic Party since 1971. Active first in party youth organization and became secretary of the party's Copenhagen branch and member of the local community council. Also active in both the Socialistic International Organization and the grouping of the socialist parties within the ten EC countries. In 1979 was candidate for post of secretary-general of Socialist International. Born May 28 1932.

Address: Jacobys Alle 12, 3. tv., 1806 København V.

CHRISTODOULOU, EFTHYMIOS
Greece, EPP (ND)

Mr Efthymios Christodoulou, who became an MEP in 1984, was President and Governor of the National Bank of Greece, 1979–81. Has participated in many international conferences on economics and in the work of international banking organizations such as the International Monetary Fund and OECD. Economist. Born 1932; educated Athens College, Hamilton College and University of Columbia. Worked as consultant director, director-general and president of a number of major banks and enterprises, including ETVA (Commercial Bank for Industrial Development) and Olympic Airways.

Address: Louki Akrita 1b, 152 37 Filothei.

CIANCAGLINI, MICHELANGELO
Italy, EPP (DC)

Sgr Michelangelo Ciancaglini, elected to the EP in 1984, is secretary of the Italian Confederation of Trade Unions (CISL) and a freelance journalist. Mayor of Furci during the 1950s and was elected to council of Campobasso, 1956. For 15 years, chairman of the INAM (National Health Insurance Fund) provincial committee. Elected to CISL executive in Rome in 1969; became member of secretariat a year later, in charge of management training and policy, agricultural problems, public employment and institutions; since 1982 responsible for organizational policy. Member, OECD trade union consultative committee, National Productivity Committee. B. Oct 6 1926. *Address: Via Giuseppe Valmarana 46, 00139 Roma.*

CINCIARA RODANO, SIGNORA MARIA
Italy, Comm (PCI)

Signora Maria Cinciari Rodano, elected to the EP in 1979, chaired the EP committee of inquiry into situation of women in Europe, set up in last Parliament. Became a vice-chairman, EP Committee on Women's Rights, in July 1984. Italian MP, 1948–68, and Senator, 1968–72. Rome City councillor, 1946–56. Member and then National chairman, Union of Italian Women. Member of Parliamentary Committees on: Home Affairs, Education and the Fine Arts, Employment and Social Security, Constitutional Affairs and Foreign Affairs. Vice-Chairman of the Lower House in the IV Legislature 1963–68. Born Jan 21 1921.
Address: Via di Porta Latina 2, 00179 Roma. Tel: (06) 75 75 984.

CLINTON, MARK
Ireland, EPP (F-Gael)

Mr Mark Clinton, elected an MEP in 1979, was President of the EEC Council of Agriculture Ministers in 1975, being Irish Minister of Agriculture, 1973–77. Born Feb 7 1915; educated Christian Brothers' School, Dublin. Former estate manager. Dail deputy, 1961–81; chairman, Joint Dail and Senate Committee on EC Legislation, 1977–79, Fine Gael front bench Opposition spokesman on various departments.

Address: Coolmine, Rathcoole, Co. Dublin. Fine Gael/Christian Democrats, 43 Molesworth Street, Dublin.

COHEN, ROBERT
Netherlands, Soc (PvdA)

Mr Robert Cohen, elected to the EP in 1979, is a former principal in the cabinets of Mr Mansholt and Mr Lardinois when EEC Commissioners; former Chef de Cabinet for Commissioner Vredeling; 'development' director at the Commission. Born Mar 4 1930; studied political and social sciences at Amsterdam.

Addresses: Van Genegenlaan 37, 1150 Brussel. Tel: (02) 762 77 57. Traay 233, Driebergen. Tel: 03438-13518.

COLLINOT, MICHEL
France, DR (FN)

M. Michel Collinot, elected to the EP in 1984. Member, National Front's political bureau. Born Nov 2 1947. Director, National Hebdo.

Address: 9, rue Palestro, 93500 Pantin.

COLLINS, KENNETH
UK, Strathclyde East, Soc (Lab)

Mr Kenneth Collins, former deputy leader, Labour Party group of European Parliament, was elected in 1979. Chairman, EP Committee on Environment, Public Health and Consumer Protection, 1979–84; a vice-chairman of the committee since 1984. Lecturer; former councillor at East Kilbride. Born Aug 12 1939; educated Glasgow University and Strathclyde University. BSc (Hons geography), MSc. Vice-president, Royal Environmental Health Institute of Scotland, European Food Law Association and Institute of Trading Standards Administration.

Address: 11 Stuarton Park, East Kilbride G74 4LA. Tel: (03552) 37282.

COLUMBU, MICHELE
Italy, ARC (UV-PSDA)

Sgr Michele Columbu, graduate in literature and professor, is President of the Sardinian Action Party. Elected to the EP in 1984. Member, Chamber of Deputies, 1972–76. The party's first representative to win a seat at Strasbourg.

Address: Is Meris, Flumini di Quarto S. Elena, Casella Postale 12, 09100 Cagliari.

115

CORNELISSEN, PETER
Netherlands, EPP (CDA)

Mr Peter Cornelissen was elected to the EP in 1984 and became a member of its Budgets Committee. Member of Dutch Second Chamber from 1967–81 during which time he was chairman of the chamber's committee on housing and town and country planning; also chairman of his parliamentary party's transport committee. Born Jan 13 1934; civil engineer. Member, assembly of Council of Europe, and a vice-president, WEU assembly, 1970–81.

Address: Willem-II-straat 47, 5682 AG Best.

COSTANZO, ROBERTO
Italy, EPP (DC)

Sgr Roberto Costanzo was elected to the EP in 1979 and became a vice-chairman, until 1984, of the EP Committee on Regional Policy and Regional Planning. Freelance journalist; vice-president of National Agricultural Press Association. Member, DC national council and central executive. Municipal councillor (1960–70), provincial assessor (1964–7) and regional assessor responsible for agriculture (1970–76). Leader, National Confederation of Owner-Farmers; chairman, European Agri-Tourism Group of COPA; member, national executive, Confederation of Italian Cooperatives. Born Nov 27 1929.

Addresses: Via Nicola Calandra 25, 821000 Benevento. Tel: (0824) 28864. Via XXIV Maggio 22, 82100 Benevento. Tel: (0824) 28696 or 24369.

COSTE-FLORET, ALFRED
France, EPP (UDF/RPR)

M. Alfred Coste-Floret, elected to the EP in 1984, is an honorary councillor of state. Public prosecutor, Nuremberg International Tribunal, 1945. MRP deputy for Haute-Garonne, 1946–59; Mayor and member of Haute-Garonne General Council, 1947–71. French delegate, UN General Assembly, 1952–55; Secretary General, International Union of Christian Democratic Parties, 1955–61, Anti-Racist International, 1960. Founder chairman, French Christian Democracy, 1978; chairman, French Association for Atlantic Community since 1977. Born Apr 9 1911.

Address: 50, rue de Berri, 75008 Paris.

COT, JEAN-PIERRE
France, Soc (PS)

M. Jean-Pierre Cot, chairman of the French Unesco delegation since 1983, became an MEP and chairman, EP budgets committee in 1984. Born Oct 23 1937. Minister of Cooperation, 1981–82; Savoie deputy, 1973–81. Mayor of Coise-Saint-Jean-Pied-Gauthier since 1971. Lecturer at the Faculty of Law first of Amiens, then of Paris.

Address: Coise-St-Jean-Pied-Gauthier, 73800 Montmelian.

COTTRELL, RICHARD
UK, Bristol, ED (C)

Mr Richard Cottrell, elected to the EP in 1979, was a television reporter and is now a member of the EP Committee on Environment, Public Health and Consumer Protection. Born July 11 1943; educated Court Fields Secondary School, Wellington, Somerset, and technical college. Vice-President, National Council on Inland Transport and European Vice-President, Association of District Councils. Married with two children.

Addresses: 48 Silver Street, Midsomer Norton, near Bath. Tel: (0761) 412100. Combeside, Back Lane, Croscombe, Wells, Somerset.

COURCY LING, JOHN DE
UK, Midlands Central, ED (C)

Mr John de Courcy Ling became a Vice-Chairman of the EP Committee on Development and Cooperation in July 1984; ED (Conservative) Group chief whip. 1979–83. Farmer, formerly a senior diplomat, his last appointment being as Counsellor, British Embassy, Paris, 1974–77. Born Oct 14 1933; educated King Edward's School, Edgbaston, and Clare College, Cambridge. Foreign Office, 1959; Second Secretary, Santiago, 1963–66; First Secretary, Nairobi, 1966–69; Chargé d'Affaires, Chad, 1973. Married with four children.

Addresses: 31 Chapel Street, Belgrave Square, London SW1. Tel: (01) 235-5655. Bellehatch Farm, Henley-on-Thames, Oxfordshire, RG9 4AW. Tel: (04912) 3878.

CRAWLEY, MRS CHRISTINE
UK, Birmingham East, Soc (Lab)

Mrs Christine Crawley was elected to the EP in 1984 and became a vice-chairman of the EP Committee on Women's Rights. Formerly a teacher, then held part-time position with Manpower Services Commission. Married with three children, including twins. Born Jan 1 1950: educated Notre Dame Catholic Secondary Girls School, Plymouth and the Digby Stuart Training College, Roehampton, London. Former member, South Oxfordshire district council; parliamentary candidate, Staffordshire South East 1983. Member of Fabians, Cooperative Party, CND, NUT and AUEW/TASS.

Address: 26 Glascote Road, Tamworth, Staffordshire, B77 2AA. Tel: (0827) 58855.

CROUX, LAMBERT
Belgium, EPP (CVP–EVP)

Mr Lambert Croux, elected to the EP in 1979, became a vice-chairman of the EP Committee on Institutional Affairs in July 1984. Member of Belgian Parliament, 1967–77; Senate, 1977–81. On bureau of CVP. Born Mar 6 1927; degree in economic sciences, Doctor of Law. Industrial legal adviser at Alken from 1954. Has chaired association of CVP delegates from municipalities and provinces. Chairman, Limburg Economic Council, 1972–77, and Limburg regional development society, 1975–77.

Address: Stationsstraat 19, 3820 Alken. Tel: (011) 312 537.

CRYER, ROBERT
UK, Sheffield, Soc (Lab)

Mr Robert Cryer, technical college lecturer, was elected to the EP in 1984. Born Dec 3 1934; educated Salt High School, Shipley and Hull University. MP for Keighley, Feb 1974–83; contested Darwen, 1964. Under-Secretary of State for Industry, 1976–78, when he resigned in protest at a decision to cut off public funds to a Merseyside workers' cooperative. Member, Keighley Borough Council, 1971–74. Chairman, Parliamentary Labour Party employment group, 1975–76.

Address: Holyoake, Providence Lane, Oakworth, Keighley, Yorks.

CURRY, DAVID
UK, Essex North East, ED (C)

Mr David Curry, a journalist, was elected to the EP in 1979; became a vice-chairman of its Budgets Committee in July 1984. Chairman, EP Agriculture Committee, 1982–84; previously ED spokesman on it. In 1975 appointed Brussels correspondent of *The Financial Times* covering EEC and Benelux affairs and the European Parliament. Became Paris correspondent in 1976 and in 1978 was appointed Foreign News Editor in London. Contested Morpeth in both 1974 elections. Born Jun 13 1944; educated Ripon Grammar School and Corpus Christi College, Oxford.
Addresses: 35 Belgrave Square, London SW1X 8QN. Tel: (01) 235 8914 and (01) 245 9382. Newland End, Arkesden, nr. Saffron Walden, Essex CB11 4HF. Tel: (079 985) 368.

DALSASS, JOACHIM
Italy, EPP (SVP)

Sgr Joachim Dalsass, a doctor in jurisprudence, was elected to the EP in 1979. Official in the Trento regional administration from 1953–56 responsible for cooperatives and the fire service. Member, Regional Council of the South Tyrol, since 1956 and chairman since 1978; deputy Councillor for Social Welfare for South Tyrol, 1956–60; member, regional executive in charge of public works 1960–72; in charge of agriculture, forestry, hunting and fishing, 1972–78. Deputy chairman, South Tyrol People's Party since 1969; President South Tyrol Regional Council, since 1978. Born Dec 3 1926.

Address: 39040 Petersberg (Bozen) (Südtirol). Tel: (0471) 615191.

DALY, MRS MARGARET
UK, Somerset and Dorset West, ED (C)

Mrs Margaret Daly was elected to EP in 1984 when she was national director of the Conservative trade unionists' organization, a CTU representative on the all-party trade union group for Europe and a member of the ED/CTU joint committee. Member, European Union of Women and of its Commission for Migration, Refugees and Demography. Former departmental head of international insurance company before becoming ASTMS official. Born Jan 26 1938. Married with one daughter.

Address: Little Cophall, Dowlands Lane, Copthorne, West Sussex, RH10 3HX. Tel: 0342 712779.

DANKERT, PIETER
Netherlands, Soc (PvdA)

Mr Pieter Dankert was President of the European Parliament 1982–84; unsuccessfully contested Presidency in July 1984. A vice-chairman of Socialist Group and member of Budgets Committee from July 1984. Member of the EP since 1977, being first elected in 1979. Former member of Dutch Second Chamber. Has also served in Council of Europe, WEU and North Atlantic assemblies. PvdA international secretary, 1975–81. Born Jan 8 1934. Former teacher; Dip Ed history.

Address: Hoogstraat 1, 1135 BZ Edam. Tel: 02993-71668.

DEBATISSE, MICHEL
France, EPP (UDF/RPR)

M Michel Debatisse, a farmer, was Secretary of State for Agriculture, 1979–81. First elected to the EP in 1979; resigned on becoming minister, returned in 1984 to become a vice-chairman of EPP Group. Member of the Community's economic and social council, and economic and social committee. Chairman, Auvergne economic and social committee since 1974. Born Apr 1 1929. General Secretary, Catholic Young Farmers. General Secretary, then President, National Federation of Farmers' Unions, 1971–79.

Address: Palladuc, 63550 St Remy s/Durolle.

DENIAU, JEAN-FRANÇOIS
France, LD (UDF/RPR)

M. Jean-François Deniau, Minister for Overseas Trade, 1978–81, and Secretary of State first for foreign affairs then for agriculture, 1973–76; elected to the EP in 1979. A vice-chairman, EP Political Affairs Committee, 1984. Born Oct 31 1928; educated ENA. Doctor of law. Former French ambassador to Spain and to Mauritania, 1963–66. Chairman, Cher county council since 1981; Cher deputy, 1978.

Address: 17, boulevard Raspail, 75007 Paris.

DEPREZ, GÉRARD
Belgium, EPP (PSC–PPE)

Mr Gérard Deprez was elected to the EP in 1984. Chairman of PSC since December 1981. Sociologist. Served on the staffs of ministers, 1979–81. Born Aug 13 1943.

Addresses: avenue des Combattants 26, 1340 Ottignies. Tel: (010) 41 85 44. Rue des Deux Eglises 41, 1040 Bruxelles. Tel: (02) 230 10 73.

DIDO', MARIO
Italy, Soc (PSI)

Sgr Mario Dido', elected to the EP in 1979, became a vice-chairman of the Socialist Group and was re-elected as such in July 1984. Former national secretary of CGIL (Federation of Italian Trade Unions); former member, Economic and Social Committee of the EEC. Member, executive, Confederation of European Trade Unions. Born Nov 16 1926.

Address: Via Filippo Civinini 37, 00197 Roma.

DIMITRIADIS, CHRYSANTHOS
Greece, DR (EPEN)

Mr Chrysanthos Dimitriadis became an MEP in 1984. Born 1933. Engineer. Professor at the air force academy. Former President, National Tourist Office.

Address: Pallados 1, 16674 Glyfada.

DONNEZ, GEORGES
France, LD (UDF/RPR)

M. Georges Donnez, a lawyer, was elected to the EP in 1979; a vice-chairman of its Legal Affairs and Citizens' Rights Committee from July 1984. Mayor of St Amand les Eaux since 1953. Deputy for the Nord (19th Division, St Amand), 1973–78. Vice-president of the Mouvement démocrate socialiste de France (MDSF). Born Jun 20 1922; educated Lycée St Amand les Eaux; Faculty of Law, Lille Licencié in law; member of the bar of Valenciennes. Member of the Conseil Général of the St Amand Rive Gauche canton, 1958, re-elected in 1964, 1970 and 1976.

Address: 51 Grand Place, 59230 Saint Amand les Eaux.

DOURO, MARQUESS OF
UK, Surrey West, ED (C)

The Marquess of Douro, elected MEP in 1979, became ED (Conservative) Group spokesman on the EEC budget and a member of the Budgets Committee in 1984. Member, EP political affairs committee, 1979–84. Chairman of Thames Valley Broadcasting (a commercial radio station) and a non-executive director of an investment company, a forest pulp-manufacturing company and a paper company. Born Aug 19 1945; educated Eton and Christ Church, Oxford. Son of the 8th Duke of Wellington. Contested Islington North in the Oct 1974 general election. Farmer. Married with two children.

Address: Friars House (fifth floor), 39–41 New Broad Street, London EC2M 1JH. Tel: (01) 628 4761. Telex: 883744.

DUCARME, DANIEL
Belgium, LD (PRL)

Mr Daniel Ducarme was elected to the EP in 1984. A vice-chairman of EP Committee on Regional Policy and Regional Planning from July 1984. EEC press and information attaché for Belgium, 1970–76. Deputy for Thuin in the Chamber of Representatives since 1981. Head of the PRL parliamentary group in the council of the French community. Born Mar 8 1954.

Address: 'Saint François', Chemin de Forestaille 15, 6530 Thuin.

DUPUY, MME ANNE-MARIE
France, RDE (UDF/RPR)

Mme Anne-Marie Dupuy, a privy councillor since 1974, became an MEP in 1984. Mayor of Cannes since 1983 and Alpes maritimes county councillor since 1982. Born Sep 18 1920. Was principal private secretary to President Pompidou. Rothschild head of personnel, 1952–63.

Address: 'Le Provence', 25 rue du Commandant Bret, 06400 Cannes.

DURY, MME RAYMONDE
Belgium, Soc (PS)

Mme Raymonde Dury, who became a member of the EP in 1982, was press attaché to the Socialist Group at the Parliament, 1976–82. Sociologist. Born Jul 22 1947. A vice-chairman, EP Committee on Rules of Procedure and Petitions.

Address: 58, rue de la Croix, 1050 Bruxelles. Tel: (02) 649 66 72.

EBEL, MANFRED
Germany, EPP (CDU)

Herr Manfred Ebel was elected to the EP in 1984. Businessman. Former district chairman, Bremerhaven boys' union. Member, Bremerhaven town council from 1967 being chairman of its CDU group for four years. Born Jul 19 1932.

Address: Pillauer Strasse 9, 2850 Bremerhaven.

ELLES, JAMES
UK, Oxford and Buckinghamshire, ED (C)

Mr James Elles, hitherto a full-time official with the EEC Commission, was elected to the EP in 1984, becoming a member of its Budgets Committee. Born 1949; educated Wagners, Ashdown House, Eton College and Edinburgh University. Worked for EEC Commission, 1976–84, being the expert responsible for fisheries negotiations, 1976–77; participated in the Tokyo Round multilateral trade negotiations in Gatt, 1977–80. Assistant to the Deputy Director General, Agriculture, with duties that included responsibility for food aid to Poland, 1980–82. Married with two children.

Address: 14 avenue Maurice, 1050 Brussels, Belgium.

ELLES, LADY
UK, Thames Valley, ED (C)

Lady Elles has been a Vice-President of the EP since 1982; unsuccessfully contested Presidency, 1984. Elected in 1979 and was a joint vice-chairman of ED Group, 1979–82. A Conservative Opposition spokesman on foreign and Commonwealth affairs, House of Lords, 1975–79. Member of nominated EP, 1973–75. Barrister (Lincoln's Inn). Created a life peer in 1972. Born Jul 19 1921; educated London, Paris and Florence; London University (BA Hons). International chairman, European Union of Women, 1973–79; chairman, Conservative Party's International Office, 1973–78.
Addresses: 75 Ashley Gardens, London SW1. Tel: (01) 828 0175. House of Lords, London SW1. Tel: (01) 219 3169/3149.

ELLIOTT, MICHAEL
UK, London West, Soc (Lab)

Mr Michael Elliott was elected to the EP in 1984 when he became a member of the Committee on Youth Affairs, Culture, Education, Information and Sport. A senior technologist/manager in food industry. Born Jun 3 1932; educated Brunel College of Technology. Former councillor and parliamentary candidate for seat in Commons. Fought EP election in Bedfordshire, 1979. Member, Cooperative Party, the Fabians, the Labour Coordinating Committee, CND.

Address: 358 Oldfield Lane North, Greenford, Middlesex.

EPHREMIDIS, VASSILIOS
Greece, Comm (KKE)

Mr Vassilios Ephremidis, a member of the previous elected Parliament, was re-elected in 1984 and became a vice-chairman of the Communist and Allies Group of the EP in July 1984. Lawyer. Elected to Greek national assembly in the 1950s; editor of *Avgi*, 1952–56. Member of central committee of his party. Born Dec 31 1915.

Address: Ithakis 41, 11251 Athens. Tel: (1) 8213788.

ERCINI, SERGIO
Italy, EPP (DC)

Sgr Sergio Ercini became an MEP in 1982; re-elected 1984. Member of the national executive and a national councillor of DC; party group leader on regional council of Umbria. Born Oct 28 1934.

Address: c/o Safim-Efim, via Nazionale 39, 00184 Roma.

ESTGEN, NICOLAS
Luxembourg, EPP (PCS)

Mr Nicolas Estgen, formerly a teacher, became an MEP in August 1979; re-elected 1984. Was at one time responsible for vocational training and secondary and higher technical education at the education ministry of the Duchy and later became an assistant government adviser. Born Feb 28 1930. Connected with family and consumer organizations.

Addresses: 1, rue P. Wigreux, Howald. Tel: 48 68 89. 3, rue de Curé, Luxembourg. Tel: 28282.

EVRIGENIS, DIMITRIOS
Greece, EPP (ND)

Mr Dimitrios Evrigenis, a judge of the European Court of Human Rights, was elected to the EP in 1984 and became a vice-chairman, EP Legal Affairs and Citizens' Rights Committee in July 1984. Elected MP on the New Democracy list in 1974. Secretary of State for Education, 1974–75; resigned on being appointed to the European Court of Human Rights. Born 1925; studied law in France, England and Research Centre in International Law in The Hague. Professor of law, University of Thessaloniki.

Address: Soulioti 23, 546 42 Thessaloniki.

EWING, MRS WINIFRED
UK, Highlands and Islands, RDE (SNP)

Mrs Winifred Ewing, elected to the EP in 1979, has been a vice-chairman of the RDE (formerly DEP) Group since that year; in July 1984 became chairman, EP Committee for Youth, Culture, Education, Information and Sport. Member of nominated EP, 1975–79. Solicitor. A vice-president of the Scottish National Party; MP for Moray and Nairn, 1974–79; MP for Hamilton, 1967–70. Contested Orkney and Shetland in 1983 general election. Born Jul 10 1929; educated Queen's Park Senior Secondary School, Glasgow, and Glasgow University. Lecturer in law, Scottish College of Commerce, 1954–56. Married with three children.
Address: 52 Queen's Drive, Glasgow S2, Scotland. Tel: (4041) 423-8060. Goodwill, 22 Kinedder Street, Lossiemouth, Morayshire, Scotland.

EYRAUD, LOUIS
France, Soc (PS)

M. Louis Eyraud, veterinary surgeon, was first elected to the EP in 1981. Became vice-chairman, EP Agriculture, Fisheries and Food Committee, 1984. Born May 18 1922. First secretary, Socialist Party federation of Haute-Loire since 1976; former member, party's national agricultural committee. Mayor of Brioude since 1971; Haute-Loire county councillor; deputy, 1976–78. Knight, Order of Academic Palms, Order of Agricultural Merit.

Address: 2, rue St Laurent, 43100 Brioude. Tel: (71) 50 07 25.

FAITH, MRS SHEILA
UK, Cumbria and Lancashire North, ED (C)

Mrs Sheila Faith, elected to the EP in 1984, joined EP Committee for Women's Rights. MP for Belper 1979–83; contested Newcastle Central in Oct 1974. Former director and company secretary of family fashion business. Member, Northumberland County Council, 1970–74, and Newcastle City Council, 1975–77. Member, Commons Select Committee on Health Social Services, 1979–83, and of executive committee, Conservative Medical Society. Dental surgeon. Born Jun 3 1928; educated Newcastle upon Tyne Central High School and Durham University.

Address: Pinewood Cottage, Sedgewick, Kendal, Cumbria.

FAJARDIE, ROGER
France, Soc (PS)

M. Roger Fajardie, a journalist, was first elected to the EP in 1981. Became a vice-chairman, EP Youth Affairs, Education, Information and Sport Committee, in July 1984. National Secretary, Young Socialists, 1958–61; member, PS steering committee since 1963, and party's executive bureau since 1973; PS national secretary, 1975–79. Founder member and administrator, national federation of Léo Lagrange leisure clubs. Mayor of La Groutte (Cher). Born Sep 4 1940.

Address: 14, rue Yvonne Le Tac, 75018 Paris. Tel: 262 71 55.

FALCONER, ALEC
UK, Mid Scotland and Fife, Soc (Lab)

Mr Alec Falconer, an insulator at Rosyth Dockyard, was elected to the EP in 1984. Born Apr 1 1940. Foundry worker, later serving nine years in the Royal Navy. Shop steward in the Transport and General Workers Union, and chairman of the Fife Federation of Trades Councils. Member, CND and Anti-Vivisection Committee. Married with one son and one daughter.

Address: 20 Burnside Street, Rosyth, Fife.

FANTI, GUIDO
Italy, Comm (PCI)

Sgr Guido Fanti, elected in 1979, was leader of the Communist and Allies Group of the EP, 1979–84. Became Italian MP in 1976. Journalist. Party member since 1945; Secretary of party's Provincial Federation of Bologna (1959–65). Elected to Central Committee, 1960; member, national leadership, since the XI Congress. Mayor of Bologna, 1966–70. Chairman, Regional Council of Emilia-Romagna, 1970–76. Former member, Presidency of the World Council on Peace. Born May 27 1925.

Addresses: Corso Vittorio Emanuele 147a, 00186 Roma. Tel: 6567777. Senato della Republica, 00186 Roma. Tel: 67061.

FANTON, ANDRÉ
France, RDE (UDF/RPR)

M. André Fanton, a barrister at the Paris Court of Appeal since 1952; MEP, 1980–81; re-elected in 1984; member of the nominated EP, 1962–69. Deputy Mayor of Lisieux. Member, RPR political council and central committee. Elected UNR deputy for Paris (11th arrondissement), 1958; re-elected 1962, 1967, 1968 and 1973. Policy adviser to M. Michel Debré, Minister of Justice, 1958. State Secretary attached to the Minister of State responsible for national defence, 1969–72. Chairman, Movement for European Independence. Born Mar 31 1928.

Address: 10, rue Danton, 75006 Paris.

FATOUS, LÉON
France, Soc (PS)

M. Léon Fatous, national treasurer, Federation of Elected Socialists and Republicans since 1972, became an MEP in 1984. Born Feb 11 1926. Mayor of Arras since 1975; town councillor, 1959. Vice-chairman, Nord-Pas de Calais regional council.

Address: 4, rue de Commandant Dumetz, 62000 Arras.

FELLERMAIER, LUDWIG
Germany, Soc (SPD)

Herr Ludwig Fellermaier first joined the EP in 1968 and was chairman of the Socialist Group in the outgoing nominated Parliament of 1979. After being elected in 1979, he was for the first part of the Parliament a vice-chairman of the group. Member of Bundestag, 1965–80, and of executive committee of Confederation of Socialist and Social Democratic Parties of the EEC. Born Jul 2 1930.

Address: Emsstrasse 8, 7910 Neu-Ulm. Tel: (0731) 81471.

FERRANTI, BASIL DE
UK, Hampshire, Central ED (C)

Mr Basil de Ferranti, elected to the EP in 1979, was a Vice-President of the EP, 1979–82. President, Economic and Social Committee, European Communities, 1976–79, member 1973–79. Joint vice-chairman, ED group, 1979–82. Chairman, Ferranti Ltd. Born Jul 2 1930; educated Eton and Trinity College, Cambridge. Conservative MP for Morecambe and Lonsdale, 1958–64; Parliamentary Secretary, Ministry of Aviation, 1962. Deputy managing director, International Computers and Tabulators, 1963; managing director, 1964. Director, International Computers Ltd, 1964–72.

Addresses: Millbank Tower, Millbank, London SW1P 4QS. Tel: (01) 834 6611. 19 Lennox Gardens, London SW1X 0DD. Tel: (01) 584 2256.

FICH, OVE
Denmark, Soc (S)

Mr Ove Fich became an MEP in 1979 in a big re-shuffle when Mr Kjeld Olsen retired from the Parliament to become Foreign Minister in Mr Anker Jørgensen's Administration. Born Mar 16 1949. Nuclear physicist at Aarhus University. General secretary, Socialist International, 1977–79. Member, EP Budgets Committee.

Addresses: Socialdemokratiet, Nyropsgade 26, 5., 1602 København V. Falkehusene 15, 2620 Albertslund. Tel: (02) 622942.

FITZGERALD, GENE
Ireland, RDE (F-Fáil)

Mr Gene Fitzgerald, who has been a member of the Dail since the early 1970s, was elected to the EP in 1984. A joint treasurer of RDE Group from July 1984. Minister of Labour, 1977–80; Minister for Finance and Public Service, 1980–81; President of EEC Council of Social Affairs Ministers, 1979; President, European Investment Bank, Jan to Jun 1981. Now Opposition spokesman on labour. Born Aug 1932.

Address: 'Cloduv', 2 Melbourne Road, Bishopstown, Cork.

FITZSIMONS, JIM
Ireland, RDE (F-Fáil)

Mr Jim Fitzsimons was Minister of State, Department of Industry and Energy, Oct to Dec 1982. Member of the Dail since 1977. Elected to the EP in 1984. Born Dec 1936.

Address: Ardsion, Dublin Road, Navan, Co. Meath.

FLANAGAN, SEAN
Ireland, RDE (F-Fáil)

Mr Sean Flanagan, elected to the EP in 1979, was Irish Minister for Lands, 1969–73; Minister of Health, 1966–69; Parliamentary Secretary to Minister for Industry and Commerce, 1965–66. Former vice-chairman of DEP (now RDE) Group in EP, now member of bureau. Born Jan 26 1922. Solicitor. Deputy for Mayo South, 1951–69 and then for Mayo East until 1977. Member, Dail and Seanad Joint Committee on EC Legislation, 1973–77. Member, Council of Europe, 1952–53, 1957–59 and 1965.

Addresses: 65 St Lawrence's Road, Clontarf, Dublin 3; St Anthony's, Ballaghaderreen, Co. Roscommon.

FLESCH, MME COLETTE
Luxembourg, LD (PD)

Mme Colette Flesch is the present Leader of the Opposition in Luxembourg. Member of nominated EP from 1969; elected in 1979 but left to take office being a minister from 1980 to 1984, when she was re-elected to the EP. Treasurer of LD Group from July 1984. Member of Chamber of Deputies 1969–80. Mayor of Luxembourg, 1970–80. Held office in Liberal group in EP, 1970–80. Born Apr 6 1937; educated Wellesley College, Wellesley, Massachusetts and the Fletcher School of Law and Diplomacy, Melford, Massachusetts. Administrator in secretariat of Council of EEC in Brussels, 1964–69.

Address: 11a, Boulevard Prince Henri, Luxembourg.

FLOSSE, GASTON
France, RDE (UDF/RPR)

M. Gaston Flosse, vice-president of the governing council of French Polynesia since 1982, was elected to the EP in 1984. Born Jun 24 1931. RPR deputy, 1978–82; member, RPR central committee since 1974. Mayor of Pirae since 1965. Territorial councillor since 1967 and for three years chairman of the Territorial Assembly. Member, National Assembly finance committee, 1978–82; special rapporteur, finance committee for overseas territories budget, 1978–81.

Address: Boîte Postale 471, Papeete, Tahiti.

FOCKE, FRAU KATHARINA
Germany, Soc (SPD)

Frau Katharina Focke, elected to the EP in 1984, became chairman of the EP Committee on Development and Cooperation in July 1984, previously a vice-chairman. Member of the Bundestag, 1969–80, of the Northern Rhine-Westphalia assembly, 1966–69. Parliamentary State Secretary to the Federal Chancellor, 1969–72; Federal Minister for Youth, Family and Health, 1972–76. Political scientist, journalist. Born Oct 8 1922.

Address: Bundeshaus, Zim. H. T. 210, 5300 Boon 1.
Tel: (0228) 163 882

FONTAINE, MME NICOLE
France, RDE (UDF/RPR)

Mme Nicole Fontaine, who became an MEP in 1984, is a former delegate to the general secretariat of the Enseignement Catholique. Born Jan 16 1942; doctor of law. Member, Higher Council of National Education and (since 1980) Economic and Social Council.

Address: 13, rue Pierre Nicole, 75005 Paris.

FORD, GLYN
UK, Greater Manchester East, Soc (Lab)

Mr Glyn Ford, elected to the EP in 1984, has been a Senior Research Fellow at Manchester University. Born Jan 28 1950; educated Reading and London Universities. Local councillor. Member of CND, the Socialist Environment and Resources Association, the Cooperative Party and British Society for Social Responsibility in Science. Member, EP Committee on External Economic Relations from July 1984. Married with one daughter.

Address: 149 Old Road, Ashton under Lyne, Lancashire, OL6 9DA.

FORMIGONI, ROBERTO
Italy, EPP (DC)

Sgr Roberto Formigoni was elected to the EP in 1984. Graduate in philosophy. Taught in state secondary schools. Assistant university lecturer, 1971–73. In 1976, one of founders of Popular Movement, organized all over Italy with the aim of promoting the participation of Catholics in cultural, social and political activities, by means of cooperatives, cultural centres and discussion groups. Now responsible for this at national level. Born Mar 3 1947.

Address: c/o Movimento Popolare, Via Copernico 7, 20125 Milano.

FRANZ, OTMAR
Germany, EPP (CDU)

Herr Otmar Franz has been an MEP since 1981; re-elected 1984. Treasurer, Mülheim CDU, 1971–75; deputy chairman, Mülheim Ruhr district association; member, Rhineland trade association executive. Born Jan 6 1935. Business executive.

Address: Werntgenshof 31, 4330 Mülheim a.d. Ruhr. Tel: 42 1137.

FRIEDRICH, BRUNO
Germany, Soc (SPD)

Herr Bruno Friedrich, elected in 1979, was a Vice-President of the EP until 1984. Member, Bundestag, 1972–80; deputy chairman of SPD in the Bundestag (1976) and of the Confederation of Socialist and Social Democrat Parties of the EEC. Member, SPD executive. Chairman, SPD Franconia district, from 1970. Editor. Born May 31 1927.

Address: Frankenwarte, Kapellenweg 37, 8700 Würzburg. Tel: (0931) 86907.

FRIEDRICH, INGO
Germany, EPP (CSU)

Herr Ingo Friedrich was elected in 1979. On staff of Institute for Politics and Communications, University of Erlangen-Nuremberg, 1967–70, taking doctor's degree in 1971. Deputy chairman, CSU for Central Franconia region, 1977; CSU chairman, Weissenburg–Gunzenhausen district, from 1972. Chairman, Nuremburg Students' Union, 1964–65. Born Jan 24 1942. Executive in electrical industry from 1970.

Address: Bühringerstrasse 12, 8820 Gunzenhausen. Tel: (09831) 2425.

FRÜH, ISIDOR
Germany, EPP (CDU)

Herr Isidor Früh, member of the Bundestag 1969–80; has been a member of the European Parliament since 1973. After election in 1979 he became a vice-chairman of the EP Agriculture Committee until 1984; still a committee member. Born Apr 13 1922; studied agriculture at University of Hohenheim; doctorate 1958. From 1952–76, head of the Bad Waldsee rural adult education institute of the Württemberg-Hohenzollern Farmers' Association. Since 1973, chairman, Federal Association of German Fruit Distillers and Small Distillers. Member, CDU, since 1956.

Address: Oberer Kirchberg 14,7957 Schemmerhofen 2. Tel: (07356) 615.

FUILLET, MME YVETTE
France, Soc (PS)

Mme Yvette Fuillet was elected to the EP in 1979; was a vice-chairman of EP Committee on Regional Policy and Regional Planning. Appointed treasurer of the EP Socialist Group in 1984. Member of Marseilles city council since 1971. Member, national executive bureau, French Socialist Party. Born Mar 1 1923. Insurance executive.

Address: Appartement 20, Le Corbusier, 280 bd Michelet, 13008 Marseille. Tel: (91) 772186 and (91) 640800.

GADIOUX, MME COLETTE
France, Soc (PS)

Mme Colette Gadioux, who was elected to the EP in 1984, is Deputy Mayor of Limoges. Born Apr 8 1945. Head of the Limoges regional service for professional training and apprenticeship.

Address: 51, avenue de la Révolution, 87000 Limoges.

GAIBISSO, GERARDO
Italy, EPP (DC)

Sgr Gerardo Gaibisso, a journalist, was elected to the EP in 1984. Member, Lazio regional council and of Catholic Action, being chairman in Grosseto. Later held regional and national posts. Member, national council, Christian Democratic Party: provincial council of CISL (Italian Confederation of Workers' Trade Unions), and director of the federation of owner-farmers in Frosinone. Editor of Catholic trade union journal *Politica Sociale* and periodical *La Zolla*. Born May 30 1927.

Address: Via Lecce, 31, 03100 Frosinone.

GALLAND, YVES
France, LD (UDF/RPR)

M. Yves Galland is national secretary of the UDF (Union for French Democracy). Elected to the EP in 1979. Company director. Born Mar 8 1941; graduate in law. A Deputy Mayor of Paris and Paris councillor. Vice-president, Radical Party.

Addresses: 36, rue Sainte Croix de la Bretonnerie, 75004 Paris. 1, rue de Platre, 75004 Paris. Tel: 272 27 69.

GALLO, MAX
France, Soc (PS)

M. Max Gallo, academic and writer, was elected to the EP in 1984. Born Jan 7 1932. Government spokesman since 1983; member, PS steering committee. Alpes-maritimes deputy, 1981. Holder of doctorate in contemporary history; former professor, Lycée de Nice.

Addresses: 5, place du Panthéon, 75005 Paris. Tel: 549664 (personal) or 5567467 (assistant). 3, rue Massena, 06000 Nice.

GALLUZZI, CARLO ALBERTO
Italy, Comm (PCI)

Sgr Carlo Alberto Galluzzi, an accountant, joined the EP in the last Parliament and was re-elected in 1984. Member, central committee of PCI. Born Dec 2 1919.

Addresses: Via Fabio Quinto Pittore 31, 00138 Roma. Tel: 3450542. c/o Gruppo Communista, Consiglio Regione Tosca, Via Cavour 2, 50129 Firenze.

GATTI, NATALINO
Italy, Comm (PCI)

Sgr Natalino Gatti was elected to the EP in 1984. Vice-chairman, National Agricultural Cooperative Organization. Assessor in local government in Modena. Member, Chamber of Deputies, 1976–83. Born Dec 24 1939. Has degree in agriculture.

Address: Associazione Nazionale cooperative agricole, Via Guattoni 9, 00161 Roma.

GAUTIER, FRITZ
Germany, Soc (SPD)

Herr Fritz Gautier entered the EP in January 1980; re-elected in 1984. Genetic scientist. Chairman, Lower Saxony Young Socialists, 1976; member, SPD management committee for Braunschweig. Born Jan 17 1950.

Addresses: Schlossstrasse 8III, 3300 Braunschweig. Tel: (0531) 18277. Romintenstrasse 17, 3300 Braunschweig. Tel: (0531) 61 18 84.

GAWRONSKI, JAS
Italy, LD (PRI)

Sgr Jas Gawronski, a journalist, became an MEP in the previous Parliament and was re-elected in 1984, being appointed a vice-chairman of the EP Committee on Institutional Affairs in July 1984. Born Feb 7 1936.

Address: Largo Fontanella Borghese 19. Tel: 00186 Roma.

GAZIS, NIKOLAOS
Greece, Soc (PASOK)

Mr Nikolaos Gazis, a lawyer, was elected to the EP in 1984 and became a vice-chairman of its Legal Affairs and Citizens' Rights Committee in July 1984. Born 1903. Elected to Greek National Assembly in 1974.

Address: Omirou 54, 10672 Athens.

GERONTOPOULOS, KYRIAKOS
Greece, EPP (ND)

Mr Kyriakos Gerontopoulos, doctor and gynaecologist, was elected to the EP in 1984. Joined ONNED, the youth movement of the New Democracy Party, in 1974; elected to students' movement central office in 1978, and to central council of New Democracy students' movement, where he held office until 1980. Member, ONNED Executive Committee, responsible for policy development, since 1982. Born 1956; educated University of Athens.

Address: ONNED, Nikitara 2–4, 10678 Athens.

GIAVAZZI, GIOVANNI
Italy, EPP (DC)

Sgr Giovanni Giavazzi, a lawyer, was elected to the EP in 1979 and became a vice-chairman of the EPP Group in July 1984. President, since 1978, of Credito Bergamasco Bank, in which he has worked for more than 20 years. President of the Bergamo Agricultural Association. 1952–56: member, board of governors of the main Bergamo Hospital. In 1956, elected to the Bergamo City Council with responsibility for town planning, finance and legal affairs. In 1964, President of the Provincial Administration. Re-elected to the Provincial Council in 1970; for five years was leader of the DC group. Born Apr 14 1920.

Address: Via Masone, 32, 24100 Bergamo.

GIUMMARRA, VINCENZO
Italy, EPP (DC)

Sgr Vincenzo Giummarra, a lawyer, was elected to the EP in 1979. Formerly assistant in the Faculty of Criminal Case Law at the University of Catania. Former member, Sicilian Regional Assembly, during five terms of office. Formerly chairman, Central Savings Bank for the Sicilian Provinces. Born May 9 1923.

Address: Via Marchese Ugo 74, 90141 Palermo.

GLEZOS, EMMANOUIL
Greece, Soc (PASOK)

Mr Emmanouil Glezos was elected to the EP in 1984. Born 1922. Journalist. Parliamentarian in the Democratic Union of the Left in 1951 and 1961. Member of the present Greek Parliament.

Address: Fedriadon 71, 11364 Athens.

GLINNE, ERNEST
Belgium, Soc (PS)

Mr Ernest Glinne, elected to the EP in 1979, was chairman of its Socialist Group, 1979–84, when he became one of its vice-chairmen. Was vice-chairman of the group in the nominated EP which he joined in 1968. Elected an EP quaestor, July 1984. Member, Belgian Parliament, as deputy for Charleroi, 1961–80. Former Minister of Employment and Labour. Born Mar 30 1931; graduate in political, administrative and diplomatic science. Burgomaster of Courcelles, 1969–77.

Address: 1, square Salvador Allende, 6180 Courcelles. Tel: (071) 45 30 66.

GREDAL, FRU EVA
Denmark, Soc (S)

Fru Eva Gredal was elected to the EP in 1979 and became a vice-chairman of the Socialist Group in 1984; previously a member of its bureau. Danish MP, 1971–75, and 1977–79; Minister for Social Affairs, 1971–73 and 1975–78. Chairman, EP delegation on relations with United States, from 1979. Took her university course at evening school when an office worker. In 1954 became a social services adviser; chairman, Danish Social Advice Association, 1959–67. Born Feb 19 1927.

Address: Østbanegade 11, 2100 København Ø. Tel: (01) 42 40 53.

GREMETZ, MAXIME
France, Comm (PCF)

M. Maxime Gremetz was elected to the EP in 1979. Member, National Assembly for the Somme, 1978–81. Secretary, Central Committee of the French Communist Party and member of its political bureau. Metal worker. Born Sep 3 1940.

Address: Comité Central du PCF, 2 place du Colonel Fabien, 75940 Paris Cedex 19. 3, place Dewailly, 80000 Amiens.

GRIFFITHS, WINSTON
UK, South Wales, Soc (Lab)

Mr Winston Griffiths was elected a Vice-President of the EP in July 1984, and remained a member of the EP Regional Policy and Regional Planning Committee. Formerly a comprehensive school teacher. Born Feb 11 1943; educated Brecon Boys' Grammar School and Cardiff University College. BA (Hons) History; Diploma in Education. Member, Vale of Glamorgan Borough Council, 1973–76. Member of Methodist Church and local preacher. Married with one daughter and one son.

Addresses: 'Ty Lion', The Craig, John Street, Cefn Cribwr, Mid-Glamorgan CF32 0AB. Tel: (0656) 740526. S. Wales Euro Office, Welfare Hall, Hope Avenue, Aberkenfig, nr Bridgend, Mid-Glamorgan CF32 9PR. Tel: (0656) 725151.

GROENENDAAL, MEVR JESSICA
Netherlands, LD (VVD)

Mevr Jessica Groenendaal was elected to the EP in 1984. International civil servant, 1973–78, and then on staff of the EP Liberal and Democratic Group, 1979–84. Born Nov 24 1945.

Address: 25, rue de l'Europe, Bereldange, Grand Duchy of Luxembourg.

GUARRACI, ANSELMO
Italy, Soc (PSI)

Sgr Anselmo Guarraci is an executive member of the Italian Socialist Party. Elected to the EP in 1984. Formerly a regional secretary and an assessor of urban development in Palermo. Born Feb 14, 1926.

Address: Via Resuttana 454, 90100 Palermo.

GUCHT, KAREL DE
Belgium, LD (PVV–ELD)

Mr Karel de Gucht has been an MEP since May 1980. Lawyer. Member, PVV executive committee; national chairman, Young PVV, 1977–79. Born Jan 27 1954.

Addresses: O.L. Vrouwstraat 35A, Bus 6, 9370 Lebbeke. Tel: (052) 21 82 98. Groenewegel 14, 9380 Lebbeke-Wieze. Tel: (053) 77 82 82.

GUERMEUR, GUY
France, RDE (UDF/RPR)

M. Guy Guermeur was elected to the EP in 1984. Customs inspector. Sub-prefect. RPR deputy for Finistère, 1973–81. Douarnenez county councillor since 1975; Paris commune administrator since 1981. President, Parliamentary Association for Educational Freedom. Born Jan 11 1930; educated École Nationale d'Administration.

Address: Pen Ar Menez, 29100 Douarnenez.

HABSBURG, OTTO
Germany, EPP (CSU)

Herr Otto Habsburg was elected to the EP in 1979. Member of the French Academy for Moral and Political Science, the Portuguese Cultural Academy and the Spanish Royal Academy for Moral and Political Science. President, International Council of the European Documentation and Information Centre, 1953–60; subsequently honorary President; President, International Pan-European Union. Born Nov 20 1912. Writer.

Address: Hindenburgstrasse 15, 8134 Pöcking. Tel: 08157/1379

HAHN, WILHELM
Germany, EPP (CDU)

Herr Wilhelm Hahn was elected to the EP in 1979, a vice-chairman of its Committee on Youth, Culture, Education, Information and Sport until 1984. Chairman of the German committee of the European Schools Council; president, Germano-Indian Association (1978); general administrator, Institute for Foreign Relations, Stuttgart (1978). Born May 14 1909; holds doctorate of theology and was Professor of Theology and then Vice-Chancellor, Heidelberg University. From 1962–64, member of Bundestag; 1964–78 Minister of Culture, Baden-Württemberg.

Address: Im Hofert 3, 6900 Heidelberg. Tel: (06221) 802817. c/o Klaus Biltor, bachstrasse 32, 5300 Bonn 1.

HAMMERICH, FRU ELSE
Denmark, ARC (Folkebevaegelsen)

Fru Else Hammerich became one of the four co-chairmen of the new Arc-en-Ciel (Rainbow) Group in July 1984, having been chairman in the last Parliament of the Group for the Technical Coordination and Defence of Independent Groups of Members. Elected in 1979. Born Sep 7 1936. Fought European elections on list of anti-EEC coalition movement. Lecturer; specializes in paedological studies at Blaagaard Teachers' Training College.

Address: Glumsøvej 40, 2700 Brønshøj. Tel: (01) 607535.

HÄNSCH, KLAUS
Germany, Soc (SPD)

Herr Klaus Hänsch was elected to to the EP in 1979. Became a vice-chairman in July 1984 of the EP Political Affairs Committee on which he served in the last Parliament. Press adviser. Chairman of Mettman local SPD. Born Dec 15 1938.

Address: Akazienstrasse 5, 4000 Düsseldorf 22. Tel: (0211) 201978.

HAPPART, JOSÉ
Belgium, NI (PS)

Mr José Happart was elected to the EP in 1984. Major of Fourous since January 1984. Farmers' representative. Born Mar 14 1947.

Address: Rullen 69A, 3792 Fouron-St. Pierre. Tel: (087) 68 76 56.

HÄRLIN, BENNI
Germany, ARC (Grüne)

Herr Benedikt (Benni) Härlin, journalist, was elected to the EP in 1984. Worked in Berlin as the local editor for *Tageszeitung* and was press relations officer for the Network-Selfhelp organization. Born Jan 1 1957.

Address: Potsdamer Strasse 130, 1000 Berlin 30.

HEINRICH, FRAU BRIGITTE
Germany, ARC (Grüne)

Frau Brigitte Heinrich, journalist and foreign editor of the Berlin *Tageszeitung*, has campaigned since her university days for a new approach by the industrialized countries to the problems of the Third World. Born Jun 29 1941; educated Frankfurt University.

Address: Humboldtstrasse 86, 6000 Frankfurt am Main 1.

143

HEMELDONCK, MEVR MARIJKE VAN
Belgium, Soc (SP)

Mevr Marijke van Hemeldonck was a civil servant before becoming an MEP in the last Parliament. Expert on labour issues at OECD, ILO and United Nations committee on the status of women. Born Dec 23 1931.

Address: Graaf Urselstraat 2, 2510 Mortsel. Tel: (03) 440 73 43.

HERMAN, FERNAND
Belgium, EPP (PSC–PPE)

Mr Fernand Herman was elected to the EP in 1979. Was Secretary-General of the Cercles populaires européens (European people's movement). Minister of Economic Affairs, 1975–77; Senator for Brussels, 1977–78, and member of Parliament for Brussels from 1978. Director of the National Society for Investment (SNI) confederation of industry, 1964–75, Born Jan 23, 1932; doctor of law and degree in economics at the Catholic University of Louvain.

Address: Rue Franklin 28, Boîte 1, 1040 Bruxelles. Tel: (02) 735 87 91.

HERSANT, ROBERT
France, EPP (UDF/RPR)

M. Robert Hersant, elected to the EP in 1984, is founder-president of the Hersant press group and, since 1972, vice-president of the National Federation of the French Press. Managing Director of *Le Figaro*. Oise deputy, 1956–57. Mayor of Ravenel, 1953–59, and Liancourt, 1967–74. County councillor, 1954–73. Born Jan 31 1920.

Address: 'Le Figaro', 37, rue du Louvre, 75002 Paris.

HEUVEL-BLANK, MEVR IEN VAN DEN
Netherlands, Soc (PvdA)

Mevr Ien van den Heuvel-Blank was elected to the EP in 1979 and in that Parliament became a vice-chairman of the Socialist Group. Chairman of PvdA from 1974–79. Member of the First Chamber, States General since 1974. Chairman of PvdA from 1974–79; chairman of PvdA's women's organization 1968–74. Born Aug 7 1927.

Address: Engelberg 8, 3956 VL Leersum. Tel: (3434) 51376.

HINDLEY, MICHAEL
UK, Lancashire East, Soc (Lab)

Mr Michael Hindley was elected to the EP in 1984 and became a vice-chairman of the External Economic Relations Committee. Born Apr 11 1947; educated Clitheroe Royal Grammar School and London and Lancaster Universities. Has been a teacher in Poland and in East Germany; at time of election was tutor at Trade Union Study Centre, Blackburn. Member, Hyndburn District Council, since 1979, leader of the council since 1981. Candidate for Labour at Blackpool North in general election, 1983. Former shop steward of the General, Municipal, Boilermakers and Allied Trades Union. Married with one daughter.

Address: 27 Commercial Road, Great Harwood, nr Blackburn, Lancs. BB6 7HX.

HOFF, FRAU MAGDALENE
Germany, Soc (SPD)

Frau Magdalene Hoff was elected to the EP in 1979. Member, federal executive of SPD. Civil engineer and lecturer on industrial safety and accident prevention. Born Dec 29 1940. Has served on Hagen Federation of SPD and on Hagen Municipal Council.

Address: Zur Höhe 72A, 5800 Hagen. Tel: (02331) 75661/70854.

HOFFMANN, MME JACQUELINE
France, Comm (PCF)

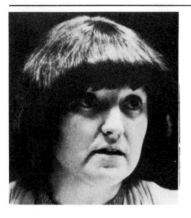

Mme Jacqueline Hoffmann, a welder, was elected to the EP in 1979. Member of the Central Committee of the French Communist Party. Born Dec 26, 1943.

Address: 32, square Eugénie Cotton, 78190 Trappes.

HOFFMANN, KARL-HEINZ
Germany, EPP (CDU)

Herr Karl-Heinz Hoffmann became a member of the EP in 1979. Vice-chairman, EP Transport Committee, from July 1984. Active trade unionist since 1945, starting in IG Chemie, then in IG Bergbau and OTV. Elected deputy chairman of OTV (public services and transport) 1968, re-elected in 1972 and 1976. Served on Economic and Social Committee of EEC from 1965, being chairman from 1970 of working party on transport and communications. Member, Konrad Adenauer Foundation advisory board on trade unions. Born Feb 14 1926.

Address: August-Lämmle-Strasse 5, 7062 Rudersberg-Steinenberg. Tel: (07183) 6670.

HOON, GEOFFREY
UK, Derbyshire, Soc (Lab)

Mr Geoffrey Hoon, a barrister, was elected to the EP in 1984; joined the EP Legal Affairs Committee, and became vice-chairman of the EP committee on Verification of Credentials from July 1984. Born Dec 1953. Worked in local furniture factory before reading law at Cambridge University. Former university lecturer; a barrister in Derby at time of election. Married.

Address: 10 Grosvenor Avenue, Breaston, Derbyshire, DE7 3AB.

HOWELL, PAUL
UK, Norfolk, ED (C)

Mr Paul Howell, elected to the EP in 1979, became ED (Conservative) Group spokesman on the EP Committee on Youth Affairs, Culture, Education, Information and Sport in July 1984. Farmer. Born Jan 17 1951; educated Gresham's School, Holt, and St Edmund Hall, Oxford (BA agriculture and economics). Desk officer for agriculture, Europe, and prices and consumer affairs at Conservative Research Department, 1973–75; political adviser to Minister of Agriculture to February 1974, and then to shadow Minister of Agriculture and shadow Minister for Prices and Consumer Affairs.

Address: The White House Farm, Bradenham Road, Scarning, East Dereham, Norfolk NR20 3EY. Tel: (036 287) 239.

HUCKFIELD, LESLIE
UK, Merseyside East, Soc (Lab)

Mr Leslie Huckfield was elected to the EP in 1984; became a vice-chairman of the EP Transport Committee in July 1984. Born Apr 7 1942; educated Prince Edward's Grammar School, Evesham; Keble College, Oxford, and University of Birmingham. Labour MP for Nuneaton, 1967–83; contested Warwick and Leamington, 1966. Under Secretary of State for Industry, 1976–79. Former member of the Parliamentary Labour Party transport group. Member of Labour Party NEC in 1978. Before entering Parliament was a lecturer and parliamentary adviser to British Safety Council.

Address: 97 Martland Mill Lane, Wigan, Gtr Manchester WN5 0LZ.

HUGHES, STEPHEN
UK, Durham, Soc (Lab)

Mr Stephen Hughes, a local government officer, was elected to the EP in 1984. Joined the EP environment committee. Born Aug 19 1952, educated St Bede's School, Lanchester, and Newcastle Polytechnic. Former research assistant to an MEP; former chairman of a local council. Member General, Municipal, Boilermakers and Allied Trades Union, and People against Loneliness. Married with one son and twin daughters.

Address: 4 Lime Street, Waldridge, Chester le Street, Co. Durham DH2 3SG.

HUME, JOHN
UK, N Ireland, Soc (SDLP)

Mr John Hume was elected to the EP in 1979 and became treasurer of the Socialist Group and then a member of its bureau, to which he was reappointed in July 1984. N. Ireland's Minister for Commerce in 1974. Born Jan 18 1937. MP for Foyle, Northern Ireland Parliament, 1969–73; SDLP member for Londonderry, NI Assembly, 1973–75, and NI Constitutional Convention, 1975–76.

Address: 6 West End Park, Londonderry, N. Ireland.

HUTTON, ALASDAIR
UK, South of Scotland ED(C)

Mr Alasdair Hutton, who was elected to the EP in 1979, continues in the new Parliament to be ED group spokesman on regional policy. From 1964–79, a British Broadcasting Corporation announcer; previously newspaper reporter. Born May 19 1940; educated Dollar Academy, Scotland, Brisbane State High School and Melbourne University. Member of Territorial Army's Scottish Parachute Battalion for over 20 years; currently second-in-command. Married with two sons.

Addresses: 34 Woodmarket, Kelso TD5 7AX, Roxburgshire, Scotland. Tel: (0573) 24369. Rosebank, Shedden Park Road, Kelso TD5 7PX, Roxburgshire, Scotland. Tel: (0573) 25262.

IODICE, ANTONIO
Italy, EPP (DC)

Sgr Antonio Iodice was elected to the EP in 1984. Was a lecturer in institutes of higher education. Former provincial secretary of Naples DC. Municipal councillor, 1973–78 and a member of the DC regional committee for Campania. Began his political career in the 'Italian Youth for Catholic Action' movement, and in the early 1960s was its diocesan president, later becoming its regional secretary. National councillor of teachers' trade union, SNALS. Born Oct 28 1941.

Address: Via G. Ferraris 2, 80014 Giugliano (Napoli).

IPPOLITO, FELICE
Italy, Comm (PCI)

Sgr Felice Ippolito was elected in 1979;
vice-chairman of the EP's Committee on Energy,
Research and Technology, until 1984; still a
member of it. Professor of Geology at the
University of Rome; editor of several scientific
magazines. Has served as vice-chairman,
Committee of the Geological and Mining Sciences,
National Research Centre; member, Upper
Council on Mining and of Technical Committee on
Hydrocarbons, Ministry of Industry. Born Nov 16
1915. Degree in civil engineering.
General-Secretary of National Committee for
Nuclear Energy.
*Addresses: Via Archimede 35, 00197 Roma. Tel:
877094. Podere Poltricia n.1, 53040 Cetonas (SI).
Tel: (0578) 23118.*

IVERSON, JOHN
Denmark, Comm (SF)

Mr John Iverson is a teacher. Age: 29. Secretary to
the Socialist Peoples' party (SF) in the EP.
Member, SF committee on Europe, Chairman,
Aarhus party, and for several years member,
party's national executive. Put as No. 2 on party
list on grounds of sexual equality; obtained only
enough votes to qualify for third place. A woman,
Marianne Bentsen-Pedersen, won the second
highest number of votes, but because the first place
was taken by a woman, Ms Bodil Boserup, Mr
Iversen was given the party's second seat in the EP,
to be taken when the Greenland MEP departs on
Jan 1 1985.

JACKSON, MRS CAROLINE
UK, Wiltshire, ED (C)

Mrs Caroline Jackson, who has been head of the
London office of the ED group in the EP and
adviser to it on employment and social policy, was
elected to the Parliament in 1984. Married to Mr
Robert Jackson, MP for Wantage, and former
MEP for Upper Thames. Former member, Oxford
City Council. Contested Birmingham Erdington,
Feb 1974. Member, National Consumer Council.
Born Nov 5 1946; educated St Clare School,
Penzance; PhD from Oxford University and former
research fellow at St Hugh's College, Oxford.
Member of the EP Committee on Women's Rights.

*Address: 74 Carlisle Mansions, Carlisle Place,
London SW1. Tel: (01) 828-6113.*

JACKSON, CHRISTOPHER
UK, East Kent, ED (C)

Mr Christopher Jackson has been reappointed ED Group spokesman on,overseas development; also specializes in EEC constitutional issues. Elected to the EP in 1979. Director of corporate development, Spillers Ltd, 1974–80. Conservative parliamentary candidate at East Ham South, 1970, and Northampton North, February 1974. Born May 24 1935; educated Rye Grammar School; Kingswood School, Bath; Magdalen College, Oxford; Frankfurt University; London University. Married with two children.

Address: Medlars, Oak Hill Road, Sevenoaks, Kent. Tel: (0732) 456688.

JAKOBSEN, ERHARD
Denmark, ED (CD)

Mr Erhard Jakobsen was elected to the EP in 1979; member since 1973. Chairman of the Centre Democrats Party; an MP in Denmark; former mayor of Gladsaxe. A leading defender of the EEC in Denmark. Originally was a Social Democrat, but broke away in 1973 to form the new party. Chairman, European Movement in Denmark, 1964–73. Born Feb 25 1917.

Address: Søvej 27, 2880 Bagsvaerd.

JEPSEN, FRU MARIE
Denmark, ED (KF)

Fru Marie Jepsen became an MEP in 1984. Member, Aarhus County Council and Silkeborg Town Council; a director of the Aarhus Theatre and vice-chairman of the county's leisure and culture committee. Also a director of the Silkeborg Seminarium and of the local tourist board. Special interests: social and cultural problems. Born Mar 27 1940.

Address: Hattenaes 19, 8600 Silkeborg.

JOSPIN, LIONEL
France, Soc (PS)

M. Lionel Jospin, who was elected to the EP in 1984, was a teacher. National Secretary of the Socialist Party (PS); First Secretary since 1981. Born Jul 12 1937; educated ENA. Paris deputy since 1981 and city councillor.

Address: 10, rue de Solférino, 75333 Paris Cedex 07.

JUPPÉ, ALAIN
France, RDE (UDF/RPR)

M. Alain Juppé, elected to the EP in 1984, has been director-general of the Paris Commune since 1980. Born Aug 15 1945; educated École Nationale d'Administration. Assistant to Mayor of Paris; city councillor since 1983. Chairman, RPR departmental federation since 1979; member of party's central and executive committees and political council. Jacques Chirac's economic adviser and deputy director of his campaign for election to the French presidency, 1981. General secretary, Club 89 (an Opposition political 'think tank') 1981.

Address: Hôtel de Ville de Paris, 75004 Paris RP.

KILBY, MICHAEL
UK, Nottingham, ED (C)

Mr Michael Kilby, manager for General Motors Components, Europe, was elected in 1984. Born 1924; educated Dunstable School and Luton College of Technology (Eng). Has experience in European and international industry, with special knowledge of European trade regulations, terms, conditions, competition and pricing policy. As European planning manager for General Motors, he worked in all European countries, including those in Eastern Europe. On EP Committee on External Economic Relations from July 1984.

Address: Grange Barn, High Street, Old Haversham, Milton Keynes, Bucks. Tel: (0908) 313613.

151

KLEPSCH, EGON
Germany, EPP (CDU)

Herr Egon Klepsch was elected leader of the European People's Party (Christian Democratic) Group in July 1984, a position he held 1979–82 and in the nominated Parliament, 1977–79. A Vice-President of the EP, 1982–84; member since 1973 being elected in 1979. CDU member of Bundestag, 1965–80. Born Jan 30 1930. PhD. Former lecturer on international politics. President, European Union of Young Christian Democrats, 1964–70.

Address: Luderitzstrasse 41, 5400 Koblenz-Pfaffendorf. Tel: 753 42.

KLINKENBORG, JAN
Germany, Soc (SPD)

Herr Jan Klinkenborg was elected to the EP in 1979. Vice-chairman, EP Transport Committee from July 1984; previously a committee member. Burgomaster of Emden. Member, SPD Council and SPD Bureau of Weser-Ems. Born Sep 26 1935. Chairman of a works council.

Addresses: Uphuser Strasse 9a, 2970 Emden. Tel: (04921) 24009. Friedrich-Ebert Strasse 70, 2970 Emden. Tel: (04921) 29017/18.

KLÖCKNER, MICHAEL
Germany, ARC (Grüne)

Herr Michael Klöckner, a journalist, was elected to the EP in 1984. Born Jun 10 1955.

Address: Ohlauer Strasse 44, 1000 Berlin 36.

KUIJPERS, WILLY
Belgium, ARC (VU–EVA)

Mr Willy Kuijpers was elected to the EP in 1984. Deputy for Louvain in Belgian Chamber of Representatives since 1971. German language teacher. Founder member of People's Union Party. Born Jan 1 1937.

Address: Swertmolenstraat 23, 3020 Herent. Tel: (016) 22 96 42.

KYRKOS, LEONIDAS
Greece, Comm (KKE-es)

Mr Leonidas Kyrkos was elected to the EP in 1981 and re-elected in 1984. Elected to Greek National Assembly in 1961, 1963, 1964, 1974 and 1977. Born Oct 12 1924. Journalist.

Address: Kalidromious 19, 10680 Athens. Tel: (1) 3633238.

LALOR, PATRICK J.
Ireland, RDE (F-Fàil)

Mr Patrick (Paddy) Lalor was elected a Vice-President of the EP in 1982 being re-elected in July 1984; a quaestor, 1979–82. Elected an MEP in 1979 and became a vice-chairman of the DEP (now RDE) Group; re-elected in 1984. Parliamentary Secretary to Taoiseach and to Minister for Defence and Government Chief Whip, 1977–79. Born Jul 21 1926; educated Knockbeg College, Co. Carlow. Member of Dail, 1961–81; Minister for Industry and Commerce, 1970–73; Minister for Posts and Telegraphs, 1969–70. Opposition chief whip, 1973–77.

Address: Main St, Abbeyleix, Co. Portlaoise.

LAMBRIAS, PANAYIOTIS
Greece, EPP (ND)

Mr Panayiotis Lambrias, a publicist, journalist and lawyer, was elected to the EP in 1984 and became a vice-chairman of the EPP Group. Member of Parliament and Secretary of State attached to the President's Office, 1974–77, Secretary of State for Tourism, 1977–81. Writes for many newspapers; director since its inception of 'Mesimvrini'. Has translated and supplemented Unesco's three-volume dictionary of social sciences. Responsible for the Greek edition of General de Gaulle's memoirs and the Greek edition of Time-Life Science Library.

Address: Vas. Sofias 7, 10671 Athens.

LANGES, HORST
Germany, EPP (CDU)

Herr Horst Langes, former headmaster, was elected an MEP in 1979; member of the Rhineland Palatinate 'Land' Assembly 1967–69. Secretary of State to the Rhineland-Palatinate Ministry of Culture, Education and Religious Affairs 1974–79. Member, Trier municipal council from 1960, and of the Trier executive and the federal committee of CDU. Born Dec 2 1928.

Addresses: Bonhöfferstrasse 32, 5500 Trier. Tel: 31659. CDU-Geschäftsstelle, Kaiserstrasse 24, 5500 Trier. Tel: 48434.

LECANUET, JEAN
France, EPP (UDF/RPR)

M. Jean Lecanuet, elected to the EP in 1979, is President of l'Union pour la démocratie française (UDF) and of the Centre des Démocrates Sociaux (CDS). Senator since 1977; chairman of the Foreign Affairs Committee of the Senate; Mayor of Rouen and President of the Conseil Général of the Seine-Maritime department. Born Mar 4 1920; graduate in literature and agrégé in philosophy. Minister of State, Lord Privy Seal, Minister of Justice, 1974–76.

Addresses: 42 bis, bd de la Toux-Maubourg, 75007 Paris. Tel: 550 34 20. 41, rue Thiers, 76041 Rouen.

LE CHEVALLIER, JEAN-MARIE
France, DR (FN)

M. Jean-Marie Le Chevallier is M. Le Pen's principal private secretary. Elected to the EP in 1984. Born Nov 22 1936. Former member, Economic and Social Council. Director general, Rennes Chamber of Commerce and Industry, 1965–76. Administrator, Pinault-Investments Society.

Address: 11, rue de la Condamine, 75017 Paris.

LEHIDEUX, MME MARTINE
France, DR (FN)

Mme Martine Lehideux, member of the National Front's central committee. Born May 27 1933. Elected to the EP in 1984.

Address: 20, rue Camille Perier, 78400 Chatou.

LEK, BRAM VAN DER
Netherlands, ARC (PSP)

Mr Bram van der Lek was elected to the EP in 1984. Professor of biology and former president of a union of scientists. Born May 20 1931. For many years a member of the Second Chamber, before being elected more recently to the First Chamber.

Address: Korte Boslaan 12, 3722 BB Bilthoven.

LEMASS, MRS EILEEN
Ireland, RDE (F-Fáil)

Mrs Eileen Lemass has been a member of the Dail from 1977. Elected to EP in 1984. Widow. Daughter-in-law of former Irish Prime Minister, Mr Sean Lemass. Member of New Ireland Forum. Elected to Dublin Corporation in 1974 and subsequently in 1979. In the Dail is member of all-party committee on women's rights; chairman of party committee on social policy. Born Jul 1932.

Address: 34 Grosvenor Court, off Templeville Road, Dublin 12.

LEMMER, GERD
Germany, EPP (CDU)

Herr Gerd Lemmer, who was elected to the EP in 1979, was State Secretary to the Federal Ministry for Refugees and War Victims, and later in the Federal Ministry for Posts and Telecommunications, 1967–69. From 1969, executive with the Buckau R. Wolf AG Grevenbroich machine factory. Member, Remscheid municipal authority, 1952–75 (First Burgomaster, 1961–63); North Rhine-Westphalia 'Land' assembly, 1958–75. North Rhine-Westphalia 'Land' minister for federal affairs, 1962–66. Born Sep 13 1925.

Addresses: Hindemithstrasse 26, 5630 Remscheid. Tel: (02191) 72316. c/o Krupp Industrietechnik GmBH, Werk Buckau Wolf, Lindenstrasse 43, 4048 Grevenbroich. Tel: (02181) 602 326.

LENTZ-CORNETTE, MRS MARCELLE
Luxembourg, EPP (PCS)

Mrs Marcelle Lentz-Cornette has been an MEP since 1980; re-elected 1984. Former secondary school teacher, holding doctorate in natural sciences (chemistry) from Sorbonne. Communal councillor from 1969 and alderman from 1970. Elected a deputy in 1979. Born Mar 2 1927.

Address: 76, route d'Esch, Belvaux. Tel: 59 45 36.

LENZ, FRAU MARLENE
Germany, EPP (CDU)

Frau Marlene Lenz became chairman of the EP Committee on Women's Rights in July 1984; a vice-chairman in previous Parliament of committee of inquiry into situation of women in Europe. Elected to EP in 1979. A vice-president of the European Women's Union since 1977; executive member, 1975–77. Member, federal executive, CDU Women's Union. Translator. Born Jul 4 1932; educated University of Heidelburg. General Secretary, European Women's Union, 1967–71; adviser to external relations office, CDU federal headquarters, 1972–75. Rapporteur to the Bundestag's committee of inquiry on women and society.

Address: Burgstrasse 102, 5300 Bonn 2. Tel: (0228) 31 38 45.

LE PEN, JEAN-MARIE
France, DR (FN)

M. Jean-Marie Le Pen, a French presidential candidate in 1974, has been president of the National Front since 1972. Elected to EP in 1984 and became chairman of the new group, Droîtes Européennes. Born Jun 20 1928; educated Jesuit college of Saint-François Xavier, Vannes, and Lorient grammar school. Licentiate of laws. Paratroop officer, Indo-China, 1954. Seine deputy (independent), 1958–62.

Address: 8 Parc de Montretout, 92210 Saint Cloud.

LIENEMANN, MME MARIE—NOËLLE
France, Soc (PS)

Mme Marie-Noëlle Lienemann, a grammar school teacher, became an MEP in 1984. Born Jul 12 1951. Member, Socialist Party's executive bureau. Massy town councillor; Essonne county councillor.

Address: 8 Square des Néerlandais, 91300 Massy.

LIGIOS, GIOSUÈ
Italy, EPP (DC)

Sgr Giosuè Ligios, member of the European Parliament since 1972 – first elected in 1979 – was vice-chairman of the Committee on Agriculture until June 1979. Member, Italian Senate, since 1972 and for three years previously was regional councillor, Sardinia. President of the provincial government of Nuoro, 1964–69. born Dec 26 1928. Former Under Secretary of State at the Treasury. Director and provincial secretary of agricultural development.

Addresses: Via Goberti 11, 08100 Nuoro. Tel: (0784) 31534. Piazza Veneto, 08100 Nuoro. Tel: (0784) 33135.

LIMA, SALVATORE
Italy, EPP (DC)

Sgr Salvatore Lima was elected to the EP in 1979. Deputy director, Bank of Sicily and a law graduate. Member of Italian Chamber of Deputies 1968–79. Several times Under-Secretary of State for Finance and for the Budget; Mayor of Palermo; Commissioner Extraordinary of Sicilian Agrarian Reform Office, 1962–63. Secretary, Palermo Province DC party, 1961–68. Born Jan 23 1928.

Address: Via Danae 19, 90149 Palermo (Valdesi). Tel: 454561.

LINKOHR, ROLF
Germany, Soc (SPD)

Herr Rolf Linkohr, a physicist, was elected to the EP in 1979. Chairman of Stuttgart SPD from 1977, member since 1972. Born Apr 11 1941.

Address: Asangstrasse 219a, 7000 Stuttgart 61. Tel: (0711) 324945.

LIZIN, MRS ANNE-MARIE
Belgium, Soc (PS)

Mrs Anne-Marie Lizin was elected to the EP in 1979. On staff of Belgian Minister of economic affairs, 1972; staff of EEC Commissioners Simonet and Davignon, 1973–77, and staff of Belgian Minister for Foreign Affairs, 1977–79. Born Jan 5 1949. Economist.

Address: 6, chaussée d'Andenne, 5202 Ben-Ahin. Tel: (085) 230864 and (02) 735 73 21 (bureau).

LOMAS, ALFRED
UK, London North-East, Soc (Lab)

Mr Alfred Lomas was elected to the EP in 1979 and serves on its Political Affairs Committee. Secretary, London Co-operative Political Committee, 1965–79, and member, London regional executive of Labour Party. Former railway signalman. Born Apr 30 1928. Councillor at Stockport, 1962–65. Director, Theatre Royal, Stratford. Labour Party secretary/agent, 1959–65.

Addresses: 342 Hoe Street, Walthamstow, London E17. Tel: (01) 520 0756. 23 Hatcliffe Close, London SE3. Tel: (01) 852 5433.

LONGUET, GÉRARD
France, LD (UDF/RPR)

M. Gérard Longuet is treasurer of the Radical Party and a member of its executive committee. Became an MEP in 1984. Civil administrator and sub-prefect. UDF deputy for the Meuse, 1978–81. Meuse county councillor. Born Feb 24 1946; educated École Nationale d'Administration.

Address: Parti Républicain, 1, rue de Villersexel, 75007 Paris.

LOO, CHARLES-EMILE
France, Soc (PS)

M. Charles-Emile Loo, a typographer, was elected to the EP in 1979; director of a workers' cooperative. Member, Socialist Party executive. Born Mar 4 1922. A vice-chairman of Socialist Group in EP until 1984. Deputy Mayor of Marseilles. Deputy, Bouches-du-Rhône, 1967–68 and 1973–78. Has been First Secretary, Socialist Federation, Bouches-du-Rhône. Vice-president, National Assembly, 1974–75.

Addresses: Socoma, 1 rue Forbin, 13003 Marseille. Tel: 959107. 8 bis, chemin du Souvenir, 13007 Marseille. Tel: 521288.

LOUWES, HENDRIK
Netherlands, LD (VVD)

Mr Hendrik Louwes, a farmer, was elected to the EP in 1979. On the EP Budget Committee formed in July 1984. Has served in Dutch First Chamber and been First Vice-President of his party's group. Born Feb 3 1921; educated Royal High School. Groningen; Wageningen Agricultural College and University of Illinois. Served as chairman of COPA working party on alcohol.

Address: Westpolder 22, 9975 WJ Ulrum. Tel: (05956) 1504.

LUSTER, RUDOLF
Germany, EPP (CDU)

Herr Rudolf Luster, member of the Bundestag from 1976 and of the European Parliament since 1978; elected in 1979. A vice-chairman of EP Legal Affairs Committee until 1984. Barrister since 1963; notary since 1970. Member, board of trustees of Gesellschaft für Zukunftsfragen. Member, CDU since 1945. For many years member, CDU executive, 'Land' of Berlin and district chairman in Berlin-Steglitz; member, Federal Party Tribunal of CDU, since 1973. Berlin city councillor, 1950–51; member of Berlin Parliament, 1967–76. Born Jan 20 1921.

Addresses: Platz der Republik, Reichstagsgebäude, 1000 Berlin 21. Tel: (030) 39772437. Holbeinstrasse 60, 1000 Berlin 45.

LYNGE, FINN
Denmark, Greenland, Soc (Siumut)

Mr Finn Lynge was elected to the EP in 1979 and leaves at the end of 1984 when Greenland leaves the EEC. Director of the Greenland radio service, a former Catholic priest. Born Apr 22 1933. Brilliant linguist, speaking eight languages, and a formidable debater on cultural topics. Educated as a Catholic priest and was an assistant parish priest in the USA. In 1965 he became a parish priest in Godthaab, Greenland. He was relieved of this post when he got married.

Address: Boks 272, 3900 Nuuk/Godthaab, Grønland.

McCARTIN, JOHN JOE
Ireland, EPP (F-Gael)

Mr John Joe McCartin was elected a vice-chairman of the EP Committee on social affairs and employment in July 1984; served on it and the Transport Committee in previous Parliament. Farmer and company director. Member of Dail since 1981; senator, 1973–81. Born Apr 24 1939; educated St Patrick's College, Cavan. Has served on Leitrim County Council, Leitrim County Committee of Agriculture; the General Council of Committees of Agriculture (chairman, 1970–72); and North-Western Health Board.

Address: Mullyaster, Newtowngore, Carrick-on-Shannon, Co. Leitrim. Tel: (049) 34 395.

McGOWAN, MICHAEL
UK, Leeds, Soc (Lab)

Mr Michael McGowan was cooperative employment development officer with Kirklees Council until he was elected to the EP in 1984. Member EP Committee on Development and Cooperation. Born May 19 1940; educated schools in Yorkshire and Leicester University. Former lecturer and BBC journalist. Member of a local council, former candidate for parliamentary election. Member of the National Union of Journalists, and Transport and General Workers Union. Married with two sons and a daughter.

Address: 3 Grosvenor Terrace, Otley, W. Yorks. LS21 1HJ.

McMAHON, HUGH
UK, Strathclyde West, Soc (Lab)

Mr Hugh McMahon, elected to the EP in 1984, was then an assistant head teacher. Born Jun 17 1938; educated Glasgow University and Jordanhill College of Education. Former Parliamentary candidate. Member, Scottish executive committee, Labour Party. Founder member and chairman of the Socialist Education Association in Scotland; member, Scottish Council of the Fabian Society, and of the Socialist Health Association.

Address: 6 Whitlees Court, Ardrossan, Ayrshire.

McMILLAN-SCOTT, EDWARD
UK, York, ED (C)

Mr Edward McMillan-Scott was elected to the EP in 1984 and became a member of the Youth Affairs etc. Committee. A political consultant. Worked for seven years in the tourist industry in Britain and the Continent, and taught English in Italy. Research assistant to two MEPs. Was adviser to the Falkland Islands Government's office in London and to companies in telecommunications and computing. As political consultant, advised companies and organizations on the impact of legislation and governmental action within the UK and the EEC. Born Aug 15 1949. Married with two daughters.

Address: Wick House Farm, Wick, Pershore, Worcestershire. Tel: 0386-552366.

McSHARRY, RAY
Ireland, RDE (F-Fáil)

Mr Ray McSharry was elected to the EP in 1984 and became a vice-chairman of the RDE Group. Member of the Dail since 1969. Minister of State, Department of Finance, 1977–79; Minister for Agriculture, 1979–81; Deputy Prime Minister and Minister for Finance, Mar to Dec 1982. During Ireland's Presidency of the EEC in 1979 he was President of the Budget Council. Treasurer of Fianna-Fáil. Born Apr 1938.

Address: 'Alcantara', Pearse Road, Sligo.

MAFFRE-BAUGÉ, EMMANUEL
France, Comm (PCF)

M. Emmanuel Maffre-Baugé, a wine grower, was elected to the EP in 1979. National vice-chairman, Union of Table Wine Producers; member, Herault chamber of agriculture; departmental federation of farmers' unions (FDSEA). Former member, EEC consultative committee on wine. Born Dec 12 1921.

Address: Route de Gignac, Belarga, 34230 Paulhan. Tel: 980058.

MAHER, THOMAS
Ireland, LD (Ind)

Mr Thomas Maher, a farmer, who was President, Irish Farmers' Association, 1967–76, was first elected to the EP in 1979. Then elected one of its quaestors, being re-elected in July 1984. A vice-chairman of the Liberal and Democratic Group which he joined. Born April 29 1922; educated in Cashel. Member, Economic and Social Committee on the EEC, 1973–78; former President, Irish Agricultural Organization Society, and of the General Committee for Agricultural Cooperation in the EEC.

Addresses: Castlemoyle, Boherlahen, Cashel, Co. Tipperary. Tel: Boherlahen 106. Ladyswell Street, Cashel, Co. Tipperary.

MAIJ-WEGGEN, MEVR JOHANNA
Netherlands, EPP (CDA)

Mevr Johanna Maij-Weggen, a teacher, was elected to the EP in 1979. Has held various posts in the ARP (Anti-Revolutionary Party) and CDA; was a member of the organization committee and the ARVC/CDA Women's Advisory Group and of the executive of the Dutch Women's Council. Member, Dutch Government delegation to 32nd UN General Assembly, New York, 1977. Born Dec 29 1943; attended the AZVU nurses school, Amstelveen, and studied social pedagogy at Amsterdam Municipal University.

Address: Aquariuslaan 53, 5632 BB Eindhoven. Tel: (040) 416310.

MALANGRÉ, KURT
Germany, EPP (CDU)

Herr Kurt Malangré was elected to the EP in 1979. A vice-chairman of EP Committee on Verification of Credentials from July 1984 Chairman of Aachen regional council from 1976. Burgomaster of Aachen, 1971–73, and Chief Burgomaster since 1973. Joined Aachen municipal assembly in 1969, becoming political group chairman in 1970. Born Sep 18 1934. Lawyer.

Address: Wilhelmstrasse 2, 5100 Aachen. Tel: (0241) 72517 or 472202 or 32002 (Büro).

MALAUD, PHILIPPE
France, RDE (UDF/RPR)

M. Philippe Malaud, diplomat and former minister, was elected to the EP in 1984. Diplômé of the School of Political Science. Born Oct 2 1925. Plenipotentiary minister since 1975. Saône-et-Loire deputy, 1973–81.

Address: 4, rue du Commandant Schloesing, 75116 Paris.

MALÈNE, CHRISTIAN DE LA
France, RDE (UDF/RPR)

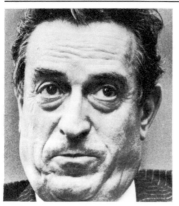

M. Christian de la Malène was re-elected chairman of the European Democratic Alliance (previously DEP) Group in July 1984. Elected to the EP in 1979; unsuccessfully contested the election for its Presidency in July 1979. Elected Chairman of DEP (European Progressive Democrats) Group in July 1979, a position he held in the outgoing nominated Parliament. Deputy 1958–77, former State Secretary for Information and former Minister for Scientific Research. Senator for Paris from 1977 and city councillor and First Assistant to Mayor of Paris. For 10 years member, UN General Assembly. Born Dec 5 1920. Doctor of law; sociologist.

Addresses: 31 rue Saint Dominique, 75007 Paris. Hôtel de Ville, 75196 Paris RP.

MALLET, JACQUES
France, EPP (UDF/RPR)

M. Jacques Mallet, a civil servant, elected to the EP in 1984. Principal private secretary to Jean Lecanuet, Minister of Justice, 1974–76. Member, steering committee, French Association for the Atlantic Community. Born Feb 5 1924.

Address: 278, boulevard Raspail, 75014 Paris.

MANCEL, JEAN-FRANÇOIS
France, RDE (UDF/RPR)

M. Jean-François Mancel, elected to EP in 1984, became vice-chairman, EP Economic and Monetary Affairs and Industrial Policy Committee. Has been national secretary of the RPR since 1981. Civil administrator. Oise deputy (RPR), 1978–81. County councillor and (since 1983) Beauvais town councillor. Deputy Mayor of Beauvais, 1971–77. Born Mar 1 1948; educated École Nationale d'Administration.

Address: 11bis, boulevard Amyot d'Inville, 60000 Beauvais.

MARCH, MME DANIELLE DE
France, Comm (PCF)

Mme Danielle de March, a former civil servant, a Vice-President of the European Parliament 1979–84. Member, Central Committee of French Communist Party. Born Aug 6 1939.

Addresses: Le Colbert, Entrée B, Avenue Colbert, 83000 Toulon. 1150A, chemin de Forgentier, 83200 Toulon. Tel: (94) 92 37 03.

MARCHAIS, GEORGE
France, Comm (PCF)

M. Georges Marchais, Secretary-General of the French Communist Party since 1972, was elected to the EP in 1979. National Assembly deputy since 1973. Former metal worker. Organizing secretary of PCF, 1961; Assistant Secretary-General of PCF, 1970–72.

Address: Comité Central du PCF, 2 place du Colonel Fabien, 75940 Paris Cedex 19. Tel: 238 66 55.

MARCK, POL
Belgium, EPP (CVP–EVP)

Mr Pol Marck, a member of the EP since 1981, was deputy secretary, Belgian farmers' union, 1957–81. Lawyer. Born Dec 6 1930. Assistant professor, Catholic University of Louvain since 1964.

Address: Schoonzichtlaan 46, 3009 Winksele-Herent. Tel: (016) 48 83 91.

MARINARO, SIGNORA FRANCESCA
Italy, Comm (PCI)

Signora Francesca Marinaro was elected to the EP in 1984. Took a degree in journalism in the University of Brussels; went to live in that city in 1963. Secretary of the federated PCI organization in Belgium. Born Nov 26 1952.

Address: Federazione PCI, 82 rue Saint-Lazare, 1030 Bruxelles.

MARSHALL, JOHN
UK, London North, ED (C)

Mr John Marshall was elected to the EP in 1979 and in July 1984 joined its Transport Committee. A stockbroker; previously university lecturer in economics. Born Aug 19 1940; educated Glasgow Academy and St Andrew's University. Contested Dundee East in 1964 and 1966 general elections and East Lewisham in February 1974. Member, Aberdeen Town Council, 1968–70; Ealing Borough Council, since 1971. Secretary, Friendship with Israel group in EP. Married with two sons.

Address: 2 Birkdale Road, London W5 1JZ. Tel: (01) 991 0162.

MARTELLI, CLAUDIO
Italy, Soc (PSI)

Sgr Claudio Martelli was elected to the EP in 1984. University professor. Deputy general secretary of the PSI, formerly responsible for information and cultural affairs. Member, Chamber of Deputies, since 1979. Born Sep 1943.

Address: Direzione PSI, Via del Corso, 476, 00186 Roma.

MARTIN, DAVID
UK, Lothians, Soc (Lab)

Mr David Martin, regional councillor, was elected to the EP in 1984 and became a vice-chairman of the Budgetary Control Committee. Born Aug 26 1954; educated in Edinburgh. Former accounts clerk and animal rights campaigner. Member, Lothians Regional Council, and Transport and General Workers Union. Married with one daughter.

Address: 34 Howden Hall Loan, Edinburgh EH16 6UY.

MARTIN, MME SIMONE
France, LD (UDF/RPR)

Mme Simone Martin became an MEP in 1979. President, Young Farmers Departmental Centre, Haute-Marne, 1972–74; vice-chairman, Young Farmers National Centre, 1974–78. General Secretary, Haute-Marne Chamber of Agriculture, 1979. Chairman, EDE (departmental stock farming board) of Haute-Marne, 1978, and member, Regional Economic and Social Committee of Champagne Ardenne. Born Apr 14 1943. Member, Republican Party. Saint Dizier town councillor.

Addresses: Thonnance les Moulins, 52230 Poissons. Tel: (25) 95 52 90. Résidence Cigny Val d'Ornel, Entrée 2, Appartement 19, 52100 Saint Dizier. Tel: (25) 05 75 86.

MASSARI, RENATO
Italy, Soc (PSDI)

Sgr Renato Massari was elected to the EP in 1984. Deputy Secretary, PSDI, from 1979, and member of its national executive. Member, Milan municipal council, 1951–63; Chamber of Deputies, 1963–83; State Under Secretary. Born Feb 24 1920.

Address: Direzione PSDI, Via Santa Maria in Via 12, 00187 Roma.

MATTINA, VINCENZO
Italy, Soc (PSI)

Sgr Vincenzo Mattina was elected to the EP in 1984. Graduate in jurisprudence. Has held important offices in trade union movement since 1960. Member, executive of PSI, with special responsibilities for the professional workers' section of the party. Chairman, Centre for Research into the Economics of Labour. Secretary General (since 1980) of the Federation of Italian Trade Unions. Member, Chamber of Deputies, since 1983. Born Jul 29 1940.

Address: c/o CREL, Piazza di Porta Pia 121, 00198 Roma.

MAVROS, GEORGIOS
Greece, Soc (PASOK)

Mr Georgios Mavros was elected to the EP in 1984. Born 1909; lawyer. He is a member of the Greek Parliament and between 1945 and 1964 was several times a minister.

Address: Pindarou 3, 10671 Athens.

MEGAHY, THOMAS
UK, South West Yorkshire, Soc (Lab)

Mr Thomas Megahy was elected to the EP in 1979; became a vice-chairman, EP committee on verification of credentials, and a member of the Parliament's legal affairs committee; now on Social Affairs and Employment Committee. Was senior lecturer in further education. Born Jul 16 1929; educated Ruskin College, Oxford, and Huddersfield Technical Teachers Training College. BSc (Economics), Dip Econ and political science, Diploma in Further Education. Kirklees Metropolitan District Council, 1973–78. Former member, Yorkshire and Humberside Regional and Economic Planning Council.

Address: 6 Lady Heton Grove, Mirfield, West Yorkshire WF14 9DY. County Hall, Wakefield, West Yorkshire WF1 2QW. Tel: 67111 Ext 2254.

MERTENS, MEINOLF
Germany, EPP (CDU)

Herr Meinolf Mertens, a farmer and forester, became an MEP in 1979. From 1966, member of North Rhine–Westphalia Land Assembly; previously a deputy district administrator. Member, district council of Arnsberg, Hochsauerland. Born Jun 4 1923; passed master's examination in agriculture.

Address: Bönkhausen 3, 5768 Sundern 6. Tel: (02933) 3680.

METTEN, ALMAN
Netherlands, Soc (PvdA)

Mr Alman Metten, who became an MEP in 1984, is a sociologist who taught in the University of Amsterdam. He has held various posts in the trade union movement. Born Oct 9 1948.

Address: Loggerhof 179, 1034 CG Amsterdam.

MICHELINI, ALBERTO
Italy, EPP (DC)

Sgr Alberto Michelini graduated in law and is well known as a journalist with TG1 (Italian Television news). Elected to the EP in 1984. He began in cultural programmes on Italian television in 1968, having worked for three years in the film industry as a scriptwriter and assistant director. From 1970, he worked with television news in Italy and abroad as a special correspondent. Since 1976, has been responsible for TG1's various studio broadcasts. Born Jul 25 1941.

Address: Via della Lungara 3, 00165 Roma.

MIERT, KAREL VAN
Belgium, Soc (SP)

Mr Karel van Miert, elected to EP in 1979, has held office as vice-chairman of the Federation of EEC Socialist Parties. Chairman of BSP (Belgische Socialistische Partij) Flemish Socialists since 1977. Born Jan 17 1942; diplomatic sciences; post-graduate studies in European Affairs. Served on staff of EEC Commissioners Mansholt and Simonet. Lecturer at Free University of Brussels.

Addresses: Merelstraat 7, 3078 Everberg. Tel: 759 87 65. Keizerslaan 13, 1000 Brussels. Tel: (02) 513 28 70.

MIHR, KARL-HEINRICH
Germany, Soc (SPD)

Herr Karl-Heinrich Mihr became an MEP in January 1980; re-elected in 1984. Metal worker. Employed at VW factory in Kassel becoming full-time chairman of the works council in 1972, and member of the general works council of Volkswagen AG Germany and of the supervisory board of the Volkswagen group. Member, SPD Federal Council; chairman, SPD group on Gudensberg Municipal Council. Born Jul 22 1935.

Address: Schwerinerweg 4, 3505 Gudensberg. Tel: (05603) 2830.

MITA, CIRIACO DE
Italy, EPP (DC)

Sgr Ciriaco de Mita, who became an MEP in 1984, is a lawyer who has held ministerial office in six Italian governments. Elected to Chamber of Deputies in 1963 and in 1968 appointed Under Secretary at the Ministry of the Interior. Minister for Industry in fourth Rumor government, Minister for Foreign Trade in the fourth and fifth Moro governments, and Minister for Southern Italy in the third and fourth Andreotti governments. Elected to DC national council in 1956 and became the party's political deputy-secretary in 1968. At the party congress in 1982 he was elected political secretary, confirmed again in 1984. Born Feb 2 1928.
Address: Direzione DC, Piazza del Gesù 46, 00186 Roma.

MIZZAU, ALFEO
Italy, EPP (DC)

Sgr Alfeo Mizzau, elected to the EP in 1984, is a business consultant. He has been assessor responsible for agriculture in the council of the autonomous Friuli–Venezia Giulia region since 1980. Joined DC in 1945 and has been active at all levels in the party, eventually becoming national adviser. Municipal councillor in Codroipo from 1952–70, he was also leader of the DC group in the regional assembly and assessor responsible for culture and measures to help voluntary associations and private schools. Member, European Committee for Minority Languages and Cultures. Aged 58.

Address: Via Codroipo, 96, 33100 Udine.

MOLINARI, EMILIO
Italy, NI (DP)

Sgr Emilio Molinari is an industrial expert and is employed at the Borletti plant. Elected to the EP in 1984. Founder of Comitati Unitari di Base (CUB) in Milan. Member, Milan city council, and Lombardy regional council. He is in the national secretariat of the Proletarian Democratic Party. Born Sep 1939.

Address: Via dei Giacinti 11, 20147 Milano.

MØLLER, PØUL
Denmark, ED (KF)

Mr Pøul Møller was elected to the EP in 1979 and became one of its Vice-Presidents, being re-elected to that office in July 1984. Member, bureau of ED Group; former group vice-chairman. Danish MP 1950–71. For many years he played a leading part in the affairs of the Danish Conservative Party and was Finance Minister, 1968–71. Former senior editor of *Berlingske Tidende* and former chairman of Dansk Arbejde, a trade promotion organization. Born Oct 13 1919. Member, Nordic Council, 1958–68; Assembly of Council of Europe, 1964–68.

Address: Carl Baggers Allé 6, 2920 Charlottenlund.

MOORHOUSE, JAMES
UK, London South and Surrey East, ED (C)

Mr James Moorhouse, elected to the EP in 1979, is a member, EP External Economic Relations Committee, being Conservative spokesman on that subject, and of ICC Commission on the Environment. Consultant and, from 1973–80, group environmental affairs adviser to Rio Tinto Zinc Corporation; previously with Shell. Contested St Pancras North in the general elections of 1966 and 1970. Born Jan 1 1924; educated St Paul's School and London University. Chartered engineer. Former member, EP transport committee. Married with a son and a daughter.

Address: 6 St James's Square, London SW1. Tel: (01) 839 2898.

MORAVIA, ALBERTO
Italy, Comm (PCI)

Sgr Alberto Moravia, who was elected to the EP in 1984, is well known as an author. His novels include *The Woman of Rome*, *Disobedience*, *Conjugal Love*, *Two Women*, *The Empty Canvas* (which won him the Viareggio Prize), *The Lie*, and *Time of Desecration*. He has also written many short stories and essays, and a number of plays. Born Nov 28 1907.

Address: Lungotevere della Vittoria 1, 00195 Roma.

MORONI, GIANNI
Italy, Soc (PSDI)

Sgr Gianni Moroni, elected to the EP in 1984, has been responsible for the running of the national office of the PSDI. Member, FINAM (National Health Service) council. A councillor and former mayor of Montecastrilli. Born Dec 13 1930 in Rome.

Address: Via Amerigo Capponi 16, 00193 Roma.

MORRIS, DAVID
UK, Mid and West Wales, Soc (Lab)

Mr David Morris, education advisor, was elected to the EP in 1984. Born Jan 28 1930; educated Central School, Llanelli; Ruskin College, Oxford; University College, Swansea; and Theological College, Aberystwyth. Worked as a labourer in a foundry, then as a minister, and then as education adviser to Gwent Education Committee. Former local and county councillor and parliamentary candidate in Brecon and Radnor, 1983. Chairman, Welsh region, Socialist Health Association. Special interests: regional policy, health service, foreign aid. Married.

Address: 118 Alma Street, Newport, Gwent.

MOTCHANE, DIDIER
France, Soc (PS)

M. Didier Motchane, an MEP since 1979, was a civil servant. Born Sept 17 1931. Member, executive, French Socialist Party.

Addresses: 5, rue Payenne, 75003 Paris. Parti Socialiste Français, 10 rue de Solferino, 75007 Paris.

MOUCHEL, JEAN
France, RDE (UDF/RPR)

M. Jean Mouchel was a member of the EP, 1982–83; re-elected in 1984 and became a vice-chairman, EP Agriculture, Fisheries and Food Committee and a joint treasurer of RDE Group. Farmer. Former vice-president, national federation of farmers' unions (FNSEA). Member, economic and social council; first vice-chairman, economic and social committee, Lower Normandy. Born May 22 1928. Deputy secretary, Permanent Assembly of Chambers of Agriculture; chairman, Normandy and Calvados regional chambers of agriculture; vice-chairman, Norman Dairy Union.
Addresses: Noyers-Bocage 14210 Evrecy. Tel: (31) 77 97 32. For correspondence: 6, promenade Mme de Sevigne, 14039 Caen CEDEX. Tel: (31) 84 42 41.

MUHLEN, ERNEST
Luxembourg, EPP (PCS)

Mr Ernest Muhlen became an MEP in July 1984. Elected a Luxembourg deputy in 1979 and was State Secretary, Ministry of State and Ministry of Finance, 1979–84; Lawyer; graduate of ISCEA in commerce and finance; doctor of economics at Law Faculty in Paris. Born Jun 8 1926.

MÜNCH, WERNER
Germany, EPP (CDU)

Herr Werner Münch, a high school teacher, was elected to the EP in 1984. Member, CDU federal cultural committee, since 1980. Born Sep 25 1940.

Address: Zur Tonkuhle 15, 2842 Lohne (Oldenburg).

MUNTINGH, HEMMO
Netherlands, Soc (PvdA)

Mr Hemmo Muntingh, elected to the EP in 1979, has served as chairman of the Fondation Européenne pour L'Environnement; was secretary of Landelijke Vereniging tot Behoud van de Waddenzee. Born Dec 30 1938; studied through Free University of Amsterdam.

Address: Westerweg 11, 9097 PD St. Jacobiparochie. Tel: (05189) 1673.

MUSSO, FRANÇOIS
France, RDE (UDF/RPR)

M. François Musso, a member of the Corsican economic and social committee, 1973–80, became an MEP in 1984. President, departmental federation of farmers' unions of Corsica, 1972–75, and of Alpes-Méditerrannée regional federation of farmers' unions, 1973–75. Member, departmental chamber of agriculture, 1973–80. Chairman, 1977–82, and founder, Land Development and Rural Establishment Company, in Corsica; chairman, Local Mutual Agricultural Credit Fund of Ajaccio; chairman and founder, Jeune Chambre Economique of Ajaccio. President, Ajaccio Agricultural Bank. Born Oct 1 1935.

Address: Domaine de la Sorba, Finosello, 20000 Ajaccio, Corse.

NATTA, ALESSANDRO
Italy, Comm (PCI)

Sgr Alessandro Natta was elected to the EP in 1984. Member, Italian Chamber of Deputies, since 1948. Chairman, central controlling committee of PCI. Born Jan 7 1918. Doctor of literature.

Address: Direzione PCI, Via delle Botteghe Oscure 4, 00186 Roma.

NEWENS, STANLEY
UK, London Central, Soc (Lab)

Mr Stanley Newens, former teacher and miner, was elected to the EP in 1984, and became a member of its Political Affairs Committee. Born Feb 4 1930; educated Buckhurst High School; University College, London; and Westminster Teacher Training College. MP for Epping, 1964–70, and Harlow, 1974–83. Organizing secretary of Harlow Council for Voluntary Service. Former president, London Cooperative Society. Chairman, Parliamentary Labour Party Eastern area group, 1974–83; vice-chairman, PLP foreign and commonwealth affairs group, 1982–83. Member, NUM 1952–56, and NUT since 1956. National chairman of Liberation.
Address: The Leys, 18 Park Hill, Harlow, Essex CM17 0AE.

NEWMAN, EDWARD
UK, Greater Manchester Central, Soc (Lab)

Mr Edward Newman, elected to the EP in 1984, became a vice-chairman of its EP Committee on Regional Policy and Regional Planning, and one of the only two males on the EP Committee on Women's Rights. Worked as a semi-skilled manual worker in light engineering and cable-making and then as postal worker in Manchester. Born May 14 1953. City councillor. Member, Socialist Health Association, Socialist Education Association, Union of Communication Workers.

Address: Flat 2, 30 Delalunays Road, Crumpsall, Manchester M8 6QS.

NEWTON DUNN, WILLIAM
UK, Lincolnshire, ED (C)

Mr William Newton Dunn, elected to EP in 1979, was previously a purchasing controller in the fertilizer division of Fisons Ltd. Born Oct 3 1941; educated Marlborough College; the Sorbonne; Gonville and Caius College, Cambridge, and INSEAD Business school, Fontainebleau. Contested Carmarthen in Feb 1974 election and Cardiff West in Oct 1974 election. Chairman, Vauxhall Conservative Association, 1975–77; former chairman, Bow Group European Energy Policy study group. Former shipping company executive. Member, EP Transport Committee, from July 1984.

Addresses: 42 Lanchester Road, London N6 4TA. Tel: 01-883-2527. 10 Church Lane, Navenby, Lincoln LN5 0EG.

NIELSEN, JØRGEN
Denmark, LD (V)

Mr Jørgen Brøndlund Nielsen has been a member of the EP since 1974, being elected in 1979. Former teacher and farmer. Member EP Agriculture Committee. Member of the Folketing for the Liberal Party (Venstre) 1971–79. Member, Danish delegation to the United Nations, 1972–73. Married. Born Aug 2 1939.

Addresses: c/o Hr Peder Porse, Boesvej 2, Svejstrup Enge, 8660 Skanderborg. Tel: (06) 577305. BS Ingemannsvej 4, 8230 Åbyhøj. Tel: (06) 154 742.

NIELSEN, FRU TOVE
Denmark, LD (V)

Fru Tove Nielsen has been a vice-chairman of the Liberal and Democratic Group at the European Parliament since 1979 when she was elected. Minister of Education 1973–75; consultant to the Danish Employers' Association. She has held a variety of posts within the Liberal Party (Venstre) and, as a teacher, she is familiar with educational problems and their political background. Member of the Danish Parliament (Folketing) 1972–73, and 1975–77. President, Nordic Council for Adult Education, from 1975. Born Apr 8 1941.

Address: Kokkedalsvej 5 B, Postbox 139, 2970 Hørsholm. Tel: (02) 57 00 65.

177

NORD, HANS
Netherlands, LD (VVD)

Mr Hans Nord was elected a Vice-President of the EP in July 1984; elected to the EP in 1979. Secretary-General of European Parliament, 1962–79. Treasurer, LD Group of EP, 1979–84. A vice-chairman, EP Committee on Institutional Affairs, in last Parliament. Born Oct 11 1919.

Address: 15, rue Conrad 1, Luxembourg. Tel: 44 02 83.

NORDMANN, JEAN-THOMAS
France, LD (UDF/RPR)

M. Jean-Thomas Nordmann became an MEP in 1982. Vice-president, Radical Party; former president, Young Radicals; former member of party's national bureau. Born Feb 16 1946; educated École normale superieure. Former technical adviser to various government ministries, including the departments of education, environment and trade. Paris councillor since 1983. Author of publications on French history and literature in the 19th and 20th centuries and two works on the history of radicalism.

Addresses: Parti Radicale, 1, place de Valois, 75001 Paris. Tel: 261 56 32. 14, rue Pirandello, 75013 Paris. Tel: 707 58 70.

NORMANTON, TOM
UK, Cheshire East, ED (C)

Mr Tom Normanton has been a member of the EP since 1973; elected in 1979. Industrialist and a director of public and private companies engaged in engineering, insurance and textiles. MP for Cheadle since 1970. Born Mar 12 1917; educated Manchester Grammar School, Manchester University and Manchester College of Technology. A director, Manchester Chamber of Commerce. Council member, CBI, 1958–64 and now a co-opted member. Member, EP Budgets Committee; former member, energy research and political affairs committees. Past president, British Textile Employers' Association; vice president, International Textile Federation.
Address: 5 Bollin Court, Macclesfield Road, Wilmslow, Cheshire SK9 2AP. Tel: (0625) 524930.

NOVELLI, DIEGO
Italy, Comm (PCI)

Sgr Diego Novelli, a journalist, was elected to the EP in 1984. Mayor of Turin since 1975. Responsible for the Turin edition of the journal *Unità*. Born May 22 1931.

Address: c/o Comune di Torino, via Milano 1, 10122 Torino.

O'DONNELL, THOMAS
Ireland, EPP (F-Gael)

Mr Thomas O'Donnell was first elected to EP in 1979, serving on its regional and transport committees. Minister for the Gaeltacht, 1973–77; Deputy for Limerick East since 1961. Born Aug 30 1926; educated Crescent College, Limerick; Salesian College, Pallaskenry, Co. Limerick; University College, Dublin. Fine Gael opposition frontbench spokesman on transport and power, 1969–73. Member, Dáil and Seanad Joint Library Committee, 1961–69; Special Committee on Company Law, 1962; Mid-Western Regional Tourism Organization, 1968–73; Muintir na Tire, 1951–61. He served as Chairman, Dromin Guild and member, Limerick Federation, 1955–58; Editor of the monthly journal *Landmark*, 1958–61.
Address: 37 Thomas Street, Limerick.

O'HAGAN, LORD
UK, Devon, ED (C)

Lord O'Hagan was elected in 1979; an Independent member of the nominated European Parliament 1973–75. Front bench spokesman in the House of Lords for the Conservatives, 1977–79, on the EEC, transport and environment. Born Sep 6 1945; educated Eton and New College, Oxford. Former deputy chief whip of ED group and former group spokesman on Political Affairs Committee; member, EP Legal Affairs Committee, from July 1984.

Address: 10 Union Street, Newton Abbot, Deven.

OPPENHEIM, FRU JEANETTE
Denmark, ED (KF)

Fru Jeanette Oppenheim, a lawyer, has been very active in her party's youth organization, and is now member of the city council of Copenhagen, and candidate for her party to the Folketing. Elected to EP in 1984. Chairman, Danish economic commission of the European Union of Women, and a member of Zonta International. Member, governing board of Danish Conservative Party. Born Aug 14 1952.

Addresses: Nikolaj Plads 26.3, 1067 København K. Tel: (01) 12 22 33 – 12 22 32. Brøndkaervej 15, 4th., 2500 Valby. Tel: (01) 46 13 31.

d'ORMESSON, OLIVIER
France, DR (FN)

M. Olivier d'Ormesson, journalist and farmer, was elected to the EP in 1979. Conseiller général for Val-de-Marne; Mayor of Ormesson-sur-Marne. Born August, 1918; graduate in economic and commercial science.

Addresses: avenue Olivier d'Ormesson, 94490 Ormesson sur Marne. Tel: 576 95 28 and 576 01 36. Château de Lézignan, Lézignan la Cebe, 34120 Pezenas. Tel: 98 12 95.

PAISLEY, THE REV IAN
UK, Northern Ireland, NI (Dem U)

The Rev Ian Paisley, leader of the Ulster Democratic Unionist Party, was elected an MEP in 1979; has represented North Antrim at Westminster since 1970; and is a member of the Northern Ireland Assembly. Moderator of the Free Presbyterian Church. Founded Protestant Unionist Party and sat as Protestant Unionist MP 1970–74. Born Apr 6 1926; educated Ballymena, South Wales Bible Colleges, and Reformed Presbyterian Theological College, Belfast. Ordained 1946. Won Bannside in 1970. MP in Stormont until 1972. Dem U MP for N Antrim in NI Assembly, 1973–75, and UUUC member, NI Constitutional Convention, 1975–76.
Address: The Parsonage, 17 Cyprus Avenue, Belfast BT5 5NT, N Ireland. Tel: 655694.

PAJETTA, GIANCARLO
Italy, Comm (PCI)

Sgr Giancarlo Pajetta, a journalist, became an MEP in 1979; an Italian MP since 1946. In 1925 joined the Communist Student Group. Called to Paris by the Party leadership in 1931, he directed the Communist Youth Federation which he represented at the IV National Congress. Became editor of *L'Unità* in 1945. Regional Secretary for Lombardy until 1948. Born June 24 1911.

Addresses: Via delle Botteghe Oscure 4, 00186 Roma. Via Pio Foà 8, 00152 Roma.

PANNELLA, MARCO
Italy, NI (PR)

Sgr Marco Pannella, elected to the EP in 1979, was a vice-chairman of its Committee on Institutional Affairs. Elected to the Italian Parliament in 1976; former chairman, parliamentary group of Partito Radicale. Journalist. One of party's founders; became Secretary-General. Chairman, League of Conscientious Objectors, since 1973. Founded 'Socialist Movement for Civil Rights and Liberties. May 13th League'. Born May 2 1930; degree in jurisprudence.

Addresses: Via Collalto Sabino 40, 00199 Roma. Tel: 65 62 557. Ufficio Studi, Gruppo Radicale, Centro Calamandrei, Corso Rinascimento 65, 00186 Roma. Tel: 65 45 112.

PANTAZI-TZIFA, KA KONSTANTINA
Greece, Soc (PASOK)

Ka Konstantina Pantazi-Tzifa was elected to the EP in 1981; re-elected 1984. Arrested in 1967 for opposition to the dictatorship. Member of Pasok's International Relations Committee and of the directorial committee of the Union of Women of Greece. Editor of Ethnos and Exormissi newspaper. Born Jan 13 1943. A graduate of the Institute of Interpreters, University of Geneva.

Address: Zatoras kai, Zichnis 2, 115 27 Athens. Tel: (1) 7707639.

PAPAPIETRO, GIOVANNI
Italy, Comm (PCI)

Sgr Giovanni Papapietro became an MEP in 1979. A vice-chairman of EP Committee in Youth, Culture, Education, Information and Sport, from July 1984. Member of the PCI Federal Committee, 1956–64, and in charge of the Cultural Committee. Secretary, Communist Federation of Bari, from 1964. Elected to the Central Committee and Central Control Committee at the XII Congress. Chief of the Communist Group at the Regional Council of Puglia. Born January 9 1931.

Address: Via Fanelli 247, 70100 Bari. Tel: (080) 41 40 78.

PAPOUTSIS, CHRISTOS
Greece, Soc (PASOK)

Mr Christos Papoutsis, an economist, became an MEP in 1984. Born 1953. Member of Pasok's central committee.

Address: Kithnou 17b, 11255 Athens.

PARODI, EOLO
Italy, EPP (DC)

Sgr Eolo Parodi, university lecturer, was elected to the EP in 1984. He graduated in medicine and surgery, and is a specialist in clinical and laboratory rheumatology. President, National Federation of Medical Practitioners, for seven years. Lectures on bacteriology in the School of Hygiene at the University of Genoa, specializing in laboratory work. Member of the Higher Health Council of Italy and of several ministerial committees. Born May 21 1956.

Address: Federazione Ordine dei Medici, Piazza della Vittoria 12/4, 16121 Genova.

PASQUALE, PANCRAZIO DE
Italy, Comm (PCI)

Sgr Pancrazio de Pasquale, elected in 1979, was chairman of the EP Committee on Regional Policy and Planning until 1984. Was secretary, Communist Federation of Messina. Member, Sicilian Regional Assembly since 1976 (chairman 1976–79); Chamber of Deputies, 1958–67; Messina Municipal Council, 1956–75. Born Aug 6 1925.

Addresses: Via Libertà 161/b, 90100 Palermo. Tel: (091) 295589. Via Consolare Pompea 51, 98100 Messina. Tel: (090) 56021.

PASTY, JEAN-CLAUDE
France, RDE (UDF/RPR)

M. Jean-Claude Pasty, civil administrator, became an MEP in 1984. Creuse deputy (RPR), 1978–81. RPR national delegate for agriculture since 1981. Deputy head, policy division, then head of research division, FORMA (agricultural markets guidance and regularization fund), 1965–67; technical adviser in private office of Robert Boulin (Minister of Agriculture), Bernard Pons (Secretary of State for Agriculture) and Jacques Chirac (Minister of Agriculture), 1968–73. Director of social affairs, Ministry of Agriculture, 1973–78. Born Jun 15 1937.

Address: 245, boulevard Saint-Germain, 75007 Paris.

PATTERSON, BEN
UK, Kent West, ED (C)

Mr Ben Patterson became ED (Conservative) Group spokesman on economic and monetary affairs in July 1984; spokesman on social affairs and employment, 1981–84. Elected to the EP in 1979. Deputy Head of London office of European Parliament, 1974–79. Contested Wrexham, 1970 general election. Born Apr 21 1939; educated Trinity College, Cambridge. Journalist and company director. Founder member, Conservative Group for Europe; member, Bow Group, since 1960 and from 1981 was member, CTU national committee. Married with two children.

Address: Kent West Conservative Office, 84 London Road, Tunbridge Wells, Kent TN1. Tel: (0892) 22582. Parliamentary Office, 44 Ridley Road, Wimbledon, London SW19. Tel: (01) 543 1840.

PEARCE, ANDREW
UK, Cheshire West, ED (C)

Mr Andrew Pearce, elected to the EP in 1979, became a member of its Environment Committee in July 1984. Was an official in the Customs Department of the European Communities Commission in Brussels, 1974–79. Founder and became chairman, British Conservative Association in Belgium. Parliamentary candidate at Islington North in general election in 1970 and by-election in 1969. Born Dec 1 1937; educated Rydal School, Colwyn Bay, and Durham University. In 1980, appointed chairman of ED group working party on agriculture. Married with four children.

Address: 30 Grange Road, West Kirby, Wirral, Merseyside L48 4HA. Tel: (051) 625 1896. Telex: 62 87 61 Bultel G.

PELIKAN, JIRI
Italy, Soc (PSI)

Sgr Jiri Pelikan was born in Czechoslovakia on Feb 7 1923. Journalist. Former Director of Radio Prague. Along with Dubcek, he was one of the promoters of the '68 'Spring'. Refugee, became a naturalized Italian. Elected to the EP in 1979; member of Czechoslovak Parliament, 1963–69.

Address: Via della Rotonda 36, 00186 Roma. Tel: 65 42 228.

PENDERS, JEAN
Netherlands, EPP (CDA)

Mr Jean Penders, elected to the EP in 1979, was on staff of Scientific Council for Government Policy, 1976–79; worked at Ministry of Foreign Affairs, 1968–72, and was Permanent Secretary to KVP Second Chamber Parliamentary Party, 1972–76. Born Apr 5 1939; holds doctorate in history (Nijmegen).

Address: Voorburgseweg 11, 2264 AC Leidschendam. Tel: (70) 27 86 91.

PERY, MME NICOLE
France, Soc (PS)

Mme Nicole Pery was elected a Vice-President of the EP in July 1984. Deputy Mayor of Ciboure (Pyrénées-Atlantiques). First elected to the EP in 1979. Born May 15 1943. A Socialist Party militant since 1967, she is a member of the 'regional identities' national committee. Former PS federal secretary for women's rights and national committee member.

Address: Rue Massy Ciboure, 64500 St Jean de Luz. Tel: 26 28 92.

PETERS, JOHANNES WILHELM
Germany, Soc (SPD)

Herr Johannes Wilhelm Peters, a miner, was elected to the EP in 1979; a vice-chairman, EP Committee on Social Affairs and Employment, until 1984; still a member of committee. Secretary, with responsibility for training, Mine and Energy Workers' Union, 1961–73. Born Dec 10 1927. Head of housing administration for Westphalia of Neue Heimst Building Society, 1973–79. Member, West Westphalian District Executive Committee of SPD; Dortmund City Council, 1969–79.

Address: Senftenbergstrasse 16, 4600 Dortmund 14. Tel: (0231) 23 03 74.

PETRONIO, FRANCESCO
Italy, DR (MSI-DN)

Sgr Francesco Petronio was an Italian MP from 1972–79. Elected to the EP in 1979. Journalist; editor of the magazine *L'Italiano*; contributor to *Il Secolo d'Italia* and several magazines. Former National President of FUAN and National Vice-Secretary of the party's youth movement. Councillor of Trieste in 1958; Rome, 1960–65; and of Milan. Member of party's central committee. Born Dec 21 1931.

Addresses: Via Felice Casati 20, 20124 Milano. Tel: 222 876. Via Quattro Fontane 22, 00184 Roma. Tel: 47 59 600.

PEUS, FRAU GABRIELE
Germany, EPP (CDU)

Frau Gabriele Peus, a lecturer, was elected to the EP in 1984. Member of the board of the International Association of Catholic Secondary School Teachers. Born Jul 25 1940.

Address: Am Schlossgarten 23, 4400 Münster.

PFENNIG, GERO
Germany, EPP (CDU)

Herr Gero Pfennig, elected to the EP in 1979, was a member of the Bundestag, 1977–80, and of the assemblies of the Council of Europe and WEU, 1977–80. Lawyer. Assistant in Faculty 09 (jurisprudence) at Free University of Berlin, 1968–73; assistant professor from 1973. Member, CDU, from 1964; district council, Berlin–Zehlendorf, 1971–75; member, Berlin Chamber of Deputies, 1975. Born Feb 11 1945.

Addresses: Waldsängerpfad 6, 1000 Berlin 38. Tel: (030) 803 6416. Reichstagebäude, Platz der Republik, 1000 Berlin 21. Tel: (030) 3977-2421/2424.

PFLIMLIN, PIERRE
France, EPP (UDF/RPR)

M. Pierre Pflimlin, elected in 1979, became President of the EP in July 1984; Vice-President, 1979–84. Mayor of Strasbourg, 1959–83. Prime Minister of France, 1958, and occupied many posts as a minister, including Minister for Overseas Territories, 1952–53, and Minister for Finance and Economic Affairs, 1955–56 and 1957–58. Elected member, National Constituent Assembly, for Bas-Rhin, 1945; re-elected 1946, 1951, 1956, 1958 and 1962. Member, Bas-Rhin General Council, 1951–70 and 1971–76; chairman, 1951–60. Born Feb 5 1907; doctor of law. President of MRP, 1956–59.

Addresses: Palais de la Musique et des Congrès, avenue Schutzenberger, 67000 Strasbourg. Tel: 35 03 00. 24 avenue de la Paix, 67000 Strasbourg.

PIERMONT, FRAU DOROTHEE
Germany, ARC (Grüne)

Frau Dorothee Piermont, elected to the EP in 1984, is an antiquarian bookseller from Bonn. A graduate in Romanist studies, she lived several years in Italy and France, among her occupations being that of lecturer in German politics and contemporary history in Paris, a worker for the independent Socialists (PSU) in France, and in the movement for women's rights. On her return to Germany, she was active in the peace activities of the Greens. Married with one son. Born Feb 27 1943.

Addresses: Postfach 210 232, 5300 Bonn 2. Rolandstrasse 13, 5480 Remagen-Rolandswerth. Tel: (02228) 1873.

PININFARINA, SERGIO
Italy, LD (PLI)

Sgr Sergio Pininfarina, elected to the EP in 1979, is a member of the board of directors of Ferrari and of the committee of the General Confederation of Italian Industry. Since 1966, chairman of Pininfarina; also chairman, Union of Industrialists of Turin. Born Sep 8 1926; qualified in mechanical engineering at Turin Polytechnic Institute and studied in England and United States. Former member, Court of Auditors, Bank of Italy.

Addresses: Piazzale Duca d'Aosta 18, 10129 Torino. Tel: 70 32 32. Unione Industriale, Via Fanti 17, 10128 Torino. Tel: 57 18 436.

PIQUET, RENÉ
France, Comm (PCF)

M. René Piquet, an MEP since 1979, has been elected to continue as one of the vice-chairmen of the Communist and Allies Group at the EP, being chairman of the French Communist MEPs. Former mechanic. Member of PCF political bureau, having been secretary of the Central Committee of the French Communist Party. Born Oct 23 1932.

Addresses: 1, allée Marc St Saëns, Boîte postale 1157, 31046 Toulouse. Comité Central du PCF, 2 place du Colonel Fabien, 75940 Paris Cedex 19. Tel: 238 66 55.

PIRKL, FRITZ
Germany, EPP (CSU)

Herr Fritz Pirkl, who was elected an MEP in 1984, is a member of the CSU executive. Area chairman of the Christian Socialist employees federation. From 1964, member of Bavarian state government. Founder in 1967 and later chairman, Hanns Seidel Foundation. Born Aug 13 1925.

Address: Bunzlauer Strasse 77, 8500 Nürnberg.

PISONI, FERRUCCIO
Italy, EPP (DC)

Sgr Ferruccio Pisoni, by profession a teacher, is a former Under Secretary of State at the Italian Ministry of Agriculture. Elected to the EP in 1984. Member, Chamber of Deputies, since 1968. Led Italian Government's delegation to Argentina to investigate the fate of people who disappeared ('Los Desaparecidos') during the period of military dictatorship. From 1972–79, was member of nominated EP, and vice-chairman of EEC–Greek Joint Committee which prepared way for Greece's entry into EEC. Chairman, Italian Association of Catholic Primary School Teachers of the Trento province, since 1965 and a member of its national council. Born Aug 6 1936.

Address: Via della Cervara 1/1, 38100 Trento.

PISONI, NINO
Italy, EPP (DC)

Sgr Nino Pisoni was elected to the EP in 1984. Expert on economic and agricultural problems. Director, Milan Provincial Federation of Direct Growers. DC national advisor; Lombardy Region regional advisor since 1970 and has acted as regional councillor for the economy. Mayor of Bernate Ticino. Member, board of Milan Chamber of Commerce, 1961–82. Born May 5 1927.

Address: Via Santa Tecla 4, 20122 Milano.

PITT, TERENCE
UK, Midlands West, Soc (Lab)

Mr Terence Pitt, who was elected to the EP in 1984, became one of the two auditors of the EP Socialist Group. Born Mar 2 1937; educated Queen Mary's School, Walsall and Aston University. Apprentice with Guest, Keen and Nettlefolds; later head of the Labour Party research department; director of Institute of National Affairs, Papua/New Guinea. At time of election was senior adviser on economic development with West Midlands County Council. Westminster parliamentary candidate.

Address: 6 Templefields Square, Wheeleys Road, Birmingham, B15 2LJ.

PLASKOVITIS, SPYRIDON
Greece, Soc (PASOK)

Mr Spyridon Plaskovitis was elected to the EP in 1981 and became a vice-chairman of the Socialist Group, being re-elected in 1984. A writer, he was imprisoned for four years during the dictatorship. Former magistrate and member of the Council of State. Member, National Assembly, 1977. Born Jun 6 1917.

Address: Aoou 6, 11523 Athens. Tel: (1) 6914717.

PLUMB, SIR HENRY
UK, Cotswold, ED (C)

Sir Henry Plumb, elected to the EP in 1979, was elected leader of the European Democratic (Conservative) Group in 1982; chairman of the EP Committee on Agriculture, 1979–82, which he has rejoined in this Parliament. President, National Farmers' Union, 1970–79; deputy president, 1966–69. Chairman, British Agricultural Council, from 1975. Born Mar 27 1925; educated King Edward VI School, Nuneaton. Past president, Comité des Organisations Professionels Agricoles de la CEE (COPA). In 1979, elected President, International Federation of Agricultural Producers.

Addresses: Southfields Farm, Coleshill, Birmingham B46 3CJ. Tel: (0675) 63133. 2 Queen Anne's Gate, London SW1H 9AA. Tel: (01) 222 1720, and (01) 222 1729. Telex: 917650.

POMILIO, MARIO
Italy, EPP (DC)

Sgr Mario Pomilio was elected to the EP in 1984. Author and high school teacher. He graduated in literature from the teachers' training college of Pisa. Has received major Italian literary awards. Born Jan 14 1921.

Address: Via Aniello Falcone 290/A, 00127 Napoli.

PONIATOWSKI, MICHEL
France, LD (UDF/RPR)

M. Michel Poniatowski, elected to the EP in 1979, was chairman of the EP Development and Cooperation Committee and became chairman of the Energy, Research and Technology Committees in July 1984. Honorary President, Republican Party (PR). Former director, cabinet of M. Valery Giscard d'Estaing; deputy for Val d'Oise, 1967–73; General Secretary, National Federation of Independent Republicans, 1967–73; President, 1975–78. Mayor of Isle Adam (Val d'Oise). Minister of Public Health and Social Security, 1973–74; Minister of State, Home Office, 1974–77. Roving ambassador, personal representative of the President of Republic, from 1977. B. May 16 1922. *Address: 22, bd Jean Mermoz, 92200 Neuilly. Tel: 745 4530.*

PONS, BERNARD
France, RDE (UDF/RPR)

M. Bernard Pons, secretary general of the RPR since 1979, was elected to the EP in 1984. Secretary of State for Agriculture, 1969–73. Doctor of medicine. Born Jul 18 1926. Gaullist deputy for the Lot, 1967–69, and (RPR group) 1973–78. Deputy for l'Essonne (RPR group), 1978–81. Paris deputy since 1981. County councillor.

Address: 123, rue de Lille, 75007 Paris.

PORDEA, GUSTAVE
France, DR (FN)

M. **Gustave Pordea** became an MEP in 1984. Doctor of law and former Romanian diplomat. Born Feb 3 1916. Literary adviser to Editions Gallimard since 1973. Author of works on political sociology and diplomatic history.

Address: 5 Passage Doisy, 75017 Paris.

PÖTSCHKI, HANS
Germany, EPP (CDU)

Herr Hans Pötschki was elected to the EP in 1984. Rector. CDU chairman at Emsdetten. Steinfurt area councillor from 1969. Chairman of Euregio from 1975. Born Jan 14 1928.

Address: Sternstrasse 53, 4407 Emsdetten.

PÖTTERING, HANS-GERT
Germany, EPP (CDU)

Herr Hans-Gert Pöttering, a lawyer, became an MEP in 1979. Was on the staff of the CDU/CSU Bundestag group, 1976–79; personal adviser to the deputy group chairman, Dr Burkhard Ritz. Born Sep 15 1945. District chairman, Osnabrück 'Land' 'Junge Union' 1974–76. From 1974, chairman of the Bersenbrück municipal CDU and member, Osnabrück 'Land' CDU district executive. From 1976, member Osnabrück-Emsland CDU executive; and 'Junge Union' Lower Saxony 'Land' executive.

Address: Sophienstrasse 8, 4505 Bad Iburg. Tel: (0541) 57060 (Dienst), (05403) 4855 (privat).

191

PRAG, DEREK
UK, Hertfordshire, ED (C)

Mr Derek Prag was elected to the EP in 1979; member of its Political Affairs Committee from 1984 and Conservative spokesman on this subject. Former spokesman on institutional committees and still a member, EP Institutional Committee. European Commission civil servant, 1955–73, being head of the Commission's Information Office in London, 1965–73. Ran own consultancy on European affairs, 1973–79. Previously economic journalist with Reuters and editor of *Financial Times* Business Letter from Europe. B. Aug 6 1923; educ. Bolton School and Emmanuel Coll., Cambridge.

Addresses: Euro Centre, Maynard House, The Common, Hatfield, Herts AL10 0NF. Tel: (07072) 71860. Pine Hill, 47 New Road, Digswell, Herts AL6 0AQ. Tel: (07073) 5686.

PRANCHÈRE, PIERRE
France, Comm (PCF)

M. Pierre Pranchère, a farmer, MEP since 1979, is a member of the Central Committee of the French Communist Party. Born Jul 1 1927. Deputy for Corrèze 1956–58 and 1973–78. Member, agrarian section, PCF; secretary, Corrèze federation, PCF, 1953–73.

Address: 5, rue Marc Eyrolles, 19000 Tulle. Tel: (55) 26 10 38.

PRICE, PETER
UK, London South East, ED (C)

Mr Peter Price, a solicitor, was MEP for Lancashire West, 1979–84, when he was elected for London SE. A member, EP Committees on Budgetary Control and Verification of Credentials. Member, Legal Affairs Committee, and Conservative spokesman on this subject. Born Feb 19 1942; educated Worcester Royal Grammar School, Aberdare Boys' Grammar School, Southampton University and College of Law, Guildford. Contested Caerphilly, 1970 general election, Aberdare 1964 and 1966. European Vice-President, Association of District Councils.

Address: 19 Station Road, Sidcup, Kent DA15 7EB. Tel: (01) 302 7294/300 3471.

PROUT, CHRISTOPHER
UK, Shropshire and Stafford, ED (C)

Mr Christopher Prout has been Chief Whip of the ED (Conservative) Group since 1983, being deputy whip 1979–82 and chairman of the EP Committee on Verification of Credentials, 1982–84. Elected to the EP in 1979. Barrister. Born Jan 1 1942; educated Sevenoaks School, Manchester University, Queen's College, Oxford, Middle Temple. English Speaking Union Fellow, Columbia University 1963–64; The World Bank Group, Washington DC, 1966–69; Leverhulme Fellow Lecturer in Law, Sussex University, 1969–79; Reserve Officer 16th/5th Lancers since 1970.

Address: 5 Oakfield Road, Shrewsbury, Shropshire SY3 8AA. Tel: (063083) 218.

PROVAN, JAMES
UK, North East Scotland, ED (C)

Mr James Provan, elected to the EP in 1979, has been a member of the EP Agriculture and Fisheries Committee since 1979 and since 1982 has been ED (Conservative) Group spokesman on these matters. Retired from Tayside Regional Council in 1982. Farmer; twice area president of NFU. Born Dec 19 1936; educated Oundle and Royal Agricultural College, Cirencester. Former member, Tay River Purification Board. Married with three children.

Address: Wallacetown, Bridge of Earn, Perthshire, Scotland PH2 8QA. Tel: (073) 881-2243. Telex: 76606 Provan G.

QUIN, MS JOYCE
UK, Tyne and Wear, Soc (Lab)

Ms Joyce Quin was elected to the EP in 1979. University lecturer and member of the Association of University Teachers. Born Nov 26 1944; educated Whitley Bay Grammar School, Newcastle University, and London School of Economics. BA (French), MSc (International Relations). Formerly researcher at Labour Party's International Department. Member, Transport and General Workers Union, Fabian Society, and Socialist Environment and Resources Association. Special interests: shipbuilding and fisheries (British Labour group's spokesperson).

Address: 41 Preston Avenue, North Shields, NE30 2BN. Tel: (0632) 591006.

RABBETHGE, FRAU RENATE-CHARLOTTE
Germany, EPP (CDU)

Frau Renate-Charlotte Rabbethge became an MEP in 1979. A district chairman of the 'Europa Union' formerly worked as foreign correspondent and interpreter with the Zeiss firm (Göttingen). In 1978, elected to executive, Lower Saxony 'Land' Association's advisory committee on the family, the executive of Einbeck CDU, became European affairs spokesman of Lower Saxony CDU Women's Union, member of CDU federal committee on women in the Middle Classes, and the agricultural committee, European Women's Union. Born Oct 14 1930. Married with two children.

Address: Haus Borntal, Postfach 170, 3352 Einbeck. Tel: (05561) 5067.

RAFTERY, THOMAS
Ireland, EPP (F-Gael)

Mr Thomas Raftery, elected to the EP in 1984, has been Professor of Agriculture at University College, Cork, since 1964. Chairman, Bank of Ireland Centre for Cooperative Studies; member, Council of the Agricultural Institute. Aged 51.

Address: 8 Bishopscourt Road, Wilton, Cork.

RAGGIO, ANDREA
Italy, Comm (PCI)

Sgr Andrea Raggio, elected to the EP in 1984, is a former chairman of the regional council for Sardinia; leader of the PCI group on that council. Born Nov 30 1929.

Address: c/o Consiglio Regionale Sardo, Viale Trieste, 09100 Cagliari.

REICHLIN, ALFREDO
Italy, Comm (PCI)

Sgr Alfredo Reichlin is a journalist and a former chairman of the board of *Unità*. Elected to the EP in 1984; member, Chamber of Deputies, since 1968, and of the secretariat of the PCI. Born May 26 1925.

Address: Direzione PCI, Via delle Botteghe Oscure 4, 00186 Roma.

REMACLE, MARCEL
Belgium, Soc (PS)

Mr Marcel Remacle, who became an MEP in 1984, was Mayor of Vielsalm, 1965. Member, Chamber of Representatives, since 1978. Born May 19 1929.

Address: Rue de Rencheux 128, 6690 Vielsalm.

RIGO, MARIO
Italy, Soc (PSI)

Sgr Mario Rigo, elected to the EP in 1984, has been Mayor of Venice since 1970. Former provincial secretary of PSI and provincial assessor. President of the independent 'Teatro La Fenice' and of the association of Adriatic ports. Vice chairman of the Venetian Biennale organization. Born Oct 4 1929; degree in economics and commerce.

Address: Findaco deo Comune di Venezia, San Marco, 30100 Venezia.

RINSCHE, GÜNTER
Germany, EPP (CDU)

Herr Günter Rinsche, an economist, was a member of the Bundestag, 1965–72. Elected an MEP in 1979. Member, North Rhine-Westphalia 'Land' assembly since 1975, being CDU group spokesman on economic affairs. Chief burgomaster of Hamm from 1964. Born Jul 13 1930. Has been member, North Rhine-Westphalia 'Europa Union' 'Land' executive and of German Council of European Movement; chairman, planning committee, Institute for International Solidarity; executive member, Konrad Adenauer Foundation; president, North Rhine-Westphalia convention of municipal authorities.

Address: Feldgarten 15, 4700 Hamm 1. Tel: (02381) 52330.

ROBERTS, DAME SHELAGH
UK, London South West, ED (C)

Dame Shelagh Roberts was appointed to the chair of the EP External Economic Relations Committee in July 1984; a vice-chairman of the EP Committee on Transport and of its Committee of Inquiry into the situation of women in Europe until 1984. Elected to the EP in 1979. Chairman, National Union of Conservative and Unionist Associations, 1976–77, and Conservative Party Women's National Advisory Committee 1972–75. Industrial relations consultant. Member, Greater London Council, 1972–75; chairman, Planning and Transportation Committee of Association of Metropolitan Authorities, 1977–79. Born Oct 13 1924; educated St Wyburn School, Birkdale.
Address: 23 Dovehouse Street, Chelsea, London SW3 6JY. Tel: (01) 352 3711.

ROELANTS DU VIVIER, FRANÇOIS
Belgium, ARC (Ecolo-V)

Mr François Roelants du Vivier was elected to the EP in 1984. Secretary General of the Wallonia Environmental Organization, 1975–83; administrator of the European Environment Bureau, 1979–83. Born Nov 5 1947.

Address: Rue de l'Abbaye 97, 1050 Bruxelles.

ROGALLA, DIETER
Germany, Soc (SPD)

Herr Dieter Rogalla became an MEP in 1981; re-elected in 1984 when he became chairman of the EP Committee on Verification of Credentials. Lawyer. On staff of the EEC Commission, 1961–81. Member, management committee of Steinfurt SPD. Born Aug 20 1927.

Address: SPD Europa Büro, Harpener Hellweg 152, 4630 Bochum 1. Tel: (0234) 23 38 97.

ROMEO, ROSARIO
Italy, LD (PLI/PRI)

Sgr Rosario Romeo was elected to the EP in 1984 and became a vice-chairman of the Liberal and Democratic Group. Professor of modern history, faculty of literature and philosophy, Rome University; rector of international free university for Roman social studies. Born Oct 11 1924.

Address: Via Adige 64, 00198 Roma.

ROMEOS, GEORGIOS
Greece, Soc (PASOK)

Mr Georgios Romeos was elected to the EP in 1984. Economist and editor. Born 1934.

Address: Tertseti 9, 15451 N. Psychiko.

197

ROMUALDI, PINO
Italy, NI (MSI-DN)

Sgr Pino Romualdi has been a member of the Italian Parliament since 1953. Elected to the EP in 1979. General Vice-Secretary, MSI-Destra Nazionale. Editor of *Il Popolo Italiano* until 1957. Twice member of the Parliamentary Committee on Industry and Commerce; member of Defence Committee in 1976. Born Jul 24 1913.

Addresses: Camera dei Deputati, 00100 Roma. Via Lucio Afranio 10, 00136 Roma.

ROOIJ, MEVR YVONNE VAN
Netherlands, EPP (CDA)

Mevr Yvonne van Rooij was elected to the EP in 1984. On staff of Dutch Christian Employers' Association dealing with European integration and government-procurement policy, previously foreign affairs section. Executive member, Dutch European Movement. Active in foreign affairs section of CDA women's organization and various CDA working parties. Born Jun 4 1951; studied constitutional and administrative law in Utrecht.

Address: Arabislaan 41, 2555 DH den Haag.

ROSSETTI, GIORGIO
Italy, Comm (PCI)

Sgr Giorgio Rossetti is a journalist and regional secretary of the PCI for the Friuli–Venezia Giula area. Elected to the EP in 1984. A member of town, provincial and regional councils. Born Aug 24 1938.

Address: Comitato Regionale di Trieste, Via Capitolina 3, 34100 Trieste.

ROSSI, ANDRÉ
France, LD (UDF/RPR)

M. André Rossi, elected in 1979, was vice-president (1965–67) and member of the nominated European Parliament from 1959. A vice-chairman of EP Budget Committee in last Parliament. Former deputy for Aisne; Mayor of Chateau-Thierry. Secretary of State, Ministry of Information, 1974–76, Minister of Foreign Trade, 1976–78. Was head of French delegation to UN Economic and Social Council. Born May 16 1921. Vice President, Party Radical. Charly-sur-Marne county councillor.

Address: Mairie Chateau-Thierry, 02400 Chateau-Thierry. Tel: (23) 83 27 14.

ROTHE, FRAU MECHTHILD
Germany, Soc (SPD)

Frau Mechthild Rothe was elected to the EP in 1984. Teacher. Member, SPD Federal Council, and of town council of Bad Lippspringe. Born Aug 10 1947.

Address: Karlstrasse 5, 4792 Bad Lippspringe.

ROTHLEY, WILLI
Germany, Soc (SPD)

Herr Willi Rothley, lawyer, was elected to the EP In 1984. Member of Rhineland assembly and deputy state chairman of SDP. Born Dec 15 1943.

Addresses: Ringstrasse 29, 6760 Rochenhausen. Tel: (06361) 693–694. Im Gothental 31, 6760 Rockenhausen. Tel: (06361) 8443.

ROUX, JEAN-PIERRE
France, RDE (UDF/RPR)

M. Jean-Pierre Roux, an engineer, was elected to the EP in 1984. Vaucluse deputy, 1968–73. Mayor of Avignon and regional councillor since 1983. Mayor of l'Isle sur Sorgue, 1965–71. Born Aug 5 1938; educated Lycée Mistral, Avignon.

Address: 27, rue Noël Bizet, 80000 Avignon.

RYAN, RICHIE
Ireland, EPP (F-Gael)

Mr Richie Ryan became a vice-chairman of the EP Budgets Committee in July 1984 having been a vice-chairman until then of the Environment Committee. Elected in 1979; nominated MEP in 1973 and 1977–79. President of the EEC Council of Finance and Economic Ministers, Jan to June, 1975, being the Republic of Ireland's Minister for Finance, 1973–77, and Minister for the Public Service, 1973–77. Lawyer. Born Feb 27 1929. Chairman, International Monetary Fund and World Bank 1977; Governor, European Investment Bank and International Monetary Fund and World Bank Group 1973–77. Member of Dail, 1959–81; Council of Europe Assembly, 1968–72.
Address: European Parliament Office, 43 Molesworth Street, Dublin 2. Tel: (01) 71 98 34.

SABY, HENRI
France, Soc (PS)

M. Henri Saby, engineer, has been an MEP since 1981 and was elected a vice-chairman of the Socialist Group in 1984. Born Aug 8 1933; educated Toulouse University. Member, Socialist Party steering committee since 1974 (vice-chairman, 1979–81); member, executive bureau, Socialist Party federation of Haute-Garonne (first secretary, 1977–80); member, steering committee, National Federation; former president, Haute-Garonne federation of elected socialists and republicans. Mayor of Aygues-Vives and Midi-Pyrénées regional councillor. Former member, directory, National Centre of Scientific Research (CNRS).
Address: Rte de St Léon, Ayguesvives, 31450 Montgiscard. Tel: (61) 81 92 95.

SAKELLARIOU, JOANNIS
Germany, Soc (SPD)

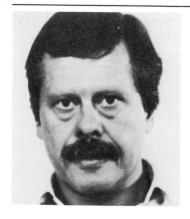

Herr Joannis Sakellariou was elected to the EP in 1984. Scientific director of the Germany army academy in Munich. Spokesman for Munich Young Socialists, 1972–74; now deputy chairman, local SDP, Sendlingen-West. Born Nov 12 1939.

Address: Grüntenstrasse 11, 8000 München 21.

SALISCH, FRAU HEINKE
Germany, Soc (SPD)

Frau Heinke Salisch was elected to the EP in 1979. Became a vice-chairman of the EP Committee on Social Affairs and Employment in July 1984; a member of the committee in the previous Parliament. Interpreter. Born Aug 14 1941. Member, Karlsruhe Municipal Council, from 1971.

Address: Sonntagstrasse 2, 7500 Karlsruhe 1. Tel: (0721) 818888.

SÄLZER, BERNHARD
Germany, EPP (CDU)

Herr Bernhard Sälzer, consultant civil engineer, was elected to the EP in 1979. Became a vice-chairman of the EP Committee on Energy, Research and Technology in July 1984; served on committee in last Parliament. Member of the CDU executive for the 'Land' of Hesse; deputy chairman, CDU Federal Committee on Cultural and Educational Policy. Born Sep 4, 1940. Mayor of Marburg since 1976. CDU group chairman, Darmstadt City Council, 1968–76; member of the Landtag, 1970–76, and CDU spokesman on cultural and educational policy, 1972–76.

Address: Dieburger Strasse 240, 6100 Darmstadt. Tel: (06151) 71240.

SCHINZEL, DIETER
Germany, Soc (SPD)

Herr Dieter Schinzel, a physicist, was elected to the EP in 1979. Born Nov 14 1942. Chairman of Aachen SPD from 1976. Member, Aachen Municipal Council, 1972–75; of Bundestag, 1972–76. Head of a North Rhine–Westphalian Land social welfare organization, 1977–79.

Addresses: Klappergasse 10, 5100 Aachen. Tel: (0241) 22180, (0241) 39393. Europe-Büro, Bahnhofstrasse 23, 5100 Aachen. Tel: (0241) 35171, (0241) 39394. Kirchrather Strasse 34, 5100 Aachen. Tel: (0241) 82001.

SCHLEICHER, FRAU URSULA
Germany, EPP (CSU)

Frau Ursula Schleicher became a vice-chairman of the EP Committee on the Environment, Public Health and Consumer Protection in July 1984; elected to the EP in 1979. Member of the Bundestag 1972–80, and chaired Bundestag committee on problems of women and society. CSU adviser on women's rights, 1965–75. Praesidium member, German Council of the European Movement; deputy federal chairman, German Catholic Workers' Movement. Born May 15 1933. Harpist.

Address: Backoffenstrasse 6, 8750 Aschaffenburg. Tel: (06021) 92901.

SCHMID, GERHARD
Germany, Soc (SPD)

Herr Gerhard Schmid has been an MEP since 1979. Member, Niederbayern-Oberpfalz SPD district executive; district chairman, Young Socialists, 1972–75; member, SPD district management in Lower Bavaria–Upper Palatinate from 1975. Born May 5 1946. Chemist; research fellow; staff of Institute of Biochemistry, Regensburg.

Addresses: Richard Wagner Strasse 4, 8400 Regensburg. (Büro). Tel: (0941) 55553. Altdorfstrasse 13a, 8400 Regensburg. Tel: (0941) 26619.

SCHMIT, MME LYDIE
Luxembourg, Soc (POSL)

Mme Lydie Schmit was elected to the EP in 1984. Vice-president, Socialist International; president, International Women Socialists; former chairman of POSL, now member of its executive committee. Communal councillor for Schifflange. Schoolteacher. Born 1938.

Address: Rue Belle-vue, Schifflange.

SCHÖN, KONRAD
Germany, EPP (CDU)

Herr Konrad Schön became an MEP in 1979. Professor of Political Science and Political Education, Saarland Teacher Training College, and then, from 1979, at Saarbrücken University. CDU political group chairman, Saarland 'Land' Assembly, 1972; Minister of Finance, 1974–77. Born May 7 1930.

Address: Hohenzollernstrasse 13, (Hansa-Haus), 6600 Saarbrücken. Tel: (0681) 53787.

SCHREIBER, HEINZ
Germany, Soc (SPD)

Herr Heinz Schreiber was elected to the EP in 1984. University lecturer 1972–83. Member of Bundestag, 1977–79. Born Nov 24 1942. Member of EP Committee on Regional Policy and Regional Planning.

Address: Dorotheenstrasse 10, 5650 Solingen 1.

SCHWALBA-HOTH, FRANK
Germany, ARC (Grüne)

Herr Frank Schwalba-Hoth, elected to the EP in 1984, became a vice-chairman of the EP Committee on Rules of Procedure and Petitions. Teacher. A foundation member of the Green movement in Hesse. From 1982–83, member of the Hesse Länd Parliament. Has pledged himself to oppose all infringements of human rights, and the threat of 'Big Brother' government, with State departments possessing computer records of all individuals. Born Dec 12 1952.

Address: Weidenhäuser Strasse 85, 3550 Marburg.

SCOTT-HOPKINS, SIR JAMES
UK, Hereford and Worcester, ED (C)

Sir James Scott-Hopkins was leader of the European Democratic (Conservative) Group, 1979–82, since when he has been on EP Political Affairs Committee becoming a vice chairman in July 1984. Member, EP since 1973; elected in 1979. Deputy leader, Conservative Group, 1974, and a Vice-President of the Parliament, 1976–79. MP for West Derbyshire, 1967–79, and for North Cornwall, 1959–66; Parliamentary Secretary, Ministry of Agriculture, Fisheries and Food, 1962–64. Farmer. Born Nov 29 1921; educated Eton and New College, Oxford, and Emmanuel College Cambridge.

Address: 602 Nelson House, Dolphin Sq, London.

SCRIVENER, MME CHRISTIANE
France, LD (UDF/RPR)

Mme Christiane Scrivener has been an MEP since 1979. Assistant General Secretary, Republican Party. Adviser to chairman of agency for technical, industrial and economic cooperation. Former Electricité de France administrator. Born Sep 1 1925; ed Paris University (law and arts), Springfield University, Massachusetts (linguistics) and Harvard Business School.

Address: 21 avenue Robert Schuman, 92100 Boulogne-sur-Seine. Tel: 8254411.

SEAL, DR BARRY
UK, West Yorkshire, Soc (Lab)

Dr Barry Seal became chairman of the EP Committee on Economic and Monetary Affairs and Industrial Policy, in July 1984; member, bureau, of Socialist Group; former vice-chairman, Committee on External Economic Relations. Senior then principal lecturer, Huddersfield Polytechnic, 1971–79. Contested Harrogate, Oct 1974 general election. Member, Bradford City Council, 1971–74; Bradford Metropolitan District Council, 1973–79, being leader, Labour group, 1976–79. TGWU and GMBATU; European consultant of Post Office Engineering Union. Born Oct 28 1937. Member, Labour Party working parties on technology and trade.

Address: City Hall, Bradford, West Yorkshire BD1 1HY. Tel: (0274) 729577.

SEEFELD, HORST
Germany, Soc (SPD)

Herr Horst Seefeld was elected a Vice-President of the EP in July, 1984, having been chairman of its Committee on Transport in previous Parliament. Elected in 1979 and became member, bureau of Socialist Group; served on its bureau in pre-1979 nominated Parliament, which he joined in 1970. Member of Bundestag, 1969–80. President of the German Council of the European Movement since 1976. Press Officer, Federal Ministry of Transport, 1967–69. Born Nov 21 1930. On board of European Union of Germany.

Address: Im Brettspiel 53, 7518 Bretten. Tel: (07252) 1903.

SEELER, HANS-JOACHIM
Germany, Soc (SPD)

Herr Hans-Joachim Seeler, a lawyer, was elected to the EP in 1979. A vice-chairman of the EP Institutional Affairs Committee from July 1984. Served in Hamburg Parliament, 1966–78; member, Hamburg SPD executive. Born Aug 9 1930.

Addresses: Kurt-Schumacher-Allee 10, 2000 Hamburg 1. Tel: (040) 24 92 29. Sonnentauweg 3, 2000 Hamburg 71. Tel: (040) 64 14 199.

SEGRE, SERGIO
Italy, Comm (PCI)

Sgr Sergio Segre became an MEP in 1979; Italian MP 1972–79. Journalist; member of editorial staff of *L'Unità* from 1945: head of foreign services, special correspondent in Berlin and Bonn (1952–57), and editor (1969–70). Editorial Secretary of *Rinascita*, 1958–61; Deputy Editor of *Stasera*. Member of party's central committee and in charge of foreign affairs section, 1970–79. Twice member of Parliamentary Committee on Foreign Affairs. Born Sep 15 1926.

Addresses: Via dei Giornalisti 64, 00135 Roma. Tel: 3454079. Via Michele Lessona 1, 00143 Torino. Tel: 772085.

SEIBEL-EMMERLING, FRAU LIESELOTTE
Germany, Soc (SPD)

Frau Lieselotte Seibel-Emmerling became an MEP in 1979. Member of the Bavarian Landtag from 1966. Born Feb 3 1932. Former school inspector. Member, SPD district management, Franconia.

Address: Virchowstrasse 15a, 8500 Nürnberg 10. Tel: (0911) 564467.

SELIGMAN, MADRON
UK, Sussex West, ED (C)

Mr Madron Seligman was elected in 1979. A vice-chairman of EP Committee on Energy, Research and Technology. Born Nov 10 1918; educated Harrow and Balliol College, Oxford (President of the Union). Director, food engineering and plant manufacturing group, which he joined in 1947. Chairman and director of other companies. Member, Royal Institute of International Affairs, the Royal Thames Yacht Club, Glyndebourne Opera Club and MCC.

Addresses: PO Box No 4, Manor Royal, Crawley, West Sussex RH10 2QB. Tel: (0293) 37457 or 27777. Micklepage House, Nuthurst, nr Horsham, West Sussex RH13 6DG. Tel: (0403) 76259.

SELVA, GUSTAVO
Italy, EPP (DC)

Sgr Gustavo Selva, a journalist on Italian radio and television, was elected in 1984 and became a vice-chairman of the EP Committee on Youth Affairs, Culture, Education, Information and Sport. Was elected to the EP in 1979 but did not take seat. As a correspondent for Italian radio and television corporation (RAI), he worked in Brussels 1960–63, in Vienna 1963–67 and in Bonn 1967–71. In March 1976, he became head of GR2 (radio news). Chairman of Italian section of Association of European Journalists, and was editor of the Venetian newspaper *Il Gazzettino* until his election to the EP. Aged 58.

Address: Via San Pio X, 5, 31010 One' di Fonte (Treviso).

SHERLOCK, DR ALEXANDER
UK, Essex South West, ED (C)

Dr Alexander Sherlock, elected to the EP in 1979, is a member of the EP Environment Committee and Conservative spokesman on that subject. Qualified medical practitioner and a barrister. Has served on Suffolk County Council. Born Feb 14 1922; educated Magdalen College School, Oxford; Stowmarket Grammar School and London Hospital Medical School. Consultant in occupational health and safety. President, Suffolk branch and Ipswich division, British Medical Association.

Address: 58 Orwell Road, Felixstowe, Suffolk IP11 7PS. Tel: (0394) 284503.

SIMMONDS, RICHARD
UK, Wight and Hampshire East, ED (C)

Mr Richard Simmonds was MEP for Midlands West, 1979–84, and elected for this seat in 1984. Elected to the EP 1984. Member, EP Agriculture and Budgetary Control committees and Conservative spokesman on latter subject. Farmer and estate business consultant, previously a surveyor. Born Aug 2 1944; educated Trinity College, Glenalmond, and studied politics and economics in Hamburg and marketing in EEC. Personal assistant to Mr Edward Heath, 1973–75; chairman, four committees, Berkshire County Council 1973–79.

Addresses: Woodlands Farm, Cookham Dean, Maidenhead, Berkshire SL6 9PJ. Tel: Marlow 4293 (office). Telex: 848248 rjssmep. Dyers, Cookham Dean, Maidenhead, Berkshire. Tel: Marlow 3269.

SIMONS, FRAU BARBARA
Germany, Soc (SPD)

Frau Barbara Simons, a teacher, was elected to the EP in 1984. Director for guidance on further education in Hanover. Member, SDP executive, Lower Saxony. Born Jun 16 1929.

Address: Lowenstrasse 11, 3000 Hanover 1.

SIMPSON, ANTHONY
UK, Northamptonshire, ED (C)

Mr Anthony Simpson, a barrister, was elected to the EP in 1979; became one of the EP's quaestors and was re-elected in 1984. Worked in the legal service of the European Commission in Brussels, 1975–79. Contested Leicester, West, in both 1974 general elections. Born Oct 28 1935; educated Rugby and Magdalene College, Cambridge. In Brussels was chairman of the European Democrat Forum; member, committee of the British Conservative Association in Belgium 1976–78. Member, Oadby Urban District Council, 1968–71.

Addresses: Avenue Michel-Ange 57, 1040 Bruxelles. Tel: 73 64 219. Bassets, Great Glen, Leicestershire. Tel: 053 759 2386.

SMITH, LLEWELLYN
UK, South East Wales, Soc (Lab)

Mr Llewellyn Smith was elected to the EP in 1984; joined the EP Committee on Energy, Research and Technology. Born Apr 16 1944; educated Cardiff University. Former labourer with Pilkington glass company and George Wimpey, builders. At time of election was tutor/organizer with Workers' Educational Association. Member, Socialist Education Association, CND, the Labour Coordinating Committee, and Cooperative Party. Married with two sons and a daughter.

Address: The Mount, Uplands, Tynewydd, Newbridge, Gwent.

SPÄTH, LEOPOLD
Germany, EPP (CDU)

Herr Leopold Späth was elected to the EP in 1984. Member, Ostenfeld municipal council, from 1959; Diet of Schleswig-Holstein, since 1971. Born Oct 30 1928. Horticulturalist.

Address: Langenhöft, 2251 Ostenfeld (Husum).

SPINELLI, ALTIERO
Italy, Comm (PCI)

Sgr Altiero Spinelli became chairman in July 1984 of the EP Committee on Institutional Affairs, on which he served in the last Parliament, being rapporteur producing the Spinelli report on the draft European Treaty adopted by the Parliament. Elected in 1979; a member of outgoing nominated EP after being EEC Commissioner, 1970–76, with responsibilities for industrial policy. Member, Italian Chamber of Deputies, since 1976. Founded European Federalist Movement, 1943; founder and director (1967–70) of the Institute of International Affairs. Born Aug 31 1907.

Addresses: Clivo Rutario 5, 00152 Roma. Tel: (06) 5896 343. Via del Tritone 46, 00187 Roma. Tel: (00396) 678 6755.

SQUARCIALUPI, SIGNORA VERA
Italy, Comm (Ind Sin)

Signora Vera Squarcialupi, journalist and broadcaster, was a member of the Italian Senate, 1976–79, elected as an independent on the Communist list. In 1979, elected to Chamber of Deputies but resigned to devote herself to work in the EP when elected to it; served in nominated Parliament 1976–79. Worked for the RAI (Italian Radio and Television Service) for 20 years both on news bulletins and programmes dealing with women's interests. Author of *Donne in Europa*, a study of the role of women in Community policy. Born Aug 5 1928.

Address: Via Losanna 16, 20154 Milano. Tel. 3458781.

STAES, PAUL
Belgium, ARC (Agalev)

Mr Paul Staes was elected to the EP in 1984 and became a member of the new 'Rainbow' group. Former journalist with *Standaard/Nieuwsblad*. Born Dec 3 1945; studied in UK and Germany at Stonyhurst College and Goethe Institute.

Address: Grote Singel 11, 2120 Schoten. Tel: (03) 658 49 71.

STARITA, GIOVANNI
Italy, EPP (DC)

Sgr Giovanni Starita, elected to the EP in 1984, is head of the DC Group on Rome City Council; for several years assessor responsible for various sectors of administration. Head of the Publicity and Press Service (SPES) for DC and vice-secretary of the Roman committee of the party. For nearly 20 years, he has been secretary of bank workers' section of CISL trade union. Born Mar 13 1926.

Address: Via Vigna due Torri 126, 00149 Roma.

STAUFFENBERG, FRANZ LUDWIG GRAF VON
Germany, EPP (CSU)

Herr Franz Ludwig Graf von Stauffenberg, elected to the EP in 1984, has been a member of the Bundestag since 1972. Member, board of European Union of Germany. Lawyer. Federal deputy chairman of boys' union, 1969–73. Member, CSU state executive, since 1972. Born May 4 1938.

Address: Klosterstrasse 8, 8196 Euraberg-Beureberg.

STEVENSON, GEORGE
UK, Staffordshire East, Soc (Lab)

Mr George Stevenson, bus driver, was elected to the EP in 1984 and became a member of the EP Committee on Transport. Born Aug 30 1938; educated secondary modern school. Former caster in pottery industry and for seven years a coal miner. Local and county councillor. Member, Transport and General Workers Union, and Cooperative Party. Married with two sons and a daughter.

Address: 11 Sherwood Road, Meir, Stoke-on-Trent ST3 7BX.

STEWART, KENNETH
UK, Merseyside West, Soc (Lab)

Mr Kenneth Stewart, elected to the EP in 1984, became a member of its Committee on Social Affairs and Employment. Liverpool city councillor for 17 out of last 20 years, being chairman of housing committee; also served on Merseyside County Council. Joiner; member of UCATT, the building trade union. Former chairman and secretary, Liverpool West Derby Labour Party; former shop steward; ex-sergeant, Parachute Regiment.

Address: 62 Ballantyne Road, Liverpool L13 9AL.

STEWART-CLARK, SIR JOHN
UK, Sussex East, ED (C)

Sir John Stewart-Clark, elected to the EP in 1979, has been treasurer since then of the ED (Conservative) Group; member, EP Committee on Social Affairs and Employment, since July 1984. Managing director, Pye of Cambridge Ltd, 1975–79; member, European Advisory Council, Institute of Directors. Born Sep 17 1929; educated Eton; Balliol College, Oxford; Harvard Business School. With J. and P. Coats Ltd, 1952–69; managing director, J. and P. Coats, Pakistan, Ltd, 1961–67; J. A. Carp's Garenfabrieken, Holland, 1967–69; Phillips Electrical Ltd, London, 1971–75. Contested Aberdeen, North, 1959 general election.

Address: Holmsley House, Holtye Common, near Cowden, Kent. Tel: (034286) 541.

STIRBOIS, JEAN-PIERRE
France, DR (FN)

M. Jean-Pierre Stirbois, a printer, is general secretary of the National Front. Deputy Mayor of Dreux. Born Jan 30 1945. Elected to the EP in 1984.

Address: 35 rue de la Ferme, 92200 Neuilly.

SUTRA DE GERMA, GEORGES
France, Soc (PS)

M. Georges Sutra de Germa is a winegrower. Born Jan 14 1930. Municipal councillor; member, National Agricultural Commission. Became MEP 1979. Member of Socialist Party since 1971. Former assistant general secretary, then vice-chairman, French Federation of Ciné Clubs. Author of Socialist Party report on enlargement of EEC to include Greece, Spain and Portugal.

Address: Campagne Montplézy, 34120 Pezenas. Tel: 98 12 77.

TAYLOR, JOHN DAVID
UK, Northern Ireland, ED (OUP)

Mr John David Taylor, elected to the EP in 1979, was Northern Ireland's Minister of State for Home Affairs, 1970–72, and Parliamentary Secretary at that department, 1969–70. MP for South Tyrone 1965–73; MP for Strangford since 1983. Member, NI Assembly, 1973–75, NI Constitutional Convention, 1975–76 and NI Assembly since 1982. Privy councillor (N Ireland). Born Dec 24 1937. Chartered engineer. Member, EP Committee on Regional Policy and Regional Planning from July 1984.

Address: Mullinure, Armagh BT61 9EL, N Ireland. Tel: (0861) 522409.

THAREAU, BERNARD
France, Soc (PS)

M. Bernard Thareau, Socialist Party assistant national secretary for agriculture, was first elected to the EP in 1981. Farmer. Vice-president, National Centre for Young Farmers (CNJA), 1966–70; president, National Porcine Federation, and administrator, National Federation of Farmers' Unions (FNSEA), 1969–77. Born Sep 2 1936.

Address: La Milsonnière, La Rouxiere, 44370 Varades. Tel: (40) 83 42 68.

THOME-PATENÔTRE, MME JACQUELINE
France, RDE (UDF/RPR)

Mme Jacqueline Thome-Patenôtre, elected to the EP in 1984, became a vice-chairman of the EP External Economic Relations Committee. Was Vice-Chairman of the National Assembly, 1960–68, and from 1947–83 was Mayor of Rambouillet. Under-Secretary of State for Reconstruction and Housing, 1957. Born Feb 3 1906. President, Society for the Protection of Animals, since 1970. County councillor for Seine et Oise, then Yvelines, 1946–79. Senator, Seine et Oise, 1948–58.

Address: 58, avenue Foch; 75016 Paris.

TOGNOLI, CARLO
Italy, Soc (PSI)

Sgr Carlo Tognoli, an industrial chemist, has been Mayor of Milan for eight years. Elected to the EP in 1984. Studied economics at the University of Bocconi. Chairman of Socialist Youth Federation, 1957. Member of the Cormano district council, 1960–70; elected to the Milan City Council in 1970, where he was assessor for social security and public employees. From 1968–70, vice-chairman of board responsible for the operation of the airports at Milan and Malpensa. Chairman of La Scala Opera House, and a director of the socialist journal, *Critica Sociale*. Born Jun 16 1938.

Address: Sindaco del Comune di Milano, Piazza della Scala 2, 20100 Milano.

TOKSVIG, CLAUS
Denmark, ED (KF)

Mr Claus Toksvig, journalist and TV reporter and correspondent, became an MEP in 1984. Has worked for BBC's Danish programmes, later two years in Rhodesia and Nyasaland. After returning to Denmark in 1958 he worked for Danish Radio and TV, was correspondent in US 1967–74. From New York he went to London as TV and radio correspondent until 1982; now works as a media consultant. Born Oct 21 1929.

Address: Søgårdsvej 9, Ravning, 7182 Bredsten.

TOLMAN, TEUN
Netherlands, EPP (CDA)

Mr Teun Tolman became chairman of the EP Agriculture Committee in July 1984. Member of the EP since 1978, being elected the following year. Member, Dutch Second Chamber, 1963–79. Farmer and stockbreeder. Born Sep 22 1924. Was politically active in Friesland as councillor and alderman of municipality of Stellingwerf, and a member of Provincial States Assembly of Friesland. Chairman, Friesland Agricultural Organization and of Dutch Christian Farmers' and Market Gardeners' Association, 1963–79.

Address: Hoofdweg 45b, 8474 CA Oldeholtpade, p Wolvega. Tel: (05610) 2463.

TOMLINSON, JOHN
UK, Birmingham West, Soc (Lab)

Mr John Tomlinson was elected to the EP in 1984, having been Head of Social Studies, Solihull College of Technology, 1979–84. MP for Meriden, 1974–79. Born Aug 1 1939; educated Westminster City School, Cooperative College, Loughborough; and Warwick University. Former political organizer and head of research department, AUEW. Parliamentary Private Secretary to Mr Harold Wilson, Prime Minister, 1975–76; Parliamentary Under Secretary of State for Foreign and Commonwealth Affairs, 1976–79. President, EEC Council of Foreign Ministers, in 1977. Married with three sons and one daughter.

Address: 23 Meriden Road, Hampton in Arden, West Midlands B92 0BS.

TONGUE, MISS CAROLE
UK, London East, Soc (Lab)

Miss Carole Tongue, elected to the EP in 1984, had been an administrative assistant to Socialist MEPs since 1980. Born Oct 14 1955; educated state schools in Harold Wood and Brentwood, and Loughborough University. Member, Women's International League for Peace and Freedom, and Quaker Council of European Affairs, for whom she acted as a lobbyist and information officer. Became member, EP Committee on Environment, Public Health and Consumer Protection in July 1984.

Address: 10 Beltinge Road, Harold Wood, Romford, Essex RM3 0UJ.

TOPMANN, GÜNTER
Germany, Soc (SPD)

Herr Günter Topmann, a retired senior police officer, was elected to the EP in 1984. Mayor of Altenahr. Member, Bundestag until 1983. Born May 7 1934. Trained cobbler.

Address: Graf-Engelbert-Strasse 24, 5990 Altena.

TORTORA, ENZO
Italy, NI (PR)

Sgr Enzo Tortora is a journalist and television presenter. Elected to the EP in 1984. Born Nov 1928.

Address: Via dei Piatti 8, 20123 Milano.

TOUSSAINT, MICHEL
Belgium, LD (PRL)

Mr Michel Toussaint, elected an MEP in 1984, is chairman of the council of the French-speaking community. Minister of State. Born Nov 26 1922.

Addresses: 14, rue Borgnet, Boîte 19, 5000 Namur. Tel: (081) 22 78 18. 105, rue Mottiaux, 5100 Jambes (Namur). Tel: (081) 30 03 57.

TRIPODI, ANTONINO
Italy, DR (MSI-DN)

Sgr Antonino Tripodi was elected to the EP in 1984. President of his party, Social Movement. Member, Chamber of Deputies, 1958–83. Born Jan 11 1911. Advocate.

Address: Via Cadlolo 140, 00136 Roma.

TRIVELLI, RENZO
Italy, Comm (PCI)

Sgr Renzo Trivelli, elected to the EP in 1984, is a member of the central committee of PCI. Born May 3 1925.

Address: Direzione PCI, Via delle Botteghe Oscure 4, 00186 Roma.

TRUPIA, SIGNORA LALLA
Italy, Comm (PCI)

Signora Lalla Trupia, elected to the EP in 1984, is in charge of the national women's section of PCI; also member of executive party. Born May 31 1948.

Address: Direzione PCI, Via delle Botteghe Oscure 4, 00186 Roma.

TUCKMAN, FREDERICK
UK, Leicester, ED (C)

Mr Frederick Tuckman was elected to the EP in 1979; serves on EP Social Affairs and Employment Committee and is Conservative spokesman on these matters. Partner in firm of management consultants. Secretary, Bow Group, 1958–59, and council member, 1955–63. Chairman, Greater London area, Conservative Political Centre, 1968–70. Contested Coventry North in 1970 election. Born Jun 9 1922; educated London University. Member, London borough of Camden Council, 1965–71; Council of Institute of Personnel Management, 1963–70.

Addresses: 6 Cumberland Road, Barnes, London SW13 9LY. Tel: (01) 748 2392 (home), (01) 748 7916 (office). 'Bassetts', 3 The Nook, Great Glen, Leicestershire.

TURNER, AMÉDÉE
UK, Suffolk, ED (C)

Mr Amédée Turner QC, patent barrister and author, was elected to the EP in 1979. Became ED (Conservative) group spokesman on energy, research and technology in July 1984; vice-chairman, EP Legal Affairs Committee until 1984. Called to the Bar (Inner Temple) 1954; practised patent bar, 1955–57; Associate, Kenyon and Kenyon, patent attorneys, New York, 1957–60; returned to London practice, 1960. Contested Norwich North in the general elections of 1964, 1966 and 1970. Born Mar 26 1929.
Addresses: 3 Montrose Place, London SW1X 7DU. Tel: (01) 235 3191. 1 Essex Court, The Temple, London EC4 9AR. Tel: (01) 583 8290. The Barn, Westleton, Saxmundham, Suffolk. IP17 3AN. Tel: Westleton 235.

TZOUNIS, IOANNIS
Greece, EPP (ND)

Mr Ioannis Tzounis became an MEP in 1984. Entered diplomatic service in 1947 and served at a number of important embassies. Served for six years as Director-General of Political Affairs at Ministry for Foreign Affairs and as Ambassador in Washington until 1982. Shortly before the restoration of democratic government, he resigned as Director-General in disagreement with the military regime and its policy on Cyprus. Born 1920 in Romania; educated Athens University. Graduate in law.

Address: Stratigou Iordanidi 11, 15452 Psychiko.

ULBURGHS, JEF
Belgium, NI (SP)

Mr Jef Ulburghs was elected to the EP in 1984. Entered priesthood in 1947 and in recent years conducted his ministry among immigrant workers. Delegate of non-governmental organizations to Unctad. Born Jun 9 1922.

Address: Zaveldriesstraat 61, 3600 Genk. Tel: (011) 38 23 68.

VALENZI, MAURIZIO
Italy, Comm (PCI)

Sgr Maurizio Valenzi, elected to the EP in 1984. Former Mayor of Naples and a member of central committee of PCI. Born Nov 16 1909.

Address: c/o Federazione PCI, Via dei Fiorentini 51, 00100 Napoli.

VANDEMEULEBROUCKE, JAAK
Belgium, ARC (VU)

Mr Jaak Vandemeulebroucke became an MEP in 1981. Former teacher. Member of his party's council since 1973. Born May 27 1943. Communal Councillor at Ostende since 1970.

Address: Anjelierenlaan 25, 8400 Ostende. Tel: (059) 800428.

VANNECK, SIR PETER
UK, Cleveland, ED (C)

Sir Peter Vanneck, member of Lloyds and former member of Council of London Stock Exchange, was elected to the EP in 1979 and became a member of its Political Affairs Committee in July 1984. Lord Mayor of London, 1977–78, and Sheriff to the City of London, 1974–75. Royal Navy and Fleet Air Arm service, 1939–49, followed by service with Royal Auxiliary Air Force. Inspector RAuxAF, 1963–73; Hon. Inspector-General from 1974 and currently Hon. Air Commodore, No. 1 Maritime HQ Unit. Born Jan 7 1922; educated Geelong Grammar School; Stowe; Trinity College, Cambridge; Harvard. Special trustee, St Bartholomew's Hospital, since 1974; trustee, RAF Museum, since 1976.
Address: PO Box 560, London SW7 5LX.

VARFIS, GRIGORIOS
Greece, Soc (PASOK)

Mr Grigorios Varfis was elected to the EP in 1984. Counsellor to the Greek permanent representative to the Community, 1964. Director-General, Ministry of Foreign Affairs, 1974. Secretary of state for Foreign Affairs, 1981–84. Born 1927.

Address: Spefsipou 35, 10676 Athens.

VAYSSADE, MME MARIE-CLAUDE
France, Soc (PS)

Mme Marie-Claude Vayssade became an MEP in 1979 and chairman, EP Legal Affairs and Citizens' Rights Committee in July 1984. Head of Workers' Education Centre, Institute of Labour, University of Nancy II, 1968–79. Member, federal executive committee, PS, and Federal Bureau, Meurthe-et-Moselle Socialist Party. Member, Unified Socialist Party, 1967–74, when she joined the Socialist Party. Born Aug 8 1936; graduate in law.

Address: 78, rue du Maréchal Oudinot, 54000 Nancy. Tel: (08) 356 16 72.

VEIL, MME SIMONE
France, LD (UDF/RPR)

Mme Simone Veil became leader of the Liberal and Democratic Group in July 1984. Elected to the EP in 1979, being its President, 1979–82, then chairman of its Legal Affairs Committee. Appointed Minister of Public Health in 1974, and became Minister of Public Health and Family Affairs in 1978, resigning in 1979. Born Jul 13 1927; qualified in law at the Institut d'Etudes Politiques in Paris. Joined prisons service, Ministry of Justice, 1957, specializing in probation and rehabilitation. Appointed Secretary-General of the Conseil Superieur de la Magistrature (Supreme Council of the Judiciary) in 1970.

Addresses: 288 bd St Germain, 75007 Paris. Tel: 550 34 11. 11, place Vauban, 75007 Paris.

VERBEEK, HERMAN
Netherlands, ARC (PPR)

Mr Herman Verbeek was elected to the EP in 1984. Author, theologian and priest. Born May 17 1936. Member of EP Committee on Development and Cooperation.

Address: Nieuwe St Janstraat 29, 9711 VC Groningen.

VERGEER, WILLEM
Netherlands, EPP (CDA)

Mr Willem Vergeer was elected to the EP in 1979; member from 1978. A vice-chairman of EPP group since 1979. Member of the Dutch First Chamber since 1971. Member and alderman, Utrecht Council, 1966–77. National chairman of KVP (Catholic Popular Party) 1975–79; member, executive, CDA. Born Mar 28 1926. Former chairman, advisory council of the Netherlands Federation of Trades Unions, the Christian National TU Federation and the Dutch Catholic TU Federation.

Address: Molenaarstraat 55, 5374 GX Schayk. Tel: (08866) 2366. Postbus 5, 5374 ZG Schayk.

VERGES, PAUL
France, Comm (PCF)

M. Paul Verges, journalist, elected to EP in 1979, is Secretary-General of the Communist Party of Réunion. Born Mar 5 1925. Mayor of Le Port.

Addresses: Temoignages, B.P. 192, 97465 St Denis Cedex (Ile de la Réunion). Tel: 21 08 07. 10 rue René Villermet, 75011 Paris.

VERNIER, JACQUES
France, RDE (UDF/RPR)

M. Jacques Vernier, Mayor of Douai and regional councillor since 1983, became an MEP in 1984. Born Jul 3 1944. Polytechnician and mining engineer. Assistant general secretary, Seine–Normandy Basin Agency, 1972–74; director, Agence de l'Eau Nord–Artois–Picardie, 1974–83. Founder chairman, Douai Consumers' Association, 1978–83. Chairman, Douai Housing Aid Association, 1976–83. Author, *The Battle of the Environment*, 1971.

Address: Mairie de Douai, 59508 Douai Cedex.

VERNIMMEN, WILLY
Belgium, Soc (SP)

Mr Willy Vernimmen, elected to EP in 1979, is Senator for Oudenaarde-Ronse/Aalst; chairman, Socialist Party group in Senate in 1978. Member, Chamber of Representatives, 1969–71. Member, bureau of EP Socialist Group. Born Dec 23 1930. Former trade union secretary.

Addresses: Brugstraat 9, 9500 Geraardsbergen. Tel: (054) 413228. Hunnegemstraat 20, 9500 Geraardsbergen. Tel: (054) 41 64 34.

VETTER, HEINZ OSKAR
Germany, Soc (SPD)

Herr Heinz Oskar Vetter, a fitter, became an MEP in 1979. Chairman, German trade union federation, 1969; chairman, Confederation of Free Trade Unions in EEC, 1970. Vice-President, 1973, and President, 1974–79, European Trade Union Confederation. Born Oct 21 1917.

Addresses: von-Behring-Platz 4, 4330 Mülheim a.d. Ruhr. Abgeordneten Büro, Heinz Oskar Vetter, Breite Strasse 13, 4000 Düsseldorf 1. Tel: (0211) 82 52 12.

VGENOPOULOS, NIKOLAOS
Greece, Soc (PASOK)

Mr Nikolaos Vgenopoulos was elected to the EP in 1981 and re-elected in 1984. Co-founder and member of central committee of PASOK. Born Jan 30 1926; doctor and university lecturer. Convicted by court-martial in 1970 for opposition to the dictatorship. MP for Achaias, 1974–77.

Addresses: Asklipiou 89, 11472 Athens. Tel: (1) 3623289. Asklipiou 10, Athens 144. Tel: (1) 3634834.

VIEHOFF-MAAG, MEVR PHILI
Netherlands, Soc (PvdA)

Mevr Phili Viehoff-Maag became an MEP in November 1979; re-elected 1984. Cartographer. Has served on executive committee of PvdA and been party secretary, Gelderland province where she has been a member of the provincial council. Also member, Hoevelaken municipal council. Has served on EP Committee on Youth, Culture, Education, Information and Sport. Born Jun 8 1924.

Address: Zuidlaarderweg 3, 9756 CE Glimmen. Tel: (05906) 2494.

VISSER, BEN
Netherlands, Soc (PvdA)

Mr Ben Visser became an MEP in 1984. At the time of his selection he was a member of Gelderland provincial council. Born Feb 6 1934. Appointed one of the auditors of the EP Socialist Group.

Address: Huygenslaan 22, 6824 JH Arnhem. Tel: (085) 42 15 01.

VITTINGHOFF, KURT
Germany, Soc (SPD)

Herr Kurt Vittinghoff, a cabinet maker, was elected to the EP in 1984. Secretary, IG-metal trade union; member, SPD federal study group on employee problems. Born Jan 9 1928.

Address: Kolberger Strasse 6, 6550 Bad Kreuznach.

VRIES, GIJS DE
Netherlands, LD (VVD)

Mr Gijs de Vries was elected to the EP in 1984. On staff of university of Leiden. Local councillor. Born Feb 22 1956.

Address: Rijn en Schiekade 63, 2311 AM Leiden.

VRING, THOMAS VON DER
Germany, Soc (SPD)

Herr Thomas von der Vring was elected to the EP in 1979. Born May 27 1937. University lecturer and former Rector of University of Bremen. Deputy federal chairman, Young Socialists, 1964–70; member, Bremen executive, SPD, from 1974.

Address: Meissener Strasse 7, 2800 Bremen. Tel: (0421) 351557.

WAAL, LEENDERT VAN DER
Netherlands, NI (SGP)

Mr Leendert van der Waal was elected to the EP in 1984. Engineer. Member of committee of Reform Church in Holland. Born Sep 23 1928. Member, EP Transport Committee

Address: Lagendijk 60, 2981 EM Ridderkerk.

WAGNER, MANFRED
Germany, Soc (SPD)

Herr Manfred Wagner was elected to the EP in 1979. President of the Saar Trade Union Federation and of the Inter-Regional Council of Trade Unions of the Saar, Lorraine and Luxembourg. Member Saarland Landtag 1970–79, being deputy chairman of the political group. Member of the Economic and Structural Advisory Council to the Prime Minister of the Saarland. Vice-chairman, Sarrebruck SPD. Born Jan 14 1934.

Address: Finkenweg 30, 6604 Saarbrücken-Brebach-Fechingen. Tel: (06892) 2786 (privat), (0681) 47711 (büro).

WALTER, GERD
Germany, Soc (SPD)

Herr Gerd Walter was elected to the EP in 1979. Member, bureau of Socialist Group, from July 1984. Deputy chairman of Schleswig-Holstein SPD. Born Apr 24 1949; graduate in political science. Further education lecturer. Former chairman, Schleswig-Holstein Young Socialists.

Addresses: Morier Strasse 45, 2400 Lübeck, c/o SPD-Landesverband, 28–30 Kleiner Kuhberg, 2300 Kiel 1.

WAWRZIK, KURT
Germany, EPP (CDU)

Herr Kurt Wawrzik was a member of the Bundestag 1969–80. In European Parliament since 1977 being elected in 1979. Member, European Union. Treasurer, Deutsche Welthungerhilfe (German World Famine Relief), since 1977. Moulder. Member, works council, Daimler-Benz, 1951–75; Mannheim Town Council, 1965–69. Held honorary offices in metal industry trade union. Member of board of AOK Mannheim. Born Feb 15 1929. Married with two children.

Address: Am Wildpark 9, 6800 Mannheim 31. Tel: (0621) 721600.

WEBER, FRAU BEATE
Germany, Soc (SPD)

Frau Beate Weber was elected in 1979 and became a vice-chairman of its Committee on Environment, Public Health and Consumer Protection, being reappointed in July 1984. Deputy chairman, SPD Federal Council; member, Heidelburg municipal council from 1975. Born Dec 12 1943. Teacher.

Address: Sickingenstrasse 1, 6900 Heidelberg. Tel: (06221) 33626.

WEDEKIND, RUDOLF
Germany, EPP (CDU)

Herr Rudolf Wedekind became an MEP since 1981; re-elected 1984. Hanover alderman, 1964–78; member, Hanover area assembly, 1968–74; member, Diet of Lower Saxony, 1974–82. Born Aug 4 1938. Businessman.

Address: Kleine Pfahlstrasse 16, 3000 Hanover 1.

WELSH, MICHAEL
UK, Lancashire Central, ED (C)

Mr Michael Welsh, elected to the EP in 1979, became chairman of its Social Affairs and Employment Committee in July 1984; member, bureau of ED Group. Former director of market development with Levi Strauss and Co Europe SA. General manager, Channel Road Services Ltd, 1966–69. Born May 22 1942; educated Betteshanger School, Deal; Dover College and Lincoln College, Oxford. Former ED spokesman on external economic relations, and former member, EP economic and monetary affairs committee. Married with two children.

Address: Watercrook, 181 Town Lane, Whittle-le-Woods, nr Chorley, Lancs. PR6 8AG. Tel: (02572) 76992.

WEST, NORMAN
UK, Yorkshire South, Soc (Lab)

Mr Norman West, a miner, was elected to the EP in 1984 and joined the EP Committee on Energy, Research and Technology. Born Nov 26 1935; educated Barnsley, and through trade union scheme at Sheffield University. County councillor (chairman of the highways committee) and chairman, an anti-nuclear working party. Member, CND and NUM. Married with two sons.

Address: 43 Coronation Drive Birdwell, Barnsley, S. Yorkshire.

WETTIG, KLAUS
Germany, Soc (SPD)

Herr Klaus Wettig was elected to EP in 1979. Compositor. Born Aug 15 1940. Treasurer of EP Socialist Group until 1984. Chairman, Hanover Young Socialists, 1969–70; member, SPD bureau, Hanover, from 1970.

Address: Rohnsterrassen 6, 3400 Göttingen. Tel: (0551) 58 150.

WIECZOREK-ZEUL, FRAU HEIDEMARIE
Germany, Soc (SPD)

Frau Heidemarie Wieczorek-Zeul was elected to the EP in 1979 and was a vice-chairman of its Committee on External Economic Relations until 1984. Teacher. Member, South Hesse SPD executive and SPD national executive. Chairman, Young Socialists, 1974–77, and then of European Liaison Office, International Youth Organizations. Born Nov 21 1942. Member Rüsselsheim Council, 1968–77.

Addresses: Michelstädter Strasse 1, 6090 Rüsselsheim. Tel: (06142) 32868. Europa-Büro, SPD Bezirk Hessen-Sud, Fischerfeldstrasse 7–11, 6000 Frankfurt. Tel: (0611) 291096. Euro-Bureau, Avenue de la Sapinière 4, 1180 Bruxelles-Uccle. Tel: (02) 35 88 328.

WIJSENBEEK, FLORUS
Netherlands, LD (VVD)

Mr Florus Wijsenbeek was elected to the EP in 1984. Born Jun 16 1944. Head of the personal cabinet of Mr Cornelis Berkhouwer during his presidency of the European Parliament from 1973 to 1975. Was secretary general of the Federation of European Liberals.

Address: J. van Oldenbarneveltlaan 71, 2582 NW den Haag.

WINTER, AUGUST DE
Belgium, LD (PVV-ELD)

Mr August de Winter, a lawyer, was elected to the EP in 1984; member of Belgian Chamber of Representatives 1963–84; senator of the party since 1981. Former minister. Born May 12 1925.

Address: G. Van Haelenlaan 180, Bus 7, 1190 Brussel. Tel: (02) 344 91 65 or (02) 343 90 80.

WOGAU, KARL VON
Germany, EPP (CDU)

Herr Karl von Wogau, commercial lawyer, was elected to the EP in 1979. Political activities in the 'Junge Union' and CDU since 1964; member, CDU 'Land' committee on economic and social policy and of the district and federal executive of the CDU/CSU Middle Classes Association. Worked for Europa Union. Born July 18 1941.

Address: Bertholdstrasse 4, 7844 Neuenburg/Breisgau. Tel: (07631) 72867.

WOLFF, CLAUDE
France, LD (UDF/RPR)

M. Claude Wolff was elected to the EP in 1984. UDF deputy for Puy-de-Dôme since 1981. Born Jan 24 1924. Mayor of Chamalières, 1974. County councillor and Auvergne district councillor.

Address: Assemblée Nationale, 75355 Paris.

WOLTJER, EISSO P.
Netherlands, Soc (PvdA)

Mr Eisso P. Woltjer, an MEP since 1979, was a member of the teaching staff at Deventer Agricultural College, Member, Limburg Provincial Council, 1978–79. Born Jan 9 1942; studied at Wageningen Agricultural College.

Address: Bergkwartier 10, 5801 PS Venray. Tel: (04780) 84324.

WURTZ, FRANCIS
France, Comm (PCF)

M. Francis Wurtz became an MEP in 1979. A vice-chairman, EP Committee on Development and Cooperation from July 1984. Member of central committee of French Communist Party. Born Jan 3 1948. Former secretary, Bas-Rhin Federation of French Communist Party, and of Strasbourg 'new university'.

Addresses: 18, rue de la Division Leclerc, 67000 Strasbourg. 33, rue Compans, Appt. 189, 75019 Paris. Tel: 200 49 20.

YANNAKOU, KA MARIETTA
Greece, EPP (ND)

Ka Marietta Yannakou, an MEP since 1984, became vice-chairman of the EP Committee on Women's Rights in July 1984. Member, executive, New Democracy. Doctor, neurologist and psychiatrist. Born 1951; educated University of Athens and in Belgium and England. Founder member, ONNED, youth movement of the New Democracy Party; played leading part in setting up section for international relations. General editor, ONNED newspaper *Dimokratiki Proptoporia*. Founder member, Pan-Hellenic Union of Women Scientists.

Address: Evrou 10, 115 28 Athens.

ZAGARI, MARIO
Italy, Soc (PSI)

Sgr Mario Zagari was elected to the EP in 1979 and became a Vice-President of the European Parliament, 1979–82 and a quaestor, 1982–84. A Vice-President of the nominated Parliament. Unsuccessfully contested Presidency in July 1979. Founder member of Socialist group of European Coal and Steel Community 1953. Born Sep 14 1913; lawyer and journalist. Director of the periodical *Sinistra europea* (European left) from 1953. Has held office in several Italian governments, being Under Secretary of State at the Foreign Ministry, Minister for Foreign Trade, and Minister for Justice.

Addresses: 161 av. Winston Churchill, Aile Waldorf App. 91, 1180 Bruxelles. Viale della Tecnica 302, 00144 Roma. Tel: 5920449.

ZAHORKA, HANS-JÜRGEN
Germany, EPP (CDU)

Herr Hans-Jürgen Zahorka, a lawyer, was elected to the EP in 1984. Former state chairman of Baden-Württemberg boys' union; communal councillor at Boblinger Kreistag. Born Jan 14 1952.

Address: Schwenninger Strasse 32, 7032 Sindelfingen.

ZARGES, AXEL
Germany, EPP (CDU)

Herr Axel Zarges became an MEP before the June 1984 elections at which he was re-elected. Lawyer and notary. Vice-chairman of the European Union of Germany and of the German Council of the European Movement; chairman of the European Union of Hesse. Member, Hesse CDU management. Born Oct 7 1932.

Addresses: Ob. Königstrasse 47, 3500 Kassel. Tel: (0561) 12477–79. Rieckstrasse 10a, 3500 Kassel. Tel: (0561) 40 34 67.

Five years spent striving for power

By George Clark
former European political correspondent of *The Times*

During its first five years as a directly elected assembly, the European Parliament strove to assert its powers as guardian of the interests of the 270 million people of the Community, but with only modest success. Fresh from the hustings, the 410 hopeful MEPs soon discovered, when they got down to work, that their powers were severely limited. Those who believed that they would be able to share effectively in the law-making decisions of the Council of Ministers, or would have the power to overrule them, were disappointed.

More often than not – after weary hours in committees, the translation of millions of words into seven languages, long periods spent voting on amendments – the MEPs' recommendations on proposed laws were sent to the Council only to get lost. Ministers either brushed the MEPs' views aside or failed to agree on the text sent to them. The EEC Commission were much more amenable.

Whatever high hopes those first directly elected MEPs may have cherished when they arrived in Strasbourg in July, 1979, the harsh reality at the end of five years was that the Council of Ministers had failed to take a final decision on at least 750 reports and recommendations submitted to them by Parliament. Renting out pigeon-holes must be a profitable business in Brussels.

The argument, from the start, had been whether it was merely a consultative body or whether its limited powers could be exploited so that the demands of the electorate could be translated into action. Was it to continue the pattern of the old non-elected assembly and try to influence the Council of Ministers simply by its weighty opinions, or had it the right to take decisions which could not be overturned?

The answer proved to be 'Yes' to the latter, but only in a very limited way. And this was essentially due to the fact that there was no Government, as such, answerable to the Parliament as there is at Westminster, the Bundestag, the Dail etc. The 'Government', that is the Council of Ministers, could not be brought down by an adverse vote in the European Parliament; it did not have to come to the MEPs for approval of the taxes which formed its Budget fund.

Parliament's essential powers were to reject the annual spending Budget when it was considered to be unsatisfactory; to decide how the non-agricultural section of the Budget (about one-third of the total) should be spent; to give considered opinions on all proposed legislation and the annual farm price settlement; to dismiss the whole of the 14-man Commission running the bureaucracy in Brussels; and to submit to the Commission its 'own initiative' reports setting out the basis for new legislation.

Most of the time, it exercised those powers responsibly. Sometimes it behaved ridiculously, for example, by repeatedly calling for higher agricultural spending while at the same time demanding that a larger part of the Budget should be spent either in the industrial field on measures to fight unemployment or on enlarging the regional fund.

A reasonable end-of-term assessment is that it has proved to be more effective than the anti-Market critics claimed in 1979, but less successful as a democratic controlling force in the governance of Europe than the enthusiasts had predicted. Because of competing national interests and the domination of the centre right majority, the Parliament did not use its limited powers as adventurously as it might have done under the pressure of a left-oriented majority.

There were many occasions when MEPs objected to the petty restrictions which proposed regulations or directives sought to impose on consumers, producers and traders but, except for a few notable instances, they did not sufficiently exploit their power to obstruct them or to force the Council of Ministers to think again. By carefully identifying the areas where the powers have been effectively used and exploiting them more systematically, the new

Parliament could in future advance from the 'base camp' which has now been established towards more democratic control of the Community.

The Parliament elected in 1979 replaced an assembly delegated or nominated from the national parliaments consisting of 198 members. The 410 members of the new Parliament were elected by the voting systems used in national parliamentary elections.† Most of the countries had a system of proportional representation (PR). Britain retained its first-past-the-post system, with PR in Northern Ireland only.

The motley group of 81 MEPs from the United Kingdom – most of them with no previous parliamentary experience – joined their colleagues in Strasbourg knowing that of all the national contingents, they had been elected with the lowest poll – only 32 per cent of voters had bothered to turn out. Overall in the nine countries, the turnout was 61 per cent. In the Federal Republic of Germany, where a fair amount of razzamatazz had enlivened campaign meetings, it was nearly 66 per cent. In France, it was 61 per cent.

British journalists who reported the first few plenary sessions in Strasbourg, discovered that MEPs from other nations, especially the French and the continental Socialists, had the feeling that the United Kingdom, having been at first spurned, then hesitatingly accepted as a member of the EEC, was still not really committed to the European ideal. Had not the low poll confirmed that impression? The Labour Party, after all, was still officially committed to taking the United Kingdom out of Europe. Would not 'the Brits' (as our MEPs came to be called) be a disruptive force in the unique Parliament which had been called into existence?

As some reassurance, it was pointed out that in spite of the low turnout, which could be interpreted as a sign of anti-Europeanism, the British electors had chosen 60 Conservatives who were committed to Britain's continued membership, as against only 17 Labour members. Within the Labour Party there had been a clash of opinion. A large section of the movement still saw great advantages in belonging to the Community. In spite of the party's official edict, many Euro constituency selection meetings chose pro-European candidates and six of them were actually elected.

Doubts about the attitude of the British MEPs were soon dispelled. They proved to be the most diligent of all national contingents in attending to their parliamentary duties. Indeed, there were some Mondays and Fridays during the monthly plenary sessions when 'the Brits' had the debating chamber almost to themselves. It seemed that a lot of the enthusiastic Europeans were not so devoted to democracy that they could spare a whole week on the parliamentary chores. For them, it became a three-day week.

Where it had power over the Budget, Parliament was able to stop the Council in its tracks and force it to take notice of European public opinion. But on the countless everyday issues, such as those involving workers' rights and restrictions on trade, the Council was able to avoid action, even when Parliament had slaved for months working out agreed proposals in conjunction with the EEC Commission in Brussels.

In our history books, labels are attached to British Parliaments in the evolution of democracy. The Addled Parliament, the Long Parliament, the Mongrel Parliament, the Unlearned, the Useless, the Dunces' . . . these are some of the adjectives used to describe their character.

The first directly elected European assembly, during most of its five-year career, I would describe as The Frustrated Parliament. It was hidebound by the restrictions imposed by the Treaties of Rome; it was crippled by the limited scope of the European Budget, which still has not been adapted to meet the needs of European people as a whole. And, most frustrating of all, it was unable to persuade the Council of Ministers to change the financial system so that substantial aid could be brought to the industrial wastelands and to the 13 million unemployed Europeans, including a high proportion of school-leavers.

It is true, however, that although Parliament could not force the Council into action, the EEC Commission, the civil servants in Brussels appointed by the member States, was brought effectively under democratic control. Some diehards in the Commission still believe that the European Parliament has been too intrusive, and that, as laid down in the Treaties of Rome, the Commission should retain its preeminent role as the initiator of legislation. Legally, the Commission remains the initiating authority. But in the course of five years, the bureaucrats have learnt that they cannot hope to get far with their plans unless they consult the Parliament and heed MEPs' views throughout the gestation period.

Acting on the principle that what is not forbidden in the Treaties is permissible, Parliament widened the interpretation of 'consultation' to include the right of MEPs to initiate reforms. These sorties into the realm of legislating are known as 'own initiatives'. In 1980 there were 90

---

† On January 1, 1981, Greece joined the Community and elected 24 MEPs, bringing the total to 434.

such initiating reports, rising to more than 180 in 1983. Nearly all the major legislation coming from the Commission nowadays is based on either a Parliamentary resolution requesting specific changes in the law, or on 'own initiative' reports which have outlined the direction in which Parliament thinks the Commission should proceed.

Parliament also won the right to be consulted on all 'framework legislation' based on pre-1979 legislation, giving the Commission the power to make changes in regulations on its own authority. Following protracted disputes over the annual budget, a conciliation procedure was devised which brought the President and senior members of the Parliament into direct consultations at Ministerial level.

In the gradual merging of initiating powers, Parliament and Commission often found themselves 'ganging up' against the seemingly obstructive or laggard Council of Ministers. Whereas in 1979 there was often talk among MEPs about using their 'ultimate weapon', the power to dismiss the whole 14-man Commission (twice they nearly came to the point of doing so!), in the last few years the idea has been pushed into the background. The axe is still there, but it is getting rusty.

As MEPs pointed out during the 1984 campaign, the EEC Commission grew to like the slightly incestuous relationship, for it enabled them to don the protective clothing which a request from Parliament for legislation gave to them. It is claimed now that 80 per cent of the 'own initiative' requests sent on by Parliament are adopted by the Commission.

Parliament set up fourteen specialist committees, divided into subjects to match the administrative sections of the Commission: agriculture; budgets; political affairs; economic and monetary affairs; energy and research; external economic relations; legal affairs; social affairs and employment; regional policy and planning; transport; the environment, public health and consumer protection; youth, education and sport; development and cooperation in the Third World; and budgetary control. Others were added later, dealing with relations between the Community institutions, and with 'the situation of women in the Community'.

More recently, the disappearance of a quantity of dangerous dioxin-contaminated waste from Seveso, Italy, and the furore which followed, led to the setting up of a special committee of inquiry into the treatment of toxic and dangerous substances in the Community. Parliament and Council have already approved new regulations on the cross-frontier transport of such wastes, allowing proper monitoring of waste shipments from point of origin to the disposal facilities.

The committees hold most of the routine meetings in the new Parliamentary building sited in Rue Belliard, Brussels, close to the Commission HQ. This enables Commissioners and officials to attend and report on their activities. In these committees, Commissioners are cross-examined about the detail of their legislative proposals at an early stage. The democratic element was introduced into the law-making process in this way without much friction.

Nevertheless, there were some clashes in which Parliament stoutly insisted on its right not only to be consulted but to have its resolutions containing new instructions to the Commission implemented. Bitter exchanges took place during the consideration of a directive on workers' rights within multinational companies (The Vredeling Directive). Eventually the Commission caved in, though the amended regulation is still held up by disagreements within the Council of Ministers.

The Commission was brought to heel by a technicality which proved over the five years to be a valuable addition to the Parliament's powers. Almost by accident, it was highlighted by a case which came before the European Court of Justice in 1980. Known as 'the isoglucose case', it ended with a judgment which stated (inter alia):

Consultation which is provided for in the Treaty is the means which allows the Parliament to play an actual part in the legislative process of the Community. Such power represents an essential factor in the institutional balance intended by the Treaty . . . Due consultation of the Parliament . . . therefore constitutes an essential formality, disregard of which means that the measure concerned is void.

MEPs latched on to the significance of this very quickly. It meant that whenever they disagreed with a regulation or directive prepared by the Commission, they could stubbornly withhold their final vote on the 'Opinion' which they were required to give to the Council of Ministers before it could act. This right of veto has now been accepted by convention.

Most MEPs were much more concerned about the Council's refusal to act on regulations and directives where the Parliament had willingly, even urgently, given them an approving 'Opinion' or sent them proposals, which , if implemented, would have improved the daily life of ordinary people.

On one issue Parliament really lost its temper. Over the period 1979–82, the MEPs passed a number of resolutions calling on the Council to produce a common transport policy in line with Treaty requirements. No fewer than 55 proposals from Commission and Parliament had been submitted to the Ministers without any satisfactory response. Deciding that this amounted to a flouting of the will of the people, expressed through Parliament, the MEPs voted by 157 votes to 12 (with 12 abstentions) to take the Council to the European Court. This was in March, 1982.

The Council is charged with dereliction of duty under Article 3 and Articles 74–85 for failing to produce a common policy aimed at securing faster, more efficient and cheaper transport throughout the Community. In this context, the Council's failure to agree on a policy which would open up the state air lines to greater competition with benefits to the traveller in cheaper fares was the subject of bitter complaint. Air fares in Europe are fantastically high, compared with those in America. The Council came forward with a draft programme for future action in the hope of avoiding the ignominy of being taken to court, but Parliament was still not satisfied. The case is pending, but a recent United Kingdom–Netherlands agreement is opening the doors to cheaper air fares.

In a way, one could sympathise with the Council of Ministers in their various groupings. It must often be the case that they say, in effect, 'These are lovely schemes, excellent! But the Community's resources could not possibly be stretched to pay for them'. The cross-Channel link is a case in point.

But, more often, there is no positive action because the argument on a regulation or directive gets bogged down in the discussion of detailed national objections. The delay in reaching agreement on a Common Fisheries Policy demonstrated how pressure groups can influence events.

Ask MEPs how the log jam can be broken and most of them will reply that a system of qualified majority voting† should more commonly be used; they claim that the Council's work is aborted time after time by member Governments, or more often just one member Government, exercising the veto. Known as 'the Luxembourg compromise' (reached in 1966 at the behest of the then French Government), it allowed a member state to insist on a unanimous decision when it considered its vital national interests to be at stake. It has been increasingly used, even on proposals not involving major questions of policy.

Several times Parliament has asked the member Governments to agree on greater use of majority voting in Council. On two notable occasions, some Conservative MEPs found themselves disagreeing with Mrs Margaret Thatcher, the Prime Minister, on the issue. The first clash happened in May, 1982, when on consecutive days the Parliament debated, first, the question of continuing to support European sanctions against Argentina after the invasion of the Falkland Islands, thus backing Britain's use of force to restore the position; and, second, the farm price settlement, where Parliament and a majority in the Council of Ministers were prepared to approve a higher award than that demanded by the British Government.

Knowing that support for Britain's tough military action was ebbing away in some European parties, Sir Henry Plumb, Leader of the 60 British Conservatives, said during the agricultural debate:

We in the Conservative group clearly recognise the deep concern of many members of this House about the problem of settling farm prices. We recognise that the Community will be a much more credible force . . . when she can settle her domestic problems with greater speed and efficiency.

Other groups in this House know very well that we are in favour of majority voting as a means towards this end . . . While representing our own countrymen, we recognise a responsibility towards the Community as a whole.

An amendment to the agricultural motion, tabled by Mr William Newton Dunn, Conservative MEP for Lincolnshire, on his own initiative, calling for the farm prices to be settled by majority vote, in the Council of Ministers, was approved by 98 votes to 31.

The Conservatives split in three ways: eleven voted for it, ten were against, 13 abstained; the rest (including Sir Henry Plumb) were not present in the Chamber. Messages from Mrs Thatcher indicated that she was not pleased.

Sir Henry wrote to her in explanation:

---

† Under such a system the United Kingdom, Germany, France and Italy have 10 votes each, Belgium, Greece and the Netherlands 5 votes each, Denmark and Ireland 3 votes each, and Luxembourg 2 votes; total 63.

Our group succeeded in getting an unequivocal decision from the European Parliament in favour of a renewal of sanctions against Argentina. This was a good deal more difficult than it had been last month, with many of our colleagues on the Right, as well as the Left, suggesting that Britain did not seem to believe that solidarity was a two-way process.

While we accept that there should be no link made between agricultural prices and the Falklands, we took the view that it was necessary to acknowledge that many European farmers are, in their view, in crisis. In my speech during the debate I deliberately referred to majority voting in this context. We felt that the renewal of sanctions by the Community should be our highest priority. I hope the decisions of the Parliament and the Commission will help towards this end.

The net result of a loss of Community support for Britain in this crisis would be disastrous for public opinion in Britain and for the cohesion of the Community as a whole.

Sir Henry Plumb was right about the changing mood in Europe. In the April session, Parliament had voted by 203 votes to 28 in support of the British response to the Argentine invasion and in favour of economic sanctions imposed by the Ten. But at that crucial May session, the voting was only 131 in favour and 79 against. The Socialist group, consisting of 125 MEPs, expressed strong reservations.

Mrs Barbara Castle, Leader of the British Labour Group, said 'The Community is turning the screw. Mrs Thatcher will clearly have to pay a high price for continuing sanctions . . .' She said her group voted solidly against the 'sell-out' on farm prices because it would allow the biggest annual increase (10.4 per cent) in the Community's history and would push food prices up to unacceptable levels.

Many speakers from other countries condemned the United Kingdom's 'intransigence' over farm prices. 'The word solidarity seems to exist in every other language except English,' M. Yves Galland, a French Liberal, complained. 'You cannot reject solidarity just because it costs money.' So the ball was passed on to the Council of Ministers where the farm price settlement for 1982, long delayed, was approved by majority vote, with only Mr Peter Walker, then the British Minister of Agriculture, dissenting. The British Government formally protested about this refusal to strive for unanimity, claiming that Mr Walker had a right to use the veto under the terms of the Luxembourg compromise.

Support for a majority system of voting in the Council became almost a test of virility. The reformers said that the Community would just stagnate if the present method of voting continued. And when Parliament produced its blueprint for the future development of the EEC institutions – Council, Commission and Parliament – in February, 1984, the veto issue was again prominent in the discussion.

Twenty-two of the 60 British Conservatives voted for the plan for a new European treaty on European union presented by Mr Altiero Spinelli, the Italian Communist and a former EEC Commissioner, who had taken a leading role in the movement for reform and had chaired the relevant committee. It was approved by 231 votes to 31.

Key clauses called for the phasing out of a member Government's right of veto in the Council of Ministers over a period of ten years; an increase in Parliament's powers; new rules to oblige the Council to take decisions more speedily; and, eventually, a power for the Community to raise its own revenue, by decision of Parliament.

Labour members voted mainly against the plan, though Mr Derek Enright (Leeds – he later failed to be re-selected for that seat), Mr Ken Collins (Strathclyde East), and Mr Gordon Adam (Northumbria) chose to abstain. In the Conservative group, Mr Brian Hord (London West), Mr John Marshall (London North), Mr Christopher Prout (Shropshire and Stafford) and Sir Fred Warner (Somerset) were against. Mr Peter Price (Lancashire West) and Mr Michael Welsh (Lancashire Central) registered abstentions. The other 36 Tories were absent from the Chamber.

This divided approach to a resolution which incorporated three key proposals to which Mrs Thatcher and her Government were bitterly opposed – ending the veto, adding to Parliament's powers, and the Community raising taxation – was not warmly welcomed in London.

Mrs Thatcher was insisting on using the veto in negotiations going on through 1983 and 1984 because she could not accept that the modest proposals for changing the Community's financing system were sufficient to remedy the injustice to Britain. Under the existing system, the United Kingdom had to pay vastly bigger sums into the EEC coffers than any other member state. The UK imports more food and other goods from outside the Community than the others, and its contributions through duties and levies are disproportionately higher as a result. Over two-thirds of the Community budget goes on farm support, but, because of the relatively small size of the British farming industry, the UK received only a minor share of the big sum paid to farmers.

The injustice built into the system, which British ministers had warned in 1973 would produce a crisis, was acknowledged by the other states, who approved refunds to the UK of £710m in 1980, £860 in 1981, £490m in 1982, and £457m in 1983 (payment of which was held up by the European Parliament to force the Council of Ministers into reforming the system).

One of the ironies of this protracted dispute was that Mrs Thatcher and her Government had – when it came to the test – stronger support from Mrs Barbara Castle, who led the Labour group, and her sixteen colleagues than that offered by the Conservatives.

When they stood for the European election in 1979, the Labour MEPs were officially committed to the party policy of taking the United Kingdom out of the EEC if fundamental reforms were not carried through. Thus it was natural that the Labour MEPs, with only a few exceptions, should be highly critical of almost everything that the EEC commission proposed. On every occasion when the question of Britain's refunds came up for consideration, or when a majority of MEPs, urged on by the strong farmers' lobby, wanted higher prices than were justified, the Labour MEPs spoke and voted for Britain's just return of overpaid contributions, and against high food prices. They said that the consumer came first, and that pushing up prices beyond people's reach would create food mountains.

This distinctly pro-British line led to strained relations between the Labour contingent and the rest of the 125-strong European Socialist group. Sometimes it seemed that they were not speaking to each other. Faced with a solid centre right majority, made up of the Christian Democrats (117 members), European Democrats (Conservatives) (63), the French Gaullists (22) and many in the Liberal group (38), the leader of the European Socialist group, Mr Ernest Glinne (Belgium), was anxious to get his force acting in unity. Often, the British were the dissenting section, especially on farm prices and also on the advance towards closer European union. Mr Glinne, for example, voted for the Spinelli proposals.

Continental socialists were baffled by the British Labour attitude. It seemed to them that 'the Brits' had renounced internationalism for 'Little Englandism' and had opted out of the main struggle in which they were engaged: the achievement of 'a socialist Europe'.

Back home, the Labour Party annual conference continued to call for a commitment to withdraw from Europe. The moderate, pro-European element in the party was swamped by the aggressive left wing, which succeeded in getting the system of candidate reselection adopted. Among other effects, this put into the hands of constituency left-wing activists the power to eliminate the pro-Europeans.

Labour leaders had a tough time in Brussels in 1982 explaining the necessity, as they saw it, for a future Labour Government to take Britain out of the community. Nevertheless, and perhaps under the influence of continental colleagues, a change of opinion against the official party line was taking place in the Labour group at Strasbourg. The breakaway of 13 Labour MPs at Westminster and their formation, with Mr Roy Jenkins, the former Labour Chancellor of the Exchequer and former President of the EEC commission, of the Social Democratic Party – firmly committed to Britain's continued membership of the EEC – also had a traumatic effect.

By the time the Labour Party came to fight the 1983 general election on a pledge to withdraw from the EEC institutions, only half a dozen of the Labour MEPs at Strasbourg remained fully committed to the party line. And in January 1984, Mr Michael Gallagher, the Labour MEP for Nottinghamshire actually switched to the SDP only to be defeated in the 1984 Euro elections.

Even Mrs Castle, former Labour Cabinet Minister and a leading critic of the EEC, argued that the party should not get itself so firmly committed to withdrawal. Her advice was that a future Labour Government should carry through its promised socialist policies, regardless of whether they would involve breaching the Treaty of Rome, and just wait and see if the rest of the Community would throw Britain out.

Meanwhile, in France, President François Mitterand was demonstrating that he could introduce Socialist measures, including further nationalisation and exchange control, without running foul of the Treaty provisions.

After the disaster which struck the Labour Party in the 1983 general election, the new leadership got conference backing for the abandonment of the 'get-out-of-Europe' policy. Research showed that it had been one of the planks in Labour's platform which had little appeal, especially when the pro-European parties emphasised that perhaps 2½ million jobs could be at risk if the UK withdrew from the EEC. Its 1984 Euro manifesto reflected a more pragmatic view of prospects in Europe but nevertheless retained the option of withdrawal.

British MEPs took a leading part in the big clashes which occurred annually between Parliament and the Commission over the shape of the annual budget, debated in December, and the fixing of farm prices, usually debated in March.

To an outsider, it seemed an amazing inconsistency that every year there seemed to be a majority in favour of a switch of Community resources from agriculture to the social and regional funds to be used in the fight against unemployment, and every spring there was a majority for increasing the subsidies to farmers. If the 65–70 per cent portion of the budget devoted to agricultural support was to remain inviolate, how on earth could the financial system be adapted to the urgent need for economic revival? The answer to that conundrum is that there were different majorities.

There is perhaps an analogy with the House of Lords (although events this year make this less so). When a Conservative Government is in power and one of its measures is threatened, the backwoods peers can be rustled up to give a majority. Similarly, the farmers' lobby is able to spur a large attendance of MEPs from areas largely dependent on agriculture when farm prices are debated.

MEPs in the 'reform majority', if it can be so styled, flexed their muscles early on. In December, 1979, Parliament rejected the draft budget for 1980, the aim being to persuade the Commission and the Council of Ministers to get some sense into the financial arrangements. A related issue at that time was the question of Britain's refund of £710m for 1980 which Mrs Thatcher had demanded at the Dublin summit meeting in November, 1979. Although the issue of funds was restricted for a time and the MEPs themselves had to exist on short commons, little was achieved. Mrs Castle was furious about the stubbornness of the pro-farmers' faction. It was pathetic, she said, to hear the farmers' MEPs asking for more money when bankruptcy loomed ahead.

Mr Robert Jackson, Conservative MEP for Upper Thames and rapporteur for the Budgets Committee, put the case succinctly when the Parliament blocked the rebate of £490m to Britain in 1982:

> Basically, Parliament is right to want a permanent solution for the different countries' contributions to be based on their relative wealth. That is what the British Government has been pressing for. Perhaps the Council of Ministers will take this suggestion seriously now – in which case, the Parliament will have done Britain and the Community a considerable service.

At Westminster the delay in paying the refund was seen as an anti-British move, but MEPs from the other countries insisted that it was merely a manoeuvre to force the hand of the Council of Ministers. Month by month, the budget crisis got worse. It was obvious that the Community would soon run out of funds. To get more money, either from a larger slice of Value Added Tax from each country, or from other duties, the Community would be in pawn to the national parliaments. And it was blindingly obvious that Mrs Thatcher would not think of providing extra sources of revenue until the basic financial structure of the Community had been reformed.

With bankruptcy looming, the Commission bravely submitted that in the year 1983–84 farm prices should rise by an average of only 4.4 per cent. But the reliable farmers' vote was called out, and Parliament called for at least a 7 per cent increase.

Time and time again, British Conservative MEPs commended the plan for a reform of the Common Agricultural Policy (CAP) put forward in 1981 by Sir Henry Plumb (later to become leader of the European Conservative Group) when he was chairman of the Parliament's Agricultural Committee. This suggested that surplus production could be dealt with by having 'standard quantities' for each crop. It would have allowed the annual fixing of the total output for each product that was required to meet consumer need, and production in excess of the quota would not get any financial assistance.

That system, Sir Henry and his committee argued, would automatically put an end to the creation of butter 'mountains' and wine 'lakes', and prevent the over-production of any commodity. In addition, the Plumb report proposed a less restrictive regime for the import of agricultural products, in particular those not produced in adequate quantities to satisfy the Community market by the European farmers. More important, in view of the continual criticism of the sale of cheap butter and grain to the Soviet Union and the East European countries, the report proposed the phasing out of subsidies on such exports.

Put briefly, the proposal was that production, if possible, should match the demand of the EEC market and that, if surpluses were accumulated, they should not be sold off at scandalously cheap prices while the European housewife was paying artificially high prices. Incredibly, this 1981 plan was scorned by the Council of Ministers until, in 1984, the imminent collapse of the whole financial system brought them face to face with realistic decisions.

The Fontainbleau summit at the end of June brought a conclusion to the five year argument. There was agreement on a new method of reckoning contributions to the EEC fund which guaranteed that the British rebates would be assured in the future without the annual wrangle, and that, subject to approval by the national parliaments, the Community's resources would be increased by raising the level of contributions from Value Added Tax from 1 per cent to a 1.4 per cent limit.

Mrs Thatcher, reporting to the Commons afterwards, found that many in her own party, as well as the Opposition, were sceptical about the value of the deal that had been struck. But she insisted that, even with a higher rate of VAT contributions, the United Kingdom would get a much better bargain.

For the Community, however, the major problem remained: how could expenditure on the Common Agricultural Policy be cut back to allow for investment in industrial revival? Mrs Thatcher had to concede that, even with the introduction of quotas to reduce milk production, spending on the CAP would rise in the coming years if further reforms were not accepted.

So, at the end of five years' struggle between the pro-farmers' lobby and the MEPs who demand action to halt the tide of unemployment, the problem confronting the new members in the European Parliament is essentially the same as that first tackled by the 1979 assembly. *Plus ça change, plus c'est la même chose!*

Northern Ireland, represented by the Rev. Ian Paisley (Democratic Unionist Party), Mr John Hume (Social and Democratic Labour Party) and John Taylor (Official Ulster Unionist) suddenly came into the headlines in February, 1983, when the Parliament's political Affairs Committee decided in Brussels by 12 votes to 7 to investigate conditions in Northern Ireland and make a report which they hoped would lead to the ending of hostility between the Catholic and Protestant communities.

Mrs Thatcher reacted strongly when it was reported on the BBC radio that the committee proposed that political as well as economic and social conditions would come under scrutiny and that representatives of all factions would be invited to give evidence at public sessions in Belfast, Dublin and London. She told the Commons – and Mr Michael Foot, the Opposition leader quickly agreed with her – that on no account would the European Parliament be allowed to touch on the delicate political and constitutional issues. That would be interference in the internal affairs of the United Kingdom.

As it turned out, reports from Brussels about the decision of the committee were inaccurate. Lady Elles, leading Conservative MEP on the committee, contradicted the unofficial 'leaks' from the committee and assured Mrs Thatcher that the investigation would not trespass on constitutional relationship matters. Naturally, there were some in the European Parliament who wanted the 'European dimension' to be brought to bear on the Irish problem. After all, there appeared to be a conflict between member states of the Community and it left the European Parliament with not much credibility if it condemned internal strife in remote countries outside the EEC while it ignored a running sore on its own body.

Later, at a private meeting with Conservative MEPs, Mrs Thatcher heard the accurate account of what was proposed, but she was not mollified. There was still going to be an investigation by an outside body; there was still going to be a report. She made it bluntly clear that she would have preferred that British MEPs had stood up for the Government and had none of this.

The Irish incident, and the Tory split over majority voting on the farm price settlement in 1982, probably represent the lowest points in the relations between the Conservative group and the party back home. Yet on both occasions there were good tactical reasons why the Conservatives in Strasbourg should have heeded the opinion of their colleagues from other countries, and taken the course they did. Later, of course, the Labour Party were to attempt to make political capital out of the apparent split between the Tory party at home and the Tory party away. But that split was minimal compared with the massive split which existed in the Labour party about Europe.

The outcome of the Irish investigation was not at all embarrassing to the British Government. It was conducted by Mr Niels Haagerup, a Danish liberal, who concluded that a united Ireland could not be brought about in the foreseeable future and that a British withdrawal would only increase the violence. He could not see the Republic of Ireland being able to incorporate Northern Ireland, to which the British taxpayers were contributing £1000m a year.

The European Parliament approved a resolution in April, 1984, strongly condemning all acts of violence and terrorism in Northern Ireland, and calling on the British and Irish Governments to set up a joint Anglo–Irish parliamentary body, containing representatives of the two national parliaments and representatives from any elected body truly representative of all the people of Northern Ireland, to try to find a way forward. It was suggested that European MPs could also join the joint organization.

Relations between British members of the European Parliament and the two Houses at Westminster were not easy, especially in the House of Commons, where the identity cards showing membership at Strasbourg were not considered enough to guarantee entry to the Central Lobby when MEPs wanted to consult Westminster colleagues. Both Labour and Conservative MEPs had sad stories to tell of their treatment as ordinary members of the public. There was no formal system of coordinating political action at Westminster and in Europe. They seemed to be treated as pariahs. Before the direct election there had been fine talk about setting up a new Grand Committee to deal with European affairs, including members from the Commons and Lords, and members from Strasbourg. But within weeks that idea was buried.

When special advice was needed in a party committee meeting at Westminster the appropriate MEPs were invited along, but very often work at the plenary session or in committee in Brussels got in the way. MEPs got their best recognition from the House of Lords Committee on the European Communities, which continues to produce the best researched and most comprehensive reports on proposed EEC legislation. They were invited to give their views – and often to interpret political moves being made in Strasbourg – on a wide variety of proposals.

The Conservatives were kept well briefed by ministers and by the Foreign Office. Their leaders, first Sir James Scott-Hopkins (Hereford and Worcester) and later Sir Henry Plumb (Cotswolds), kept in close touch with the Prime Minister when international events were the subject of emergency debates, or there were issues before the Parliament involving Britain's vital interests. The Labour group had two or three meetings each year with the full national executive of the Party to discuss current topics and also contributed a section to the annual report setting out the record of their activities in Strasbourg.

On a national basis, however, the system of consultation and coordination left much to be desired. Many British MEPs think that the scheme adopted by the West German Bundestag in June, 1983, provides a model for a joint committee. It enables members of the Bundestag and German MEPs to determine jointly what recommendations shall be placed before the Bundestag on matters of basic policy.

Looking back on the controversies of the last five years, the dispute over the directive on workers' rights in multinational companies – the Vredeling Directive, named after the commissioner who introduced it in 1980 – was fiercest. The directive sought to give workers in multinational undertakings the right to information about their firm's sales and production figures, profits, investment programmes and – crucial to the argument – advance information about any plant closures.

The directive became the focus for intense lobbying by the employers on one side, and the European trade unions on the other. In the Chamber it became a battle between the centre right and the Socialists and their allies. During three hours of voting, the built-in centre right majority† carried a series of amendments which the unions said emasculated the modest reforms that the Commission had drafted. Mr Ivor Richard, the commissioner for employment, was a disappointed man and did not conceal his anger. He went back to the Commission with the mauled directive, but they refused to accept several of the changes carried by Parliament. The centre right would not stand for this and again tore into the amended version.

Using the isoglucose case as their precedent, the majority refused to pass the final Opinion until they got their changes accepted. Without an Opinion, the Council of Ministers could not act. As it happened, the directive got bogged down in the Council and at the time of Parliament's dissolution, Ministers had still not reached agreement on it.

Sir David Nicolson, Conservative MEP for London Central, summed up the right's objections to the original directive: 'It would undermine management authority, delay decision-making, weaken our cost competitiveness and discourage inward investment,' he said. It was the wrong priority. Parliament should have been debating ways to restructure and stimulate industry.

The Confederation of British Industry still argue that even the modified draft would create 'very great risk' of confidential information leaking to rival firms, would undermine local managers by allowing unions direct access to the HQ office, would impose new costs, and risk industrial conflict by giving rise to demands and expectations which could not be fulfilled. The British Government is still opposing the directive.

M. Mitterand, when he addressed the last session of Parliament before the 1984 election,

---

† In this context it is worth recording that the centre right could usually muster up to 240 votes out of a total of 434 members.

shocked British pro-Europeans when he hinted that Britain might be relegated to a subordinate position in a 'two-speed Europe'. He and his Foreign Minister, M. Cheysson, referred to British demands for a restructured financial system as 'petty quarrelling'.

Referring to Parliament's approval of the Spinelli report calling for a new treaty to advance the Community towards closer union, M. Mitterand said that France was ready to take part in such a move. 'I suggest, to that end, that preparatory talks are started which could lead to a conference of those member states who are interested,' he said. Any country could opt not to join in the new union if it did not want to be further involved in this new vision of Europe, he added.

The Spinelli report proposed the phasing out of the veto in the Council of Ministers. M. Mitterand supported this: Mrs Thatcher is adamantly opposed. 'It is time,' said the French President, 'to find some more normal and promising approach than that offered by the insistence on unanimity in Council decisions. The practice has gone way beyond the limits of the Treaty and even beyond those envisaged in the Luxembourg agreement. Recourse to unanimity should be restricted to specific cases. Once again, it is time to go back to the Treaties.' He also emphasized the need to restore to the Commission its proper authority. 'It is not the role of the European Council to be a generalized court of appear,' said M. Mitterand.

In Paris two days later, Sir Geoffrey Howe, the Foreign and Commonwealth Secretary, rejected the idea that Britain should be a second-class or associate member of the Community. Britain was determined to pursue its important contribution to the modernization of Europe, he emphasised.

Signifying the Labour Party's backing for reforms to remove the injustice to Britain, Mr Neil Kinnock later told M. Mitterand it was not a petty quarrel. 'It is not petty,' he said. 'It is a symptom of the inadequacies of the system.'

These exchanges set the scene for MEPs as they assembled for the new Parliament.

Policies of Parliament's political group

THE SOCIALIST CONFEDERATION
Fight for jobs is top priority

The manifesto of the Confederation of Socialist Parties of the European Community was agreed at a congress of the confederation in Luxembourg on March 8 and 9, 1984. With its publication in the United Kingdom came a foreword by Mr James Mortimer, general secretary of the Labour Party, pointing out that for obvious reasons it represented a compromise and not all of the many detailed proposals contained in it were supported by all the parties. Indeed, each of the parties would in any case be presenting their own manifestos to their own electorate.

It was clear, he said, that there was a very wide measure of agreement on the principal issue in the elections – the policies needed to defeat unemployment. At the same time, however, the British Labour Party did find it necessary to enter some reservations on certain other issues.

The foreword continued:

We were unable to reach agreement on three quite important issues. These were the European Monetary System (of which Britain is not a member); the powers of the European Parliament; and a proposal to increase the community's 'own resources'. On these issues, our reservations are included in footnotes to the text.

The Labour Party delegation to the Congress also considered it necessary to put onto the record further reservations about the actual wording of the document – even though there were no serious problems over policy. In particular, the delegation was concerned that the text was sometimes less specific than the party would have liked. These points included:

That the Labour Party interprets the first paragraph of the manifesto as meaning that we would use the EEC to further our objectives.

That the commitment to the 35-hour week must involve no reduction in pay.

That the references to energy policy in no way detract from the Party's policy for the coal industry and, in particular, our call for a major increase in investment in coal.

That the reference to the reduction of nuclear arsenals in no way detracts from the Labour Party's own policy on nuclear weapons.

In these EEC elections, the Labour Party will be fighting on the policies set out in its own EEC manifesto. As we make clear in our manifesto, the framework of policy for Labour's campaign is set by the programme on which we fought the general election. This confederation manifesto, therefore, should be read alongside the Party's EEC manifesto, and other relevant policy statements.

Jobs and industry
It is important to stress, however, that the central theme of this manifesto is strongly supported by all of the member parties of the Confederation – as well as by all the trade unions in the Community. This concerns the absolute priority that needs to be given, by the Community, to the issue of jobs – with the Confederation calling on all member states to act together now to create jobs and cut unemployment. Among the measures included here – and upon which we all agree – are:

A massive increase in public investment and in investment in industry, so as to encourage economic expansion throughout the Community.

A huge increase in training and retraining.

A new priority to be given to regional development.

Rapid progress towards a 35-hour week.

Action to support the development of effective industrial democracy.

Positive action to help provide equal rights for women.

These are the real issues in these elections. These are the issues upon which all of us – socialists parties and trade unions alike – will be fighting. For Labour's aim, the aim of our socialist allies, is to achieve a new deal for the people of Europe.

A joint declaration on June 1, 1984, by the leaders of the parties to the confederation, stated that the overriding issue was the fight for jobs. On this they stated:

Public investment must play a key role in the recovery of economic activity. That is why we support the proposal – put forward by the European Trade Union Confederation (ETUC) – for a coordinated investment push by the European members of the OECD, amounting to 1 per cent of GNP of all the countries concerned.

We are convinced that a policy for economic revival will require positive employment policies, which must include redistribution of work. This could be done in different ways:

the 35-hour week
lowering of the retirement age
extension of holidays
policies for vocational training and continuing education

We support the trade unions in their current struggle for the 35-hour week and for more jobs.

The following are extracts from the Confederation Manifesto of nearly 10 000 words:

Jobs – Peace – Freedom

As European Socialists, we are internationalists by definition. The European Community, of which our countries are members, represents a supplementary instrument for the realisation of our goals: social justice, solidarity and freedom.

The strength of the Labour movement which originated in our countries, the quality of our trade union traditions, the alliance of democracy and socialism, the richness and diversity of the socialist experience mean that the European Community remains a decisive region for the future of socialism and the democratic and progressive forces throughout the world.

We need a European Community which is not a commercial and technocratic Europe, but a fraternal Europe of the people. The 1984 elections can contribute to this transformation.

It is in this spirit that the Socialist members of the European Parliament have led and are leading a continuous battle in all the fields for which the European Parliament is at present competent: social, economic, industrial and agricultural policy, the fight against unemployment, control of multi-national companies, cooperation for the development of the poorest countries, respect for human rights in the world. We need support in extending and intensifying these activities and in making them more effective.

It is in this spirit that we are proposing three themes for a line of action for the European Socialist Group: JOBS, PEACE and FREEDOM.

The fight for jobs is our absolute priority

The fight for jobs is at present our top priority. The social breakdown and the human suffering caused by the present mass unemployment are unacceptable. It is imperative that we offer new prospects for the millions of unemployed in Europe. Moreover, only an immediate reaction aimed at casting out the curse of unemployment can enable us to resolve the growing economic and budgetary imbalances in Europe. We are determined to maintain and develop our social security systems in Europe. It is therefore necessary to create jobs.

Over the past years, we have noticed the refusal of employers to develop real economic and social cooperation on the European level. Nevertheless, in order to make a reality of the social entity which the Community should constitute, a European employment plan, containing a clear commitment to the creation of jobs in the private and public sectors, would be an important step.

Public investment can play a key role in the recovery of economic activity. Moreover, there are many opportunities for organising investment programmes, especially in the fields of energy saving, construction and urban planning, transport, environmental protection, the sectors of high technology, etc.

An important role can be played by public demand within the Common Market. Furthermore, the impact of an expansionary policy would be greater if it was carried out simultaneously in all European countries. This is why we support the proposal – put forward by the trade union movement (the ETUC) – in favour of a major public investment push.

According to the European Socialists and the ETUC, this must be coordinated at the level of the European members of the OECD and must amount to 1 per cent of GNP. In this context, the member states of the European Community can play a determining role, by concluding an agreement within the Council of Ministers.

The international environment must also change. As a first step towards progress in the North–South dialogue, all the countries of the Community should put into practice their commitment to contribute 0.7 per cent of the GNP as net official development aid (NDA) as soon as possible. A policy on transfer of capital towards the Third World is an important part of a policy for economic recovery.

Structural policies
The European Commission, in close association with the European Parliament, should propose a European industrial programme. More than ever before, the economic crisis and the anarchy of the markets prove the necessity of democratic planning. Furthermore, in some of the European countries, the conservatives have completely destroyed all instruments for planning. The privatisation of public companies is the latest example of this negative approach. We are strongly opposed to this policy.

Any industrial policy must be accompanied by a consumer policy (consumer protection to defend their purchasing power and their economic interests, through their participation in economic decisions, through the development of safe products which are neither dangerous to the health of consumers nor to the environment, and through an improvement in the quality of products and services). These questions should be dealt with and particularly on the European level.

The Energy Council must promote tangible measures with regard to the development, better use and external supplies of energy, bearing in mind that Europe's vulnerability in the field of energy can best be reduced by the more effective exploitation of European energy resources and the development of research into sources of renewable energy.

A substantial increase in the resources of the Regional Development Fund is of crucial importance. We support a reform of the way in which the Regional Fund operates, especially:

an increased concentration of grants on the poorer regions of the EEC, taking account of the problems of urban concentrations, which are often pockets of poverty within the richest regions;

the part of the Fund which can be freely allocated outside the national quotas should be increased to 20 per cent.

The inadequate substance of the proposal for a Fifth Directive on the structure of public limited companies and of the Vredeling proposal for a directive, adopted by the European Parliament, makes it necessary to draw up more complete European legislation on industrial democracy applicable both to national and multinational firms. This would constitute a major advantage in view of reinforcing the present legislation within the European countries.

An active employment policy
If we really want to attack unemployment, a radical redistribution of work is indispensable. In accordance with the proposals of the ETUC, this can be achieved by a number of different measures, such as the reduction of the working week to 35 hours, the lowering of the retirement age, the extension of annual holidays, etc . . . .

In order to have a real effect on employment, the reduction of working hours should proceed with relatively important steps at once, which are well planned. The 35-hour week should be a first common target in the whole of the Community.

The reduction of the working week is not only an instrument for creating jobs, but is also a vital component of social and cultural development. In the coming years, this reduction should remove the artificial barriers between work and leisure, manual and intellectual work and the existing inequalities between men and women.

The European Social Fund, whose financial resources must be extended, will play a major role in this field, especially in the field of job creation and of vocational training for young people.

The scale of unemployment among young people under 25 has become monstrous. This is a truly alarming situation. We rely on young people to guarantee the economic and democratic future of our society. It is essential that opportunities for school and vocational training for young people are improved. We call for more jobs for young people and also for social training schemes.

Monetary stability and economic recovery
The countries of Europe together constitute an economic area and a market which are superior to the United States and Japan. However, they are suffering the full effects of American monetary policies which are financing a record budgetary deficit through high

interest rates, which in turn lead to an erratic rise in the value of the dollar, the only currency for international settlements.

From our point of view, monetary stability is an important component of economic recovery and of a greater independence vis-à-vis the United States. It is essential that the monetary policy of the member states should reinforce our expansionary policy and contribute to the convergence of economic policies to promote the recovery.

From our point of view, a strengthened European Monetary System would be an important asset. We note however that Great Britain is not a member.[†] It could for example constitute a basis for increased independence of the European countries vis-à-vis the United States in economic and monetary affairs. However, in order to use the European Monetary System as an instrument for economic recovery in Europe, several problems must be dealt with:

> The burden of adjustment (upwards or downwards) within the EMS must be shared equally between all the partners, and the adjustment mechanism should be independent from short-term capital movements.

> The potential of short-, medium- and long-term loans, which are in principle available within the EMS, should be used; close cooperation between central banks must support the EMS and offset speculative capital movements.

> The reinforcement of the EMS logically necessitates the creation of a European Monetary Fund which will control the evolution of the EMS in close contact with the political authorities of the Community.

> In the short-term, the ECU must be given a larger role to play. Its role as payment currency should be more widely recognised within Europe. In the medium-term, this currency could act as monetary focal point in the constitution of a new international monetary order. The creation of conditional drawing rights attached to a European Monetary Fund should be considered, to which the developing countries could subscribe.

> The European countries should form a resolute bloc in order to exert as much pressure as possible upon the United States so that they will change their restrictive monetary policies and stabilize the exchange rate of the dollar.

A renovated Common Agricultural Policy

The Common Agricultural Policy (CAP), the only integrated policy which relies upon common financing, represents an important component of European policy. The CAP has led to an expansion in European agriculture by means of a great increase in productivity and in the level of production in several sectors. The CAP has to a great extent assured the independence of the European Community in food supplies.

However, a critical balance sheet for the CAP must equally be drawn up. The major principles which were supposed to govern the CAP are less and less respected nowadays. The imbalances and inequalities have grown to such an extent that they have become intolerable. The CAP needs to be reformed, with due regard to the fundamental principles upon which it is founded.

Measures must be taken to eliminate structural surpluses, for these represent a major misuse of resources, and the cost of these surpluses, which has become too high for the Community, distorts the equilibrium of the Community budget. Thus, for milk, measures for production control must be set up, which take into account the importance of milk production in the economy of the various countries.

A price policy based upon an unlimited quantity does not in itself constitute a true agricultural policy. Therefore a threshold of guarantee should be introduced. A more vigorous structural policy must be set up with a view to improving rural infrastructure and to helping the most deprived regions. The importation of cereal substitution products originating from outside the Common Market and designed for use as cattle fodder must also be examined, for this is a major cause of dairy surpluses.

The CAP must contribute to the protection and the creation of jobs in the rural areas through concerted action by the agricultural, social and regional funds and it must direct Community expenses more towards structural improvements, social well-being and regional equilibrium.

The CAP must achieve a greater degree of fairness in the support of agricultural incomes in favour of small and medium-sized producers, family farmers and agricultural workers, through a better planning of production in order to avoid structural surpluses.

The Community must install a true Community policy for the Mediterranean products and

---

† The British Labour Party does not subscribe to the rest of this section.

regions which eliminates the present inequality of incomes and which, while avoiding the creation of surpluses, institutes a price mechanism capable of safeguarding the incomes of the farmers in these regions. We want to preserve the unity of the market, and this means progressively dismantling the monetary compensatory amounts.

The interests of consumers must be considered equally with those of farmers. Consumers must be able to buy good food at fair prices. We will seek to improve the quality of our food by restricting the use of potentially harmful additives and by encouraging the consumption of more natural foods. We need to ensure that our agricultural policies do not encourage the destruction of the natural environment.

The process of integration of Spain and Portugal should be carried out on a parallel with the internal reforms of the European Community, and this makes it even more necessary to set up a CAP based upon an equilibrium between farmers from Northern and Southern Europe and upon the respect of the interests and the living standards of all European farmers.

Our agricultural policy must take due account of the Community policy on aid and development. We must develop, in the framework of the next Lomé III Convention, a common food policy for the poorest parts of the Third World, where food is as far as possible replaced by aid to develop agricultural production in Third World countries. We must encourage the countries to develop their agricultural industries and to export towards the EEC.

International relations

The European Community must be capable of speaking with one voice on the major questions of international policy. The Socialists of the Community want to see the EEC playing a more active and independent role in international relations, whether in East–West or North–South relations.

An EEC open to the world has a vocation for enlargement to all European democratic countries. It is currently due to open its doors to Spain and Portugal. It is in its own interest that the EEC should expand its Mediterranean policy, in particular with the sixteen associated countries. The enlargement of the EEC to include Spain and Portugal is an urgent political imperative for the Socialists, who are aware that such an enlargement must contribute to the consolidation of democracy and to economic progress in the countries concerned. The European Socialists are equally aware that the new enlargement is essential for the EEC itself: it will especially contribute to a more active solidarity between the North and the South of the EEC as well as to a reinforcement of the EEC's influence in the world.

On a parallel with a positive solution to the internal problems of the EEC, the negotiations on the enlargement to include Spain and Portugal should be concluded as quickly as possible, with the aim of the entry of these two countries into the EEC in 1986.

The Socialists want the Community to play a more positive role in international relations. The EEC also has a specific role to play in the European continent's search for true security based upon the reduction of tensions, détente, the dissolution of the blocs, cooperation and disarmament. Furthermore, the EEC cannot remain neutral or indifferent towards the conflicts and injustice in regions such as the Middle East and Africa, as in South-East Asia and Central America.

The EEC must not exert its influence through traditional power politics and military means, but through political relations and diplomatic initiatives in the East, West and South.

The Socialists thus want the EEC to provide a real contribution to the creation of areas of freedom, democracy and development in the world and to the fight for human rights and the establishment of a new international order. This new internationalism will naturally lead Europe to favour any contact it can establish with those social and political forces who, throughout the world, share these preoccupations.

More democratic and more efficient institutions

The Socialists consider the Community institutions firstly as the means of achieving the objectives they want to assign to the Community. The existing institutions must therefore be made as effective as possible. But the democratization of the community will come about through the constant improvement in the functioning of its institutions. The Community needs good institutions, for without democratic institutions, there can be no good Community policies.

Democracy also implies that each Community policy should be controlled or controllable by the national parliaments or by the European Parliament; whatever happens, no area of Community affairs can escape parliamentary control.

Institutional improvements in favour of the European Parliament are hoped for[†]

The European Parliament must be in a position to increase its influence in the decision-making process. The Parliament must participate more directly in the legislative process by extending the consultation procedure giving it the right of initiative. As a result, the Parliament would be able to adopt proposals which, after the opinion of the Commission, would be examined by the Council in the same way as those of the Commission.

In the budgetary field, the European Parliament already possesses, since the reform of 1970, the power of decision-making. It is now necessary to simplify and clarify the budgetary procedure in order to put an end to the 'budgetary guerilla warfare' which each year sets the Parliament and the Council at loggerheads over the interpretation of the Treaties. In this context, the European Parliament has taken into consideration the prospect of institutional progress in favour of the European Parliament.

An improved financial system[‡]

A solution to the financial problem of the EEC is indispensable. The insufficiency of its present resources forces it, moreover, to find adequate funds and to rethink its system of financing. But this system affects the fundamental aspects of the Community: the Community preference, the Common Agricultural Policy and the commercial solidarity with regard to third countries.

The solution to the financial problems must be fair to all the member states of the EEC, but this does not mean overthrowing the Community system and adopting the theory of 'juste retour', whilst taking into account the individual capacity of each country to pay. The solution to the financial problems must go hand in hand with a necessarily larger budgetary discipline, which should affect all Community expenditure and which should be translated by a containment of the budget of the EEC.

The attribution of new funds to the Community is essential so that it can face up to its new assignments and to the prospects of enlargement. But it can only justify this by the implementation of new common policies.

Adequate finances represent means for new policies: social, economic, industrial and regional policies and enlargement. Expenditure must be established in relation to the available means and not vice versa. These new resources should essentially stem from an increase in the present limit of the funds originating from VAT and from a Community borrowing and lending policy in favour of developing investment in industrial sectors of the future.

Member parties of the confederation are:
Parti Socialiste, Socialistische Party (Belgium)
Socialdemokratiet, Sozialdemokratische Partei (Germany)
Parti Socialiste (France)
Labour Party (Ireland)
Partito Socialista Democratico (Italy)
Partito Socialista (Italy)
Letzeburger Sozialistesch Arbechter Partei/Parti Ouvrier Socialists (Luxembourg)
Partij van de Arbeid (The Netherlands)
Social Democratic and Labour Party (Northern Ireland)
Labour Party (United Kingdom)
(Also socialist parties in Spain and Portugal)

---

† The British Labour Party and the Danish Socialdemocratic Party do not support this section.
‡ The British Labour Party does not support this section.

THE EUROPEAN PEOPLE'S PARTY
'Towards a United States of Europe'

The European People's Party – the Christian Democratic Group – issued an action programme for the second legislature of the elected European Parliament. It concluded that the EPP was the party which worked constantly, steadily and unanimously towards the building of the United States of Europe. 'The Christian Democrats are federalists. They aspire to ideals of harmony in social justice. They uphold the realistic belief that only through European unification can our citizens prosper.'
The following are extracts from the 11 000 word 'Action Programme':

European unification is a historic mission for the present generation. The European Peoples' Party (EPP) remains the motivating force. To continue on the road prepared by the Community founding fathers is a primary obligation for Christian Democrats.

The economic situation in Europe is greatly influenced by international factors which give the recession a world-wide character; large currency fluctuations, huge increases in raw material and energy costs, extensive social and technological change are all factors. There are more than 13 million unemployed in the Community, almost half of them under 25. The EPP considers it a priority to offer these people future prospects.

Recent experiences have taught us that we have been: living beyond our means and neglecting productive investment; permitting labour costs to rise too rapidly at the expense of innovation; relying excessively on the public sector thus creating established rights, whose costs cannot be controlled.

The opportunities offered by the Community are not being sufficiently used. In certain cases measures can be taken at national level but they will remain ineffective if they are not coordinated with the other Community member states. The individual member states are simply too small to solve many of the major problems. The Community must have the scope and framework for the coordinated approach that is essential in tackling the problems of unemployment.

The Community should not turn in on itself but rather it should shoulder its responsibilities to the world including that of creating a more just international economic order. The EPP is committed to the principle of a socially and ecologically responsible market economy, which is the cornerstone of its policy. Simplistic approaches are incompatible with the philosophy that determines our party line. A responsible policy requires both a sound economic and a sound social base.

Economic policy
Our principal economic policy objectives are: lasting, balanced economic growth with a subsequent reduction in unemployment, due to an increase in investment and advances in structural reform, and continuation of the struggle against inflation and an improvement in competitiveness, thus pre-supposing a national socio-economic policy which is adapted at Community level.

Efforts for stronger convergence are absolutely essential for the member states socio-economic policy and ought to be given priority. Agreement on policy is essential if the Community is to assert its economic position and associated political influence in a changing world and if its internal problems are to be overcome. The economic climate can only be improved by coordinated, convergent and indeed Community-wide policy.

This policy should aim to increase the overall expansion of the private sector, particularly small and medium size enterprises; create favourable economic conditions, providing new possibilities for jobs; encourage investment from Community business and attract foreign investment; develop and complete the internal market.

This is the way to increase the opportunities for meaningful paid employment, particularly in the socially and economically less-favoured regions. We simply cannot allow the waste caused by the present piecemeal approach due to border formalities and protectionism. Europe must wake up and take common action.

The EPP is therefore committed to a policy with the following objectives:
> Coordination of the member states' policies for economic recovery. Such a policy must be designed to reduce national Budget deficits to a level compatible with available

resources; improve industrial profitability; stimulate production at sectoral as well as individual level; undertake initiatives and justifiable coordinated action to stimulate growth on an international level; create conditions where interest rates can be controlled; bring inflation rates down as much as possible.

Economic growth that is subject to social and ecological constraints, taking into account the specific position of the Third World and to an appropriate and fair distribution of work throughout the world.

Rapid dismantling of all money-wasting administrative, fiscal and technical border formalities and the abolition of regulations of a nationalist protectionist character, an extravagant waste of time and money. The Community must become a single market, attractive to investors.

Conditions of equal competition for passenger and goods transport in Europe by the creation of a common market for transport and allied services.

Progressive tax harmonisation on capital returns, more effective cooperation at European level to combat tax fraud and flows of capital towards non-Community countries; common company law and taxation rules.

Further development of the European Monetary System:

> better coordination of credit, monetary, budgetary, social and economic policies of the member states, thus strengthening common exchange rates,
>
> the creation of an autonomous European Monetary Fund.
>
> The ECU could be used increasingly as a reserve currency in central banks, promoted as a means of payment in transactions and strengthened in its role in the international monetary system.
>
> Introduction of travellers cheques and deposit accounts in ECUs

This would contribute considerably to the stability of the world money market.

> Application of joint measures for the development of key industries and innovation; the encouragement of cooperation between European firms, in particular in the area of research, in projects that are of general interest to the future development of Europe and/or capital intensive projects. To achieve this the Community must make the necessary finance available.

Gradual abolition of national subsidies to industries and sectors that are not structurally viable, taking the problems of the frontier regions into account. According to the Treaty, national subsidies must be presented to the Commission for approval first.

Greater solidarity in action to combat energy shortages, in line with the commitment made by the member states in case of a crisis; in such cases existing gas and oil stocks should be released to ensure European energy supplies; more long-term contracts for imports and exports of electricity.

A European investment programme particularly to develop alternative sources of energy and raw materials and to improve the environment and infrastructure and for research into raw material and energy savings.

Active suport for small and medium-sized undertakings (SMUs), as well as co-operatives and craft industries through such facilities as loans, tax incentives, access to research findings and export promotion, by the harmonization of tax systems and by simplifying administrative formalities. In particular, the setting up of undertakings should be made easier (enterprise creation saving schemes similar to those for housing).

Encouragement of private or cooperative SMUs that are developing new ranges of products or services, in particular those related to the environment, research, energy and technical assistance.

Concentration of available resources under the European regional development fund in the least developed regions and areas suffering from large industrial decline. This policy is an expression of mutual solidarity within the Community and it must aim at strengthening the particular development opportunities of the regions concerned.

Effective promotion of structurally weak areas of the Community. Regional policy must contribute to closing the gap between rich and poor regions. The goal of such efforts is that people find work in their own region; people should not be forced to migrate to other regions or even other member states.

As far as the EPP is concerned, regional policy must contribute to regional decision-making. By proposing a 'Mediterranean Plan' for example, the EPP can point the way for Southern Europe.

Social policy

The EPP is working towards a flexible system for the redistribution of paid working hours taking into account practical possibilities in working life, what is feasible for industry and the personal circumstances of workers. Such measures must not lead to a fall in the average level of productivity. The policies of the two sides of industry must be backed up by a Community framework agreement laying down the basic conditions for the many ways and means of redistributing work. Furthermore such a redistribution of work implies strict limits on both work and overtime and calls for a more active battle against those working on the side or illegally.

There should be continuing harmonisation of legislation on health and safety on the shop floor with a comprehensive programme of exchanges for officials and factory inspectors within the Community; issuing of directives to protect workers handling harmful substances or working in dangerous conditions; strengthening and improvement of the European social fund and the concentration of its resources in areas and groups severely affected by long-term unemployment, particularly women.

Agriculture and fisheries

The EPP demands:

The maintenance and completion of the basic principles of the present Common Agricultural Policy, namely, free movement of agricultural and fisheries products within the internal market, as well as common prices; joint financing of the policy; Community preference over imports from third countries.

A common fisheries policy designed to achieve a fair balance between the need to protect fish stocks and the socio-economic conditions linked with fishing.

The position of women

The EPP stresses the need for:

Greater participation by women in the political, economic and social decision-making process and in employment, by means of a fair distribution of these tasks and family responsibilities between men and women.

Free choice for a father or mother to work in paid employment. Social policy must: on the one hand, aim to create sufficient measures concerning the family to allow parents to reconcile work and family obligations, on the other hand, prevent a situation forcing parents to work purely for financial reasons at the expense of family obligations.

The three directives (equal pay, equal right to work, equal social security) should be implemented. In addition the directive on social security should be extended to cover labour regulations. This means that the principle of equal pay would apply not only to statutory provisions but also to social provisions (such as pensions) governed by agreements between social partners within specific vocational groups.

In the short term, a European directive to improve the legal status of women working in family businesses in the agricultural, commercial and craft sectors. The status of this group of women should be improved in both legal terms and in the area of wages, social security and tax.

Environment

Action to combat air, water and soil pollution is very much a task for the Community. Action to combat the pollution of soil and water must be taken without delay in order to protect Western European flora and fauna (woods). The Council of Ministers must adopt a directive for the introduction of lead-free petrol in the European Community. The Community must negotiate with the countries of Eastern Europe to ensure that there, too, the emission of substances harmful to the environment by industry and vehicles is curbed. The EPP also calls for immediate enforcement of European legislation on the transfrontier transport of dangerous waste; adoption of regulations for the destruction and storage of chemical, industrial and nuclear and urban waste. Dumping at sea should be strictly controlled.

A general European Convention to prevent the pollution of the North Sea should be drawn up to coordinate existing national and international legislation. The European Commission should take action to combat pollution of the Mediterranean.

East–West relations

The EPP believes that democratic Europe must be prepared to participate in any agreement on arms control. The dialogue within the Conference on Security and Cooperation (CSCE) should clearly be pursued without evading the fundamental issues of Human rights, the right to self determination and the renunciation of any acts of aggression. The European

Community and its member states must continue to examine the possible means of economic cooperation with the Eastern bloc.

EPP parties from NATO countries believe that: collaboration in a strong Atlantic Alliance and the up-keep of its forces are essential to any European policy aimed at preserving peace. In this context it is vital that relations between the United States and Western Europe should develop on a basis of equality, mutual understanding and solidarity between allies. Such relations can only be achieved by joint conciliation on matters of a political and strategic nature.

Greater Democracy in Europe

The Christian Democrats commit themselves to European unity. European integration represents much more than material gain. Our first political objective in European unification is to transform the European Community into a European Federation. Cooperation between the member states in a spirit of solidarity and joint action is consistent with our Christian principles.

The allocation of responsibilities and political powers between local, regional, national and Community bodies follows and ought to conform with the principle of subsidiarity. This allocation of responsibilities ought to contribute to the desire for justice, solidarity and honest management. The tasks which national governments cannot accomplish alone should be undertaken by larger bodies (the Community). National and other authorities maintain their own significance in this context. It goes without saying that the national differences which ensue must be respected.

As a democratic party, we attach considerable importance to achieving a fair balance between Parliament, the Commission and the Council, a legislative process that is subject to democratic control, with scope for initiatives and flexible decision-making procedures.

A great many initiatives have been taken during the last legislature by the EPP and the Commission that will benefit the citizens of Europe. Unfortunately far too many of these initiatives have come up against strong opposition due to the re-emergence of national egoism creating serious difficulties for the development of Community policies. Take note here of the abuse of the 'Luxembourg Compromise' Agreements, which means the Treaties are undermined and the Community itself is paralysed. The Community cannot allow such nationalistic approaches. Also with the growing awareness of the European citizens in the European idea, a climate in which the Council of Ministers can make decisions in the common interest must be created.

We can and ought to expect a great deal of the European Parliament, but then it needs greater resources and legal powers if they are to achieve the results they should in the best interests of European citizens.

The EPP therefore desires that we should remain no less committed to the objective of European union as the ultimate goal of the integration process: 270 million citizens represented in the European Parliament and administered by a European government. The EPP is the main supporter of the proposals to create a European Union, as formulated to European Parliament. The achievement of European Union is the next important step towards the creation of a United States of Europe. The EPP consequently encourages the member states' national Parliaments to ratify a treaty of European Union.

In the meantime, the possibilities offered by the present European Treaties should be utilized to the full to solve society's problems. Following the adoption of the necessary framework legislation by the Council, legislative powers should be delegated to the Commission to increase the Community's decision-making authority. The Commission must become the driving force of European Unification once more. In order to achieve this it must abandon its bureaucratic nature and take its political responsibilities.

Links between Parliament and the Commission should be further consolidated by:

The appointment of the President of the Commission by the European Parliament.
Submission of the Commission's multiannual programme to Parliament for approval.
Regular monitoring by Parliament of progress in the implementation of that programme.

Greater effort should be made to render the Community's administrative procedures more transparent. This would enable the European Parliament to strengthen its supervisory role. We wholeheartedly support any measures that would increase the degree of popular representation in Europe. This applies particularly to extending the powers and influence of the European Parliament in the area of decision-making and legislation, in the conclusion of agreements with third countries and in increasing the Community's own resources.

The extension of Parliament's powers is a dynamic process and a step on the road towards European union.

EPP demands

In a number of sectors national policies should be replaced by a European policy. Greater effectiveness and efficiency can be achieved by transferring political decision-making from the national to European level. Examples of areas in which this is feasible include parts of development policy, capital-intensive scientific research, industrial restructuring, the energy sector and many other policies that are discussed in this action programme. This will make it possible to observe strict spending limits that will promote European development and reduce the growing burden on the taxpayer.

Importance should be placed on statutory cooperation in border zones, therefore strengthening the European ideas already entrenched in these regions. Enlargement of the Community to include Spain and Portugal should be pursued in order to support these democracies and to enhance relations between the European Community and Latin America. So that such an enlargement can succeed, the necessary conditions for growth and the effective operation of the EC must be created.

The operation of present policies, the creation of new policies and the membership of Spain and Portugal should be guaranteed by an increase in the Community's financial resources and an effective cost control policy. The effectiveness of the decision-making process and the legislative and administrative services of the European Community should be improved; a European company law be created; the role of administrative tribunal should be handed over by the Court of Justice to specialized bodies; and a European passport should be introduced to underline the solidarity and unity of the citizens of Europe. In addition a decision should be taken on the creation of a European driving licence.

THE LIBERAL AND DEMOCRATIC GROUP
'For a Liberal and Democratic Europe'

In December 1983 the political parties adhering to the Federation of Liberal and Democratic Parties of the European Community adopted a common programme to put before the electorate. They stated they believed its underlying principles and the practical proposals it contained corresponded to the needs of the Community's states and peoples in the 1980s. The following are extracts from that programme – in total length it was well over 10000 words:

EEC institutions

In the interest of the Community and its states and peoples, the Council must take its decisions by a majority vote in those cases where the treaties so provide. Although the member states must be given the possibility of invoking their essential interests in specific cases, it is nevertheless unacceptable that Community action should be blocked by their doing so. The practice of unanimity is contrary to the treaties, does great harm to the Community and cannot continue in its present form.

As a matter of urgency, legislative authority in the Community must be exercised jointly by Parliament and Council. In addition, Parliament must be given a real say in the appointment of Commissioners by having the power to consent, or withhold consent, to each appointment. It must be granted powers of ratification of treaties concluded between the Community as such and third countries. Parliamentary control over the Community budget must come to include the revenue as well as the expenditure side. Loans taken up are also to be considered as revenue while loans granted should be counted as expenditure, over and above budgetary expenditure for all Community policies.

European parliamentary elections must be based on a uniform system of proportional representation, in order to ensure fair representation of the political forces taking part. The law should guarantee the right to vote and to be a candidate to every EC citizen irrespective of which member state he is a resident.

The member states of the Community must place their national law enforcement agencies at the full disposal of the European Court of Justice in order for it to enforce its judgements. Furthermore, where the complaints procedure provided for in the EC Treaties is concerned, the Court of Justice should be granted the power to verify the compatibility of national and European law.

The financing of the Community by its own resources must be upheld. These resources should be adjusted to meet agreed commitments through Community procedures. This should not mean that the contributions and returns of individual member states must always be in balance.

At the moment the citizens of the United Kingdom (and in future, Portugal) – who have lower average earnings – contribute more per capita to Community revenue than citizens in other countries who have higher average earnings. This is clearly against the basic principle of either proportional or progressive taxation accepted at the national level in all Community countries. In the long term new principles for the raising of Community revenues must be adopted which makes all Community taxation at least proportional to regional wealth and income.

In view of the scale and gravity of the Community's current problems, the paralysis of the decision-making process, the financial crisis and the need substantially to increase its external and economic policy powers, Liberals and Democrats maintain that there is a need to reinforce European integration as a matter of urgency and thus to come out in favour of adopting a new treaty establishing the European Union. We want the present Community to develop into a free European Union of equally respected states and peoples within which national, regional and local powers of decision-making are placed in the context of the new European dimension and thereby given added significance. The task of the Union will be to complete the Community process of integration and unification, on the twin foundations of liberal democracy and human and civil rights. Furthermore, it must assume its role in ensuring European security and in the world at large, it must stand for the principles on which it itself is founded: peace, freedom, equal rights, individual responsibility and social justice.

Human and civil rights

European Liberals and Democrats call on the European Parliament to draw up a charter of human, civil and political rights for the Community, confirming the human and civil rights spelled out in the Human Rights Convention of the Council of Europe, which should include the right:

to open government,

to participate in political decision-making through representatives elected by universal suffrage,

for any citizen to inspect and correct any information held on her or him by public or private bodies,

to participate in the organisation of his/her workplace.

This charter would establish standards to be observed by member states and by Community institutions. The European Parliament should monitor progress towards the implementation of these rights. The rights thus established should eventually be incorporated in European law and in the European Convention on Human Rights and become binding law.

European Liberals and Democrats will seek to add a number of new rights in the European Convention on Human Rights, including the unconditional ban of the death penalty, the right to asylum for political refugees and the right to conscientious objection to military service, thus making these rights enforceable in most of Western Europe.

Liberals and Democrats also call on the European Parliament to draw up a charter of social economic and cultural rights including the right to equal pay for work of equal value, safe working conditions, collective bargaining and collective action, social security and social assistance, free and equal education.

The European Community must accede to the European Convention on Human Rights and thereby accept the ultimate jurisdiction of the European Human Rights Commission of the European Court of Human Rights at Strasbourg.

Economic policy

Liberals and Democrats demand quick and steady progress towards the establishment of a uniform European internal market, with equal competitive opportunities for enterprises and with free consumer choice for European citizens in the member states. They particularly insist on:

The further reduction of trade barriers, customs formalities and controls; in particular, the task of collecting Value Added Tax on imports should be transferred from the customs authorities at EC frontiers to the national tax authorities.

The harmonisation of those framework conditions important to the functioning of the Common Market, especially in the field of tax and company law, as well as other commercial and economic laws.

The elimination of subsidies creating unfair competition.

Liberals and Democrats affirm the need for Government to favour free enterprise by improving the competitive climate, with a view to stimulating economic recovery and reducing unemployment, in order to enable existing industries to strengthen their positions and to provide opportunities for new activities which will create more jobs, especially in the labour-intensive sector. The economic crisis will be best overcome, present jobs guaranteed and new ones created if excessive public debts are contained and if the total investment rate is increased by reducing bureaucratic barriers and through tax incentives. European Community and national policies to stimulate employment and renewed growth must be harmonized to secure more complete integration.

European Liberals and Democrats recognise the vital role of the workforce in the creation of wealth. They consider it essential that a higher proportion of the active working population find employment in the private and social market-regulated parts of the economy in order to fight overall unemployment and reduce public deficits and inflation at the same time. The European Community must respond to the challenges of information technology and other sunrise industries by developing a European telecommunications strategy backed by a major joint Research and Development programme. The development of democratic participation and profit-sharing is a key element of economic policy.

The Social Fund should support a Community-wide programme (with additional help to the poorest regions) to assist people of all ages.

We believe the reduction of working time to be a gradual process, not necessarily linked to growth and prosperity. We do not regard this restructuring process as a solution to the problem of unemployment as such, but as a possible instrument to spread the available work over more people. The various formulae for reducing working time can also be applied differentially, sector by sector, or even from enterprise to enterprise.

The solidarity of the EC member states within the European monetary system is a determining factor in the future of the European Community itself. European Liberals and Democrats support further progress towards economic and monetary union with greater coordination of financial systems. As a first step, those member states not yet part of the European monetary system EMS should join as soon as possible. On this basis, together with the USA and Japan, a durable world monetary system could be developed.

On the basis of EMS, EC member states most promote the wider application and use of their common currency, the ECU, including creating ECU banknotes and coins.

National discriminatory practices, especially non-tariff trade barriers, on the internal market must be eliminated and the EC Treaty provisions on free movement respected. These provisions must also be applied to services, transport, insurance etc. Tenders for public contract should be put out in a European context. We advocate as free as possible a world trade system, based on reciprocity. This brings the greatest advantages for all states concerned and for their citizens. The European Community itself must pursue these principles and take an active role in implementing them. It should not to try to limit Third World countries' exports of any lawful merchandise to EC markets, and should seek to ensure that its own aid, assisted exports, etc. avoid distortion and are compatible with market economy conditions.

Social policy

Social security systems must primarily aim at enabling individuals to secure their basic material needs (the insurance principle) and at guaranteeing a minimum standard of living for all (the solidarity principle). Citizens and those working within the Community should be able to collect benefits they have paid for through taxation, contributions to pension schemes etc., wherever they settle. Harmonisation of social security schemes in the member states should begin in those areas affecting citizens of member states living in another member state.

European Liberals and Democrats would give higher priority to vocational training and part-time working, with special emphasis on the needs of young people and women, and to measures to reduce the social costs of unemployment. We back current plans for reform of the Social Fund with a view to establishing closer and more efficient coordination between its projects and general EC priorities in the field of youth employment and vocational training, and to heightening its overall flexibility. We realize this will require a strengthening of the financial means at the Fund's disposal.

European Liberals and Democrats believe that greater employee participation in enterprise and capital-sharing is necessary to the development of a healthy economy. The European Community must promote the principle of free movement of its citizens throughout its territory, regardless of their occupation. Diplomas at all levels must be made reciprocally comparable and be recognized as proper professional qualification.

The European Liberals and Democrats demand abolition of personal controls at the internal frontiers of the Community, in order to give European citizens a stronger sense of belonging to the same Community. We demand that the countries of the European Community develop and apply a uniform strategy to fight drug abuse, drug addiction and drug-induced criminality. This also requires preventive and therapeutic measures, in particular a wide-ranging plan to reduce illegal drug sales. We support the proposed renewal of the EC anti-poverty programme.

Environmental policy

The three basic principles of a European environmental policy on which all further developments depend, should be:

The principle of prevention: concerted action should be taken within the framework of a long-term environmental strategy, geared to prevention of environmental problems.

The causal principle: those responsible for any adverse impact on or damage to the environment should be liable for their elimination and future avoidance; the polluter pays for all costs incurred, also in the case of cross-frontier damage.

The principle of cooperation: all bodies and states concerned should cooperate in good understanding to solve environmental problems.

Standards of environmental and public health protection must be defined. All EC member states should introduce comparable tests to establish the environmental compatibility of new products, constructions and technologies. Air pollution, the rapidly expanding death of forests and the deterioration of cultural sites in Europe must be fought at source by setting rigorous, compulsory limits. A European programme of forestry aid is required. Further action can be taken through market-economic means, such as a bonus/malus system.

The protection of nature, especially of moorlands and wetlands, forests, seas, including the

North Sea shallow sea area, as well as the conservation of farmland are vital to the ecological balance in Europe. Europe's fauna and flora are a vital component of its heritage. All possible provisions should be made to protect species threatened by economic, industrial and social needs. An active policy for animal protection must be promoted and strict standards applied to vivisection.

European Liberals and Democrats will work for the establishment of an environmental charter, which should treat infringements of environmental legislation as criminal offences.

Agriculture, food and fisheries

While European Liberals and Democrats firmly support the aims of the CAP and believe them correct, they nevertheless regard vigorous reforms geared to a more market-oriented agricultural policy with market-oriented prices as unavoidable in the light of the increasing surpluses and the growing constraints of the financial deficits of the CAP.

We seek a continued and speedier integration of national policies into one Community policy for food supply and farming, and believe that the successful pursuit of this aim requires the establishment of economic and monetary union. In the interim, monetary compensatory amounts must be eliminated on the lines proposed by the Commission. It will also be in our interest for the Community to continue to work for harmonization of food legislation. Uniform rules on quality, ingredients, plant health conditions and labelling need not, by definition, limit the variety of products or the range of choice available to the consumer. A better balance in production should be sought and production of crops of which Europe is a net importer encouraged.

We will adopt a more rigorous attitude towards food supplies in structural surplus and in this context apply the principle of co-responsibility whenever appropriate. At the same time, we will ensure that adequate stockpiles of food are maintained both to meet our own needs and as a contribution to a world stockpile for famine relief.

We see a revised CAP as being a positive policy for all kinds of land use. We therefore believe that as well as its economic aspects it must continue to have social and environmental dimensions. We would seek changes in the method of financing so that costs fell more properly on the Social and Regional Funds.

The fish stocks of the waters around the Community are a common resource. Liberals and Democrats believe that the Community should adopt a more rigorous policy in favour of the conservation of fish stocks and look for development and encouragement of the Community Fisheries Service.

Small and medium-sized enterprises

Small and medium-sized undertakings play a key role in the economic life of EC member states both by reason of their productivity and their impact on employment.

Liberals and Democrats call for the implementation of a programme specifically geared to the problem of small and medium-sized businesses in the Community. Such a programme should aim at minimizing or abolishing excessive or unnecessary governmental interference. A further considerable contribution to the promotion of small and medium-sized enterprises is to be made by a more determined fight against concentration processes and price agreements at a European level.

National arrangements in respect of profit and income taxes, industrial taxation and estate duties must be harmonized to make them more flexible and to encourage enterprise and new businesses. With regard to value added tax, the thresholds for full or partial exemptions should be raised to allow for inflation in recent years.

The supply of energy

Faced with economic crisis and mass unemployment, the European Community must encourage the development of the most efficient sources of energy. Liberals and Democrats recognize that all the major sources of energy available to us involve disadvantages and a number of risks. It is clear that energy saving and the increased use of coal, natural gas and alternative energy sources cannot, in the short and medium term, be relied upon fully to meet the Community's energy requirements. Hence nuclear energy necessarily has an important contribution to make. But the ways in which nuclear power is used must be subject to a series of guarantees. Effective Community safety standards must be drawn up, and waste storage techniques and processing of the waste itself must be improved.

Moreover, European Liberals and Democrats recognize that the public must be kept fully informed, both as to the problems of securing supplies and questions arising from the use of power stations and the processing of waste.

As the Community's response to the energy challenge, we propose a Common Energy

Policy (CEP) which would ensure the pooling of a proportion of available financial resources and direct them towards basic research in the energy sector. Meanwhile, the research and development programme into energy conservation and renewable energy sources must be expanded.

Research and technology

European Liberals and Democrats advocate more cross-frontier cooperation in science and research. Cooperation between institutes of higher education should be improved. When fixing new research objectives for the Community, particular attention should be paid to the coordination, preparation and implementation of the relevant programmes, as well as to the assessment and distribution of results.

Regional development

The exclusive goal of the European Regional Development Fund (ERDF) is to provide financial back-up for the economic development of underprivileged regions in the Community, in conjunction with national support for specific projects. Its resources must be increased to reflect the fundamental importance of regional economic convergence in the Community in combating the economic crisis. In addition, it should coordinate its activities with those of the other EC financial instruments (Social Fund, EIB, Agricultural Orientation and Guidance Funds, ECSC Fund), all of which have a regional dimension.

We insist that all Community expenditure in the regions should be additional to existing national government expenditure. Regional and local authorities should have more opportunity of direct access to the Community institutions for the exchange of information and mutual consultation. They should also have the right to apply directly to the Regional Fund and the Social Fund without the intervention of national governments.

Foreign and security policy

The European Community must be developed into a union with a common foreign and security policy whose instruments and objectives should enable it increasingly to determine its own destiny. In the immediate term, European Liberals and Democrats demand the establishment of a permanent Secretariat for European Political Co-operation (ECP).

Atlantic cooperation remains fundamental to our freedom, peace and prosperity. The policies of the United States are crucial in this respect and it is vital that we develop a united European voice to influence those policies.

The European Community should promote the negotiations on disarmanent – in which it should itself take part – and take its own initiatives in this respect.

European Liberals and Democrats consider that the cause of peace is served neither by an uncontrolled arms race nor by unilateral disarmament. We argue strongly in favour of balanced reduction of nuclear and conventional weapons down to the lowest possible level. Both the Community as such and its member states should promote strict implementation of existing treaties against chemical, biological and toxic weapons. In addition, they should seek the conclusion of better, properly verifiable treaties so as to impose a complete ban on producing, storing or using these weapons.

The European Community must persist in its efforts to facilitate and contribute to the peacemaking process in the Middle East.

The enlargement of the Community should be seen primarily in political terms. We call for an early and favourable conclusion of negotiations with Spain and Portugal so that they can become members as soon as possible. At the same time, enlargement must not be allowed to jeopardise the steady and effective development of the Community itself. A firmly united Europe within clearly defined boundaries is a prerequisite for the smooth integration of new member states.

Community policies towards the Third World should ensure that help reaches the poorest countries and the poorest people in those countries. European Liberals and Democrats believe that preference should be given to self-sufficiency in food and the development of small-scale rural projects and of small and medium-sized enterprises.

The Community should not make the granting of aid subject to the existence of a Western-type democracy in the beneficiary countries. However, no support should be given to regimes which flagrantly and persistently violate human rights. The European Community should help the developing countries gradually to reduce the heavy financial burden by suggesting appropriate measures for each country or group or countries. The European Investment Bank should be asked to increase its investments.

THE FRENCH COMMUNIST PARTY
Europe at centre of capitalist crisis

Early in 1984, the French Communists at the European Parliament published a review of their activities at the Parliament since the first direct elections in 1979. The following are some extracts.

In the section of the review on the functioning of the EEC and dealing with the Communist refusal to agree to unlimited extension of the jurisdiction of European institutions, it is stated:

Instead of trying to remedy the problems afflicting the countries of Europe – unemployment, dependence on other countries, unsatisfactory relations with the US – certain people, particularly the Right in the Assembly, have preferred to try to change the institutions with the aim of reducing the jurisdiction of national parliaments and governments. Some of these plans directly challenged the right of veto still possessed by each of the ten countries of the Common Market in the process of Community decision making. Of the four main French parties, only the Communist Party and its associates have come out clearly against abandoning this right of veto.

They have also spoken out against the temptation to have discussed in the European Assembly subjects manifestly outside its jurisdiction: the defence of Europe or the world situation, as if the Assembly in Strasbourg was a mini-United Nations. It is this extension of the range of matters covered by the European Assembly which over the years has sapped its credibility, particularly following accusations, subsequently shown to be groundless, made by rightist groups against governments of third world countries (Ethiopia, Vietnam, Nicaragua, for example).

The Community's budget, like those of the member states, is economic and political choice translated into figures. It also reflects the contradictions between member states and becomes the principal means whereby the European Assembly strengthens its political powers and widens its jurisdiction.

Communist and associated delegates have shown that, without waiting for new resources, it was possible to direct the Community budget towards a new economic advance, a reinforcement of commercial policy to counter American pressure, real incentives for industrial cooperation and solidarity with poor countries.

If new resources are shown to be necessary for new common policies, they could be provided by limiting the too numerous derogations to Community preference costing 25 billion francs each year and by ceasing to make financial presents to Great Britain.

The action of the communist and associated deputies in the European Assembly as well as the firmness of the French government in the Council have been decisive in limiting to a large extent the refunds to Britain accepted by Giscard in 1980, but it is necessary to put an end to this system of compensation from 1984.

The EEC is today in an impasse, as is indicated by the failure of the Athens summit. The present impasse is not due, as certain people make out, to the growth of major problems but rather to a political refusal to solve them. Today it is a question of knowing which Europe we want to build: one dedicated to fighting unemployment or one which, like Mrs Thatcher's government, fights the unemployed. One which tries to free itself from the grip of the dollar or one which denationalizes. One which works for peace and detente or one which works for a resumption of the arms race.

Europe is at the centre of the capitalist crisis. It suffers from its effects, and the unrestrained 'liberalism' dear to Reagan, Kohl and Thatcher shows what that capitalism is capable of. One more reason for exploring alternatives.

These alternatives have names: the fight for employment, industrial cooperation between the Ten, the preservation and development of the gains of the common agricultural policy, the promotion of equality by increasing the rights and social benefits of the workers, reduction of the trade imbalance between the Ten, the defence of Europe against commercial attacks from abroad, especially those from the US, better use of our currency against the hegemony of the dollar by using eventually the ECU for settling certain contracts, cooperation with the developing countries, Community initiatives in regard to security, disarmament and democracy.

THE GREENS
Towards a Green Europe

This manifesto represented the culmination of over a year's discussion and it was adopted by the Ecology Party (UK), Les Verts (France), Ecolo and Agalev (Belgium), De Groenen (Netherlands), Dei Greng Alternativ (Luxembourg), Comhaontas (Republic of Ireland) along with parties in Sweden and Austria which were not involved in the elections. In addition these parties and Die Grünen (West Germany) signed a technical alliance for the European elections, pledging themselves to work together when elected to form a 'Green' group within the EP. The ten-point programme for Europe was as follows:

Defending the environment
Establish a European Environmental Agency to oversee tests on innovations and take action to remove common pollution problems like acid rain.

Food for the future
Stop CAP payments to farmers on foods in surplus and provide money for research and development of organic farming.

Working for a future
Move from growth-oriented to sustainable economies, sharing available wealth and resources, regulating the activities of multinationals, and encouraging the conversion of military industries to socially useful production.

Jobs for keeps
Reform the Social Fund to make it a device for encouraging local employment agencies and savings banks to help small businesses, co-ops and the self-employed. Restrict job-training to jobs that will last – especially in energy conservation, recycling and repair.

Sharing the wealth
Ensure that the Regional Fund acts to aid conversion of declining industrial areas to sustainable alternatives. Establish direct relations between authorities in regions with self-government and the EEC institutions so that they can cooperate on practical issues of Community aid and economic and social restructuring.

A nuclear-free Europe
Work with those inside the Community, and those from East and West, to promote a nuclear-free, non-aligned Europe. Call an immediate halt to the nuclear power programmes throughout the EEC and work for the immediate removal of nuclear weapons from Europe.

Transport for tomorrow
Use the Transport Fund to encourage and promote energy-efficient transport. Introduce restrictions on energy-intensive private transport to help the development of more efficient public transport.

European democracy
Make the Council of Ministers more accountable. Ensure that all countries use proportional representation in direct elections to the European Parliament.

Rich and poor
Recognise our responsibility to the poorer nations of the world by putting an end to our exploitative economic superiority and providing direct help (through grants, not loans) to help create self-sufficient sustainable economies.

Towards international responsibility
Increase cooperation between the EEC, the European Free Trade Association (EFTA) and Eastern European countries such as those in COMECON. Explore the potential of the Economic Commission for Europe and the Council of Europe as mechanisms for improving relationships within Europe and developing regional bodies for a future European Federation of Regions.

Manifestos of the main UK political parties

THE CONSERVATIVE PARTY
'The Strong Voice in Europe'

Mrs Margaret Thatcher, the Prime Minister and Leader of the Conservative party, in a foreword to the party manifesto for the European elections, said:

Britain joined the European Community with a vision. We saw opportunities for trade and greater prosperity. But we also saw in the Community the promise of peace and security, an alliance in which endeavour, enterprise and invention could flourish.

For the first time in history, the very idea of an armed conflict between the countries of Western Europe has become unthinkable. As we celebrate the anniversary of D-Day, we shall also be celebrating almost 40 years of peace among the nations of Europe.

Membership of the Community has had its problems. But we have tackled them with courage and vigour.

When the European Parliament was directly elected five years ago, we Conservatives promised that our Government would defend Britain's vital national interests. We have kept our promise. Today, Britain's voice in Europe is strong and clear, and its message is respected by our partners.

We have been right to fight for improvements to the Common Agricultural Policy and for a fairer system of finance. We want these things so that we can put behind us the endless haggling over money and begin to develop the full potential of the Community.

These coming European elections are part of our commitment to peace with freedom and justice. It is vital that Britain's voice remains strong in Europe. We do not want to see our accomplishments and our future damaged by those who seek only to destroy what has already been achieved.

That is why I ask for your support on June 14.

The Conservative Commitment
These elections are about who can best represent your interests in the European Community. This manifesto explains why the policies of the Conservative Government, together with a strong Conservative team in the European Parliament, are the best guarantee of British interests in Europe and the best means of securing a prosperous and successful European Community. We are in the Community to stay because that is in Britain's interest and in Europe's. We intend to see that it succeeds.

Conservatives share the ideals which underpin the Community – safeguarding peace, stability and democracy in Europe, recognising our common destiny, and making the best use of our resources so as to secure the prosperity of our citizens. We want to see it playing an important role in strengthening democracy across the world. We have made, and will continue to make, a positive and constructive contribution to turn those ideals into reality. This requires practical proposals and a resolute approach to negotiations rather than empty rhetoric.

Five years ago, therefore, we called for an end to the confused and half-hearted approach to the Community which was all that a deeply-divided Labour Party could offer. In both the general election and the European elections of 1979, the Conservatives won a clear victory.

Since then we have shown that it is possible to be true to Britain and true to Europe. We have set to work to win agreement on essential reforms; to assert the major role which Britain should play in the Community; to establish a more effective Community voice in the world; and to secure, in cooperation with our partners, an economic recovery which will provide jobs for our people on a lasting basis.

After five years we have a record of solid achievement in Europe.

Our firm economic policies at home are restoring the economic health of Britain, giving us the fastest growth rate of the Ten, and we are helping to lead the Community out of recession.

We have won agreement that there must be a fairer Community budget system. Pending its achievement, we have negotiated budget refunds of £2500m for the last four years.

We have won Community agreement that there must be effective and guaranteed control of spending, including agriculture.

For the first time in the history of the Common Agricultural Policy, support prices have been reduced and open-ended guarantees removed for products in surplus. While bringing about these reforms, we have fought for a fair deal for British farmers, who now produce more of our food than ever before.

We have secured a Common Fisheries Policy which provides a good deal for British fishermen and long-term security.

We have helped consumers by keeping the rise in food prices below the rate of inflation.

We have secured reforms in the European Social Fund so that it provides more help to Britain's unemployed, particularly young people training for new jobs.

We have secured important new measures under the Regional Fund to help create new industrial opportunities in the steel, shipbuilding and textile areas of the UK.

We have won agreement on measures to make the Common Market more effective, to move towards freer trade in insurance and transport services, and to give greater priority to scientific and technical cooperation.

Our record is in sharp contrast to that of the Labour Party. We have had to make good its failure to secure any reforms when it was in office, or to develop Community activities in ways of benefit to this country. The warring factions within the Labour Party have made it incapable of achieving anything for Britain in Europe. Its irresponsible threat to withdraw from the Community has damaged the reputation of Britain and made our negotiations more difficult.

Nor do the Liberal and SDP parties offer an alternative. Their policies are vague, they are inexperienced, and they are united only in their unwillingness to defend British interests.

In the European elections on June 14 we are seeking fresh endorsement of Conservative policies designed to promote British interests in the Community, and the election of a strong Conservative team in the European Parliament. Over the next weeks and months the work of these last five years of tough and persistent negotiations will come to fruition. We look to the electors to support us, to vote Conservative – for Britain and for a better Community.

A Community with a world role

Conservatives believe that Community membership increases the influence of the United Kingdom and strengthens our ability to direct our own destiny in the world. The Ten working together can have more influence on matters of foreign policy, economic policy and trade than they can have separately.

Improving cooperation on foreign policy

Conservatives want to see the Community taking the initiative on world problems, not just reacting to them. We want to create a more hopeful relationship between East and West. That is why we have taken the lead in improving cooperation among the Ten on foreign policy. We will continue to strengthen the arrangements for working together, though we will insist that the procedures remain flexible and unbureaucratic.

We recognise the importance of preserving and strengthening our friendship with our great ally, the United States, which since World War II has done so much to secure liberty and prosperity in Europe. We share the objectives of maintaining peace and protecting our freedoms. We believe that a stronger and more united Europe is in the interests of the Western Alliance as a whole.

Nato is the right forum for coordination of Western defence. Closer European cooperation on the purchase and production of defence equipment is in Britain's interest and in Europe's, and can help to promote European industrial development and innovation. We would also like to see even greater cooperation on defence and security among members of the Community. We welcome recent moves towards more discussion among the Ten of the political and economic aspects of security.

Enlargement

Enlargement of the Community to include Spain and Portugal will strengthen democracy and security in Western Europe. We wish to see these negotiations brought to a conclusion as soon as possible, so that the wish of both countries to join on January 1st 1986 can be met.

A trading community
The trading strength of the Ten combined is unrivalled; their share of world trade is half as large again as that of the United States. The Community has numerous trading agreements with developed and developing countries. Its potential influence is therefore very great.

Free trade is essential for world prosperity. The Community should use its strength to increase freedom of trade. It must not try to solve its internal problems by adopting protectionist measures. The protectionist policies of the Labour Party are bad for consumers, bad for industry, and bad for Britain.

Conservatives will work for:

Freer trade in services, a field in which Britain leads the world.

A Community policy to roll back protectionism, in agricultural as well as industrial products.

Action to ensure that Japan opens her markets more rapidly to imports and investment. The opening up of markets in newly industrialised countries.

Measures to deal effectively with unfair practices by other countries and to provide breathing space for Community industries in difficulties. Conservatives in the European Parliament have taken a leading role in making Community action against unfairly subsidized imports more effective.

Action to solve our trading differences with the United States in a way which defends our legitimate interests, notably in agriculture, company law and taxation.

Action to promote economic coordination and greater exchange rate stability.

Helping the Third World to help itself
The less developed countries take 40 per cent of the Community's exports. In turn they supply us with many of our raw materials. The Community's trade and aid policies towards these countries should reflect this degree of interdependence and be designed to meet humanitarian needs, to encourage self-sufficiency and to further our trading and political interests.

The European Community and its member states provide more than a third of all the aid given to the developing world. The Lomé Convention, now being renegotiated, provides 63 African, Caribbean and Pacific States (34 of them Commonwealth members) with the most comprehensive trade and aid arrangements between the developed and developing worlds. In addition, the Community programme of aid to other countries in the Third World, including India, has been growing steadily.

Resources are limited, but we will work to maintain an open trading environment, to avoid waste in aid programmes, and to promote investment in developing countries.

We want British industry and commerce to be able to make more of the opportunities offered by the Community's aid programme. We will continue to make the quality of Community aid more effective, particularly so that it contributes to self-reliance in food production. Food aid plays an important part in fighting famine in the Third World, but it should not be used merely as an outlet for Community surpluses.

Recovery in Europe: policies for jobs
Conservatives recognize that the member states of the European Community are today more dependent upon one another than they have ever been. So we each have a vital interest in our collective success. That is why relaunching and reviving the Community is of major importance to this country. Our policies in Britain have cut inflation and restored business confidence. Our partners in Europe, regardless of party or ideology, are now following similar policies with positive results.

These policies provide the essential foundation for sustained European recovery with improving job opportunities. The more Community member states work together to promote them, and the more we exploit the potential of a common market of 270 million consumers, the greater will be the benefits. We look at Community policies on their merits. When it is clear that Community action is more effective than national action alone, we wholeheartedly support it.

At Community level, just as in Britain, practical Conservative policies to control expenditure, eliminate waste and set industry free, provide the best prospect of creating new jobs which will last. That is why Conservatives believe that the greatest single contribution from the Community need cost no money at all – it is to make a reality of the common market.

Removing obstacles to trade within the Community and opening up a genuine common market in goods and services will boost industrial competitiveness, reduce costs, extend consumer choice, and improve prospects for employment. But if we are to exploit fully the opportunities this provides, we also need to ensure fair competition and make our economies more flexible and responsive to change.

Fair Community competition rules must be enforced, small businesses encouraged, new technologies developed, and older industries made more competitive. Community funds and financial instruments should be used to help achieve these ends. These policies will strengthen Europe's future as the centre of invention and creative endeavour which it should be.

Already over two million British jobs depend on our trade with the rest of the Community, which provides by far our largest market. Furthermore, much investment from other countries such as the United States and Japan comes to Britain, bringing new jobs in advanced industries, because we are guaranteed tariff-free access to this vast common market.

Opening up the market

Although customs tariffs and quotas have gone, too many barriers to trade remain. The French lorry drivers' protest vividly illustrated the problems. We must make faster progress towards a Community-wide market where those with goods and services to sell can go about their business with a minimum of restrictions and burdens. In particular, we shall strive to:

Eliminate costly delays and bureaucracy at frontiers within the Community.

Make public purchasing more open and competitive.

Create a common market for financial and other services, which is particularly important to Britain as the financial centre of Europe.

Promote faster progress towards mutual recognition of proper professional qualifications.

Agree a definite and detailed timetable for the removal of non-tariff barriers to trade.

These changes will help businesses. But they will also help the individual as consumer, as traveller, as student, as earner, or as job seeker.

Trade within the Community is too often obstructed by a jungle of conflicting national laws. We shall work for simpler laws and common trading standards across Europe. But we shall resist harmonization for its own sake.

Small businesses

Experience shows that small businesses can generate many of the new job opportunities. Our policies for simplifying trade, reducing frontier formalities and easing bureaucratic burdens will help small firms grow and create more jobs. We shall continue to champion their interests.

Developing Europe's technological and industrial potential

This is a key to the future prosperity of the Community. We will:

Promote common efforts on research and innovation such as the ESPRIT programme on information technology, and the new programmes on telecommunications and biotechnology: the costs of such work are often too great for individual countries or companies.

Encourage training programmes for the new technology industries.

Seek to remove obstacles to joint European ventures and investment, and encourage industrial cooperation.

Continue to support Europe's aerospace industry through collaborative efforts such as Airbus Industries' A320 and the EH 101 helicopter, which the Conservative Government helped to launch.

Support Community efforts to rationalise traditional industries such as steel and shipbuilding on a fair basis.

Community funds

We recognise that Community funds can play a useful role in supporting these policies. The UK benefits from these funds, and from the activities of the European Investment Bank. We will:

Continue to insist on an increase in the share of non-agricultural spending in the Community Budget, including the Regional and Social Funds.

Ensure that resources are used where they are most needed.

Work to ensure that enlargement does not lead to our own problem areas being deprived of a fair share of Community support.

Ensure that lending by the European Investment Bank particularly benefits small businesses.

Conditions of employment

We have strongly supported the Community's efforts to promote high common standards of health and safety at work. But the Community should not impose detailed and binding rules without regard to differing national practices. Such rules are more likely to destroy jobs than create them.

Good employers need no urging to consult their employees and inform them properly. We want the practices of the best firms to become the norm. But the emphasis must be on voluntary arrangements. We shall therefore resist attempts to impose excessively rigid systems of legislative compulsion in matters which are better agreed between employers and employees.

Monetary cooperation

Uncertainty about interest rates and exchange rates is bad for trade. We support the objectives of more stable exchange rates and financial conditions, which require above all a common commitment to policies which will master inflation. The question of sterling participation in the exchange rate mechanism of the European Monetary System remains under regular review. We should only take that step when the conditions are right, both for us and for our partners. We support the increasing commercial use of the ECU in Community trade and finance. We have already removed all serious obstacles to its use in this country, and will urge our partners to do the same.

Transport

We attach a high priority to increasing freedom of competition in transport. We are pressing for:

Easing of the unduly restrictive quota of Community road haulage permits, and their eventual abolition, to enable free movement of goods across the EEC.

Community agreement to counteract protectionism in world shipping and to act against unfair and disruptive action from Eastern bloc countries.

More competition in air passenger transport to provide a greater variety of service and encourage lower fares.

Energy policy

We will work to:

Encourage energy conservation and development of our own energy resources.

Continue moves to realistic and fair energy pricing throughout the Community.

Ensure contingency arrangements in case of future oil crises.

Promote a healthy and competitive coal industry.

Environment and conservation

The UK has long been a pioneer in fighting pollution. Much pollution crosses frontiers, in water or in the air. So policies for the environment are a proper concern for the Community if they are to be effective, and if there is to be fair competition within European industry. Measures must strike a fair balance between the protection of the environment and the need to contain industrial costs. Within the Community we will work for:

The elimination of lead in petrol for new vehicles by 1990.

Community action to control cross-frontier movements of hazardous wastes. More research to find practical answers to the problem of acid rain.

Proper assessment of the environmental effects of major industrial development projects before approval.

Community assistance in cleaning up polluted rivers such as the Mersey.

We have taken the lead in promoting Community action for a ban on the import of whale products, and secured measures for the protection of seals and wild birds.

Consumers

A concern for consumer interests runs right through our policies on the Community. Our commitment to a realistic agricultural pricing policy, and to creating greater Community-wide competition and choice, will benefit the consumer. The consumer interest is not best protected by excessive intervention in the market-place in the name of consumer protection.

But Community consumer measures are justified when barriers to trade are caused by different national approaches to consumer protection; and when safety is involved.

Securing reforms

In Europe as in Britain we are the radical party leading the way to necessary change. Since 1979 we have worked to persuade our partners that the Community must set its own house in order if it is to tackle the major external challenges. We have argued that a budgetary system which imposes unfair burdens on Britain or any other country and which provides no firm control of spending, is damaging to the unity and effectiveness of the Community. Prolonged annual haggles are not a sensible way of dealing with the problem. We are seeing a solution which takes this item off the agenda, so that we can all devote our energies to making the Community more of a force to be reckoned with in the world.

We have put forward this case with determination and persistence – and with increasing success. While continuing to press for long-term reforms, we have secured interim arrangements for British refunds of £2500m, two-thirds of what our budget contribution would otherwise have been. In contrast, the Labour Government presided over a rapid increase in Britain's budget burden, approaching £1 billion in their last year of office. Its formal 'renegotiation' used up much goodwill towards Britain, yet it failed to secure any relief whatsoever.

At the Stuttgart Summit last June, the Prime Minister secured the agreement of our partners to launch a major negotiation to establish a fairer distribution of burdens; to curb the growth of expenditure, particularly on the CAP; to develop new policies; and to examine the Community's revenue needs. And in the European Parliament, our MEPs won agreement that long-term budgetary arrangements were necessary if the Community was to make progress.

Since then we have been involved in long and tough negotiations to complete this agenda. Once again, it is the Conservatives who, by their commitment to the Community, their consistent approach, and their resolute defence of British interests, are securing real progress and real reform.

The Budget: discipline and fairness

Conservative policies of financial prudence must apply in the Community as well as in Britain. More has to be done, in addition to the work of the Court of Auditors and the budgetary control activities of the European Parliament, to bring Community spending under control.

We have now secured the agreement of our partners to a system of budgetary discipline. A maximum level of overall expenditure will be fixed each year, and the rate of growth of agricultural expenditure (which accounts for two-thirds of the total budget) will be held below the rate of growth of Community revenue. We shall ensure that budgetary discipline becomes a full part of the Community's procedures.

Strict budgetary discipline will not in itself guarantee a fairer distribution of budget burdens. This is why we have persuaded our partners to accept a new system which will ensure that in future no member state will bear a budget burden disproportionate to its relative prosperity within the Community.

Agriculture

In the last two decades we have seen major improvements in efficiency and productivity in farming throughout the Community. Meanwhile the Common Agricultural Policy has given farmers guarantees of good prices for what they produced, whether or not there was market for it. As a result, the Community is faced with surplus production on a scale which has been getting out of control. Demand is stagnant and attempts to dispose of surpluses on world markets threaten to bring us into conflict with our trading partners outside the Community. The rapid rise in agricultural spending has brought the Community up against the limit of its financial resources.

Conservatives recognize the benefit of secure food supplies and more stable prices brought about by the CAP, and the part the policy has played in easing difficult social changes in the countryside. But the CAP has become the victim of its own success. We must tackle the problems of costs and surpluses now so that it can be placed on a basis which will safeguard the future of a healthy agricultural industry, and preserve the quality of our rural heritage.

Our new system of budgetary discipline, combined with the package of measures agreed by Agriculture Ministers in March this year, marks a significant reform of the operation of the CAP and a first major step towards control of agricultural spending.

British agriculture Under the Conservatives, British agriculture has prospered while the price of food in the shops has risen less quickly than other prices. This is a record of real achievement. Conservatives, as the national party, have to strike a balance between farmers, consumers and taxpayers. We wholly oppose the anti-farmer attitudes of the Labour Party. Its policies for the CAP, and for the rerating of agricultural land and nationalisation of tenanted land, would drastically cut British agricultural production and drive tens of thousands of farmers and agricultural workers off the land. Labour talk of cutting agricultural costs, while advocating a policy which could cost the British taxpayer £2.25 billion per year.

Controlling surpluses The removal of open-ended guarantees for products in surplus, or likely to be in surplus, has now been agreed by Ministers. The Plumb Report, drafted by the leader of Conservative MEPs, and adopted by the European Parliament, was the first Community document to recognise the need for this.

A rigorous price policy is essential in order to help reduce surplus production and the costs of disposal and to make the agricultural industry more responsive to market conditions. We have agreed this year, for the first time in the history of the CAP, price reductions or a price freeze on nearly all major products.

Problem sectors Because of the huge cost of surpluses in the *milk* sector, a special sup-plementary levy has been introduced for milk production for five years. All dairy farmers face a difficult period, but we believe that this system is the fairest and most effective that could be secured. It is also important that the real price of cereals should be reduced in order to restore the balance between the livestock sector and the major arable crops. The agreement to reduce the price of most cereals this year is a step in the right direction.

Agricultural trade Conservatives insist that the Community must not try to solve the problems of the CAP at the expense of our trading partners elsewhere. As the European Parliament stated, in adopting the Resolution on Sir Fred Catherwood's Report on this subject, Europe must guard against exporting heavily subsidised agricultural surpluses at the expense of important industrial products. In line with this approach we have successful-ly opposed an oils and fats tax. We will also work to ensure that the Community stands by its obligations, for example to the ACP countries and, above all, to New Zealand.

Community revenues

In accordance with the agreement at the Stuttgart Summit last year, we have been prepared as part of the overall negotiations to consider an increase in the Community's revenue. But we have made it quite clear that we cannot recommend any such increase to the British Parliament unless there is a final and satisfactory agreement on the new arrangements for effective control of agricultural and other expenditure, and for a fair sharing of the budgetary burden.

Fisheries

The Conservative Government has succeeded in negotiating a Common Fisheries Policy providing British fishermen with secure advantages in our own waters. This policy provides the stability the industry needs for long-term investment and, with effective conservation measures, should secure expanding stocks of fish.

Our achievements contrast with the abject failure of the last Labour Government to make any progress in defending the interests of British fishermen or in negotiating a satisfactory policy. The lost opportunities under Labour made our negotiations longer and more difficult than they need otherwise have been.

We shall continue to ensure that our fishermen get a fair share of the resources available to the Community, and that the policy is enforced even-handedly and managed efficiently. We shall continue to help our industry adapt to the new circumstances that face it with the loss of deep-water fishing opportunities.

The European Parliament and Community decision-making

Since 1979, the directly elected European Parliament has established for itself a position of real influence at the centre of the Community's decision-making. Its role is to scrutinise and, where necessary, to amend or check proposals for new legislation from the Commission; to control spending; to curb bureaucracy; and to act as the forum where the problems facing the Community can be debated and solutions proposed.

Conservatives have used the Parliament not only to criticise Commission action and bring it into line with Conservative thinking, but also to draw attention to the major reforms the Community needs if it is to survive. They have pressed for the economic and social policies essential to longer-term prosperity.

In their constituencies, the Conservative members are a vital link between the Community and the voters of this country. They have helped to safeguard the rights of individuals and businesses threatened by bureaucracy or administrative action, and they have fought to ensure that firms and projects in their constituencies receive a fair share of Community resources.

All this has been done by making more effective use of the Parliament's existing powers. Over the next five years the Parliament must consolidate its influence. This can best be done if a direct link is maintained between the Members and their constituents, which is why in the discussions on a uniform electoral procedure Conservatives will continue to attach great importance to the retention of such a link in Britain.

The newly elected Parliament must give high priority to developing a more consistent and responsible stance on the central issues, notably those relating to the Community Budget. Over the years, the Parliament's say in how Community funds are spent has increased, but it has little direct responsibility for how the money is raised. It has shown itself unwilling to make cuts in some areas of Community expenditure so that within the limits of available resources other areas might benefit. Conservatives will work to ensure that the Parliament shows itself capable of making political choices of this kind.

On a growing range of issues, the Parliament is regarded as 'the voice of Europe'. It has an important part to play on human rights questions, for example. Conservative MEPs will help to ensure that the European Parliament makes a responsible contribution to the maintenance and expression of the democratic ideals upon which the Community is founded.

These three criteria – effectiveness, consistency and responsibility – allied to a concern to keep the Parliament closely in touch with the electorate, are fundamental to the Conservative approach. This approach has helped us to work very closely on key issues with members from many other like-minded parties across the Community. With these parties the Conservatives have held the initiative on all important issues since 1979, from the Falklands crisis and cruise missiles to policies for economic recovery.

Conservatives have insisted that member states should retain the right to protect their vital national interests in the Council of Ministers by being able to invoke, where necessary, the principle of unanimity. However, we recognise that if the Council is to be an effective decision-making body, a member state's right to block a decision should be used only as a last resort. It is not in our interest that other member states should, without proper justification, veto agreement on measures which would benefit the United Kingdom.

We welcome practical reforms in the workings of the Community institutions. But we do not support attempts to force the pace of institutional reform, especially in ways which might jeopardise the defence of genuinely vital national interests or which would not command the necessary degree of common agreement and public support.

A strong Community

The Community is founded on a great deal more than the pursuit of ten differing national interests. Compromises have to be reached and differing aspirations reconciled. The Community may, on occasion, be troubled by short-term conflicts. But these should not obscure the immense progress made in building a new Europe over the past few years. With the right leadership the Community is an association of immense potential, whose achievements in the future should dwarf what has been achieved to date. If the leadership of the Community were to fall into the wrong hands, the price of stagnation will be high in the short term but far greater for future generations.

In Europe, as in Britain, we are in the vanguard of those seeking modernization and change. Our policies in Britain and our policies in the European Community stand together. Strict control of finance and elimination of waste; economic growth and employment created through enterprise and initiative; a commitment to the Western Alliance and to working with our friends abroad to safeguard our common interests.

The implementation of Labour Party policies would destroy jobs and prosperity across Europe just as they would in Britain. A protectionist Europe is no more likely to secure our interests than a protectionist Britain. A non-aligned Europe is no more likely to safeguard our liberties than unilateral disarmament in Britain. Withdrawal from the Community, whether plainly advocated or disguised in Labour's call for a new Messina Conference to tear up our treaties, would do serious damage to British interests in Europe.

It would be equally wrong to plunge into a federal Europe, as the Liberals propose, and thus lose our capacity to protect British interests.

A resolute, strong Conservative team in Government and in the European Parliament is the best protection for British interests and for the future of the whole Community.

We do not change our policies every time there is an election. That is why people trust us. And that is why we seek your support on June 14 for the strong Conservative voice in Europe.

THE LABOUR PARTY
'The Way Forward'

Labour's manifesto, supported by the Socialist Group of the European Parliament, stated:

On June 14, the British people will have the chance to demand a new start – for Britain and for Europe. In these elections Labour will be fighting for a Fair Deal for Britain and a New Deal for Europe.

New policies, new priorities
Labour demands an end to the waste of resources – and wasted opportunities – brought about by Tory policies. We call on the Government now to create new jobs, rebuild British industry and save our National Health Service.

Labour demands new policies for Europe – for an end to mass unemployment and industrial decline. We need to give a new priority to investment in industry, to training, and to economic expansion.

Labour demands a break with the past in the European Community – for an end to its squabbling, its stagnation, its man-made mountains of surplus food which go stale while millions in the Third World starve, its agricultural system which has made the Community virtually bankrupt and brought sky-high prices for food.

The real issues
These are the real issues in the European elections: the need to provide jobs for our people. The need to invest and modernize our industry. The need to provide food at fair prices. The need to safeguard and extend our health and social services.

These are the issues which make the elections to the European Parliament so vital to us all. They are the issues which are at the heart of Labour's campaign for a better future.

Labour's principles
Putting people first
We are a democratic socialist party. Let there be no doubt about it. We are on the side of the people because we are part of the people. We put people before profit or institutions. We both want the same things:

A fundamental right to employment for everyone.

The best health care for all – regardless of ability to pay.

Social services and benefits available to all in need, young or old, disabled or unemployed.

A first-class education for our children, with a secure career to follow.

Decent homes in a clean environment.

An end to discrimination. The protection and extension of our democratic rights and freedoms.

And peace in a world working together to end poverty and fear.

These are the values which inspire our policies. We are proud to put them in the forefront of our manifesto. Proud to be judged upon them.

A crusade for jobs
There is one issue to which we must give priority. One issue upon whose solving everything else depends. And that is the issue of mass unemployment.

There are more than 14 million people out of work in Europe. It is the shadow which darkens their lives, blots out their future and destroys hope. We must lift that shadow. It cannot be done quickly and it cannot be done easily. But unless we start soon it may never be done at all.

The way out of crisis
Labour's way out of the crisis is to use the wealth of the Community to rebuild our industries and public services – creating new jobs and new opportunities for the people of Britain and

Europe. Labour calls for all member states to work together – with others – to pull Europe out of the slump.

We demand that the share of the Community budget going on industry and jobs is sharply increased. Two-thirds of the budget is now spent on agriculture – ten times more than investment in training and retraining people, through the Social Fund. Ten times more than the regional fund – money which is desparately needed for investment in declining industrial areas.

Labour's plan

Labour will fight to give a new priority to jobs and industry. We will campaign on a ten-point plan of action:

To rebuild our economies with new public investment in housing and the renewal of our inner cities. In more efficient transport – especially public transport – and communications. In creating a better environment and curbing pollution. In a more efficient energy supply and the conservation of energy.

To invest in industry and especially in the high technology industries of the future. Cooperative ventures such as the ESPRIT programme in electronics, and the Airbus in aerospace, must be given full support. But we will campaign to extend projects like this to other fields, such as biotechnology and new materials.

To encourage cooperative enterprises with new initiatives that will enable working people to draw on modern management methods and on wider financial support.

To invest in modern training and retraining to be financed by a much larger European Social Fund – and especially for young people, women, and black and Asian people, to give them a fair chance of decent work with equal pay.

To invest in depressed regions through giving a new priority to the Regional Development Fund, and by giving a major boost to regional development by member states.

To ensure that our North Sea oil wealth is invested in Britain instead of it being wasted on unemployment, or flowing overseas to build up the industries of our competitors.

To help British industry win markets at home and abroad Labour will resist any attempt to take Britain into the European Monetary System, for this would make British goods even less competitive than now. And we will press our partners to accept the sensible planning of trade, so as to protect economic expansion and help create and safeguard jobs.

To achieve rapid progress towards a 35-hour week without loss of pay throughout the Community as called for by European socialists and trade unions. This will ensure that economic expansion in Europe really does feed through into new jobs.

To use our energy resources more efficiently with a new energy policy that will help to create more jobs. We need to develop renewable resources, and above all, we must safeguard and develop Europe's own energy resources. We will fight to defend and develop British coal – and to protect our coal industry from subsidized imports.

To extend Labour's democratic principles into industry to ensure that working people have a fair say in decisions that affect their lives. Labour supports the EEC proposal that workers should have the right to be informed and consulted by their employers. We condemn the British government for refusing to extend the rights of workers.

In Britain, as in Europe, there is still a great wealth of natural resources. And there is even greater wealth in the skills and expertise of the people. Yet these resources, these skills, are being cruelly wasted.

To end the waste

We can no longer afford this waste. The idle factories and the millions unable to work. The loss to tax revenues and the cost of benefits for the jobless – over £17000 million a year in Britain alone.

Labour, socialists and trade unionists throughout Europe, are committed to put this wealth to work – to help build a better life for all the people of our countries.

We need a crusade for jobs to help build that better life.

A new policy for food

Shoppers in Britain and the Common Market pay far more for food than they need – a direct result of the Common Agricultural Policy.

The need for fundamental reform

Labour will fight for the fundamental reform of this policy – so that it works on behalf of shoppers, not big business agriculture.

269

We demand a system which encourages lower prices in the shops.

We oppose a food policy which makes rich farmers even richer but squeezes others unfairly. Whole groups of farmers are penalised. Our farm labourers continue to work for appallingly low wages – among the lowest in Britain.

Our fishing industry has been devastated by the Community's fishing policy – bringing unemployment and hardship to many communities.

Added to the waste of food and resources, there is the damage to our countryside from the constant pressure to increase production at any cost.

A way to cheaper food
For the sake of all our futures, we need to end the waste generated by the Common Agricultural Policy. We need to:

Put an end to high food prices.

Lift the burden of agricultural subsidies from the shoppers.

End the system of farm support that leads to food mountains.

Open the Common Market to cheaper food from elsewhere.

Guarantee a decent living for farmworkers and those farmers who work in the worst conditions.

Protect Britain's fishing industry.

Safeguard our environment.

Only the Labour Party has the strength and determination to press these reforms home in Europe.

A fair deal for all
In Britain, as in Europe, the crisis brought on by reactionary Tory governments threatens not only our jobs, but also our social services and our democratic freedoms.

We need to end discrimination wherever it is found. We need to protect and rebuild our social services and the communities they serve. We need to protect local democracy and trade union rights.

We need to save our health service
Labour created the National Health Service to be an efficient and modern means of providing the best health care for everyone who needs it. We will not allow it to be destroyed.

We will not accept the destruction of what successive Labour governments have built up. We will fight to improve our schools and to extend the provision of nurseries and services like meals on wheels and residential care.

In Britain, millions live on poverty-rate benefits. We will campaign to improve them.

Equal opportunities for women
Labour is working, in Britain and in Europe, for a fair deal for women.

Positive action for women
Special funds are available through the EEC to enable women to have the training they need to have a fair chance of working on equal terms with men. The Tory Government has refused to take up all the money on offer. It has consistently opposed legislation to help women – both in the European Parliament and at government level in the Council of Ministers. The Government had to be taken to the European Court of Justice before it would adopt the EEC policy of equal pay for work of equal value.

Labour will insist that we use every penny available, so that women can gain their rightful place in the new industries of the future.

A better environment
Working for a safer environment
Socialists in Britain and all over Europe are concerned at the neglect of our environment, and the pollution of our rivers and countryside.

We will press for immediate action to end the havoc caused by mismanagement and pollution. We will work to end the threat from acid rain. We will insist that a greater proportion of Community funds be used to help protect our environment and defend our wildlife.

Better transport for all
Labour is committed to a transport policy which serves the people and is accountable to the people.

We will campaign in Europe for an efficient, integrated transport system, one which gives first preference to public transport and which takes full account of the impact of transport on the environment.

A wider democracy

Labour believes that the institutions of the Community must be made fully accountable to the people, through their own Parliaments. The basis of democratic control of the Community must rest on the rights of people, in their own countries and communities, to govern themselves.

Protecting our rights

We do not believe that the European Parliament should be given more powers – for this would take power and decision-making even further away from ordinary people.

But we do need to improve our own democratic procedures in Britain. And, especially, we need to return to our own Parliament the powers so foolishly ceded by the Tories to the EEC in the 1972 European Communities Act.

Peace and security

Above all, we need to make sure we all have a future.

The urgent need for peace

As the nuclear arms race grows more dangerous, the need for peace becomes more imperative. We must work to stop both the nuclear arms race and the build-up of chemical weapons.

The EEC has no authority on matters of defence. And Labour will resist attempts made by the Liberal and SDP Alliance – and others – to give it that authority.

But Labour believes it is vital to all our futures that we work with socialists and all others who desire peace.

Labour believes in effective and sound defence for Britain, through Nato. But every new cruise missile and every Trident submarine raises the tension of the nuclear arms race. We are opposed to both – just as we are opposed to Soviet missiles in the East.

We are campaigning to remove cruise missiles as a vital step to help build a lasting peace. We are calling for a freeze on the testing, production and deployment of nuclear weapons; for a change in Nato strategy, to 'No First Use' of nuclear weapons; for the removal of all nuclear bases in and around Britain.

Labour is working in Europe for a future free from the threat of war, any war. Our aim is the removal of all nuclear weapons from the continent of Europe. Labour will start by removing them from Britain.

The Third World

Labour's commitment to peace is part of our basic socialist beliefs and principles, shared by all who want a better future, free from poverty and exploitation.

A commitment to people

These same principles underlie our commitment to the peoples of the Third World. While the Common Market builds its food mountains, millions of people in the Third World lack the basic necessities of life.

In the name of fairness and commonsense, we must help undo the damage. The EEC's aid programme has been a failure. We need:

To improve access to the markets of the Community for Third World products.

To concentrate aid on the poorest people in the poorest countries.

To improve the Lomé Convention, to bring in all the poorest countries of Asia and use it to help agriculture and industry.

To act against multinational companies which make profits by exploiting the poorest peoples of the world – by selling as hard as they can unnecessary or harmful products such as milk powder.

To support community agreements and the rescheduling of the debts of Third World countries.

More aid, less red tape

We must cut the red tape that stops aid from reaching the poor. We must encourage all members of the Community to increase their aid to the target set by the United Nations.

We must use the wealth of Europe to bring new hope to the Third World. By doing so we will help to create new jobs for all.

A fair deal on the budget
Mrs Thatcher pretends that settling Britain's payments to the European Budget will be the answer to all our problems. It won't.

Of course, we need a fair deal on these payments. There is no reason why we should continue to pay money to those countries richer than ourselves. Contributions must be related to ability to pay.

Tackling the real crisis
But the real issue is how the money is spent. The real crisis is about jobs and industrial decline.

The Tories claim they are fighting on the budget issue in the national interest. But for them the national interest is to cut public spending, so that they can cut the taxes of their rich City of London friends and big business.

Our priorities are different. They are set out in this manifesto.

What Britain needs, what the people of Europe need, is a strategy that gives priority to rebuilding and reinvesting in our countries. It is a socialist strategy which recognises that the national interest can only be served by meeting the basic needs and hopes of the people.

And unless the reforms we demand are carried through, Labour is not willing to consider any call for the Community's resources to be increased.

Labour's MEPs fight for change
This is why we need more Labour members in the European Parliament.

To fight for the people of Britain. To insist on the reforms we have set out in this manifesto.

Tory opposition
Over the past four years, Labour MEPs have led the campaign for change in the Community – on food policy, on jobs, on more help to the regions, on new rights for all.

They have been opposed, at every turn, by Britain's Tory MEPs. For the Tories in Europe – as in Britain – prefer to defend the interests of big business and big farming against those of ordinary people.

But the Alliance would be no better. They believe so fervently in the EEC, as it stands, that they would not – they could not – fight effectively for change. Indeed, their only friends in the European Parliament – the liberals – have blocked reform time and again.

The Labour Party is the only party with the determination to fight for reform.

Britain's role in the Community
Since we joined the Community in 1973 our economic position has deteriorated beyond even the most pessimistic forecasts of those who opposed entry.

Membership has helped to speed up our economic decline. It has cost Britain jobs. It has helped to reduce our standard of living.

A radical programme
The framework of policy for our campaign in these elections is set by the programme on which we fought the General Election. It is a radical programme because we believe that the country's problems are now so serious that only radical policies can match them.

We stand by the arguments we presented in our election manifesto. However, our programme is not static. It was moulded through democratic debate and that debate will continue. It responded to current problems and concerns. And these problems will change.

Fighting for the best deal for Britain
Britain will remain a member of the EEC for the term of the next European Parliament, and Labour will fight to get the best deal for Britain within it. At the end of that time Britain will have been a member of the EEC for 15 years – and this will be reflected in our pattern of trade, the way our economy works and our political relations overseas.

But we also recognize the fundamental nature of the changes we wish to see made in the EEC and that its rules may stand in the way of a Labour Government when it acts to cut unemployment. It is in this context that we believe that Britain, like all member states, must retain the option of withdrawal from the EEC.

The issues before us
But the elections of June 14 have another significance, just as deep, just as important, to the voters of Britain. Because they will be the first nationwide test of the most disastrous Government this country has known since the heyday of Neville Chamberlain.

The Tories' grim record

These elections cannot replace the Thatcher government. But they can pass judgment upon it.

We have now had five years of ceaseless failure dressed up, by a Tory press, as endless success.

Unemployment, even on the government's fiddled figures, has nearly trebled. Bankruptcies reach a new record every year. Our National Health Service is scarred by cuts. Our public transport system is being slashed. Council house building for the million-long housing list has virtually stopped. Education and social services are savaged in each new round of spending cuts.

We must keep shouting until the whole country heeds us: *There is a better way.*

We can have free and efficient health care. We can have cheap and reliable transport. We can invest to provide the jobs we need in a modern industrial economy.

There is a way forward for Britain. It is Labour's way. It is the way forward for Europe, too.

A new beginning

Labout believes it is time for a fresh start. It is time for us to look to tomorrow – and make sure it is more secure, and more hopeful, than today. We need a strategy that will put people – and people's needs – first.

A sound, socialist approach

On June 14 we can all make that start with Labour's sound, socialist approach: one that will put the Community's resources to work for the people in Britain and the rest of the EEC.

We can begin to work together to revitalise the economies of Europe and invest in industry and our public services. We can direct the wealth of the Common Market to the regions and the people who most need it.

We can bring hope where there is decay. Inspiration where there is now stagnation. We can help create a new Europe.

THE LIBERAL / SDP ALLIANCE
'Let's get Europe working together'

Mr David Steel, Leader of the Liberal Party and Dr David Owen, Leader of the Social Democratic Party, in an introduction to the Alliance manifesto said:

The Alliance of our two parties, Liberals and Social Democrats, has been committed to Britain's membership of the European Community from the beginning, believing that it is essential to Britain's future prosperity and security and her influence in the world. But being much more seriously concerned and informed about Europe, we can be more critical and more constructive than the other parties about its very real problems.

Too many British political leaders have concealed their inability to provide imaginative direction to the Community behind a surly anti-Europeanism. We have no patience with these attempts to play to the gallery of outdated nationalism. True leadership should make it clear that Europe has got to work better – and that Britain's vital interests will be best served if it does. We recognise that the European budget has been unfair to Britain and that the agricultural policy has got out of hand, and that these must be rectified. But these arguments have been allowed to eclipse the real crisis of the Community, which is not agricultural but industrial.

European industry has to work together to compete with Japanese and American industries which have left Europe behind. Our industries are so desperately vulnerable that they are tempted to turn to protection – which will only make them still more backward and Balkanised, with each country's industry looking to its own government for help.

Only by working on a European scale can we establish the high-technology industries which hold the key to the future, and without which Europe will become increasingly dependent on Japan and America. And in information technology the British, with their expertise in communications and software, have a specially valuable role to play.

The economic recovery of Europe depends on concerted policies to ensure growth without dangerous inflation, and to limit the wild fluctuations of currencies which hamper our trade. The creation of new jobs and the attack on unemployment is far more effective on a continental scale. Only common action can produce a more efficient infrastructure and transport system, and bring down the absurdly high air-fares within Europe.

The need for closer European collaboration is still more urgent in defence. We believe that we must build a stronger 'European pillar' within Nato which will both strengthen the Atlantic Alliance and give Europe a more independent role, to hold her own with the superpowers. The European armed forces must work with common equipment, which should increasingly be provided by European suppliers.

A stronger European force within Nato makes it easier, not harder, to press for disarmament and a genuine deal with the Soviets. We are determined to move Nato's policy towards 'no first use' of nuclear weapons, and are pressing for a nuclear-free zone on either side of the iron curtain, which can lead to a wider agreement to limit nuclear weapons. Firm and united European leadership will have far more influence on both Moscow and Washington.

Both our parties are deeply committed to pushing actively for disarmament, not only to make the world safe from war, but to allow far greater funds to be devoted to helping the developing world. We seriously champion a unified European Community working steadily for peace, disarmament and development. Even on the difficult question of Northern Ireland, the Community could provide an appropriate framework for discussions between the member states, ourselves and the Irish Republic.

In social fields the Europeans can achieve far more together than separately. The environment can only be protected effectively by common regulation and safeguards. The defence of human rights and rights of women and minorities are matters of common European concern. In all these areas the British, once they take Europe seriously, can play a valuable role.

The reform of the European system is in part the responsibility of the European Parliament, which should exert much more effective control over the Brussels bureaucracy and bring a human perspective to technology. That is why our Alliance takes the European elections more seriously than the other parties. The more British people vote and concern themselves with Europe, the more we can bring the common touch to the workings of Brussels.

We cannot evade the fact that our future lies in the European context. It is hopeless to try to fight in Brussels in a negative, chauvinist spirit, obsessed with the past. Our Alliance of Social Democrats and Liberals has the qualifications to work for the Europe we need – a dynamic industrial grouping which can mobilize the skills of over two hundred million people, to create new prosperity and security, to hold their own in the world, and to contribute to peace and a fair deal for the poor countries.

Economic recovery
The Alliance manifesto stated:
Europe, since the 1973 oil crisis, has failed to meet the challenge posed by the end of a period of unprecedented expansion and prosperity. Instead, the last ten years have been dominated by economic recession and stagnation.

There is now a real danger that Europe will not be equipped to benefit from the gradual recovery in world trade. We lag behind in two senses: first, our governments continue to pursue restrictive fiscal policies thus slowing the pace of recovery; secondly, emergence from recession has highlighted the need for restructuring industry – yet Europe is well behind in applying new technologies. A divided Europe is in grave danger of being elbowed out of many growth sectors, becoming an economic and technological satellite of America and Japan.

The Alliance proposes a coordinated programme for economic expansion and job creation. We call for the abolition of the remaining barriers to a true common market for trade. We want more investment in new technologies. We want to retrain and re-equip Europeans for success in today's competitive markets. Ours is a programme to make the most of Europe, to make it work.

Working together for economic recovery
Europe's economies are now too closely tied together for any one country to reflate alone.

The Alliance wants to see a concerted Community programme for economic recovery. Particular emphasis should be put upon measures which promote jobs and investment, with special help for small and medium-size businesses and for cooperatives. Finance should also be provided for investment in infrastructure – road, rail, tunnel, port and other facilities. In these ways Europe can set in motion a sustained recovery which puts people back to work and strengthens our international competitiveness.

Britain should become a full member of the European Monetary System (EMS), which would help to stabilize exchange rates and prevent the wild and damaging variations in sterling which we have seen in the last five years. Europe should take the initiative in developing cooperation between the three main currency blocs – the US, Japan and the EMS, to help keep world-wide currencies stable. This would facilitate general expansion and promote world trade.

We support the rapid implementation of the next planned step in the EMS, the creation of a European Monetary Reserve Fund, which, by providing drawing rights in times of crisis, would further strengthen the stability of the European economies.

Getting industry moving again
Major problems of change in the structure of industries throughout Europe have come to crisis point in the ten years of recession. While some industries such as textiles and shipbuilding have suffered major contraction, even the growth industries of the 1960s – chemicals, cars, consumer electronics – have been in difficulty. It is now clear that to remain competitive in today's world, all these industries must adapt to new technologies which will have far-reaching effects on production methods and employment. Yet today, Europe lags behind the US and Japan in these new technologies, particularly micro-electronics.

The Alliance wants to see all the countries of the Community working together to help industry meet this challenge and to generate new jobs. The policies now needed are:

Greater cooperation in basic research.

Substantial new investment in joint research and development (R & D) in advanced technologies including more support for the European Strategic Programme of Research in Information Technology (ESPRIT).

A build-up of the aerospace and electronics industries.

Coordinated Community measures to help restructure industries in difficulties, such as steel and textiles.

Community investment in major transport links, including a Channel tunnel.

The rapid achievement of a real common market in Europe by:

the removal of national regulations which impede access to the service sector, including insurance and banking;

275

common codes of practice agreed as quickly as possible in fields such as health and safety;

the development of a truly European market for public purchasing in areas like telecommunications with Community-wide standards in industries such as electronics;

the development of a unified European-based telecommunications infrastructure – integrating cable, radio and satellite;

the elimination of frontier controls and barriers which restrict the free movement of goods between member states.

Managing change for the benefit of Europe's people

New technologies mean higher productivity which in the long run means higher incomes. In the short run, however, it can mean unemployment and disruption to people's lives. We must not ignore these social effects of industrial change. Earlier industrial revolutions brought much injustice and suffering. The European Community needs to coordinate and to assist national governments in their efforts to deal with these problems. The Alliance proposes:

A substantial increase in resources going to regional and social funds. These funds support investment in infrastructure, industry and services, job retraining and community service programmes in the areas that are worst hit. Particular help is essential to find new jobs for the long-term unemployed. Today in Europe there are 13 million people out of work compared with only 8 million farmers, yet over six times as much Community support goes to agriculture as to industry. If Europe is to work these priorities must change.

A full range of choices for young people leaving school, offering them training, education and employment opportunities, with a link to continuing and adult education schemes, and retraining, particularly in the use of new technologies.

The right to have a say in decisions at work. The Alliance supports in principle the now modified Vredeling proposals on disclosure of information to employees, and wishes to see the Community approve the draft Fifth Directive guaranteeing to employees, or their representatives, the right to full participation in the key decisions made by the firms they work for. The Alliance believes that these rights should be implemented flexibly in different countries and company structures but their implementation is an essential preliminary step towards full industrial democracy.

Europe is often in a much better position than national governments to protect the interests of the consumer. Community competition laws should be used to check the abuse of economic power by big business, multinationals and nationalized industries. In this way the cost of air travel in Europe and the price of new cars in Britain could be brought down. We support common policies on consumer protection and health and safety standards which directly benefit consumers.

Europe and the world

The Alliance believes that the present highly dangerous world situation underlines the urgent need for the members of the Community to act in a more united way in world affairs. The Community is, despite the recession, an economic giant. In international affairs it remains a political dwarf. To make the world a safer place it is essential that Europe works effectively for peace, speaking with one voice. We want to see the countries of the Community on equal terms with the United States and Soviet Union in taking positive initiatives in world affairs.

One voice for Europe

The Community must build on successful collaboration in foreign affairs which is firmly based on 'European Political Cooperation', the system whereby foreign ministers and ministers consult regularly on the main international issues. It is in Britain's interest to promote even closer collaboration so that a more united and dynamic Europe can exercise a stabilizing influence in areas of world tension and defend human rights wherever they are threatened by undemocratic regimes. In the longer term this should lead to joint European diplomatic representation overseas.

The members of the Community share a common interest in developing closer political and economic links with Eastern Europe in order to lower tension between East and West. Europe should also exercise a more active and united role in the Middle East in order to reduce the risk of conflicts that could threaten world peace. The Community should also assist the development of democracy and elimination of poverty and the protection of human rights in Central and Southern America and in Africa.

Europe as a force for peace

The Alliance would seek to build a European pillar within the Atlantic Alliance which can express Europe's distinctive interests in defence and disarmament, reduce Europe's dependence on nuclear weapons and take a greater share of responsibility for our own defence.

We must strengthen Europe's conventional forces through:

Integration of command structures, closer collaboration in training and standardization of equipment.

Coordinating and pooling defence research and development and closer coordination in procurement to ensure that Europe's conventional defence is more cost effective and therefore stronger. This would also help to correct the present 7:1 imbalance in defence trade between the US and Europe.

We should reduce Europe's dependence on nuclear weapons by:

Moving towards 'no first use' of nuclear weapons.

The creation by Nato of a 150km Battlefield Nuclear Weapon Free Zone in Central Europe which could provide the basis for negotiations with the Russians on a wider verifiable nuclear weapon free zone.

Europe should launch the following initiatives in disarmament and arms control:

The inclusion of the British and French independent nuclear deterrents in East-West arms reduction talks with a European voice in the negotiations.

Suspend further deployment of cruise and Pershing missiles to give the Soviet Union an opportunity to come back to the conference table.

Mutual reductions of conventional forces in Europe.

The creation of a register of sales of arms to third countries and ending sales of arms to regimes which persistently violate human rights.

A ban on the production and use of chemical weapons. We must ensure that agreements banning biological weapons are observed.

Europe and the developing countries

The Alliance believes that Europe must work together with the developing countries of the world, both for humanitarian reasons and because of the need to stimulate world trade and economic recovery. We urge:

All Community members to meet the UN target for aid of 0.7 per cent GNP within five years. Britain currently spends a mere 0.4 per cent of GNP on aid to developing countries thus placing it with Italy at the bottom of the league table of Community countries.

That aid should be targeted mainly on the poorest countries and the poorest in all countries.

That more aid should be channelled through non-government organizations because of their effectiveness in reaching the needy.

Policies which encourage self-reliance and self-sufficiency in food production, and long-term guaranteed prices for the developing worlds' primary products including food. Food aid should be concentrated on emergency and disaster relief.

That the European Development Fund should be part of the Community budget so that it can be scrutinized by the European Parliament.

The Community to work with the Third World countries to develop technologies appropriate to their needs.

Only the Alliance wants to see the Community united in making a far greater contribution to peace, disarmament and development.

Reform of the Budget and CAP
The budget problem

Mrs Thatcher's stubborn and blinkered pursuit of 'her money back' from Brussels has dominated and distorted the debate about Britain and the Community over the last five years. And it has not worked! There is a budget problem but it is a problem for the whole Community and not just for Britain. The problem is twofold: first, the Community spends too much on the common agricultural policy (CAP); second, too little is spent on other important sectors of the economy. Common sense, economic logic and political equity all demand reform. The Community budget must be both acceptable to all member states and sufficient to finance the programmes needed to generate economic recovery in Western Europe.

Failure to achieve a durable reform will leave Europe weak and divided. But we must not exaggerate the importance of the budget as such. Budgetary transactions represent only a small part of the total economic picture of the effects on the UK of British membership. Over-concentration of spending on agriculture is as much a result of failure to establish other common policies as a consequence of the way the CAP works. The Tories have blocked the development of just those policies that would make the Community work better for Britain.

Reform of the Budget
The Community budget must reflect the needs of the 1980s, not the assumptions of the 1960s. Expenditure on agriculture must become a smaller proportion of the Community budget, leaving more room for other important programmes. The Community, as a whole, can only suffer from an unacceptable balance in the burdens and benefits falling on individual member states. Revenue raising must be linked to relative wealth and poverty. British payments to the Community's resources and those of our partners should be broadly proportionate to each of our shares of Community GDP.

Over the longer term we should aim for a Community budget which seeks explicitly to transfer funds from richer to poorer regions on lines similar to those long established to equalize tax burdens and benefits among the regional governments of the Federal Rupublic of Germany.

A budget constrained by the current ceiling on revenue-raising will not allow sufficient headroom for the other expenditures necessary to achieve the other policy objectives which we advocate. We can fund the industrial, regional and social policies which Europe so badly needs only if we are prepared with our partners to find the money to pay for them. While in the short term this should come from VAT, in the longer term we must look to other sources of taxation, such as excise duties.

A larger Community budget need not mean net increases in British taxation. British and other Community governments waste scarce resources on separate and competing national programmes in many fields. Pooling those resources in common programmes can achieve more for less to the benefit of the UK and the Community as a whole.

The Alliance supports an agreement for reform of the budget:
Linking revenue raising to the proportionate wealth of each member state.
Reform of the CAP so that agriculture becomes a smaller proportion of the budget.
Growth in the Community's income for new common policies, particularly for industry, and significant increases in the regional and social funds.

Reform of the CAP
The CAP must be made to work by ensuring that production is related to demand, that farmers have stable markets within a healthy rural environment and that consumers have food at fair prices. The Alliance proposes the following reforms:
Establish production targets for major commodities, set in the light of world and European demand, and translating these to quotas where this is appropriate. The question of making these quotas tradeable should be examined. Production in excess of these targets would be sold at world prices.
Relate guaranteed prices to quality particularly to reduce cereal support prices.
Vary the level of support so as to discourage the large factory-type of producers whose operations provide too few jobs.
Use agricultural structural funds to help the young, new entrants to farming and the small family farm – particularly for those in difficult areas such as hills and uplands.
Halt unfair assistance to farmers by individual member states in the Community.
Phase out the Monetary Compensation Amounts – the so-called green currencies – as a step towards the creation of a genuine common market in food.

Fisheries
The world's supplies of fish are dwindling by the hour. The common fisheries policy will only be effective in conserving fish stocks, protecting them from pollution and ensuring sustainable yields when there are agreed standards of enforcement. To that end the Alliance supports:
A much stronger common fisheries inspectorate.
Area fishing plans to improve conservation of stocks.
Stock preservation by licensing individual boats within a national catch quota agreed within the CFP, the licensing system to be agreed with the industry.
Protection of the fishing interests of existing members of the Community on the accession of Spain and Portugal with their large fishing fleets.

Protecting the environment
The essential unity of Europe is most apparent when we come to deal with the environment. We share our atmosphere and the seas which surround us on three sides with our European neighbours. Our coasts, mountains and countryside are visited by millions from the rest of

Europe each summer, and millions of us visit the coasts, mountains and countryside of the rest of Europe. The common protection of the common environment is the goal of the Alliance.

Without a stronger Community presence any individual nation's attempt to control acid rain, to eliminate lead from petrol, to halt the misuse of dangerous chemicals, to protect animals and wildlife and to reduce other environmental threats will be thwarted by the failure of its neighbours to achieve similar high standards of environmental care. All industries throughout the Community must bear their true environmental cost so no country can steal an unfair advantage.

The protection of the environment and economic prosperity need not be mutually conflicting goals. Europe must tackle the twin evils of poverty and unemployment, but this must be through a 'green' growth, a growth that is compatible with and not at the expense of the environment.

Integration of environmental policies

The Alliance believes that within the Community we should:

Reduce our dependence on oil by shifting the balance of Community spending on energy research and development towards a more efficient use of energy, energy conservation and the development of environmentally benign alternative energy sources.

Alter the structural policy of the CAP so as to place strict environmental conditions on improvement grants and ensure that conservation improvements and productivity improvements are given equal treatment.

Allocate funds for the development of conservation-compatible agriculture.

Encourage recycling, re-use and the development of longer-life products.

Require mandatory environmental impact statements for all major industrial, agricultural and transport projects and for all major projects receiving Community funds.

Controlling pollution

We would extend the role of the Community in controlling air and water pollution, particularly at source, through:

More vigorous efforts to control acid rain and other trans-frontier pollutants.

Leadership in developing technical, financial and administrative methods for substantially reducing noise pollution, especially from transport.

A commitment to set 1990 as the target date for Community-wide adoption of lead free petrol.

A substantial increase in both the powers and funding of the Community's Action Programme on the Environment to encourage the development of clean technologies.

Protecting the living environment

The Community has an important role to play in protecting wildlife and promoting animal welfare. We believe that:

Community funds should be more readily available to protect habitats of European importance.

The Community should toughen the conventions governing trade in wildlife products by closing existing loopholes.

The Community should insist upon high standards of welfare for livestock and allocate research funds to develop alternative means of animal production. Europe should coordinate the development of humane techniques for testing and research to drastically reduce the stressful use of animals.

The Community's role in the monitoring and control of harmful effects from pesticides, toxic wastes and misused fertilizers should be strengthened and Europe should ensure that chemicals found unsuitable for use in Europe are not exported.

The rights of the European citizen

The member countries of the Community share a common heritage of human rights and they, together with eleven other European countries, are all parties to the European Convention on Human Rights (ECHR). But the citizens of the Community need stronger protection of their fundamental rights and freedoms against the misuse of power by public authorities, whether at Community or national level. The demands of modern, complex, urban societies and rapid advances in technology have made governments and officials much more powerful. In the absence of new safeguards and remedies for individuals and minorities these increased public powers could menace personal freedom and the rule of law. Such safeguards should cover the protection of access to centrally held personal information and very considerable extension of legal aid.

The Alliance believes that action should be taken on two fronts to defend and extend citizens' rights. First, to strengthen the effectiveness of the ECHR. Second, to establish a Community charter of political, social and economic rights for the citizen.

Our aim must be the effective guarantee of all the basic rights of the citizens of the Community. People should be entitled to a common European citizenship and passport, providing free movement and equal treatment throughout the Community.

The European Convention on Human Rights

The Alliance believes that a wide range of measures to strengthen the ECHR are necessary:

The UK and all member states should no longer impose time limits on acceptance of the jurisdiction of the European Court and Commission of Human Rights.

The UK and all member states should secure the rights and freedoms of the European Convention on Human Rights to everyone within their jurisdiction and provide effective national remedies for claims of violation.

The UK and all member states should accept the obligations not only of the Convention itself but also of the additional Protocols which guarantee further rights and freedoms.

The Community institutions should formally accept and become bound to comply with the European Convention.

The procedures of the European Court and Commission should be streamlined and their resources should be increased (including legal aid) so that everyone within the Community has access to speedy and effective remedies for violations of fundamental human rights.

Rights for women

Among the few fundamental human rights already enshrined in Community law are the rights to equal pay and to equal treatment in employment and social security without sex discrimination. These rights need to be translated into practical reality in all parts of the Community. This is especially important in the present recession when economic problems and changes in the labour market are undermining past progress and creating new obstacles to equality for women at the workplace. Community law has played an important role in compelling the present British Government to introduce legislation on equal pay for work of equal value.

The British Government's record shows its lack of commitment to the equality of the sexes. Britain fails to take advantage of the money available for positive action projects under the Social Fund. For example, in 1981 West Germany applied for almost £53m of assistance for special training projects for women while Britain applied for a mere £5924!

Although Community law has played a valuable part in protecting women's rights, its role and effect remain too narrow.

The 1982–85 action programme for women should be fully implemented and put on a more permanent basis and the growing body of Community laws on equality for women should be strengthened by means of directly applicable regulations.

Community measures are needed to clarify imprecise concepts such as indirect discrimination and there should also be acceptance of the use of a standard male salary as a basis for comparison to enable women in segregated jobs to utilise equal pay rights, with a further requirement to utilise job evaluation schemes which are free from sex bias when making comparisons.

Private occupational pension schemes should be brought clearly within the ambit of the equal treatment principle and aspects of general social security not so far covered by the equal treatment Directives (eg differing pensionable age provisions, survivors' benefits, etc) should be included.

All diminution of individual rights on grounds of marital status should be removed.

Workers should be able to rely on an effective means of exercising their rights to equal treatment, in all the member countries.

The Community should also play a role in safeguarding the civil rights of immigrant workers from countries outside the Community.

Minimum standards should be laid down at Community level giving immigrant workers from outside the Community defined legal rights, which apply equally to men and women, and protect them from arbitrary dismissals from their jobs, removal or deportation by the authorities, harassment by the authorities and arbitrary administrative action.

An effective democratic Europe

Our programme describes the new tasks and priorities which face the Community. It is against Britain's interests for the Community to remain static. It is in Britain's interests for the Community to develop the means to meet Europe's political and industrial crisis. But reform is urgently required if the Community is to act decisively on behalf of the peoples and states whose interests it serves. For the Community to work for Europe's people its leaders must learn to act together.

At present, Community institutions are close to deadlock and its cumbersome structure is beset by national bureaucracies and national governments pursuing short-term goals. We want to streamline the Community's structure and its methods of decision-making. This can be done without changing the treaties. Power should be exercised at the most appropriate level and with clear accountability to the people through their elected representatives.

More effective and democratic decision-taking

The attempts by the Parliament to influence budgetary and agricultural policies during the last five years have made it clear that co-decision-making between Council and Parliament would be more likely to protect Britain's interests than continuing to depend on Britain's veto in the Council. We believe that:

The first urgent reform is that Parliament and the Council should jointly exercise legislative authority in the Community.

The practice of requiring unanimity and the frequent use of the veto based on spurious claims of vital national interest have done great harm to the Community. The use of the veto in the Council must be severely restricted.

The powers of the Parliament over expenditure of the Community should be extended to the revenue side.

Fundamental matters such as Community law and Community taxation should be exercised by a fully democratically elected Parliament. Co-decision-making between the Council and Parliament need not mean indefinite delay. Each body must operate within strict time-limits.

An accountable Commission

The authority and accountability of the Commission must also be strengthened. We propose:

The appointment of the Commission should take place in two stages. The Council should first appoint the President and then, on the President's recommendation, the remaining members.

Each appointment should be subject to a public hearing before a committee of the Parliament which should have the power to consent, or withhold consent, to each appointment.

The Parliament should be able to censure individual Commissioners in addition to its present power to censure the whole Commission.

There should be a right of public access to documents relating to decisions taken by the Commission.

Fair Votes

If the European Parliament is to have real 'muscle' it must become fully representative of the peoples and parties of Europe. It is intolerable that the Conservatives have twice blocked the road to real democracy in Europe by opposing a common and proportional system of voting. As a result Britain is misrepresented in the Parliament and the whole political balance of the Community is distorted. We demand:

A common electoral system based on fair votes by proportional representation.

That British citizens living outside the UK should have full voting rights in future European elections; it is unfair that many of them are deprived of a vote on June 14.

These reforms will endow a democratic Community with the capacity to act and to achieve. Such a strengthening of the Community is urgent to meet the challenge of further enlargement, and with it the adaptation of structures designed for a compact group of six countries to a wider grouping of twelve. We see the prospect of Spanish and Portuguese membership both in political terms and as an expansion of the Community's markets. All truly free and democratic countries of Europe should be welcome in the Community. We call for an early and favourable conclusion of negotiations.

We have outlined the democratic direction in which the Alliance hopes to see the Community develop. Most people in the Community want it to work, want it to succeed. Voters everywhere are frustrated by the missed opportunity of Europe. Liberal and Social Democratic MEPs will seek to join with like-minded MEPs from the other Community countries in the construction of an ever closer union among the peoples of Europe. Our aim is a relevant, effective alliance of the energies, skills and resources of Europe's peoples. That way lies a better deal and a fuller life for the whole Community.

THE SCOTTISH NATIONAL PARTY
'Scotland's Voice in Europe'

The following are extracts from the Scottish National Party's manifesto:

Without self-government, Scotland's bargain in the Common Market is not nearly as good as it could be. Throughout the United Kingdom's negotiations to join, Scotland's national interests were flagrantly ignored by London politicians. Since the UK entered the EEC eleven years ago, this familiar London process of 'government by neglect and omission' has continued. Repeatedly, deals have been hatched with the Commission and other countries by English ministers who know nothing of Scotland and care less. The most notorious case of this was in the marathon argument on fishing when the London government caved in and accepted fishing limits of 12 miles when international law gave 200 miles to Scotland.

Not only has Scotland been badly served by English ministers on the Council of Ministers but Scotland has only eight MEPs as part of the UK when our national entitlement as an independent country like Denmark or Ireland would be 16.

Provided Scotland's national interests in relation to steel, oil, fishing and other vital industries can be sorted out satisfactorily, an SNP Government would be happy to recommend membership to the Scottish people who will have the final decision in a referendum. But independence is vital if Scotland is to participate in and benefit from the development of the Community. Our vision of the EEC is that of a highly decentralised confederation where sovereignty resides with the members but where all are prepared to cooperate for the common good.

So what then in short-term can Scotland achieve?

Greater national and international prominence so that we are not treated as at present as an insignificant province whose needs are of no account.

A more substantial share of EEC funding to boost vital industries.

Protection for our steel, fishing and hill farming industries now under threat.

A research institute of the EEC, comparable with those established in other member states. These institutes add thousands of first-class jobs to the areas in which they are located. Scotland would be the ideal location for such an institute studying the Community's problems of remote areas.

European Parliament

The SNP favour an increase in the democratic power and influence of the Parliament over Europe's bureaucracy. For example, we support:

An increase in the proportion of the budget over which the Parliament has direct control.

More substantial power to initiate proposals for implementation by the Commission.

Right to first consideration and amendment of proposals by the Commission.

Where the Council of Ministers ignores the Parliament's advice, the right to impose delay upon them.

Where essential and vital national interests are involved, the right of veto shall remain to member states as at present. The SNP rejects the creation of a unitary European State and will resist trends in that direction. We believe that the best international harmony stems from the widest representation of national interests.

Agriculture

In this context, the SNP MEPs will press for implementation of the Agricultural Development Programme (ADP) which Mrs Ewing persuaded the EEC to establish but which has been held up at national level. Reform of the common agricultural policy is urgent if the EEC is not to become insolvent.

The SNP will press for transfer of a proportion of CAP spending to national governments and for extensions to the deficiency payment system at UK level. Current spending policies which assist wealthy grain producers but hit diary and pig farmers and those on hill and marginal land will have to be reformed, to benefit less favoured areas. As well as giving aid to these farmers who need it, the agricultural policies will require to reflect consumer interests to a greater extent. Let's have cheaper food for our people – not for the Russians!

Fisheries

An independent Scottish Government will re-open negotiations with the aim of establishing an exclusive 100 mile Scottish zone and overall control up to 200 miles. The SNP will cooperate over conservation and more effective policing of the fishing areas. We favour aid to enable the processing of fish within, or close to, traditional fishing communities. And we favour a degree of local management of resource conservation and allocation. The promises made by the common fisheries policy of certainty of fishing opportunities, fair quotas and efficient policing have not materialized; we insist these promises to be kept.

The SNP will renew its fight to persuade the European Parliament to establish a Separate Fisheries Committee to look after the industry and in particular to establish protection for existing fishing communities if Spain and Portugal with their large fishing fleets are to be admitted to Community membership.

Industry and Training

The SNP will initiate and support campaigns to transfer a higher proportion of the Community Budget to social and industrial development. The SNP will insist that the national governments use EEC funds as 'additional' funds, and not as recompense to the national Treasury for sums outlaid or committed under domestic regional policy. The worst offender in the Community on this count has been the British Government, using EEC grants as a *substitute* for UK spending, not, as intended, as an increment. What Europe votes to give us, London grabs – quite illegally.

SNP MEPs will press for a larger social fund budget to provide help to the deprived areas of the EEC, undergoing social and economic trauma from the sharp decline of traditional industries. Unfortunately, many of these areas are in Scotland, thanks to the callous negligence of UK governments.

The SNP will support the UK government's claim for equitable refunds provided conditions are imposed to allow the refunds to be ploughed into investment and employment and not swallowed by the Treasury.

Energy

While the SNP favours cooperation on energy research and development, it will not support any future common energy policy which does not reflect Scotland's extraordinary strength as an energy exporter. The fact is that Scotland produces over 88 per cent of all the oil in the EEC. It will be an essential element of the negotiations that Scotland will expect concessions from the EEC to reflect the energy and resource advantage that the Community would gain from Scotland's adherence.

One of the concessions will be acceptance by the Community of Scotland's need to retain control over labour and equipment content in relation to offshore oil development. Rate of exploration, development and production will remain in Scotland's control. And we, unlike London, recognize that Scotland is Europe's natural centre for research into all forms of alternative energy – wind, wave, solar, hydro and peat.

PLAID CYMRU
A voice for Wales in Europe

Plaid Cymru, the Welsh nationalist party, fought the European elections on a manifesto seeking a stronger voice for the Principality in the Community. Extracts from its manifesto are:

The crisis in Wales is deep-rooted. We have no government to defend our interests, no government to plan our future. Our economy is in decline, and we suffer 17 per cent unemployment. Our coal industry is starved of investment and many pits are under threat. Our steel industry has been cut more savagely than any other in Europe. While the barley barons of England get richer and richer, many dairy farmers in Wales face ruin as a result of the cut in the milk quota. In the league table of prosperity Wales has dropped to 48th place among the 54 regions of Western Europe.

The fundamental weakness of the EEC is the status of the old imperial powers, France and England. Both see the EEC as a machinery to enable them to continue as world powers. Both have used the power of veto in the Council of Ministers to block any change in the rules of the Community. Hence the structure of the EEC is inflexible and dominated from the centre – according to the old imperial pattern.

The cornerstone of our policy is that Wales must win full national status within the EEC. Our present position is the worst of all worlds. While Ireland has 15 members in the European Parliament, can nominate a Commissioner and is represented at the Council by a minister with the power of veto, Wales has only four members in the Parliament and is not represented in any other way. There is an EEC office in Wales – but no Welsh Office in Brussels. It is no surprise that Ireland has benefitted so greatly from membership of the EEC while Wales has suffered so badly. The recent decision to allow an increase of 4.6 per cent in the milk quotas for Ireland while cutting the milk quota for Wales by 10 per cent is a clear example of the advantages Ireland enjoys.

Plain Cymru will press for:

A greatly increased Regional Development Fund which should be the first call on the EEC budget.

Grants to be given according to the spirit of the 'additionality rule' so that allocations from the ERDF are truly additional to allocations from Westminster.

Grants which are closely tied to the number of jobs provided and which are allocated according to the priorities of an overall plan.

More autonomy for Wales so that the Welsh Office can bid directly for grants and loans and shall be wholly responsible for the deployment of the ERDF.

Greater access to European Social Fund monies for the training of women and young people, helped by the implementation of a scheme of reimbursement by central government to local initiatives which financially assist such projects.

Plaid Cymru will therefore press for:

An energy strategy to secure the long-term future of energy supplies in Europe based on indigenous energy sources with a proper priority given to workable coal reserves; such a policy would recognize the Welsh coalfield as an important long-term resource.

A directive to the UK government to provide operating support to the coal industry at the same level as our partners in the ECSC, and also to authorize adequate investment in the Welsh coalfield.

Tariffs on imported fuel to be used to finance investment in alterative sources of energy that are renewable, pollution-free and in harmony with the ecology of Europe.

A halt to all new fission power stations.

A fully integrated coal and steel policy within Wales with the future of the Welsh steel industry linked to the development of the coking coal reserves at Margam and investment in continuous casting technology at Llanwern.

The present Common Agricultural Policy takes up 65 per cent of the EEC budget, much of which is misdirected. Too large a proportion of the CAP budget supports the cereal and sugar beet industries, producing large surpluses and high prices for imported foodstuffs. Plaid Cymru will fight for a complete change of emphasis in the CAP to encourage the grassland-based livestock farm which is ecologically and economically more sound in the long term than 'high-tech monoculture agribusiness'.

The European Commission

The existing EEC Commission under its President, Mr Gaston Thorn, leaves office on January 5 1985. In July 1984 Dr Garret Fitzgerald, President-in-office of the Community, announced that M. Jacques Delors, the former French Finance Minister, was to succeed Mr Thorn. At the first session of the new European Parliament in July, the bureau of the Parliament signified its concurrence when it had a meeting with Dr Fitzgerald.

The membership of the present Commission, their nominating countries and their portfolios are as follows:

President M. Gaston Thorn (Luxembourg) – Secretariat General, Legal Service, Spokesman's Group, Cultural Affairs. **Vice-Presidents** M. Francois-Xavier Ortoli (France) – Economic and Financial Affairs, Credit and Investment. Herr Wilhelm Haferkamp (Germany) – External Relations including nuclear matters. Sgr Lorenzo Natali (Italy) – EEC enlargement, Information, Mediterranean policy. Viscount Etienne Davignon (Belgium) – Industrial Affairs, Energy, Euratom Supply Agency, Research and Science, Joint Research Centre. Mr Christopher Tugendhat (United Kingdom) – Budget and Financial Control, Financial Institutions, Taxation.

Commissioners Sgr Antonio Giolitti (Italy) – Regional Policy, Coordination of Community funds. Mr Richard Burke (Ireland) – Personnel and administration, Interpreting and Conference Services, Statistical Office, Office for Official Publications, President's delegate. Mr Giorgios Contogeorgis (Greece) – Transport, Fisheries, Coordination of tourism questions. Herr Karl-Heinz Narjes (Germany) – Internal Market and Industrial Innovation, Customs Union Service, Environment, Consumer Protection and Nuclear Safety. Mr Frans Andriessen (Netherlands) – Competition Policy, Relations with European Parliament. Mr Poul Dalsager (Denmark) – Agriculture. M. Edgard Pisani (France) – Development.

Newly appointed Commissioners are: Lord Cockfield and Mr Clinton Davies (UK); Mr Willy de Clercq (Belgium); Mr Henning Christoferson (Denmark); and Mr Peter Sutherland (Ireland).

The Commission and its secretariat are based at: Rue de la Loi 200, 1049 Brussels. Tel: 235 11 11. Telex 21877 Comeu B.

Presidents of the European Parliament

Common Assembly of the European Coal and Steel Community

Henri Spaak (Belgium, Soc)..................................... .... Sep 11 1952 to May 11 1954
Alcide de Gasperi (Italy, CD)..................................... .... May 11 1954 to Aug 18 1954
(On Mr de Gasperi's death, Jean Fohrman, Luxembourg, Soc, assumed the office but not the title of President from Aug 19 1954 to Nov 29 1954 until a successor could be elected.)
Giuseppe Pella (Italy, CD) ....Nov 29 1954 to Nov 27 1956
Hans Furler (Germany, CD) ....Nov 27 1956 to Mar 19 1958

European Parliament

Robert Schuman (France, CD) ....Mar 19 1958 to Mar 28 1960
Hans Furler (Germany, CD) ....Mar 28 1960 to Mar 27 1962
Gaetano Martino (Italy, LD) ....Mar 27 1962 to Mar 21 1964
Jean Duvieusart (Belgium, CD) ....Mar 21 1964 to Sep 24 1965
Victor Leemans (Belgium, CD) ....Sep 24 1965 to Mar 7 1966
Alain Poher (France, CD) ....Mar 6 1966 to Mar 12 1969
Mario Scelba (Italy, CD).....................................Mar 12 1969 to Mar 9 1971
Walter Behrendt (Germany, Soc).....................................Mar 9 to Mar 13 1973
Cornelis Berkhouwer (Netherlands, LD) ....Mar 13 1973 to Mar 11 1975
Georges Spénale (France, Soc) ....Mar 11 1975 to Mar 8 1977
Emilio Colombo (Italy, EPP) , ...Mar 8 1977 to July 17 1979
Simone Veil (France, LD) ....July 17 1979 to Jan 18 1982
Pieter Dankert (Netherlands, Soc) ....Jan 20 1982 to July 24 1984
Pierre Pflimlin (France, EPP) ....Jul 24 1984 to

The bureau of the European Parliament consists of the President and Vice-Presidents and the enlarged bureau consists of those appointees plus the political group leaders. The five quaestors, elected to look after the interests of MEPs, sit in on the deliberations of the enlarged bureau which arranges the Parliament's agenda and supervises all its activities.

European Parliament funds to political groups

In addition to what the member states and political parties themselves spend, the elections to the European Parliament are also assisted by a budget laid down by that Parliament which goes to the political groups. As part of the background information to the 1984 elections, the European Parliament Information Office in London put out the following release explaining the rules of these funds and how their distribution is calculated. It stated:

In three European Community states – Denmark, Federal Germany and Italy – financial aid is granted to political parties from public funds to cover the parties' general and electoral expenses. The sums concerned and the rules governing their use vary considerably.

In three other states – the United Kingdom, Ireland and France – government aid is granted for electoral purposes. In the UK and Ireland public buildings are made available for meetings and candidates are allowed to send free of charge one communication to each elector. In France, the cost of paper, electoral posters and leaflets is refunded to candidates getting at least 5 per cent of the votes. In the UK also, opposition parties in the House of Commons receive financial aid for research and running parliamentary offices (£325000 in total each year).

Before the 1979 elections, the European Parliament decided to provide funds to the political groups to prepare an information campaign and a total equivalent to £8.4m was provided for this purpose. The same is being done for the 1984 elections. In order to take account of the enlargement of the Community and inflation, it is proposed to provide a total of 43 million European currency units (ecus) under Item 3708 of Parliament's budget, or £24.6m (at the exchange rate of November 30 1983). The total of 43m ecus includes an appropriation of 19m ecus in the draft 1984 budget which is subject to confirmation on December 15 1983.

In relative terms the total of 43m ecus is equivalent to about 14p per elector in the ten Community countries.

Basis of 1984 Distribution
This total is being distributed as follows:
  (i) 7 per cent (or £1.72m) on an equal basis between the seven political groups in the European Parliament (or £246000 each);
  (ii) 62 per cent (or £15.27m) to be divided among the political groups on the basis of one 434th part of this sum for each group member (i.e., £35200). Members not attached to a political group will each receive one 434th part.
  (iii) 31 per cent (or £7.64m) will be placed in a reserve fund for distribution after the elections on June 14–17 1984. This will be distributed, in proportion to the total number of votes cast, to political parties and groupings which obtain more than 5 per cent of the valid votes cast in a member country, or which obtain more than 1 per cent of the valid votes cast in each of three or more member countries in which a grouping puts up candidates.

The purpose of retaining 31 per cent of the total until after the elections is to reserve funds for members elected or re-elected in 1984 and for political groupings which do not obtain a seat but which obtain a specific percentage of the votes cast. Moreover, the Bureau of Parliament decided that Parliament should 'endeavour to make some allowance for the problems facing parties which in political terms will have to take part in the European elections but which will have great difficulties in obtaining a seat as a result of their national electoral system'.

The Official Journal of the European Communities, issue C293 of October 29 1983, gives details of the rules and procedures governing reimbursement of expenditure by political groupings having taken part in the 1984 elections.

Groups' Allocations
Calculations as to the distribution of funds from the 31 per cent post-election reserve are hypothetical, but under headings (i) and (ii) above the total distribution before the elections between the political groups is as follows:

Socialists (125 seats at end 1983)	£4 645 000
European Peoples' Party (117 seats)	£4 363 000
European Democrats (63 seats)	£2 463 000
Communist and Allies (48 seats)	£1 935 000
Liberals and Democrats (38 seats)	£1 583 000
European Progressive Democrats (22 seats)	£1 020 000

Group for the Technical Coordination and defence of independent groups and Members (11 seats)	£634000
(Ten unattached Members	£352000)

How each group distributes its funds to its constituent parties at national level is its own decision.

The funds made available to the groups are 'to cover a contribution to the costs of preparations for the information campaign leading up to the second direct elections in 1984'. The main items of expenditure are likely to be on meetings, publications, posters, travel and other administrative costs. The conditions under which they may be used are laid down by the Bureau of Parliament and the expenditure will be checked by Parliament's Budgetary Control Committee and the Community's Court of Auditors.

The funds allocated may be utilized until at the latest 40 days before the date of the elections to cover any payment commitments, provided that payment is actually made not later than 40 days after the date of the elections. Any monies which are not covered by these two provisions shall be repaid to Parliament.

Results in 1979
In 1979 the 110.97 million valid votes were cast Community-wide and a further 5.68 million votes were cast in the Greek election to the European Parliament in October 1981. Taking the two polls together the approximate percentage break-down of votes between the political groups was as follows*:

Socialist Group parties	27.4% in ten countries
EPP parties	30.1% in nine countries
European Democrat Group parties	5.9% in two countries
Communist and Allies Group parties	13.7% in nine countries
Liberal and Democratic Group parties	9.5% in ten countries
European Progressive Democrat Group parties	3.3% in four countries
Technical Coordination Group parties	1.8% in four countries

* After adjustments for members whose electoral lists or groupings are split between different political groups.

Addresses

The European Parliament and the office of its President is situated at the Centre europeen, Plateau du Kirchberg, Luxembourg (Telephone: 4300 1) with offices also at 97–113, rue Belliard, 1040 Bruxelles (Telephone: 234 21 11). Sessions are held at the Palaise de l'Europe, Strasbourg (Telephone: 88/37 4001).

Information offices of the European Parliament are in:

	Tel:
Athens	
2, avenue Vassilissis Sophias – Athènes	1/723 34 21
Bonn	
In der Raste 12 – 5300 BONN 1	0228/23 10 01
Bruxelles	
97–113 rue Belliard – 1040 Brussel	2/234 21 11
Brussel	
Belliardstraat 97–113 – 1040 Brussel	2/234 21 11
The Hague	
Lange Voorhout 27A – 2514 EB 's Gravenhage	70/62 49 31
Dublin	
43, Molesworth Street – Dublin 2	1/71 91 00
Copenhagen	
Børsen DK- 1217 – København K	1/14 33 77
London	
2 Queen Anne's Gate – SW1H 9AA London	1/222 04 11
Paris	
288, Bld St. Germain – 75007 Paris	1/550 34 11
Rome	
Via Poli, 29 – 00186 Roma	6/679 06 18
	6/679 05 07